THE APLEY LEGION

THE
APLEY
LEGION

A PARADE OF SERVICEMEN FROM A SHROPSHIRE ESTATE

GRAHAM JONES

For Val,
Best Wishes
Graham

SilverWood

Published in 2014 by the author
using SilverWood Books Empowered Publishing®

SilverWood Books Ltd
30 Queen Charlotte Street, Bristol, BS1 4HJ
www.silverwoodbooks.co.uk

ISBN 978-1-78132-137-9

British Library Cataloguing in Publication Data
A CIP catalogue record for this book is available from the British Library

Set in Sabon by SilverWood Books Ltd
Printed in Great Britain by TJ International, Padstow, Cornwall

Dedicated to
all those who were true to the motto of the Legion
Service not Self

Contents

THE APLEY LEGION

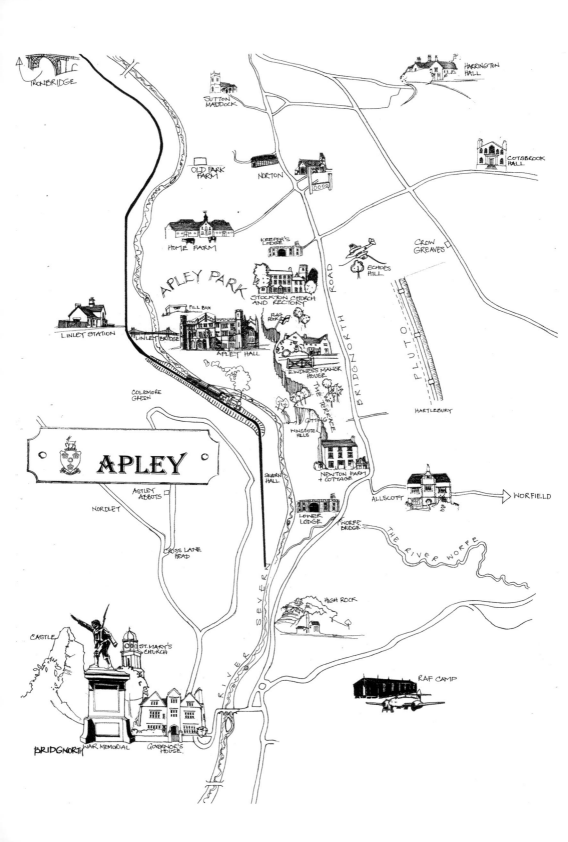

Map of Apley

The natural features that made Apley Park a special place are the River Severn and the Apley Terrace. A huge lake formed on the Cheshire Plain at the end of the last Ice Age. The melt waters broke though the Ironbridge Gorge and the river carved a new course south to the sea. The red sandstone cliffs that form Apley Terrace were shaped by the river over thousands of years.

The River Severn was the main artery of trade for the Industrial Revolution. It gave access to the outside world for the products of the mines and ironworks of Coalbrookdale. Construction of the railway was completed in 1862. The Fosters entertained lavishly and visitors from London and all over Britain could then arrive in style.

The Estate covers more than eight thousand acres, with about three hundred residential properties. It is administered from the Governor's House in Bridgnorth. Built around 1630, it was the Royalist headquarters during the Civil War, King Charles visited twice. Other properties in the town are no longer part of Apley Estate. There is however a valuable open space within the town that has not been sold to developers. It is the cricket ground.

The RAF camp is now an industrial estate and Dr Beeching closed the railway. Under the fields fuel oil still flows through the pipeline that fed PLUTO and was poured into the tanks that crossed Normandy on the way to Berlin.

Foreword

A FINE PROSPECT

© Vicki Norman 2011 in the collection of Dr Christopher Gillie

And a fine view it was from The Queen's View along Apley Terrace to High Rock and across the Severn to Bridgnorth with the tower of Saint Leonard's and the dome of Saint Mary's standing out above the town. What Queen Mary made of this when she visited Apley in the 1930s we do not know but we do know what King Charles had to say in 1642 when he looked out in the opposite direction from Bridgnorth Castle: "… this is the finest in all my kingdom." Looking north to the Whitmores' Estate the outstanding feature in the landscape was High Rock, a bare outcrop on the red sandstone ridge that formed Apley Terrace. The ledges on High Rock and some of the ancient trees rooted on the dangerous crags were ideal nesting places for the buzzards. These keen-eyed birds patrolled the meadows and parkland on both sides of the river, soaring effortlessly on moth-like wings. In time man took to the skies and could share the thrill of flying with birds of prey.

Airmen flying over the English countryside have often remarked on the patchwork pattern of the fields below, neat, orderly and manicured. The finest examples can be seen over the parkland and fields surrounding the great country houses. The airmen circling Apley Hall would observe the river to the west and the drive emerging from woodland sweeping to the front door.

In bygone days visitors arrived in horse-drawn carriages to be pampered and entertained, likewise in wartime soldiers and airmen came to rest until their wounds were healed. They explored their surroundings, the woodland pathways, the gardens of the Hall, the tiny station at Linley and the line that led to Bridgnorth and the many welcoming ale-houses.

Before they returned to do battle in the skies one or two airmen flew back to thank the staff. Gliding carefully down onto a riverside meadow one young airman walked back across the lawns to flirt with the nurses again, flew off, waggled his wings over the Hall and was gone. Another made an awkward landing, left his damaged aircraft in the Park and returned to camp for a reprimand.

Not all the airborne visitors were welcome. The moonlit river was a useful guide for Luftwaffe pilots making for Liverpool. One, returning with bombs to spare, dropped a 'stick' harmlessly in fields near Home Farm, another destroyed houses in Bridgnorth and killed residents.

Lancaster bombers of the RAF returning after a night raid dropped fragments of 'window' over Apley fields. Small boys collected the long strips of 'silver paper' and coiled it carefully, hoping to exchange it for something more valuable, a piece of shrapnel perhaps. Over Hamburg and Cologne the bombers dropped clouds of 'window' to confuse enemy radar.

At war's end Mosquitos and Spitfires flew off the airstrip at Chatham's farm and the milking cows returned to their pasture. The relics of war began to disappear. Scratch the surface, dig deeper and past history is revealed.

Ancient History

The Romans occupied Britain for four hundred years and during that time must have explored much of the county from their garrison town of Viroconium, an important staging post on Watling Street. They probably established a settlement at Stableford, which was later fortified by the Anglo-Saxons. These invaders from across the North Sea took over the land from the Romans and gave names to the hamlets of simple cottages they built at Winscote, Allscott, Burcote and Swancote.

The modern history of Apley begins in 1620 when Sir Thomas Whitmore became lord of the manor. At the outbreak of the Civil War the landed gentry of the county were divided. The Myttons and Clives were for Parliament, some of the Corbetts for the King and some for Cromwell. The merchants of Bridgnorth and Shrewsbury were not whole-hearted in their support for the Crown. To raise funds for his cause King Charles demanded 'Ship Money', a tax on ports that included inland ports. Much as they may have wished to avoid it everyone became involved.

Prince Rupert and King Charles visited Shrewsbury and Bridgnorth to drum up support. Troops were billeted at Apley and all around the town. The Whitmores declared for the King and a blockhouse was built in the Park to guard the Severn waterway, a vital supply line. A few local lads trudged off to the indecisive Battle of Edge Hill and trudged back again. Sir William and his son stayed at home.

The Civil War came to an embarrassing end for the Whitmores when Roundheads appeared uninvited at the Hall and took them and the garrison troops to Wem as prisoners of war. It may have been quite a jolly affair; the captors sampled the wine in the cellars, carved a few words of thanks on the walls and confiscated the lot. More hurtful to the Whitmores was the £5000 fine Parliament imposed on them for joining the wrong side. The monarchy was restored and it was business as usual for the Whitmores. They had the satisfaction of watching the products of their ironworks being shipped through the Estate into the wider world. The ironmasters of Coalbrookdale made huge profits and in time this wealth would transform Apley.

The County Regiment

In 1755 Lieutenant General William Whitmore of Apley raised the 53rd Regiment of Foot. The uniform definitely, adventure possibly, and the pay certainly attracted local lads. More recruits came from the neighbouring counties and from as far afield as the west coast of Ireland.

They first saw action in The American War of Independence and went on to serve against Napoleon's army in the Peninsular War. They battled tribesmen in the Sudan and helped plague victims in Hong Kong. The King's Light Infantry, formed from the 53rd, found themselves in Afghanistan in the 1870s. At the beginning of the twentieth century they were fighting the Boers in South Africa.

During the Great War Shropshire lads joined the county regiment in droves and fought on every front. Following the Battle of Bligny in June 1918 the 1st/4th Battalion was awarded the Croix de Guerre. Only a handful of British regiments were honoured in this way. Village boys were still serving in the county regiment in 1968 when the 1st battalion of the King's Shropshire Light Infantry became the 3rd battalion of The Light Infantry.

The first Colonel of the Regiment.

© Shropshire Regimental Museum

MONEY WELL SPENT

The profits from cold black iron, cast and forged in the Cradle of the Industrial Revolution were used to create a lush green playground at Apley. The Napoleonic Wars certainly helped. Thomas Whitmore's lucrative contract to supply arms and cannon to the navy financed the remodelling of the Hall in grand style. Teams of navvies more used to digging canals transformed park and woodland. When their work was complete they moved on to the next back-breaking enterprise. Decades passed and the stands of trees matured; a magical landscape appeared that would endure for a century.

Unfortunately Captain Whitmore overspent or maybe he gambled away some of the family fortune. To clear his debts he sold his estate. William Orme Foster paid a handsome price for Apley in 1867. The Fosters were also ironmasters, manufacturing blast furnaces to produce iron, rolling mills for steel, locomotives for the expanding American railways; all solid Black Country products.

With their vast fortune and an understanding of the technology of the time the Fosters put the finishing touches to the work begun by the Whitmores. According to the eccentric Gerald Tywhitt, the 14th Baron Berners, who was born at Apley, they created 'an earthly paradise for children' The Fosters entertained in lavish style at the Hall. This together with the unique surroundings even attracted the attention of Queen Victoria. Apley offered similar seclusion to Sandringham and it is said that the Queen and Prince Albert did consider buying the Estate.

BRIGHT YOUNG THINGS IN DEPRESSING TIMES

The Great War bankrupted many but not the Fosters. The whole nation celebrated the victory over Germany and at Apley the celebrations continued. House parties and dinners were laid on in the same style as in pre-war days. The guests were a mixed bunch, the literate, the frivolous, the brave, the sporting, the political and the Royal.

Evelyn Waugh and P G Wodehouse may have drawn some inspiration from the 'goings on' at the Hall. 'Clivedenesque' was how it was described which meant a lot of booze and slack morals. Waugh's best known work, *Brideshead Revisited*, was published in 1945, later it was adapted for television. It portrayed some of the glamour of the inter-war period which he knew well. A snob and a drunk he was well qualified to comment on the behaviour of the wealthy. He didn't mind offending anyone and satirized his own class in his first really successful novel, *Vile Bodies*. It was to have been titled *Bright Young Things*, a phrase used to describe frivolous young socialites with more money than sense and a fondness for fast cars and free love. After the tragedy of the Great War those who could afford it 'let their hair down'.

As a boy P G Wodehouse spent summer holidays cycling the lanes around Apley, his parents rented a cottage at Ackleton. In adult life he visited the Hall that may well have been the inspiration for Blandings Castle, the scene of some of Bertie Wooster's misadventures. This wealthy buffoon's childish behaviour got him into all sorts of difficulties. Jeeves, his faithful man servant, with his superior manner and superior intelligence was always able to solve Wooster's problems. Apley Hall may have been Blandings Castle but servant and master were definitely not modelled on Tom Gray and Major 'Jimmy' Foster, they were not Jeeves and Wooster.

The 'guns' that made up the shooting parties came from far and wide, from the stately homes of England and castles in Bavaria. There were parties made up of officers who had served in the most prestigious regiments of the British army and Austrian aristocrats who had fought for the Kaiser. All was forgiven, they were good company and the Major made regular trips to their estates in Austria until the outbreak of the Second World War.

With shooting and fishing, tennis courts, a billiard room and swimming pool there were plenty of distractions for the guests. No one was going to refuse an invitation, the guest list was long. Joe Kennedy arrived with his son, JFK, the future President of the USA. Queen Mary and her son, Edward , Prince of Wales, came separately.

Gala balls and house parties at the Hall seemed far removed from real life in the outside world. The Fosters' wealth came from trade, they were realists and understood industry and the lives of working men and they could afford to be generous. The business empire of William Orme Foster made him a multi-millionaire but for twenty years he did not receive any of the profits, partly because he was reluctant to shed labour.

This public-spirited tradition was handed down from one generation to the next. The Fosters financed an educational institute and hospital in Bridgnorth. They renovated the parish church at Stockton. In Norton they built the village school and a community hall.

When work was done estate workers came for relaxation and recreation. The men spent time playing darts and billiards and less time in the village pub. The hall was called the Reading Room. In warm comfortable surroundings hard-pressed housewives chose romantic novels from the bookshelves and were transported into another world. Daily papers were provided, the news was often depressing.

Industries geared up for war had collapsed overnight, unemployment and poverty was widespread. The 'land fit for heroes to live in' did not materialise. There were strikes and hunger marches. Men, mutilated by war, were reduced to begging on the streets of London. Jimmy Foster had some understanding; he too had lost a leg in battle and would never regain the full vigour of his youth. He might have brooded on his condition but he did not intend to allow it to blight the rest of his life. His father did not intend to abandon responsibility for his tenants and estate workers who had given so much in the war years. "Work will be found". The pay was poor but there some security. It was a better life than that of the miners families in the pit villages north and south of the Estate.

In 1924 William Foster died and Jimmy Foster inherited the Estate which he intended to maintain as a 'sporting estate'. Norman Sharpe, the newly appointed head gamekeeper was the man charged with establishing Apley Park as the place where country sports could be enjoyed to the full. Within a decade this was achieved. For those who were part of it this was a Golden Age.

THE OLD ENEMY

War was inevitable. Adolf Hitler was not a man who listened to reason. Professional soldiers were sent to France, Territorials were called up and on the home front Local Defence Volunteers put on arm bands. When Churchill turned them into Home Guards they were given stripes and pips to sew on their uniform. The Major was promoted to Colonel, corporals in the Great War became lieutenants overnight, farmworkers and craft apprentices filled up the ranks.

Jimmy Foster was a bachelor. He never saw the need for lavish accommodation and lived simply in his 'flat' in the servants' quarters. When the Hall was turned into a convalescent home he stayed where he was. Trooper Tom Gray carried on; making sure that the Major was always well turned out. This he had done for thirty-six years and he would continue to do so for the next two decades. Tom wasn't a servant he was an old comrade, a companion and general factotum, the sort of man every bachelor-soldier needs.

Although Apley was well out of harm's way there were daily reminders that there was a war on. Home Guards dug trenches, filled sandbags, and let fly with 303 rifles at targets in the Park. At least half of them had done it all before in Flanders a quarter of a century earlier. Village shopkeeper, Ted Lewis, sometimes slipped out of his store onto the main road dressed in police uniform. No one knew exactly what the duties of a 'special constable' were. Ted certainly made no attempt to direct traffic when convoys of American trucks raced through the village. They were a law unto themselves.

The nation was encouraged to 'dig for victory' in gardens and allotments. In the fields farmers worked tirelessly to increase food production. They needed help. They got it from Manchester girls and Italian boys. The Land Girls learned quickly from old farmhands and applied new skills with enthusiasm. The Italian boys were not so keen. They performed badly in the desert of North Africa, surrendering in droves, and they performed no better in the Apley fields. The girls were a distraction. The hot-blooded young POWs needed a lot of 'prodding' to help them concentrate on the job in hand.

THE END OF EMPIRE

Europe had been wrecked by war, recovery was slow. Britain was bankrupt and it took some time for her to realise that she was no longer a world power. Politicians in the colonies were clamouring for independence, it was granted gracefully and painlessly in some cases. In other parts of the Empire there was bloodshed. A bitter, protracted campaign was fought in Malaya. British troops were sent to trouble spots worldwide and to man lookout posts on the border between a divided Germany. They were not professional soldiers, they were the National Servicemen. Everyone who completed their two year stint had something to say about it. Some moaned, most lads agreed, 'it was an experience'.

It was all in the 'luck of the draw'. Alex Smith, a farmhand, had a rough time on the front line in Korea. The Honourable James Hamilton, destined to inherit Apley Estate, had an entertaining time with the British

Army of the Rhine. It might easily have been the other way round. A whole generation of young men were thrown together, shaken up, and required to 'rub along' at a time of great social change.

WE WILL REMEMBER THEM

In 1922 'old soldiers' in their twenties, Comrades of The Great War, met in the Reading Room and formed an association to honour those who had died and aid those whose lives had been shattered by war. They elected a committee and formed the Apley Park Legion. Only one man could be considered for President of the Branch, Major Jimmy Foster.

The Presidency was handed on over the years from Major to General to Brigadier, to Lord James Hamilton, a subaltern in the Coldstream Guards and on to his son Major Ben Hamilton who served in the same regiment. Rank wasn't particularly important all the Apley Legionnaires had once had a rank and a number and they were not all soldiers, there were sailors and airmen too.

In the early days Apley was special. The members were bound together not only by military service but by the very nature of the Estate itself. Closest to Nature were the farmhands, foresters, gamekeepers and the gardeners at the Hall. Their love of the countryside was shared by the 'gents' who rode to hounds and bagged the pheasants and coaxed the salmon from the Severn.

As time went by the butler, the chauffeur, the maids and footmen all disappeared. The kitchen, dining room and corridors were silent until the boarding-school boys swarmed in. For twenty years school masters in baggy tweed jackets did their best to educate inky ruffians. Then silence again. The Hall was empty. Thieves came for all they could carry away. The swelling roots of unkempt shrubs began to prise apart the masonry everywhere until parts of the garden resembled a neglected temple in a tropical land.

OLD COMRADES FADE AWAY

The Major died. Trooper Tom Gray, who had stood by Jimmy Foster for nearly sixty years, passed away soon after. The General took charge.

General Eddie Goulburn, who had commanded thousands of troops on the battlefield, now faced the problem of administering the estates of Betchworth and Apley. He was a 'no nonsense' man and set about his task with a will. Eddie's younger brother Cuthie, retired from the army. He moved into the Manor House and turned his hand to farming. Brigadier Cuthbert Goulburn and his brother Eddie were both bachelors, they both needed looking after.

Some care was needed when choosing the right team. It helped if there was common ground, a military connection, and similar personality. General Eddie Goulburn DSO found the ideal couple, Sam and Nell Coles. Sam was given just twenty minutes to familiarise himself with controls of the Daimler, The General knew that was enough. Sam had spent the war defusing bombs; this was a man he could rely on totally.

'The Brig' threw himself into the life of the community. Charming and sociable he needed a man to match his personality and in Tom Hopper, a Black Country gunsmith, he found just the man. Sergeant Hopper of the Royal Engineers spent most of his life getting out of scrapes; this was a very useful skill, because the Brigadier took a lot of risks, physically and socially. The bonds between all these military men were not unique, it was called comradeship.

HANDING ON THE TORCH

A 'special operator' with the Royal Signals, Roy Coles flew home from Kenya for 'demob' in 1961, the last village lad to complete National Service. The professionals were left to carry on the Apley tradition of service to the Crown for the next fifty years.

Company Sergeant Major Tommy Roberts completed more tours than most in Northern Ireland. Alwyn Barnett, a cheeky little boy, was commissioned in the RAF. Alwyn flew up the ranks to retire as an Air Commodore. Submariner Adrian Connolly was unique. He flew over the equator, he sailed over the equator and he sailed under the equator, on board HMS Conqueror.

Framed in the library of the Union Jack Club in London is an embroidered replica of the battle honours of the King's Shropshire Light Infantry. Some visitors are surprised to see a familiar place name, Afghanistan, and the date, 1872–80. A new-comer to the village, Trooper Jamie Chater of the Queen's Dragoon Guards came home unscathed after a tour of duty in Afghanistan in 2012. Sergeant Steven Draper had been there too. Steven joined as a Fusilier. He was all over the place collecting medals, in Northern Ireland, Iraq, Afghanistan, and bringing them back to show his folks on Windmill Lane. He spent some time in Basra.

Apley men had been to the Gulf before him. Gunner Botley of the Royal Garrison Artillery kept an eye on the oil refinery at Abadan, kept back the invading Turks and watched gunboats and supply vessels sail up the Tigris towards Baghdad. In 1919 he sailed home and did his best to keep down the rabbit population on the Estate.

Gunner Ern Ewins, painter and decorator, manned an anti-aircraft battery at RAF Shaibah, near Basra in the early days of The Second World War. The protection of oil supplies from The Gulf was still a priority. From the Gulf Ern went on to Cairo to join the Desert Rats. They crossed North Africa and did not stop until Rommel's Afrika Korps withdrew from Tunisia.

For more than a hundred years Apley men have been serving world wide on land and sea and in the air. British troops are scheduled to withdraw from Afghanistan in 2014 and Jamie Chater will probably be there for his second tour of duty to witness this episode of modern history.

A New Beginning

Against all the odds Apley survived the financial storms of the twentieth century. Responsibility for steering The Estate through the choppy waters at the beginning of the new millennium then rested with Lord Gavin Hamilton.

Nature could not be allowed to have her own way. The fabric of farms and cottages had to be preserved. Stockton Buildings once housed one of the finest herds of Shorthorn cattle in all England. Fine cheeses matured in the dairy where now cream teas and tasty meals are served. The stockyard has gone, replaced by a play-barn. Lord Gavin and Lady Harriet have a young family and know how difficult it is to keep children amused. The play barn is a memorial to John Pigg, the old farm manager, and a symbol of Gavin Hamilton's commitment to the community. We look forward with optimism.

In the darkest days of the Second World War Winston Churchill gave a speech to prepare the nation for the Battle of Britain. If we were victorious he predicted, "that all Europe may be freed and the life of the whole world may move forward into broad sunlit uplands."

When the opening shots of the Great War were fired in 1914 Apley men were there. In defence of the nation they 'soldiered on' and served in practically every campaign of the twentieth century. They still strive to keep the peace and protect us from evil.

Chapter 1

At the Turn of the Century

Daddy Pots

There was no duck pond beside the village green in Norton. There was no village green, just a triangle of grass with an oak tree planted in 1937 for the Jubilee, and an ancient elm that was finally finished off by a moth from Holland. This was at the heart of the village where Cheswardine Lane and Village Road crossed the Bridgnorth Road. The village school nearby was rather grand with its elaborate Victorian brickwork and an unusually tall clock tower; strangers thought it was a church. The pub opposite had been the administrative centre for 'The Hundred', an area of land capable of sustaining roughly a hundred households. 'The Hundred Man' was responsible for raising local troops and leading them; he was also expected to enforce the common law.

Local villains and petty criminals were tried in the court room. Sometimes justice was done and sometimes injustice was done. Punishment could be immediate. Opposite The Hundred House were the stocks and whipping post where vindictive villagers chastised their wayward neighbours for such serious offences as 'gossiping'. This was no cure; gossiping continued for centuries inside and outside the village pub.

In the middle of the twentieth century the stocks were still there beside the remains of an ancient elm. Soldiers young and old assembled here every year in November to make their March of Remembrance up the hill to the parish church. Although they complained that it was often 'a bit fresh', few of them wore overcoats and they jostled and joked around the stocks to keep warm. They milled around awaiting orders the way soldiers have always spent much of their time. Some glanced up at the school clock. The Legion Chairman looked anxious. His eyes were

25

fixed on a cottage gate just beyond the tithe barn. He turned to the parade marshal, "Here he comes. Thank God for that! Sort 'em out, Tom!"

Regimental Sergeant Major Thomas Dovey, late of the Oxford and Buckinghamshire Light Infantry, had not lost his voice. He could bark and bawl as loudly as ever, but he seemed to have lost his grip on discipline. His 'troops' – representatives of all three services – formed a casual column that chattered and muttered as the standard bearer carefully unfurled the blue and gold standard, and took up his post at the head of the squad. Across the road the latch clicked on the cottage gate and out stepped a stocky old fellow in a dark suit and a bowler hat. He straightened his shoulders and set off briskly to join the column of men. "Ah – ten – shun. L–eee-ft turn!"

The man who had held up the parade was not Major Arthur Foster of Apley Hall. It was Bill Philpot, 'Daddy Pots' to the village children. He attached himself to the rear of the column. "By the left! Quick march!"

Off they went with standard flying, arms swinging and medals jingling. Everyone knew where these men had served by the colour of their ribbons. They had fought in the trenches of France and Belgium, in jungles and deserts, on icy seas and in flak-filled skies. Bill Philpot wore medals that were different from all others; one bore the head of Queen Victoria, the other that of her son Edward VII. Bill was the oldest man there, the only one on parade who had fought in the South African Wars. That was why they had to wait. They couldn't leave him behind.

At the beginning of the twentieth century, men of the county regiment were camped on the banks of the Orange River that flowed out of the Orange Free State, a stronghold of the Boers. From here they marched up to the battlefront under the blazing South African sun. They arrived at Paardenberg Drift in the afternoon, loosened their packs and dusted themselves down; they were not going to rest for long. In just over an hour they were sent into action. To attack the Boer positions they had to ford the Modder River. They waded across in full battle kit with the water up to their armpits. The engagement lasted twelve hours but the outcome was indecisive. The Shropshire Battalion's casualties were few; although several were wounded only four were killed.

While his mates were getting their feet wet, Trooper Philpot (3818) was high and dry, cantering around the veldt in pursuit of an elusive enemy.

A troop of the 10th Hussars going out on patrol wearing pith helmets for protection against the sun. During the Boer War they were covered with khaki cloth, earlier in the Zulu War they were white and easy to spot by the enemy.

© National Army Museum (92817)

"Call for the Cavalry!"

The 18th Hussars had a proud history; they had fought at the Battle of Waterloo and taken part in the Charge of the Light Brigade. The task in hand now was to relieve the garrison at Ladysmith. Bill and his troop were called upon to play only a minor part and then add another clasp to their South African medal. The Battle of Talana Hill was an altogether more unpleasant affair; after that Bill was ready to come home.

In 1902 the Peace Document was signed and the Volunteer Service Company of the KSLI was welcomed home at a ceremony in the county town. Two years later a fine memorial, in white marble, was unveiled outside St Chad's in Shrewsbury to honour the men who had died in the South African War. This would not be the last war memorial to be erected in the county. Within twenty years they would appear in every town and village.

Trooper Philpot settled down to a peaceful life on the estate.

He watched, with some sadness, lads leave to serve in the Great War, the Second World War and the Korean War. Daddy Potts said, "They never seem to learn."

Hello Dolly

Young Tom Gray lived near Wimbledon Common and watched Queen Victoria's Horse Guards exercise almost daily. His earliest memories were of straight-backed troopers, the jingle of harness and the smell of polished leather. He wanted to be part of this, and in time he was.

The opening shots of the South African War were fired in 1899. Patriotic fervour swept the nation and music hall audiences everywhere bellowed with extra gusto the chorus of 'Goodbye Dolly Gray'. The twentieth century was only five months old when Thomas John Gray gave up his job as a waiter and agreed to serve the Queen for twelve years as a trooper in the Household Cavalry.

For any young recruit, life was going to be hard. They were all barked at and bullied by drill sergeants. This was supposed to be part of the process of producing a disciplined force. Many unfortunate lads with unfortunate names suffered terrible ridicule in front of the squad. Poor Trooper Turvey was always going to be called 'Topsy'. "Topsy-turvy, Topsy-turvy, stand still will you! You don't know y'r arse from y'r elbow, Topsy-turvy."

The sergeant always invited the rest of the squad to join in the fun. "Na then lads, lets 'av' a chorus of 'Goodbye Dolly Gray'. I'll start you off…Goodbye Dolly I must leave you…Come on sing up…No, no not you, Gray…March on Doll…That's it…Hark I hear the bugle calling, Goodbye Dolly Gray." To put up with this sort of nonsense a man had to be made of strong stuff and Trooper Tom Gray was made of strong stuff.

The Royal Horse Guards saw plenty of action during the South African War, but not Tom Gray. He was nineteen at the time and not drafted. For ten years it was the routine of drill, exercises, manoeuvres and ceremonial duties. Tom Gray admitted that he was no great horseman, but he was chosen to be one of the escorts for the King of Spain when he came to London on a state visit, and he took part in the coronation ceremony of George V in 1911.

A more memorable event occurred earlier in 1905, something that would determine the whole course of Tom Gray's life. He was introduced to Sub-Lieutenant Arthur William Foster. Every officer had a batman, his own personal servant. This arrangement usually lasted until one of them left the regiment. Arthur Foster and Tom Gray were together for fifty-seven years. This was not the usual arrangement. They moved back and forth, London to Windsor, Windsor to London for ten years. When they were allowed leave Captain Foster went home to Apley, and Trooper Gray went back to Wimbledon.

The dark storm clouds of war gathered over Europe. Soon young men would be clamouring at the doors of recruiting centres eager to join in what they believed would be a great adventure. They were quite wrong.

LITTLE JIMMY FOSTER

Upstream from Apley Hall was the birthplace of the Industrial Revolution. The products of the forges and foundries were shipped down the Severn to Bristol and beyond. The most famous of the ironmasters, Abraham Darby, built the first iron bridge, and another, 'iron mad' Wilkinson, was buried in a cast iron coffin.

A view of Apley Hall from across the Severn. Some of the trees in the middle distance are imaginary, placed there for 'artistic effect'.

"Idyllic Surroundings"

All the families in the iron trade prospered and that included the Whitmores of Apley. At the time of the Napoleonic War, Thomas Whitmore watched with some satisfaction, from the grounds of Apley Hall, barges laden with cannons gliding steadily south to fulfil his lucrative contract with the Royal Navy. However, this did not get him out of financial difficulties, and so in 1867 the family sold the hall and the estate to another ironmaster, William Orme Foster.

The Fosters had no difficulty raising the money to make the purchase; their company was at the forefront of the technology of the time producing blast furnaces, mills for rolling steel and some of the first locomotives for the expanding rail networks of the world. They were fabulously rich and could afford to be generous, a family characteristic that passed down from one generation to the next. It wasn't all work and no play. William Foster was fox-hunting mad and put his only son, Arthur, in the saddle as soon as he started to toddle around. "Might make a cavalryman!"

The little lad had heard it all before but he didn't interrupt his Uncle Jimmy when he opened up again with, "Tel-el-Kebir, it was a walkover. They were no match for us; no spirit, no discipline."

Young Arthur could have told the tale himself, he had heard it so often, but he was in no hurry to get away. The French mistress was waiting to give him more language instruction, but he found battlefield stories far more interesting.

There was always something romantic about military uniform especially if there was a horse included to add a bit of dash and daring. Victorian prints and paintings captured many heroic events. At Waterloo, the Royal Scots Greys were depicted ploughing into Napoleon's infantry squares. In the Crimea, Hussars in tight red breeches were shown charging towards blazing Russian cannons. Small wars were best, against half-naked Africans, like Zulus, armed with spears and cow hide shields. When the action was over the heroes could dust off their red tunics and return swiftly to London to pick up a bright new Victoria Cross. By comparison, the life of a country squire was rather dull.

Old soldiers like Uncle Jimmy told tales of daring deeds. They missed out the bits where cannonballs bounced through breastplates and limbs were ripped off by shrapnel; in any case it always happened to somebody else. In June 1905, twenty-year-old Arthur William Foster presented himself at Hyde Park Barracks and was taken in as a Sub-Lieutenant in the Royal Horse Guards. He responded well to training at the Cavalry School and the Veterinary School. He impressed his superiors and was marked out for promotion. He demonstrated soldierly skills at Netheravon and musketry at Hythe. On promotion to captain he was appointed assistant adjutant after only four years with the regiment.

The regiment was everything; a family where lifelong friendships were founded. The junior officers socialised in the town houses that most well-to-do families kept in London, and for sport there was hunting and shooting on their country estates. Ceremonial duties in the capital or at Windsor could be tiresome for troopers and their officers alike. On the other hand, the glamour of the uniform made them popular with the ladies. It was Tom Gray's job to make sure that Captain Foster was always 'presentable'. "Thank you, Gray. Where would I be without you?"

Tom trooped along the Mall behind 'Jimmy', as he preferred to be called, at the Coronation of George V. The captain got a medal for it. Both men had missed out on the medals for the South African War, but they didn't have to wait long for the next war.

The assassination of the Archduke Franz Ferdinand of Austria, on the steps of the town hall in Sarajevo, lit the fuse that set Europe aflame. There was a chain reaction; Austria declared war on Serbia, Russia mobilised in support of Serbia, Germany declared war on Russia and France. Finally Britain declared war on Germany to protect Belgian neutrality. The 14th of August 1914 was the fateful day.

The German generals had drawn up elaborate plans for mobilising their forces in the event of war, and had devised a strategy for the invasion of France. This involved marching across Belgium; there was no room for manoeuvre. Belgium was in the way. A few politicians and members of the public voiced their opposition, but the majority of Britons, always sympathetic to the under-dog, were swept along on a tide of nationalism and cheered the troops on enthusiastically, to war.

Less than three weeks after the declaration of war the Royal Horse Guards, Trooper Gray and Captain Foster among them, crossed the Channel as part of the British Expeditionary Force. They moved inland immediately and took up a position west of Paris alongside French forces. The support they gave to their ally at this stage was crucial; until then the German invasion plan had been working like clockwork.

Chapter 2

The Contemptible Little Army

First Blood

The first major encounter between the German Army and the British Expeditionary Force took place in the third week of August 1914. In the coalfields near Mons, the well-rehearsed rapid fire of the British infantry held up the German advance, and the cavalrymen used the tactics they had been trained for. They engaged in skirmishes, dashing from hedge to hedge, as if they were fox-hunting. The German war machine ploughed on. The French and Belgians were in retreat and the outnumbered British also began to withdraw.

Sir John French's divisions had learned much during the South African Wars and were stubborn in retreat. The German 'Schlieffen Plan' was designed to knock France out of the war in six weeks, but the British got in the way and Wilhelm II, 'Kaiser Bill', was furious. He wrote to von Kluck, commander of the First Army:

> *...address your skill and all the valour of my soldiers to exterminate the treacherous English, and walk over John French's contemptible little army.*

The British regulars were delighted and adopted the title. Captain Arthur Foster and Trooper Tom Gray were young then. In time they were proud to be known as 'Old Contemptibles'.

There was poor co-ordination between the French and British commanders. As a result the British were left high and dry and had to pull back. The retreat from Mons was a sad event in British military history; there was worse to come. It was clear even now that the war would not be 'over by Christmas'. For four years the front line between the opposing armies hardly moved. The war of attrition claimed the lives of tens of thousands of men.

A White Christmas

A trench system was established that stretched from the Channel coast to the Swiss border. The ancient market town of Ypres was on the front line, and it was here in October 1914 that the 3rd Cavalry Division took up position. Captain Bowlby of the Royal Horse Guards had been sent ahead to organise billeting for the regiment. Arthur Foster and Geoffrey Bowlby had served together for nearly ten years. They were like brothers. The main contingent of the Royal Horse Guards sailed for France on the 6th of November and disembarked the following day. They were dispatched immediately to Ypres. From their base to the east of the town they sent out patrols along the Menin Road.

A quiet moment on the Menin Road. The nearest horseman, standing in his stirrups, is looking in the direction of a shell that has just exploded in the distance. This photograph and the next are from a collection belonging to Major Arthur Foster.

Apley Estate Archives

"Who was that disturbing the peace?"

33

Aware that he was a witness to history in the making, Captain Foster made notes and took 'snaps' for the family album. A tide of refugees swept down the Menin Road making for what they believed was a safe haven in the ancient market town. In November it snowed, and a miserable winter lay ahead for everyone. High casualty rates, erratic supplies and poor equipment meant that morale was going to suffer.

"Gray, according to Napoleon an army marches on its stomach."

"So I understand, sir."

"We need something warm inside us. See what you can do."

Scrounging was something that everyone did but not from a mate – unless he happened to be the company cook. With nearly fifteen years service Trooper Gray knew everyone. "What 'ave you got goin' spare, cookie?"

"Raspberry jam, plenty o' that, and bread. This stuff from the town is 'ard as a rock in a day."

"That'll do nicely, thank you very much, an' a few o' them cotton flour bags."

Tom Gray had all that was necessary to create his 'Ypres Pudding'. After lashing the jam onto fragments of stale French bread, a sprinkling of water made it pliable enough to cram into the cotton bags. Gentle simmering for twenty minutes and it was ready to serve. In civilian life Tom Gray had been a waiter; he knew how to present fine food.

"Splendid, Gray. Absolutely delicious!"

In years to come back at Apley Hall, in the company of old comrades, Jimmy Foster would ask Tom Gray to prepare this speciality 'for old time's sake'. The Ypres Pudding never tasted quite the same.

ALL HELL LET LOOSE

Captain Arthur Foster got his first real taste of action in February 1915, his 'baptism of fire', at Zillebeke, south-east of Ypres. The same month he was 'mentioned in dispatches'. Shortly afterward his name appeared in the *London Gazette*. He was among the first to be awarded the Military Cross.

From a strategic point of view it would have been sensible to withdraw from the town of Ypres and leave it to the Germans. Sir John French would not hear of it. On the high ground surrounding the town, the Germans set up a ring of fortified gun emplacements and a network of deep interconnected trenches. During the course of the war their artillery reduced Ypres to rubble and disrupted the efforts made by French and British forces to establish a stable front line from which to mount an attack. The Germans had the advantage – high ground and greater numbers.

In March 1915 the trench system under Frezenberg Ridge was a rudimentary affair. In places the trenches held by British infantry were no more than two feet deep, hardly enough to cover a man. Troops holding these positions did so under the nose of the enemy guns. Constant shelling made the building of a strong line of defence impossible. Every move of the harassed men of the 85th Infantry Brigade was watched by Germans on the ridge above. Men from Kent, Surrey and Middlesex who had held on so stubbornly were finally relieved. They withdrew in good order, their trenches taken over by cavalrymen. The Lifeguards and the Leicestershire Yeomanry were going to fight as infantry. Their horses, so carefully groomed for the parade ground, were stabled well out of harms way. Briefings were given by the infantry commanders at 'White Chateau', close to the notorious Hellfire Corner. Under cover of darkness, fresh troops were led to the front line by guides of the 85th Brigade. They worked feverishly all night to dig themselves in. This activity did not go unnoticed.

In the early hours of the morning on the 13th of May, the cavalry were subjected to a violent bombardment. The 2nd Lifeguards could not hold their position and fell back across ground scarred by shells and turned into a quagmire by the persistent rain. With no second line of defence they were pursued by German infantry. The Leicestershire Yeomanry made a brave attempt to cover the withdrawal of the Lifeguards despite rifles jamming in the muddy conditions. Their flank was exposed and they sought refuge in trenches held by Dragoon Guards. The Yeomanry were decimated by machine gun fire as they attempted to cross open ground on each side of a railway track. Two squadron leaders and practically all their troopers were killed. After six hours of battle only one officer and twelve men had made it to safety. Five hundred men of the 7th Cavalry Brigade were casualties.

A counter-attack was launched. At 2.00 in the afternoon the Royal Horse Guards, Captain Arthur Foster and Trooper Tom Gray among them, advanced across open ground into a hail storm of machine gun fire. A few of the remaining Leicestershire Yeomanry attempted to cover the Horse Guards' advance, and then went forward with them to set up a new line of defence near a farm. There followed three hours of battle then a lull. Men of the Leicestershire Yeomanry searched cautiously for fallen comrades. Near the farm they discovered a party of the Royal Horse Guards, two officers and five men, only two of which were unwounded. The senior officer was Captain Arthur Foster. He had serious injuries to leg and shoulder; the rest were hardly in better shape. They were isolated, the sound of battle still echoed around them, but there were no Horse Guards to be seen. Trenches to left and right were empty. "What's happened to the Blues?"

No one could offer an explanation. The regiment was lost. A trooper was sent back to the command post to report the situation and request orders; he never returned. The mixed party of Yeomanry and Horse Guards remained in the trench until nightfall, and then withdrew carrying the wounded to safety and collecting casualties of the Lifeguards that had been lying on the battlefield all day. They assembled on a road to the rear where remnants of all the cavalry regiments that had gone into action on that day were gathered. It had rained all day; wet, wounded and dejected, they clung together, a band of weary warriors.

A medical officer is treating a trooper of the Royal Horse Guards wounded in one of the opening skirmishes of the war. French troops look on. The pine wood surrounding them would be shredded by enemy artillery as the war progressed. At this stage in the war 'tin hats' had not been issued and men went into battle in soft forage caps.

Apley Estate Archives

"Aren't we the lucky ones?"

36

It was difficult to imagine that these men had once paraded in the capital, immaculate in their ceremonial uniform, with breastplates and helmets gleaming. Few had survived the battle uninjured. Tom Gray was one of the lucky ones.

The losses on the 13th of May were such that none of the cavalry regiments that had gone into action that day could now operate as a fighting unit. Some of the men who had lost their lives were recovered from the battlefield and eventually laid to rest near their comrades; others had simply disappeared from the face of the Earth. After the war their names were carved into panels on the Menin Gate.

The fighting was over for Captain Foster and Trooper Gray. Arthur Foster's wounds were treated at a dressing station, and then at the nearest field hospital. His left foot was so badly shattered that it was decided to amputate. Gangrene, feared by everyone who underwent surgery in these conditions, set in. His leg was amputated again, just below the knee and again some days later above the knee. Only a man with a robust constitution could have survived this repeated trauma. Within a fortnight the captain and his trooper were back in England. A long period of convalescence followed. As time went by they were able to reflect on the cost in human life. That battle in May 1915 cost the lives of over nine thousand men.

Chapter 3

Joining the Colours

Run for Your Life

No sooner had war been declared on Germany than the call went out to 'Join the Colours'. On battlefields of old the colours had been the rallying point for the troops; the colours were defended at all costs. Artists captured the scene in romantic pictures that appealed to young men. This was going to be a great adventure; this was a chance to get away from the daily routine, do brave deeds and return as heroes. Boys in industrial cities and the slums of the capital had nothing to lose; theirs was a miserable existence. By contrast, for a Shropshire lad working in the open air, every season had its rewards. Life was good.

At the outbreak of war, Albert Nicholls was working as a gardener in a place of peace and tranquillity on an estate overlooking the Menai Straits. His employer was a man who believed in duty to king and empire. "Have to let you go, Nicholls."

Nicholls may not have been ready to volunteer at this early stage. He might have wanted a bit more time to consider his position but he didn't have a position anymore. "Sorry. Duty and all that. You understand."

Albert packed his few possessions and boarded the Shrewsbury train. He walked through the Park from Linley Station to the family home in Cheswardine Lane. It was a brief stay. Less than a fortnight after the declaration of war, Albert journeyed to Birmingham and together with countless other young men completed Army Form B111. He gave his occupation as 'Gardener'. Anyone examining the form would have supposed that this recruit was at least a solicitor's clerk judging by his copper-plate handwriting. He agreed to 'serve three years with the colours', longer if required.

He was drafted into the 11th Battalion of the King's Royal Rifle Corps. Blackdown Camp was not as bad as it sounds; the surrounding countryside, on the Devon/Somerset border, must have reminded Albert of the Apley parkland. He spent Christmas at Blackdown. In France, in some sectors of the battle front, there was a Christmas truce. It was never repeated. This was war not a party.

The battalion moved to Witley in Surrey in February 1915, and finally to Larkhill within a few miles of Stonehenge. In May an advance party, including Rifleman Nicholls, left for France. The rest of the battalion landed at Boulogne in July, and moved up to the front line as part of the 41st Infantry Brigade. They had trained for eight months, read the newspapers, examined the casualty lists and listened to tales told by men who had been there before them, yet nothing could have prepared them for what they were about to experience. Rifleman Nicholls was in and out of the front-line trenches for well over three years. He survived the first year unscathed; some of his comrades were not so lucky.

The seasons passed: the summer of 1915, the misery of winter, the New Year, spring came, blackbirds sang and poppies grew again in the wasteland of Flanders. 'Flaming' June arrived in 1916 and the 11th Battalion of the King's Royal Rifle Corps were in 'Divisional Reserve', putting their weary feet up in Rue de Furnes, Poperinghe.

'Pop' was described in the battlefield guide as 'a centre for recreation, for shopping and for rest'. This little town had a quarter of a million troops billeted nearby; it must have been quite a busy shopping centre and not very restful. The town hall in Poperinghe was an imposing building but there was a dark side. Cells in the basement, built to accommodate the town drunks and petty thieves, were also the last place of rest for men condemned to be 'shot at dawn'. Young soldiers were taken from the cells here, bound to a post in the yard, blindfolded and shot.

Seven new boys appeared in Albert's billet, replacements for riflemen who were on their way home with 'Blighty' wounds, and replacements for others who would never go home. When the word spread that they were going up to the front again everyone knew what to expect. They were going back to the same line of trenches they had defended months earlier. The battalion entrained at 'Pop' and detrained at Asylum; the sidings were in the grounds of a mental hospital. "They've brought us to the right place. We must be barmy!"

Back in the trenches they were welcomed by the cheerful faces of the Duke of Cornwall's Light Infantry. The KRRC were also given a warm welcome by the German artillery doing their best to hit a nearby ammunition dump. They only succeeded in wounding Rifleman Tudor. The Royal Artillery replied the next day, the German gunners responded and the barrage continued. Six more riflemen were wounded in this exchange and the colonel was taken off to the nearest dressing station. Major Swaine sent off a message to all the company commanders to inform them of a change of command. "Thank you, Nicholls. It's quietened down a bit. Should be alright."

To be a runner required special qualities. Physical fitness of course, total reliability and self-reliance, and a great deal of good fortune. There was always the possibility that something would jump up and bite or drop on you from a great height. Albert didn't always 'run'. Sometimes he had to scramble about on all fours in rubble and mud, sometimes he swished along the lanes on his bike or cantered back and forth on a borrowed pony. Keep moving, that was the secret to survival. He set off on his rounds of the forward positions at midday and was back at the command post in the late afternoon. It was a fine evening with not a cloud in sky. The black clouds that drifted across the land were man-made. The shelling continued. "Now, was that a 7.7 or a 4.2?"

The artillery exchanges across the front line had provided 'the entertainment' for over a year. At twilight the guns fell silent; stars appeared and filled the sky. Albert knew the patterns they made and the names of some of the constellations. He could easily make out the Plough with its pointers to the North Star. He knew that these same stars were shining down on Echoes Hill above the village. Albert pulled his blanket around his shoulders and his 'tin hat' over his eyes and slept. No one got much sleep for the next three nights. The following day two riflemen were killed. "We're not having that!"

Major Swaine was a determined man. Officer patrols were sent out into 'no man's land' to reconnoitre, and raiding parties were organised for the following night. Nearly one hundred and fifty men were involved. 'The show' began with a release of gas. Smoke grenades added to the confusion. This little skirmish cost the lives of seven more riflemen, and in the next three days at least a dozen men of all ranks were wounded. Throughout, messages flew back and forth, tactics changed, orders given and then withdrawn. Albert Nicholls and the other runners were kept busy. When it was over the general commented, "I consider the behaviour of all troops could not have been better and showed great dash and determination." He didn't mention Rifleman Nicholls by name although he had certainly been dashing about. The battalion was relieved by the Essex Regiment. The KRRC trudged back to Asylum, then took the train to Brandhoek and spent five days in the luxury of billets.

"Where to next, does anyone know? We're taking the bus for a change." After a mystery tour of half a dozen shelled out hamlets with unpronounceable names they finally flung down their kit at Kortepyp Camp. "Come on, Albert. You must know something. Where to next?"

"Back to the front. Taking over from 'The Queens'" (West Surrey Regiment).

These trenches were better than some they had known and the names were understandable. Albert was at Battalion Headquarters at Stinking Farm. 'A' Company was in Spring Lane and the Machine Gun Section in Well Lane. Both were damp even in mid-summer. 'B' Company was in Winter Trench, an inhospitable place at any time of the year. This was unfamiliar territory. What they did learn was that a tunnel was under construction by Royal Engineers. It passed under no man's land in the direction of a concrete gun emplacement. It was difficult work in sandy conditions. During their three-day stay here there were no casualties, but the riflemen were on the receiving end of some 'friendly fire' from the French. This came in the shape of an eight inch mortar packed with high explosives. It landed in their trench with a thud. It was a dud.

They were relieved by the Royal Irish Rifles and then spent two days being shunted by train. They were crammed into trucks and marched from sidings to huts and finally to billets at Neuvilette. There were few complaints; everyone came to accept this as normal procedure.

From the relative safety of the billets at Neuvilette they were marched up to the front again, and here they stayed for three weeks until the Scots Guards arrived. They didn't see much of the enemy but the days did not pass without incident. Lord Cavan dropped in and pinned on medals, cheers all round. All were grateful to be alive and in one piece.

41

Arras, April 1917. These men of the King's Royal Rifle Corps have just come 'out of the line'. They are celebrating a victory at Monchy-le-Preux in what was known as the Battle of the Scarpe.

"The King's Royal Rifles rejoice!"

The iron cross painted on the side of the flimsy spotter plane that circled the village was plain to see and harmless enough. When the ruffians of the Rifle Corps jeered and shook their fists at the pilot he buzzed off. He must have told his mates about the rude behaviour of the riflemen because German gunners sent over a single shell which burst overhead wounding ten riflemen. The battalion moved to more comfortable quarters in a nearby orchard; it wasn't very fruitful. The neat rows of trees were no more than skeletons, stripped and shredded by shrapnel; this was not a place of safety. Another shell wounded six more men. "We might as well be in the front line!"

That night during the changeover with the 10th Battalion two more men were wounded. Albert's pals settled in and waited for the dawn. The landscape was just what they had come to expect; ragged leafless trees, stone barns reduced to rubble, the land bare and pock-marked with shell craters, tangled wire held up by twisted iron stakes. What appeared to be a shredded sandbag was hanging on the wire and swaying gently. A patrol went forward cautiously to investigate. They found that the bundle of field-grey rags was a young German infantryman. "Must have been shot last night, poor lad. He won't do that again; wandering about in the dark."

No one was safe, even in a deep dug-out. Three more riflemen were killed when a shell landed in the entrance to their shelter. Patrols scurried out from both armies probing each other's defences; neither side was inclined to make a full-scale assault.

"What's happened to Nelsby?" Nelsby went out with a couple of specialists; they were looking for a suitable site for a new gun emplacement. They only got as far as the wire when they came under fire. Sapper Cooper ran back and fell into the arms of his comrades and died. Gunner Horley lay out by the wire. Nelsby had disappeared. Had he gone over to the other side? Had he been captured? Was he dead or alive? The official war diary that recorded this event gave no clue. The National Archives have no service record. Did he ever exist? Of course he did. His mate, Sapper Cooper, was buried nearby in the Hebuterne Cemetery along with fifty-eight others. There are six graves there that say simply 'A Soldier of the Great War'. Nelsby must have been one of these; he was lost but he was never found.

The day after Nelsby disappeared two dozen men went out to attack a machine gun post. To their surprise they were unopposed. The Germans had retreated to a stronger position; the trench was deserted. On the way back to the safety of their own trenches Lance Corporal Smith was wounded. Three more men were wounded the next day as the battalion was being relieved by Scots Guards, and in the final stage of the operation a dozen more were wounded by a shell as they stood on the road outside Battalion Headquarters. Rifleman Albert Nicholls was standing inside. For a fortnight the KRRC continued with what was known as 'attrition', the wearing down of enemy resistance. The Germans were attempting to do the same. There were artillery exchanges every day. There were no pitched battles, but nevertheless during this brief period twenty-one men were killed, one hundred and fifty-one were wounded and fourteen were listed as 'missing'. Some, like Nelsby, were never found. Mothers and wives waited for years hoping that one day they would hear the click of the latch on the garden gate and see 'the lost boy' sauntering up the path.

By the autumn of 1918 the Germans were starving. It had to end soon. Albert came home on leave on the 3rd of November, a week before the armistice. He skipped down Cheswardine Lane and into the family kitchen. There was peace at last and Albert had two weeks in a warm bed. He had a hot meal every day and not everyone was dressed in khaki. The Great War came to an end. The fighting was over; now it was time to count the cost. The King's Royal Rifle Corps alone had lost one thousand two hundred men. That Albert Nicholls survived the war was miraculous; of his original company of over a hundred men only fourteen came home. He had seen many close friends die, heard the wounded scream as they were carried from the battlefield and in the weeks that followed waited for news of those who were 'missing'. The bells of St. Chad's at Stockton rang out over the parish. There was little to celebrate; there had been too much pain.

Leave was soon over. Albert walked down the lane, passed the hall and took the train from Linley south to the coast. The war was over, Christmas over and a New Year was on its way. He was going back to France; there was nothing to fear now. He met up with other riflemen from the KRRC on the ferry, and as they crossed the Channel they began to think of their comrades still there in France waiting to take their leave. He had arrived with the advanced party. They had been constantly on the move for three years never knowing from one day to the next where they might be, or if they would live to see another day. It is astonishing that they never broke; individuals did but not the 11th Battalion of the King's Royal Rifle Corps, and not Rifleman Nicholls. Of all the Apley men who fought in the Great War, no one spent more time in 'a place of danger' than Albert Nicholls, and he came home without a scratch.

SHARPSHOOTER

The Sharpe family travelled from Essex to Shropshire in 1902 and moved into Apley Lodge. Edward Sharpe had been appointed head gamekeeper on the estate, and he held this position for over a quarter of a century. He had an infectious enthusiasm for all things natural. His sons, Ted and Norman, learned to love the countryside and both in turn became gamekeepers. Norman was five-years-old when he started to explore the woodlands around the lodge. In the course of his lifetime he came to know every corner of the estate; woodland, stream, dingle, parkland, field and hedgerow. Perhaps the places he loved best were on the banks of the Severn; the six-mile stretch from Coalport Bridge to the town mills, upstream from Bridgnorth.

Norman Sharpe was not a model pupil at the village school. He didn't always see eye to eye with the schoolmaster Mr Davies. The schoolroom windows were built high deliberately so that pupils would not be distracted by villagers going to and fro, and gossiping in Village Road. Above the windowsills there was always a clear view of the sky, the thatched top of the tithe barn and the giant elm next to the stocks. Norman could imagine all the wildlife hidden in the foliage, birds, insects and the resident squirrel. Maybe he wasn't paying much attention to Mr Davies but, Sharpe by name and sharp by nature, he did learn. On leaving school he might have taken up his father's trade as gamekeeper, and he would have been delighted to do so. Instead, the agent offered him a job in the estate office in Bridgnorth. He was given responsibility immediately; collecting rent. He did his weekly rounds of properties in every street in the town and became a familiar figure as he carried out his duties.

In the evenings and at weekends, Norman was in the woods; this was where he knew he belonged, but he would have to wait. At the outbreak of the Great War, Norman Sharpe was eighteen-years-old. They said it would be 'over by Christmas'; if it had been he would have missed it. The British Expeditionary Force was bloodied in the early months, but despite this young men were eager to join. The Sharpes' ancestral roots were north of the border. Norman made his own way to Scotland to join the clan. In 1915 he was in the uniform of a private in the Argyll and Sutherland Highlanders and he served with them to the end of the war.

The 14th Battalion of the Argyll and Sutherland Highlanders was formed at Stirling in 1915 and moved to Plymouth in June that year. Three months later he was under canvas on Witley Common in Surrey. Thousands of front-line infantry were trained here, and at this stage of the war the training was thorough. Norman believed that recruits who joined later were ill-equipped for the conditions they were expected to face. The final phase of training took place at Aldershot. In June 1916 the Argylls landed at Le Harvre; they were in the thick of it from the start. In four years the 'Argylls' won six Victoria Crosses.

45

The Scottish 15th Division was 'mobile', directed to sectors of the front that had been hardest hit and in need of reinforcements. The reputation of the Sutherland Highlanders dated back to the Crimean War where they had formed 'The Thin Red Line'. Their commander had thought it unnecessary for them to form a defensive square; he believed that they could be relied upon to stand firm against all odds.

A youthful Norman Sharpe, proud to be wearing the uniform of an Argyll and Sutherland Higlander.

"Highlander from the Severn Valley."

On every soldier's record of service there was a section where any special skills were recorded; the examples given were 'swimming' and 'chiropody'. Private Sharpe's skills were, 'sniper', 'bomber' and 'runner'; he was clearly a very busy man.

Letters from home kept up morale but there was often sad news of village lads killed or maimed; lives blighted. Norman had lost touch with Bob Howard. As scrapping schoolboys they had blacked each other's eyes in playground fights. Between 'hostilities' they were good friends. Bob got into another fight in the trenches of the Somme and he lost. Norman was saddened to learn that his old sparring partner was one of the fallen.

In the summer of 1917 Norman was laid low with 'trench fever'. This was a condition that afflicted all armies. There were flu-like symptoms together with skin rashes and leg pains. It was not particularly serious, but the cause baffled the medical officers. By the end of the war the culprits had been identified – body lice. There were plenty of them about and they thrived in the trenches, especially in warm weather.

Bullet and bomb, shell and shrapnel killed and maimed men daily. They came to accept it. Above all, there was one weapon they feared most – gas. There seemed to be no defence against it. The allies were as guilty as the Germans; General Haig ordered gas to be used during the Battle of Loos and both sides continued to use it to the end. The effects, particularly of mustard gas, were horrifying. A change in the wind direction was just as catastrophic as a gas attack by the enemy. The Argylls suffered in this way.

Norman was dispatched with a message to a company of the Black Watch. There was no one to receive it. They were dead to a man. The sight of their frozen faces, black and purple, haunted him all his days.

To 'inculcate the offensive spirit' the Argylls spent ten days in 'The Bullring' at Etaples. This training establishment was infamous, the discipline unnecessarily harsh and the restrictions unreasonable. There was a permanent undercurrent of discontent. Many of the troops had front-line experience and did not need instruction from NCOs who had never been under fire. On the first day the Argylls were given bayonet practise, hounded over an assault course and lectured on how to face shrapnel. Norman did not need any of this. A mate answered for him when his name was called at the next muster parade. From then on he spent his days in a railway siding, writing letters home and waiting to be sent back into the line. Lying in his bunk one evening at Etaples, Norman was disturbed. "Get up, Sharpe! You are in trouble. You've been absent on parade."

"And you, Sergeant, are in trouble because you marked me present.

The worst thing that can happen to both of us is to be sent to the front."

The treatment of troops in the Bullring forced weary soldiers to the point of mutiny. One long night Norman was ordered to stand guard over a young soldier. At dawn he was taken from the cell and shot. The general who signed his death warrant never met the man, or even examined the court martial documents. He just signed. Norman blamed the politicians not the generals. Boys, untrained, undisciplined and totally unprepared had been sent to war and were expected to stand firm when all hell was thrown at them. Years later, in Apley woods, when Norman heard the crack of gunfire from an unexpected quarter, that night in France flashed back into his mind.

Private Sharpe saw action in major battles and minor skirmishes. As a runner he managed to dodge danger. His conspicuous conduct earned him a 'mention in dispatches'. "The next Military Medal will have your name on it, Sharpe."

Norman's luck ran out. At Dickebusch, a village not far from Ypres, together with two other runners, he guided artillerymen to a forward gun emplacement. They moved cautiously to avoid the German shells. The enemy gunners were both methodical and predictable. An experienced soldier could tell by the sound of the shell as it whistled overhead where it would land. This particular one had the names of his companions on it. The shell fell amongst them; two gunners of the Royal Artillery were killed, and the three escorts were wounded. Norman was hit. Hot splinters ripped through his leg. His war was over. It was July. Within four months the war was over for everyone.

There was still a place for Norman in the estate office but he wanted the outdoor life. At last, after four painful years, he threw away his sticks. He was now ready to take responsibility for one of the beats as under keeper to his father. In due course he became head keeper. Apley became famous as a sporting estate. Norman was the man in charge during the golden age between the wars.

FALL FROM GRACE

Christopher, the parson's son, joined the King's Shropshire Light Infantry as an officer, and went off to war alongside the village lads. He shared the horrors of trench warfare with them; he did rather well. In October 1917 he was promoted to captain and appointed 'Brigade Bombing Officer'.

The war didn't seem to do him any harm, indeed it helped his career. He landed a 'plum job' as Aide de Camp (ADC) to Lord Reading, the Viceroy of India.

Life in the tropics, outside the British compound, could be very unhealthy. There were things to be avoided; the open sewers, the flies that swarmed over them and any poisonous snakes that lurked near them. Contact with any of 'the native species' was risky. Even contact with the native people was discouraged. "Silly chap spends a lot of time with the natives. Bad form."

At the viceroy's residence in Delhi, Captain C M W Noel-Hill was mixing with the very cream of society. On Christmas Eve 1923 they gathered for a festive photograph. The viceroy and Lady Reading were seated at the front, standing behind them secretaries, ADCs and advisors, several in splendid uniforms. All appeared confident and rather serious; smirking was 'not the done thing'. Ladies sitting to left and right of the viceroy appeared more relaxed, among them Megan Lloyd George the twenty-one-year-old daughter of the war-time prime minister. She had not yet embarked on her own political career. The guests at the residence did look a bit starchy, but Megan knew that even at the very top they misbehaved. Her own father was a fine example of infidelity.

What happened to Captain Noel-Hill to cause his fall from grace we do not know, except that the decline and fall was rapid. In 1924 he was on 'light duties', in 1926 he was given a gratuity and retired on the grounds of 'ill health'. Then in January 1927 he had some explaining to do in front of the Chief Justice of Bhopal. How had a man in his position got into financial difficulties with a Mr Laiquat Ali? "Tried to warn him, wouldn't listen." Bankrupt and in disgrace Christopher Noel-Hill was shipped home.

In a cheap lodging house in Shrewsbury he had time to consider what might have been. In the long run some of the 'sons of the soil', privates in the county regiment, men he had commanded in France, fared better than the rector's son, ADC to the Viceroy of India.

Chapter 4

With the Sun in Their Eyes

ON A GREEN HILL FAR AWAY

A twisted tangle of barbed wire stretched from the Channel coast to the Swiss border. For four years shell-shocked troops from trenches on either side gave their lives attempting to cross no man's land. There was no way round it, except perhaps the long way round, through the Straits of Gibraltar across the Mediterranean Sea and into the Black Sea. The problem was the Dardanelles, the narrow passage between these two seas, and the Turkish guns on either side.

Churchill was First Lord of the Admiralty in 1914 and with his usual bruising enthusiasm set about persuading the war cabinet that a campaign against the Turks had merit. He believed that the Turkish forces were weak and would be easily overcome, Germany would lose an ally and at the same time we could help our ally, Russia. John Fisher, the First Sea Lord, regarded by some as the finest admiral since Nelson, was not convinced.

Attempts made to force a passage through the Dardanelles in February 1915 ended in failure. In April, troops were landed at Cape Helles. They were held on the beaches and made little progress. In an attempt to break out and secure the Gallipoli Peninsula more troops were landed to the west at Anzac Cove and Sulva Bay.

The Australian and New Zealand Army Corps mounted a series of heroic attacks against the Turks. To engage a determined enemy they had to advance not over level ground but up near vertical cliffs. Green Hill and Chocolate Hill were well over a thousand feet high. These hills and all the neighbouring features such as the Salt Lake and Scimitar Hill were named by the military map-makers.

The bare slopes of Chocolate Hill were the scene of bitter fighting against the Turks who held the high ground.

© National Army Museum (94462)

"Chocolate Hill? I can think of a better name for it."

British, French and Anzac forces fought side by side. They were there in strength and made yet another attempt to dislodge the Turks from the high ground. Reinforcements were brought in to attack what was thought to be a weak point in the Turkish defences.

The 2nd South Midland Mounted Brigade formed up including troopers of the Warwickshire Yeomanry. Richard Humphrey Wainwright from Ackleton was in their ranks. His is the last name to be read out at the memorial service at Stockton every November. He died on Scimitar Hill in September 1915 and is buried on a Green Hill, far away, overlooking Salt Lake and the beautiful blue Mediterranean beyond.

Within four months all troops had been withdrawn from Gallipoli except those who died there. Early on in the campaign when it was clear that there was little hope of success, Admiral Fisher resigned. Churchill was also a casualty. He lost his job at the Admiralty, but he soon got another one serving in the army on the Western Front.

More than Just a Scratch

Troops of the British Empire were assembled in Egypt where they were kitted out and given training before being shipped to the battlefront. Both the training and the kit were inadequate. The generals who directed operations were not up to the job either. Field Marshall 'Bill' Slim, a lieutenant at the time, later described the Gallipoli commanders as the worst since the Crimean War.

Eric Watson was working in Manchester at the outbreak of war. For recreation he played lacrosse. Lacrosse is a rather unusual sport normally associated with public schools, but actually devised by Native American Indians. They were supposed to settle their differences by competing at lacrosse rather than resorting to tribal warfare. The tribes of Europe used bombs and bullets instead. Eric and his teammates at the lacrosse club were keen to join up and join in. "It'll be good sport. We don't want to miss it."

Eric joined the Manchester Regiment. Things moved quickly. He enlisted on the 19th of August, spent a week at Littleborough and sailed from Southampton on the 10th of September. In less than a fortnight the Manchester Regiment was off to war.

Carrying all their new kit they were assembled under the great cast iron arches on the platform of Manchester's London Road Station. They were in high spirits; there was backslapping, handshaking, gentle embraces, a few flags fluttering, handkerchiefs waving and dabbing damp cheeks. On the photographs of the day there was eagerness on the faces of the young men leaning from the carriage windows. Behind them there must have been some who could not find room at the windows to wave. They sat back in the compartment with their kit around them, glancing up at the backs of their comrades, perhaps thinking, "Have I done the right thing, volunteering?"

Too late. With a whistle and a wave of the green flag the train pulled away from the platform leaving behind a sea of anxious faces. Before they had gone more than a dozen miles some lads were opening up their ration packs. Somewhere south of Birmingham they stopped and tea from an urn on the platform was handed in through the carriage windows. No one was allowed off. After that things got a bit unsanitary; men relieving themselves where they could. There was great relief when the train came to a halt at Southampton docks.

The flag waving was over; the boys were barked at and herded like sheep. With a tubby little army sergeant snapping at their heels they were bunched together and urged up the gangplank of SS Avon, a packet boat requisitioned from the Royal Mail.

They set sail and most soon found their sea legs. Those who couldn't find them were grateful that they had decided to put on khaki and not navy blue! The passage to Alexandria took three weeks. They crossed the Bay of Biscay and passed through the Straits of Gibraltar with the towering wedge of the Rock on the port side; they knew left from right by then. In Valletta Harbour they took on more supplies; the troops were not allowed ashore. The Avon steamed on. The Manchester Regiment disembarked at Alexandria.

The young soldiers journeyed by train across the Nile Delta towards Cairo. They looked out through the carriage windows on scenes unchanged since biblical times; turbaned men in flowing robes, veiled women and scampering children everywhere. Lads from Cheshire saw their first camel, animals on the move, goats and cattle and the occasional dog stretched out in a dusty doorway. In the lush green fields watered by the Nile there were crops of grain, sugar cane and beans. The date palms often pictured around desert oases were, here in the delta, planted in regimented lines along the irrigation channels. In the coming months the boys became accustomed to all this but never to the wailing of the imams, calling the faithful to prayer from the minarets of the mosques in Cairo and every town and village in the country.

The British formally took charge of Egyptian affairs in 1861 and, as colonial powers always do, brought with them their lifestyle, customs and sports, including horseracing. The Manchesters were camped on the racecourse at Heliopolis, just outside Cairo. They were kitted out, and serious training for war was started in January 1915 when they moved from their bell tents on the racecourse to the more substantial Abbassia Barracks. In common with foot soldiers in all wars they were treated like mushrooms, 'kept in the dark and fed on shit'. They moved again to Kantaraand and then were told, "You're off to the Dardanelles. That's the passage to the Black Sea. There's the Turks on both sides".

"Well that's a job for the navy."

In the first week of March 1915 the navy had some success. They silenced the batteries at the entrance to the Dardanelles. Marines went ashore a number of times but met with increasing resistance. The Turkish shore batteries were concentrated about ten miles inland on both sides of the Narrows; the channel was heavily mined. Under the guns and in broad daylight attempts were made to clear the mines using fishing trawlers manned by civilians. Understandably this exercise failed. There was worse to come. On the 18th of March a task force was ordered in to force a passage from the Aegean to the Black Sea. It was a disaster. In a matter of hours, out of nine battleships, three were sunk and three were crippled.

The army was keen to show what they could do. British, French and Anzac forces first landed around Cape Helles on the Gallipoli Peninsula on the 25th of April. They might have made better progress had they not been hampered by poor organisation on the part of their commanders, and the stiffening resistance of the Turks. Trenches were dug as deep as those in France; it was the same old story. A series of bloody skirmishes and full-scale battles followed. One of the allies' main objectives was the village of Krithia.

The 1st/6th Battalion of the Manchester Regiment embarked at Alexandria on Tuesday, 4th of May. The passage to Gallipoli, aboard the captured German liner *Derflinger*, took two days. They were put ashore at V Beach and found things 'very busy'.

GIVEN EVERY PROTECTION

Eric Watson prepared for battle. Standard-issue headgear for this part of the world was the pith helmet. They were light and gave excellent protection from the sun. Some were made of cork; the best were made from the sola plant, from India. No matter what the material, protection from the harmful rays of the sun was guaranteed, but these helmets provided little protection from anything the enemy might throw at men in the front line.

Getting into the front line to relieve the troops already there was tricky; 'bullets flying in all directions'. Among the wild flowers, marguerites and poppies, on the surrounding hills were little mounds of earth where fallen comrades lay. They drew breath at the battle front before the order was given to go 'over the top'. Private Watson's company advanced 'one hundred and fifty yards nearer to Constantinople' and held their ground.

The Third Battle of Krithia began on the 4th of June. There were casualties. Eric Watson 'caught a packet'. It was more than just a scratch. A 'tin hat' might have saved him from serious injury but his pith helmet gave no protection. The head wound he received at Gallipoli ended Private Watson's war. Casualties were taken off the beaches and ferried to hospital ships.

His Majesty's Hospital Ship *Britannic* was a sister ship to the *Titanic*. She was launched from the Harland and Wolff shipyard in Belfast in 1914 and immediately requisitioned for war service. To man this great ship required a crew of over eight hundred men; although the medical staff numbered nearly five hundred they still had their hands full with over three thousand wounded on board. *Britannic* was fully occupied throughout the Gallipoli campaign. In two years she made five successful trips from Southampton to the eastern Mediterranean.

Back in England, recuperation for Eric Watson was a slow process. There was a lot of sitting about, chatting, playing cards, reading. Reports in the daily papers were generally optimistic, but the casualty lists could not disguise the fact that a terrible price was being paid, and there was little to show for it. It was clear by now that the operation in Gallipoli had failed. After months of misery all allied troops were withdrawn. They dispersed; some back to England to regroup and recruit more into their depleted ranks. Some battalions were sent straight to France including Australians and New Zealanders who had suffered greatly. French forces and the Irish Brigade sailed across the Mediterranean to the port of Salonika.

Any movement in these waters was dangerous. German U-boats were active everywhere and mines had been laid in all the sea lanes. Before the end of the Gallipoli Campaign the *Britannic* made one last trip. Taking the familiar route from Southampton into the Mediterranean she stopped at Naples to take on coal and water and then set course for Gallipoli. As *Britannic* passed between the island of Kea and the Greek mainland doctors and nurses, relaxing in the dining room, were alarmed by the sound of an explosion. They reacted immediately and rushed to the wards. It may have been a mine or it may have been a torpedo but the result was the same. *Britannic* sank. Mercifully there were few casualties. She had carried Eric Watson to safety and now she was a casualty, lying at the bottom of the Mediterranean Sea.

The Forgotten Army

The British Salonika Force and the allies that fought alongside them were regarded as a 'forgotten army'. It was difficult to see how so large a force could be overlooked when the battle front extended for over 200 miles, from the Adriatic to the Aegean across Albania, Serbia and Northern

Greece. The area had not yet recovered from the Second Balkan War fought between Greece and Serbia on one side and Bulgaria on the other. It came to a miserable end in 1913. A year later Bulgaria sided with Germany. The French gave support to the weakened Serbia forces; Britain, Italy, Romania and even Russia sent troops in support. This multinational force was no more successful than the forces sent to Bosnia and Kosovo in more recent years. Greece remained neutral.

Andrew Jones, a stockman at Astol Farm for many years, had been surrounded by farm animals all his life. When he enlisted at the Agricultural Hall in Bridgnorth High Street, he gave his trade as estate carter; he was then working at Aldenham Hall in the service of Lord Acton. He could handle a team of horses harnessed to a cart, a plough or a field gun. He trained as a gunner in the Royal Field Artillery at barracks near Edinburgh, and remained attached to Scottish brigades during his service overseas. "I'm being shipped off with 'The Jocks' to Salonika. Top end of Greece they tell me."

Andrew's two elder brothers were already in uniform, Charlie in the Shropshire Yeomanry in Palestine, Albert in the county regiment in France. One of his cousins, Eli Jones, had lost his legs in Flanders and another, Bertram Sargent, had lost his life at the Battle of Loos.

The German fleet was so active in the Mediterranean that some troops and supplies were taken to Greece by train across France and Italy, and then made the short crossing to the Albanian coast. Gunner Jones and 'The Jocks' were going to make the dangerous journey by sea. It was January and hard to imagine a more dismal place than Edinburgh's Princes Street Station; no cheery send off, no flag waving. For earlier contingents there had been bands and speeches. The war was more than a year old by now and everyone knew what lay ahead at journey's end.

The station platforms were awash with a sea of khaki. The blackened steel girders above supported panels of smutty glass. A pale grey light filtered through onto the shuffling crowd below. The greasy black engine, impatient to be off, snorted like a bull and sent out angry bursts of steam. Harsh words echoed over the heads of the troops. They took up their packs and began to edge towards the carriages. Gunner Jones and his battery stood apart, distinguished from the rest by the badge of the Royal Artillery on their forage caps and the spurs on their boots. The glengarries of the Highlanders with silk ribbons behind, silver badge and chequered bands were the only glints of colour in this drab scene.

The conditions on the journey to Liverpool were no better than those experienced by Eric Watson. At the docks the battery embarked with all the paraphernalia of war; field guns, limbers and startled horses. They were not mere beasts. They were individuals that the drivers and gunners treated as friends. They were cared for, groomed, fed and watered, their stalls cleaned daily. It was a full-time job, but at least it meant that the gunners were excused the tedium of inspections. The air down on the lower decks was not very fresh; the officers saw no reason to venture below.

Almost every ship stopped at Malta, the headquarters of the Mediterranean Fleet. Moored in Valletta Harbour for a few days, this gave everyone the opportunity to 'get spruced up' before the final leg of the voyage. The captain set course for Salonika.

Mount Olympus, home of the gods of ancient Greece, was sighted as they approached their destination. It was a dramatic sight. Most of the supplies for the campaign were brought in through the port of Salonika. There was heavy traffic in the sea lanes and the troopship moved cautiously towards the dock. From a distance the most prominent feature was the White Tower on the waterfront. The town spread out beyond on rising ground. The network of narrow alleys could be made out and above the rooftops were the spires and towers of mosques and churches. This was a very different scene from the one they had witnessed as they sailed away from Liverpool and out into the Irish Sea. The blue Mediterranean rippling around them, the smoky town ahead, bustling waterfront, steaming ships and the mountains rising up to the clouds. It was difficult to take it all in. The scene was best viewed from a village in the hills to the east, a village called Panorama.

Looking over the rail as they approached the dock, Andrew and his comrades were reminded that they were entering a war zone. At the entrance to the harbour they passed the wreck of a steamer, victim of a U-boat attack. Fortunately there had been no loss of life. She had managed to reach the shore and beach herself; all were saved including six hundred mules. Horses, stores and men slowly assembled on the quayside.

"What's that smell?" Sergeant Ivor Morgan was almost lost for words. "This enchanting place was destroyed utterly once we set foot on the ground and marched from the dock to the base camp. For the place absolutely stank. If there was a stronger word I would use it."

From the base camp Gunner Jones' battery made their way east to the front line. This was well defined by the Struma River. The enemy, the Bulgarians, were on their own soil on the opposite bank. The British were on Greek soil. There was very little to fight over here. To advance the enemy faced a stiff climb to the British stronghold at Lahana.

A battery of the Royal Field Artillery. The Bulgarians in the valley below, across the Struma River were content to hold their positions. From time to time gunners of the RFA reminded them that it would be unwise to attempt to advance.

"There's plenty more where this came from."

Andrew Jones and the other gunners were comfortable enough in their tents near the gun emplacement with a fine view over the Struma valley. The weather improved, spring flowers were everywhere and the surrounding area was very pleasant. A few more trees and they could have been in the Clee Hills. There was entertainment, football, cricket, concerts, truly amateur dramatics and the RAF. An airstrip was built for this new force. They had the skies to themselves, more or less, and could swoop over the Bulgarian lines, 'just t'see if they are up to anything'.

The real danger lurked down in the marshes below where the Struma drained slowly into the Aegean. Roughly a quarter of the hospital beds were filled with soldiers suffering from malaria. The mosquito killed more than the bullet. The enemy in Salonika was disease; only one in twenty of the casualties were the result of enemy action.

Andrew Jones became one of the casualties. A bout of measles developed into a chest infection. He was soon up and about and able to walk around the field hospital at Lahana. Less lucky ones were buried nearby, their graves marked with a simple cross painted crudely with number, rank, name and regiment:

T/143630 Driver S Thomas Army Service Corps

Gunner Jones sauntered away and went back to his tent for a lie down. Many years later at a church parade in Worfield he learned that George and Fanny Thomas had lost their son in Salonika. Unknowingly, Andrew had walked past his grave. Driver Thomas was one of the oldest men from the district to die in uniform. He was forty-six.

The greenery of the spring soon disappeared under the scorching Mediterranean sun. Hot air rising from the parched earth created little whirlwinds that spiralled through the tented camps. Dust got everywhere. In the mess tents the troops did their best to fend off the clouds of flies anxious for a share of the 'bully beef'.

Andrew Jones was back in hospital again, and this time it was more serious. He contracted blepharitis, an eye infection that would plague him for the rest of his life. This condition was aggravated by stress, smoke and dust; there was plenty of all three around at the time. He was sent back to the coast for treatment, but little could be done before the age of antibiotics. Ulcers, formed on the cornea of the eye, did not respond to any medication. The treatment in extreme cases was to stitch the eyelids together to rest the eyes.

Number 4 Base Hospital at Kalamaria was very pleasant, well away from the smells and dust of the port of Salonika. Charming Canadian nurses cheered up the troops and chatted to them as they sat out in the fresh air on the lawns that went down to the water's edge. With his eyes bandaged Gunner Jones could feel the sea breeze, but could not appreciate the view out into the blue Mediterranean.

Another cemetery was established nearby where those who succumbed to wounds and disease were laid to rest. Also buried here were nursing staff; girls from the Canadian prairies who had simply come to help. Patrick Downey came to fight. He was no coward; he did not run from the enemy. His crime was to disobey an order from an officer. His cap fell in the mud, when ordered to pick it up and replace in on his head he refused. The court martial found him guilty. He was sentenced to death. He was 'shot at dawn' right there at the water's edge by a firing squad made up of men of the Durham Light Infantry and buried without ceremony. More than a year had passed since this tragic incident but it was still talked about in the hospital wards. "If you wus picked for a firin' squad would you do it?"

"You'd 'ave to. Couldn't disobey an order or you'd be the next."

Hospital ships made regular trips back and forth to Malta where better medical treatment could be given. Those who recovered were sent back to Salonika; those no longer fit for front line duties were sent home. Ben Sankey from Bridgnorth, a Private in the KSLI, only went as far as Malta. He never came home to his wife Elizabeth in Severn Street. The crossing to Malta was not without danger. German U-boats were a menace.

Troops embarking on the hospital ships leaving the port of Salonika knew that they were sailing into hostile waters, and the Red Cross painted on the side of the vessel was no protection. The *Britannic* had been sunk and lives lost, and the *Burma Castle* had also gone down.

On the 12th of May 1917, Gunner Jones embarked with over six hundred other patients on the hospital ship *Dover Castle*. She was intercepted by U-boat *UC-67*. She was sunk on the 17th. This wicked act was reported in the British press; if nothing else it was a useful piece of propaganda. When a hospital ship was sunk in the Channel, an artist in the offices of the *Illustrated London News* painted a particularly vivid picture; a scene of panic and confusion as the ship sank stern-first with ant-like figures scurrying across the decks, leaping from the rails into choppy waters, struggling to reach the rescue boats circling the doomed vessel.

Salonika Harbour. The sick and wounded are being helped on board a lighter that will transfer them to a hospital ship bound for Malta.

"Looking forward to the cruise to Malta?"

It wasn't like that when the *Dover Castle* went down. The first torpedo fired from the German U-boat hit the engine room and killed half a dozen sailors instantly. Medical staff above began to arrange the immediate evacuation of their patients to the escort ships. It was an orderly, disciplined operation and no lives were lost. The *Dover Castle* was not sunk by enemy action. After the evacuation she was judged to be a hazard to shipping and was sunk by the Royal Navy. Nevertheless, for Andrew Jones, a young man unable to swim and scarcely able to see, the transfer to the lifeboats with the possibility of another torpedo attack was an experience he did not want to repeat.

Gunner Jones made the return passage to Salonika in September and settled in to No. 3 Convalescent Camp, inland from the port. While he had been away Salonika had experienced 'The Great Fire'. Once again this was nothing to do with enemy action. Like the Great Fire of London, it started in one of the overcrowded alleys near the waterfront. Hundreds of homes were burned to the ground and the refugees had to be rehoused by the British Army. The conditions in the camps were probably better

61

than those they had left in the town.

"Gunner Jones, you can handle a plough."

"Yes, sir, I can."

The British Army had set up smallholdings and market gardens to supply fresh food for the troops. Ploughing, feeding the stock, milking twice a day, this suited Andrew just fine until the ulcers on his eyes came back. Christmas 1917 was spent in No. 50 General Hospital.

In January he boarded the hospital ship *Glenart Castle*. She had only recently returned to service. In calm weather off Southampton she had struck a mine. All the passengers were evacuated safely and she was towed into harbour and repaired.

Andrew disembarked in Malta for repeat treatment; the *Glenart Castle* steamed on. Everyone on board was looking forward to the first glimpse of the English coast. Twenty miles west of Lundy Island she encountered *U56*. The German U-boat sent a torpedo into her; there were only thirty-eight survivors. Stopping for treatment in Malta had saved Gunner Jones' life. He came home on the *Wandella*. With bandages off he saw Arab dhows and flying fish along the coast of North Africa, the mighty Rock of Gibraltar and dolphins in the Bay of Biscay.

From the docks at Southampton he was dispatched immediately to Harrow, to the Holmleigh Military Hospital. As one of the 'walking wounded' he was allowed to wander about the streets of Harrow. The masters from the famous public school flapped about the pavements in their black academic gowns doing their best to ignore the boys in straw boaters and high collars. It wasn't just the school uniform that set them apart. They called out to each other with the confident, hoity-toity tones of 'born leaders'. These were the lucky ones too young to join 'the regiment' and their seniors at 'the front'. Over six hundred Old Harrovians were killed in the Great War.

No longer considered fit enough to be a gunner in the Royal Field Artillery, Andrew was transferred to the Royal Engineers and sent for training at a unit near Liverpool. Three months later he was posted to 604 Fortress Company at Gosport; no longer a gunner he was now an engine driver. Until the war's end he shunted munitions and stores around the docks and the fortress. His last Christmas in uniform was spent at Haslar Barracks in Gosport. In February 1919 he was on Prees Heath handing in his kit. He never went to sea again and never took the controls of a locomotive ever again. He went back to what he knew best, the land and livestock.

He rarely talked about the war but did occasionally comment on educational matters. When asked about his own schooling, he had left Morville School at the age of twelve, he would say, "I finished up at Harrow; didn't enjoy it much."

Chapter 5

Battle Scars

Was It Worth It?

The Battle of Mons in 1914 was the first taste of things to come for the British Expeditionary Force. Although the rapid fire of highly trained regular soldiers inflicted terrible casualties on the German infantry, it didn't stop them. In British military history, Mons became famous for 'The Retreat'. The cost was counted in lives lost. Well over a thousand British 'Tommies' were dead; 'Fritz' lost many more.

Soon after, the battle to defend the market town of Ypres resulted in fifty thousand British casualties. The slaughter continued and yet there was still enthusiasm for the war – at least in the papers and among those who had not been on the battlefield.

The image of Lord Kitchener, with stern face and moustache like the boughs on a fir tree, was everywhere; in magazines, on postcards, in the windows of private houses and around the plinth of Nelson's column. It was almost three dimensional; his huge gloved hand thrust forward and an accusing finger pointing out at every young man in the land.

'Join your Country's Army', he demanded, and 'God Save the King'. It was very effective and millions flocked to the recruiting centres. Some were still reluctant.

Silly girls handed out white feathers, a badge of shame, to boys not yet in uniform. They would have acted differently had they nursed men blinded by cordite, mutilated by shrapnel or choking to death with mustard gas. Many lads at the front, weary of the senseless war, prayed for a wound just serious enough to send them home, but not bad enough to blight the rest of their lives. If the result was their discharge from the army, so much the better. A lost arm would mean an empty sleeve; then it would be clear 'he had done his bit' and no white feather would be presented. The gratitude of the nation was shown to men such as this when the Silver War Badge was struck. It was awarded 'For Services Rendered, to King and Empire'. Not everyone was deserving of it but Eric Watson, of the 1st/6th Manchester's, certainly was as were at least half a dozen other Apley men.

Too Hot to Handle

Charlie Webb was back in uniform during the Second War. Charlie was tall, and in his dark uniform with silver buttons and medal ribbons he was an imposing figure. Rowdy children dashing out of school and down Village Road went quiet when they saw him pushing his bike in through the garden gate. Little girls were bravest; they knew there was nothing to fear. "Hello, Mister Webb. Hello."

"Hello, my girl. What have you learnt today?"

The little gang shuffled closer. Mr Webb was not really scary. It was just his gruff voice; 'gravelly' if you wanted to be polite. That was the way he had always been. He knew how to talk to little girls; he had one of his own, Ailsa. She was bigger now, and the village girls wanted to be like her. They wanted hair like Ailsa; long and dark.

Looking up at Charlie the children studied his lined face, like a road map printed on crumpled parchment. Gypsy fortune tellers convinced some people that the lines on the palm of their hand revealed their life history, and foretold their future. Small wonder Charlie's forehead was so furrowed. He had lived through troubled times and in the future there was tragedy.

Like all men of his generation, the Great War took away their youth and gave nothing in return, except the ability to adapt and endure whatever life threw at them. Charlie began his service as a private in the Gloucestershire Regiment. He transferred to the Royal Horse Artillery and the Field Artillery; if the war had lasted longer he would have flown with the newly created Royal Air Force. Charlie did not come through unscathed.

In some parts of the battle front the trenches were so close that an athletic youth could throw a cricket ball at the enemy. Instead they made up packets of explosives and sent them across no man's land using crude 'tennis rackets' to launch them. Both sides soon developed more reliable hand grenades. The British produced the Mill's bomb, a bit like a knobbly cricket ball. This was very effective; the casing shattered when it exploded and sent metal fragments in all directions.

This image is taken from a 'magic lantern' slide. Shows were put on in the Agricultural Hall in Bridgnorth High Street to raise the morale of a war-weary public. These soldiers may well have posed for the camera but certainly the German trenches were often close enough for grenades to be thrown in either direction.

"Bowling right arm over the wicket."

The Germans replied with the 'potato masher', a grenade on a stick which could be thrown twice as far as the Mill's bomb. When a cord was pulled there was a delay of about five seconds before it went off. The sooner the grenade was flung in the direction of the opposition the better. The 'potato masher' that came cart-wheeling through the air was easy to spot before it landed at the feet of startled soldiers. In the crowded trench there was no room for manoeuvre and often some brave lad would step forward, snatch it up and fling it back.

The Germans called their weapon the *Stielhandgranate*. Charlie Webb called it the 'Piss-quick' because if you were going to handle it then speed was of the essence. Charlie didn't make much of his wound; it wasn't obvious hidden under the back of his shirt. Something had ripped a piece out of him leaving a hole big enough to take a man's fist; a chunk of hot metal from the casing of a 'piss-quick'. Charlie just hadn't been quick enough. A mortar bomb gave Norman Sharpe his limp, Bob Ridge lost his hair after a gas attack and Alf Rowley ran into something even more deadly, a virus.

A SURVIVOR OF THE PLAGUE

Alf Rowley's folks had not moved far in over six hundred years. Forests cleared near Worfield gave them fields to till. The Rowleys took their name from these rough meadows, 'row leas'. Down the years they prospered. William Rowley appeared on Shrewsbury's roll of Guild Merchants in 1252. The Rowleys married profitably and gave the public what they wanted – good cloth and plenty of beer. They built a mansion in the centre of the county town in the early 1600s, and Roger Rowley was sufficiently well off to be able to 'help out' Sir William Whitmore of Apley when Cromwell asked him for £583, a fine for foolishly deciding to support the Crown during the civil war.

Alf's father had the name but not such deep pockets; he was still working in the 'rough meadows' near Worfield. At twelve years of age little Alfred left school and started work as a 'garden boy' at Hilton. He grew to be a sturdy youth and learned new skills. When he was called to join the county regiment he gave his trade as wagoner and well suited he was for such work; steady and powerfully built like the shire horses he harnessed in the early morning, and worked with all day long.

He went to France in 1918 with the 1st Battalion of the King's Shropshire Light Infantry, arriving in time to take part in the final skirmishes of the war. Neither side had much fight left in them at this stage. The fittest troops should have been the Americans, freshly arrived in France in great numbers early in 1918. They brought vigour and enthusiasm but many now believe they also brought a deadly flu virus. They called it Spanish Flu. Spain was neutral; the press there was not censored and was able to report the full impact of the epidemic that became a pandemic. In the months before the armistice more men on both sides died of flu than were killed by weapons of war.

Peace came and gleeful troops poured onto the ferries which were to take them home. Private Alf Rowley was on the coast at Etaples-sur-Mer. He was in bed in No. 26 General Hospital; he had 'a touch of flu'. Worldwide, hundreds of thousands were in the same position. Stay in bed and keep warm was the treatment. Alf was shipped home and lay in the military hospital at Colchester for a fortnight. In February 1919 Alf came home. He had fought off the virus that had infected half the world's population. It killed more people than any other single outbreak of disease, more even than the Black Death of the Middle Ages. The Rowleys had survived the Black Death, and Alf survived the Spanish Flu. He regained his youthful vigour and carried on working the land for the rest of his days.

When We Were Two Little Boys

As they passed the school on the way to the village shop, mothers could join in with the morning hymn. Urged on by the schoolmaster and the battered piano the children screeched out the words of 'All Things Bright and Beautiful'. They knew the words by heart, as did their mothers outside on Village Road. One of the verses reminded all of them that there was a 'rich man in his castle and a poor man at his gate' and that God had 'made the high and lowly and ordered their estate'. They took that to mean the Apley Estate. That was just the way it was.

The tune changed in the dark days before Christmas when carols were rehearsed. The children then bawled out the story of 'Good King Wenceslas' as their mothers scurried past for provisions. The carol told the story of how bread, wine and firewood had been carried by the good king and his manservant, through the snow, to 'yonder peasant'. It just went to show that the rich man in this castle was aware of the plight of those outside his gates.

Little Arthur Garbett was very slight but he was very willing. He got a job at the hall when he left school at the turn of the century. The staff had 'meals provided' and he should have put on weight. The trouble was he soon worked it off. Twice a day he made the two mile round trip from the hall to the Home Farm under the yoke. This device, carved from a single baulk of timber, fitted over the shoulders and made life easier for milkmaids. They could carry two buckets of milk at a time; it took the weight off their arms. "Off you go, Arthur. They'll be squealin' for it."

He hooked up a bucket, full of kitchen waste, on each end of the yoke and plodded off out of the side gate of the hall, and up the hill and on to level road. After another half mile he passed the cricket square, neatly fenced off to keep out the cattle grazing in the meadow in front of Home Farm. The 'pig-mun' greeted him and so did the pigs. "Well done, lad. Just listen to 'em. They're pleased to see you. Now you sit down 'ere for a minute. There's no need to rush back."

Arthur couldn't saunter, it wasn't in his nature, but he did pause at the top of the hill overlooking the hall. He had always meant to count the number of windows; the top two floors were easy enough, after that it was confusing, and in any case someone might be watching.

Another youth, just three years older, looked out and studied Arthur as he strode downhill with the yoke slung over one shoulder, like a rifle.

"Who's that, father? What does he do?"

"That's young Garbett from the cottages. Quiet lad. Helps out with anything. Why do you ask?

"Just like to know, father."

Arthur Foster and Arthur Garbett were not acquainted. World events would give them something in common and in time Arthur Foster would give the 'Hall Boy' a helping hand.

In the summer months cricket was everything for village boys. There was practise in the week for the match at the weekend, mowing and rolling the pitch, oiling the bats, cleaning the pads; they all joined in with enthusiasm under the keen eye of Edward Sharpe, head gamekeeper. The boys played together for a decade and then prepared to fight together.

Almost every family sent a boy to war; the Sargents sent three. George went to the KSLI, Bertie went to 'The Devons' and Ted was a gunner in the Royal Field Artillery.

Arthur Garbett stood in line with other volunteers in front of the medical orderly. "Jump on the scales. You're a bit light. Are you a steeplechase jockey?"

"I'm a farmhand."

"Right, put your boots on. Up on the scales again. That's better. Off you go. A1."

Arthur was in. He trained as a gunner and went off to France with Ted Sargent.

If the Germans threatened to break through the British lines troops

69

were moved quickly to plug the gap. Hundreds moved on foot, in trucks and even double-decker buses along the rutted Belgian lanes towards the front. With them went the artillery, horse-drawn gun carriages and cartloads of shells. They moved through a landscape scarred by shelling, pock-marked like the face of the moon.

The gunners loved their horses. Seated astride their favourite mount the warmth from the animal's flanks, felt through the rough khaki of their breeches, comforted the riders. In return a reassuring voice gave encouragement to the horse, even in the heat of battle. "Come on, my beauty. You can do it."

When the worst happened and a shell burst and shrapnel tore through the air, horse and rider felt the same pain. Men screamed and called out for 'mother'; the warhorse bore it better.

Ted Sargent wasn't far behind when it happened. He recognised the limber, lying in a shell hole, by the number on the side. In the bottom, in the mud and mess, uncomplaining, was the lad he had stepped out onto the cricket pitch with that hot summer before the war. Now he couldn't move at all, his leg broken in two places. "Come on, Arthur. Let's get you out of here. You're goin' 'ome."

'Two Little Boys' was a desperately sentimental song, but Margaret Thatcher liked it. It was top of the 'hit parade' for seven weeks over Christmas 1969. In four or five verses Rolf Harris told the story of Jack and Joe who played at soldiers and went to war together. Joe lay wounded and dying; Jack popped up on his horse and carried him off to safety. Ted and Arthur could have taken the parts of Jack and Joe, only the Apley boys' story happened to be true.

Gunner Garbett was patched up at the dressing station, given morphine and with a stiff cardboard label tied to his collar dispatched to the base hospital. They managed to save his leg although it was still in bad shape. Within days he sailed across the Channel and came to rest much closer to home in Birmingham.

His luck was beginning to change; now he was in the hands of a dedicated surgeon. "Do you want to walk with a limp for the rest of your days?"

"No, sir. I do not."

"Then you have to trust me. I can straighten you out, but it's going to be painful."

Arthur endured traction, a series of operations and the pain that went with them; all this at Selley Oak Hosptial, the same hospital now treating casualties from Afghanistan.

Arthur had another bit of luck. It came in the comfortable shape of 'Beattie' Edwards. Nurse and patient romances were very common. Often they lasted no longer than the cheap novels read by teenage girls. When the soldier got back on his feet he went off home. This could be a hundred miles away and the romantic bond formed in the hospital ward was strained and then snapped. Not so in this case.

Miss Edwards had been one of Lord Acton's parlour maids. She had watched young men from the estate, footmen, gardeners, carters and farmhands, go one by one to war. Beatrice went into the service of a doctor in Birmingham and she took it upon herself to help out on the wards of Selley Oak.

The fortunate part of this affair was that Lord Acton's estate at Aldenham was 'just across the river' from Apley. For young lovers it was a twenty-minute bike ride from Morville, through the 'damson valley' along the lanes to Colemore Green and down the path to Linley. In 1919 they began their married life together in 'The Sheepcote'. Arthur was back at Home Farm and walking the same route he had trudged along as a boy with the yoke and 'slops' for hungry piglets.

When the tenancy of Yew Tree Farm came vacant and Arthur Garbett wanted to take it on Major Arthur Foster approved. Ted Sargent often passed the farm on his waggon carrying timber from the woods to the estate sawmill. He gave an encouraging wave to his old comrade working in the fields. Arthur and Beattie Garbett lived out their days at Apley, and so did Ted.

Chapter 6

A Land Fit for Heroes

There was political turmoil in Germany for more than a year before the end of the Great War. While the politicians in Berlin cast about for an 'exit strategy' disillusioned troops were stuck in the trenches of France and Belgium.

The war had started well for Germany and her allies, particularly the submarine war; it seemed that this would be decisive. Warships and merchant vessels were sunk at an alarming rate. In May 1915 a Royal Mail Ship was sunk off the coast of Ireland by the U-boat, *U20*. This was a propaganda disaster for the Germans. Over a thousand passengers lost their lives when the *Lusitania* sank. World opinion turned against Germany and this was part of the reason why America decided to enter the war on the allied side.

Exhausted by three years of war it seemed that Germany might have to be content with the 'status quo', to hold on to the territory they had overrun in the early days of the war. The allies would never have agreed to this. Only a military breakthrough would force the hand of Germany. In September 1918 the breakthrough came north of the port of Salonika. The Allied Army of the Orient, the odds and sods of Britain and France, fighting side by side with Greeks and Serbs faced the Bulgarians. Fighting on home ground the Bulgarians had defended stubbornly until now, but without the support and supplies from Germany they faltered.

British troops, with Greeks in support, moved up from the shores of Lake Doiran and made the stiff climb towards the Bulgarian positions. The 8th Battalion of the King's Shropshire Light Infantry played their part, advancing in khaki shorts and overburdened with equipment.

They were led from the front: Captain Frank Nalder died, Regimental Sergeant Major Holden died, others with familiar local names, Pointon, Dyke and Jones all died in the assault; a third of the battalion were casualties. Lieutenant Colonel Erskin was forced to withdraw and regroup. The Bulgarians were well entrenched above them on Pip Ridge. Further along the line the French and Serbian forces broke through and the Bulgarians were forced to retreat all along the front. Bulgaria was out of the war.

The next nation to sue for peace was Turkey. The Turks were dogged fighters but they had been steadily driven back through Mesopotamia, Palestine and Syria. In September 1918, the British general, Edmund Allenby, gathered his forces for a final push north towards Constantinople. The colourful Colonel T E Lawrence (of Arabia) rode into Damascus on the 1st of October. The Turks made a final stand at Aleppo. There was little resistance. Demoralised and ravaged by illness they simply faded away.

Captain Arthur Foster, despite the loss of a leg, was still a lively young officer with a desk job in London. Trooper Tom Gray's job was to make sure Captain Foster was always well turned out. At Hyde Park Barracks, Tom gave 'Jimmy's' tunic a final flick with the clothes brush in the morning before he went off to the War Office. Staff officers were easily recognised by the red tabs on their collars. They were the people who were 'in the know', the link between the military and their political masters. It called for diplomacy. When the war was over governments on all sides had to work together to restore some sort of order; embassies reopened and diplomatic relations were restored.

The document from the War Office that confirmed Captain Foster's appointment to a post in military intelligence was written in pencil which seemed rather odd as if it might be erased at any time. The captain was promoted to major.

The victory celebrations were hardly over when Tom Gray packed their bags and they sailed off to the Orient. Near the end of the voyage they edged through the Dardanelles, the ship guided by a Turkish pilot to avoid any floating mines still not cleared from the waterway. This was the passage the Royal Navy had tried to open up early in the war. They might have pressed on and shortened the war if only they had known that the Turkish shore batteries had hardly any shells left to throw at them. The ship carrying diplomats and their staff passed through the Sea of Marmara and entered the Golden Horn; on the port side Europe on the starboard side Asia. Crowds at the quayside watched their arrival. Even at a distance the red fezzes of the men could be seen bobbing about as they strained to get a better view. From the rail of the ship the skyline of Constantinople was spectacular, dominated by the minarets and huge domes of the mosques. It was unlike any other city on earth.

The atmosphere in the streets was remarkably relaxed. German and Austrian troops still walked about freely, almost indifferent to the arrival of the British. Diplomats arriving to reopen the embassy and members of the military mission moved into the Pera Palace Hotel, overlooking the Bosphorus. As they arrived German officers were packing methodically and preparing to take the Orient Express back to Berlin, and an uncertain future.

"We'll be comfortable enough here, Gray. You'll be able to see the sights."

Trooper Tom Gray striking a casual pose in front of one of the huge mosques in Constantinople. He tugs on his pipe and positions his arm so that the long-service stripes on his sleeve are clear to see.

Permission given by his son, Tom Gray

"Let's see, where to next?"

74

Tom was given a 'chit', a slip of paper from the embassy which allowed him to roam the alleys and markets of Constantinople. If he wished he could 'take refreshment' in the cafés. He had complete freedom just as long as he was back in his quarters by ten o'clock and didn't neglect his duties. He was unlikely to do that. Tom made the best of it taking in the sights and sounds of the city and the view across the water to Asia. For a few coins he could take one of the ferries to the other side and land near the railway station. This impressive piece of architecture was the gateway to another continent.

Nearby on high ground was the Haidar Pasha Cemetery. About six thousand soldiers from the Crimean War were buried here, despite the best efforts of Florence Nightingale and her nurses in the wards at the Scutari Barracks. There were also close to four hundred graves for those who had died in the past four years. Nearly all of them had been taken prisoner by the Turks and died in captivity. Sailing back into the setting sun, choppy waves produced a sparkling magic carpet laid out below the silhouette of the city with its spires and domes.

For seven months after the end of the Great War, civil servants and politicians argued over the wording of the peace treaty. The victors agreed that Germany must be punished. Germany had to pay; her armed forces disbanded and never allowed to threaten her neighbours again. Her colonies in Africa and the Pacific must be handed over. Germany's allies also had to be punished; the Empire of Austria-Hungary ceased to exist and so did the Ottoman Empire. The spoils of war were shared out; not everyone was satisfied. Italy had been promised bits of Austria, Turkey and Germany. France and Britain wanted to enlarge their empires. Poles wanted independence. Arabs wanted independence from the Turks and the Jews were promised a 'National Home' in Palestine. The Treaty of Versailles did not please everyone.

The Greeks also wanted a reward for their efforts late in the war. It was less than twenty years since the Greeks and Turks had squabbled over Crete. Neither side was satisfied with the outcome of that little war. The Greeks laid claim to part of the Turkish mainland and the British Prime Minister, Lloyd George, promised support.

In the free and easy atmosphere of Constantinople it wasn't difficult to gather military intelligence. Major 'Jimmy' Foster wasn't a spy; he was the military attaché, which sounded better. Conversations with Turkish

Army officers were not strained; they had nothing to hide, and they had fought honourably and talked openly. Nevertheless, the major had to be sure that they were complying with the terms of the ceasefire. He had to know the strength of the garrisons for instance. This information was useful to the Greeks and there was no reason for it to be kept from them. After all, they were allies of Britain.

Twenty thousand Greek troops landed on Turkish soil on the 1st of May 1919. They were escorted to the port of Izmir by French and British naval forces. At the end of the month Foster and Gray made their way home and prepared for life on 'Civvy Street'.

The campaign did not go well for the Greeks. They fought on against an enfeebled Turkish Army for three years and then withdrew. They gained no new lands and lost over thirty thousand men. What part Jimmy Foster played in this affair is not clear. No doubt he was in a position to provide useful information to the Greeks as they prepared for the initial invasion. Before the conflict came to an end he received the Greek Medal for Military Merit.

Major Foster's military career came to an end in August 1919. Trooper Gray collected his silver medal for long service and good conduct and he too came out of uniform after eighteen years. For all that time, Tom's address had included the word 'Barracks'. Now he had a smart new address, 89 Piccadilly. "This will do nicely. Thank you very much."

The Ritz Hotel was just down the road. In the opposite direction, at 127 Piccadilly, was the Cavalry Club, where the major could relax. For many others life was not so comfortable. Limbless soldiers were begging on the streets of London. Thousands more could not find work; the years ahead were not going to be easy. The 'Land fit for Heroes', they had all fought for, looked bleak.

IT'S THIS OR THE DOLE

Victory had been hard won and celebrations were joyful but short-lived. Lads pressed into service 'for the duration' were eager to get out of uniform, go home and repair their lives. Some were a bit too eager. In their haste to leave the services many declared themselves fit even though the war had scarred them for life. Mental scars were disregarded unless the unfortunate was literally 'barking mad'.

From the Dispersal Centre on Prees Heath, Shropshire lads made their way home to every town and hamlet in the county and put up their feet for a day or two. Those that came back to Apley were some of the lucky ones; they just picked up their tools and went back to their old trades. Unlike some landlords the Fosters still had money. Others who had enjoyed the same lifestyle pre-war had been brought to the brink of ruin. Their fine country houses could not be maintained and estates were broken up. Factories that had produced the materials of war closed down overnight. Somehow the country had to get back on its feet. Desperate men went 'on the tramp' looking anywhere and everywhere for work.

Charlie Webb was an adaptable man; he marched away from the School of Aeronautics, at Shorncliff in Kent, and made his way back home to Swindon. He was full of confidence; prepared for anything. He could ride, fire a mortar, drive a car and by the end of the war he was ready to take to the skies.

Facing a hostile enemy across no man's land, the troops had needed something to get them 'over the top': courage, grit, determination and a large shot of rum. The men had a 'swig' from a tin mug, the officers 'just a nip' from the hip flask. The fiery liquor burned their throats, warmed their bellies and made them brave. Away from the battle front the government recognised how dangerous alcohol could be, and in 1916 nationalised some pubs near munitions factories. Licensing hours were fixed at the outbreak of war; publicans were expected to behave more responsibly. To ensure that standards were kept an association was formed, the People's Refreshment Houses Association. Only managers of good character were appointed. One such man was Henry Shord who held the licence of the village pub in Norton. Mr Shord, manager of the Hundred House Hotel (PRHA accredited), began his career in the British Army as a drummer boy and served for twenty years; clearly this was a man of good character.

His good wife got a letter from Swindon. Her brother Charlie was home safely and looking for work. Henry's wife made an appeal. "After all he's been through, couldn't you find a place here for our Charlie?"

"I suppose I might. He can do some chauffeuring for us."

Charlie made regular trips to the railway stations at Wolverhampton and Shrewsbury to bring respectable guests to the respectable inn managed by the respectable Mr Shord.

Henry Shord was a changed man when his wife fell ill. Little could be done to control the cancer, and Charlie's sister went back to the family home in Cirencester to die. The men left behind at the village pub both grieved, Charlie for his sister, Henry for his wife. The loss they both felt should have brought them together. Instead they quarrelled. "Get out, Charlie. There's nothing here for you now."

Charlie Webb did not go far, just two hundred yards down Village Road, and there he stayed for the rest of his days. He liked the work well enough at the Crowgreaves Farm but he wasn't a 'man of soil', and when the opportunity came he left. The construction of what would become a key training unit of the RAF began at Cosford in the 1930s. It was further to ride the bike but working on a building site was better paid than working on the land.

RAF Cosford opened its gates in 1938; Charlie stayed on. At the beginning of the Second World War he was back in uniform; dark blue, a member of the security team. With trouser clips firmly in place, chrome buttons on his tunic and three ribbons from the Great War over his breast pocket, he looked the part as he cycled along the lanes to the camp. As he passed by his old workmates labouring in the fields one remarked, "Charlie's landed on 'is feet. See, they've even given 'im a new bike!"

BACK TO THE LAND

Ted Sargent left his gun carriage in France, hitched up a timber wagon at the estate yard and drove off into the woods. George Sargent handed in his rifle at Copthorne Barracks, opened up his tool box, sharpened his chisels and set about repairing doors and windows that had been neglected for four years. Albert Nicholls and Alf Rowley went back to the land. William Foster declared, "Work will be found here for anyone who wants it."

Frank Jasper looked further afield. He had fought alongside Canadians; they talked of home, and they made it sound like the sort a place to make a fresh start. On the plains of Saskatchewan and Manitoba the wheat grew well, and in the fertile soil the grass grew well to nourish herds of beef cattle. Breeds like the 'Hereford' Frank already knew. With clear skies, clean air and the wide open prairie all around, what could be better? "It could 'ave bin a bit warmer. The ground froze hard as iron." Frank's daily task throughout the first winter was to pump up water from deep below the cattle yards. Whatever the weather the beasts had to be fed and watered. Frank came back to Kemberton to a milder climate.

Far from the capital, with fields and woodland all around, Apley and the surrounding hamlets were shielded from world events and, to some extent, the misery caused by the war. That did not mean they were out of touch or unaware of what was going on beyond the parish boundaries. The Reading Room, built by the Foster family before the war, was the community centre for the village. The craftsman-built hall was well lit and warm; centrally heated. Rather than spend the evenings in the pub men were encouraged to play darts and billiards there, and to read. There was a generous stock of books, not all dusty rejects from the hall, and daily newspapers.

At the Fosters' London 'town house' in Chapel Street and at the hall they entertained politicians, military men and captains of industry. News of the outside world came direct from the men at the top. The worry for everyone must have been civil unrest. Miners and dockers, men in the shipyards and factories struggled to feed their families. This was a class struggle. Mine owners and factory bosses often lived in comfort well away from the dust and grime where their money was made. Things were different in the countryside; the gentry and the cottagers looked out on the same landscape. The wages of farm labourers were the lowest in the land, but with a kitchen garden, a pig sty and a plentiful supply of rabbits on the doorstep, no one was going to starve.

Chapter 7

In Memoriam

BROTHERS IN ARMS

The casualty lists in the opening months of the Great War were alarming and grew ever longer. Some were buried where they fell, others buried in makeshift cemeteries behind the front line, and tens of thousands had no known grave. The loss was felt in every street in Bridgnorth town and in every nearby hamlet. The parishioners of Saint Mary's at Sutton Maddock put up a simple plaque as a memorial to the handful of boys who never returned to the place of their birth. Memorials to the fallen took many forms. Chiselled on walls, arches and bridges were the names of thousands who had no grave. The last resting place of the lost sons of a few wealthy families were marked by private monuments with headstones more elaborate than those set up, after the war, in rank and file in many lands.

The Nevetts of Cotsbrook Hall put a marble surround over the grave of one of their sons in the cemetery of Stockton Church.

Lone Pine Cemetery is on high ground on the Gallipoli Peninsula overlooking the beaches where troops from Australia and New Zealand showed such courage in 1915. On a panel here is carved the name of Sergeant William Nevett of the 12th Battalion Australian Infantry.

On the evening of the 24th of April 1915, battleships, minesweepers, troop transports and lighters sailed out of harbour from the Greek island of Limnos and made for the coast of Turkey. The main force of French and British troops arrived in total darkness on the tip of the Gallipoli Peninsula. Further north Anzac forces were ferried ashore at 'Z' Beach. In the poor light of the early dawn there was confusion. One of the naval officers ferrying the troops ashore believed they were too close to the promontory of Gaba Tepe and steered north crossing the path of other units. The battalions were mixed and the chain of command broken. They finally landed in what became known as Anzac Cove. The Australians and New Zealanders expected to land on a gently shelving shore with cultivated land and orchards ahead of them. The planners were quite wrong. When the troops scrambled ashore they found themselves on a narrow beach with near vertical cliffs above them. Many of these young men were recent immigrants to Australia; they had 'get up and go' and how well they displayed it.

Platoons commanded by individual soldiers and junior officers pushed inland. With heavy packs (40kg) they began the climb to the plateau where 'Jacko' was dug in. A mixed bunch of about fifty men of the 11th and 12th Australian Infantry Battalions, under the command of Colonel Clark, fought their way up to Russell's Top and forced the Turks back. Commanding the enemy forces at this point was Mustafa Kemel, a formidable opponent and a fearless front-line commander. His leadership qualities were outstanding; within a decade he became the first President of Turkey.

These Australian troops appear orderly and disciplined as they come ashore on the 25th of April 1915. They are under fire from the Turks who are entrenched above. On the water's edge lies Sapper Fred Reynolds believed to be one of the first men to die on what would become Anzac Day. Major Francis Irvine with his rolled greatcoat slung across his shoulder looks on, he too will soon be among the dead. The photographer, Lance Corporal Joyner was killed in France in December 1916.

© Imperial War Museums (Q 112876)

"Anzac Beach, where history was made."

Those already ashore looked down across the beach to the water's edge at the body of Sapper Reynolds. Troops wading ashore filed past the 'poor bastard' without a word. By late afternoon on the 25th of April it was clear that the Australians could not hold their positions. Too many were lost in the fighting and the few that remained withdrew to Anzac Cove. On this day Colonel Clarke was killed. Sergeant William Nevett (857) of the 12th Battalion of the Australian Imperial Force was lost. He has no known grave.

At Cotsbrook Hall the Nevetts received the letter informing them of the death of their son. They passed on the tragic news to his younger brother, Tom, serving with the 5th Battalion KSLI. Within days Tom sailed for France. From the docks at Boulogne the battalion was dispatched to the front line. In the trenches there was death all around and good friends were lost, yet none were as dear to Tom as his brother Bill. In action near Hooge, Shropshire lads faced the first flame-thrower attack by the Germans. Skirmishes continued throughout the summer and there were daily casualties.

The generals made elaborate preparations for the Battle of Loos. Casualties were anticipated. Dressing stations and clearing stations were set up capable of handling at least ten thousand men. Transport to evacuate men to the coast was arranged including seventeen ambulance trains. Even barges were put on standby.

Before the battle had even begun Lance Corporal Tom Nevett was wounded, carried from the battlefield and carried home. Medical officers at the front and the staff of the military hospitals could do little for him. He came home to die.

The church was well attended in those days and full on special occasions such as Christmas, Easter, or the funeral of a well-respected parishioner. In mid-October 1915, a line of villagers trooped up the hill and met with staff from the hall who arrived in orderly groups out of the woodland across Church Field. The Nevetts came from another direction to lay their son to rest.

The lane from Cotsbrook to the church was long and straight. In the pasture close to Barker's Rough cattle grazed contentedly. A sudden gust of wind disturbed them. The hearse sped past; autumn leaves blew into the air in its wake. At the crossroads the mourners could see the outline of the ancient stone farmhouse at Astol set back from the road, and surrounded by barns and stables. As they approached a dog ran out from one of the farm cottages and barked through the hedge as they passed. The dog was on guard; there was no one at home. The Howells and their neighbours were making their way to the church to pay their last respects to Tom Nevett.

The hearse and the gleaming black saloon that carried the family mourners slowed on the long pull uphill out of the valley. The Howells and others stood reverently in a gateway as they passed. The women, all in black, looked up anxiously. The men standing behind them, their caps clasped in rough hands, looked down at their freshly blackened boots. Mrs Nevett looked out and nodded gently in their direction.

Tom Nevett was laid to rest close to the lych-gate of the cemetery of Stockton Church. Mourners drifted away quietly in twos and threes. The family went home the way they came, along the lanes past the farm cottages and the grazing cattle. The Howell's dog made no sound. Sitting upright, alert beside his kennel, he watched in silence as the Nevetts passed by. Lizzie Howells was upstairs changing from widow's black to an everyday frock, putting her 'funeral hat' carefully back in its box and folding the tissue paper over it. Until the next time.

Two years later, almost to the day, Percy Price rode up from the village post office – On His Majesty's Service – with a brief message:

Regret to inform you...
Pte William Edward Howells, 10ᵗʰ Battalion Royal Welsh Fusiliers...

Lizzie Howells read it, looked up at Percy, looked down and read it again, folded it carefully and put it into her apron pocket. "Thank you, Percy. That's our Billy gone now."

He did not come home to familiar fields; there was no memorial service except the one arranged when the Tyne Cot Cemetery in Belgium was dedicated. There, on one of the panels, his name is carved alongside over thirty thousand others who 'have no known grave'.

The Nevetts arranged for a white marble surround to be placed over Tom's grave at Stockton to remind folk that he had died of wounds received in France, and also that his brother William was at rest near Gaba Tepe. The family moved away, to Church Stretton, to ease the pain of their loss perhaps.

William Howells and the Nevett brothers are among those remembered every November at Stockton Church. On the other side of the world, Sergeant William Nevett, and thousands like him are remembered on Anzac Day, the 25th of April, the day he died in 1915.

GRAND DESIGN

Memorials were being erected in every corner of the land; the demand was such that an Exhibition of War Memorials was set up in London. A delegation from Bridgnorth went to the capital to decide on the form of the memorial. William Foster of Apley, the committee chairman, announced, "It is to be of statuary form. We have commissioned a sculptor, a Shropshire man, an army man, Captain Adrian Jones."

He may have had local origins but his work was well known. His largest sculpture could hardly be missed, *The Quadriga*, a four-horse chariot on top of the Wellington Arch at Hyde Park Corner. The Angel of Peace held a wreath high above her head as she descended into the Chariot of War. Between the horses a boy with a cheeky grin looked out. He clung to the reins as they reared and plunged to left and right confident that when their hooves came to ground he would not be under them. It was all larger than life. When the sculpture was unveiled in 1912 it was the largest bronze sculpture in Europe. His sculpture for the Bridgnorth memorial was also going to be larger than life.

To commission a sculptor with such a reputation would be expensive, but the committee was determined that the memorial would be 'dedicated free of debt'. Captain Jones waived a good proportion of his fee. His sketches were approved for a bronze figure; a soldier moving forward in full battle order, his arm outstretched frozen in the act of hurling a grenade. Adrian Jones thought that an appropriate site for the memorial would be at a crossroads on the High Street. William Foster offered a corner of the castle gardens. The committee readily accepted this generous offer. On summer evenings couples, arm in arm, sauntered round the Castle Walk and came into the gardens to sit among the flower beds and listen to the efforts of the town band. An ash tree, at a high point in the gardens, conveniently fell down so that work could begin on the site. The pedestal of Alveley stone was put in place by Mr Banks, a local mason. The bronze plaques were cast at Thames Ditton, and Jones' inspiring sculpture arrived from the foundry. The assembly was complete.

The soldier with arm raised looks out over the railway station. Townsfolk used to joke, 'He's waving to the engine driver, he thinks he's going to miss the train!'

Photograph by the author

"Goodbye my friends."

CEREMONIAL DUTIES

More than eight years had passed since the first volunteers had taken the train down the valley and off to their training camps. Within a matter of weeks many of them were part of the British Expeditionary Force crossing the Channel and moving up to the front line. Some never returned; their names were now cast in bronze so that, *those who come after see to it that they be not forgotten.*

It was the second week in March, the year 1922. The weather had been unkind earlier in the week, but on the day it was fine. The town folk assembled quietly in the gardens. Every street in the town had sent young men to war; the names of one hundred and forty-three of those who had *given up their own lives that others might live in freedom* were recorded on the memorial. A special place was set aside for the families of 'the fallen'.

In the High Street the bandsmen tried out their instruments, blowing a few notes on bugle and flute. The Mace Bearer fidgeted. He knew that all eyes would be on him at the head of the column. The mayor adjusted his chain of office, again, and spoke to the man in charge of the escort of 'town bobbies'.

"Superintendent Phillips, are we right?"

"We are, sir".

Behind the mayor and his escort was a large contingent of ex-servicemen. They were a mixed bunch. The officers stood out in Saville Row suits, the 'other ranks', wearing jackets from the fifty-shilling tailor, shuffled uncomfortably. Medals had been sent through the post in crude cardboard packets. An inscription on one reminded them that they had taken part in *The Great War for Civilisation*. Some didn't bother to pin on their medals. "We all got the same."

The solemn sound of muffled bells rang out from the tower of Saint Leonard's. The clock above the ringers struck two, then the town hall clock and then the clock of Saint Mary's, one after the other.

Alerted by the command of Captain Woolley, the 'old soldiers' straightened their backs and set off from the High Street for the castle gardens. It was a very orderly affair, everyone conscious of the beat of the drum and doing their very best to keep in step. Latecomers to the ceremony paused at the roadside as the column of marchers passed by. Scanning for familiar faces in the ranks of the ex-soldiers, Territorials, Scouts, Guides, and Grammar School boys in scarlet jackets, the onlookers smiled weakly when they spotted a friend and made shy gestures of acknowledgement putting up an open hand now and then. Once in the gardens they were arranged in their allotted places on three sides of a square facing the memorial, and prepared for the unveiling.

The sculptor, Captain Adrian Jones, addressed the crowd. He had been a soldier for twenty-three years and served in earlier campaigns in Abyssinia, Egypt and the South African War; he was comfortable in the company of military men.

"I set out to create a monument that would demonstrate the vigour, determination and heroism that Shropshire men have always displayed in the defence of the empire. You must decide whether I have been successful or not."

He went on to explain the wording of the plaques on the sides of the pedestal and repeated his admiration for those who had died in the service of their country. Then he took up the cord that would release the union flag covering the figure standing out clearly against the sky. He handed the cord to Eli Jones.

Who better to perform this duty than a man who had served in France as one of the King's Foot Guards? He had been a familiar figure in the town; a cheerful lad running errands in the High Street. He joined up as soon as he was eighteen and looked particularly pleased with himself when he stood smartly to attention in front of the camera in the uniform of the Coldstream Guards.

Superintendent Phillips salutes. The mace bearer looks straight ahead. In top hat, the mayor, Mr A E Jones, stand stiff and formal. Captain Adrian Jones, the sculptor, hands the cord to Eli Jones. He looks up from his wheelchair as the union flag floats away to reveal the memorial.

"The Unveiling."

On this important occasion he remained seated. He edged cautiously towards the memorial, the cord resting across the oilskin apron covering his lap. He had lost both legs in France. He drew himself up in his wheelchair, and with a determined snatch pulled back the cord. The red white and blue of the union flag cascaded down and settled gently around the plinth. There was almost complete silence; just a few sighs of satisfaction were heard, as if to say, "What a marvellous memorial."

Eli spoke, an ordinary man, who despite the occasion spoke confidently, thanking the Memorial Committee for selecting him as 'the privileged person' to perform the unveiling.

The band struck up with 'Oh God our Help in Ages Past'. The printed order of service was hardly necessary; everyone knew the words. After prayers and readings came the dedication to the *ever glorious dead*. The hymn, 'Fight the Good Fight' was sung heartily, and 'The Last Post' was sounded by the bugler.

William Foster of Apley and the mayor both spoke briefly before the wreath laying. Emotions were restrained, contained; it was the way of things then. As the bereaved drew close to the memorial to lay their tributes some glanced up hesitantly at the tablets. They knew that somewhere, among the rest, frozen in cold metal, was the name of a son, husband or brother. This finally confirmed that they would see them no more.

'The Reveille' sounded, the column of marchers reformed, the band struck up again and with arms swinging and medals jingling they swept past the memorial, out of the gates and down to the High Street to disperse.

LOOK TO THE FUTURE

Fires had been laid in the cottages off the High Street; the women walked quietly away and 'put a match to them'. Thin columns of smoke drifted from the chimney pots. In sombre Sunday clothes they offered comfort to neighbours and friends from out of town. "You'll come in for a drop o' tea won't you?"

The fires brightened, the kettles boiled, the best china came out, home-made cake was handed round and the talk turned to the antics of children and the price of coal. The men drifted into their favourite pubs;

there was nothing more to be said about the war. Dockers were striking, miners too, farm workers wages were low and farmers were mean. Far more distressing was the poor performance of the town football team in their last match against Wenlock. There was little merriment. "Go on, 'ave another drink. You'll feel better for it."

The clergy, the councillors and Captain Jones quietly congratulated each other that it had 'all gone well'. In turn, they all had a word with Eli and thanked him yet again.

Of all the dignitaries, William Foster could understand better than the rest what lay ahead for Eli. In the early evening William and Henrietta Foster made their way home, chauffeur driven, along the riverside, under High Rock towards the estate. The gates of the lodge were open. A small boy heard the car and scampered out. When they had passed by he stood bolt upright in the middle of the road and watched them disappear into woodland. The carriageway, cut through the sandstone of Winscote Hills, opened out into parkland; the hall appeared straight ahead. A few deer looked up as they glided past. The weather had been favourable; it had stayed fine all day. The dark clouds that had threatened rain were edged with gold by the setting sun as it dipped below the trees on the ridge above the Severn. Spring was on its way; there were signs of new life emerging. "It's looking a bit brighter, don't you think?"

LEST WE FORGET

One by one more modest memorials were unveiled. Village carpenters at Worfield made one for their comrades and set it up on a grassy triangle at the end of a row of black and white cottages. In the cemetery at Stockton a stone cross was erected.

Every Sunday morning for decades a ritual had been performed at the parish church. Members of the Foster family drove up from the hall and took their seats at the front. The pews filled up behind them and everyone took up a place appropriate to their rank. Nearest to the altar sat the 'lord of the manor' and his family with guests of 'quality'. Behind them sat the agent and his wife, tenant farmers, the butler, head gamekeeper. Everyone knew their place; foresters and farm labourers at the back.

In churches throughout the land clergymen were praying for

victory. Every day for four years the Reverend Loftus Meade Owen made a personal plea to God to end the war and save the lives of village lads. At last his prayer was answered and there was peace. Phillip, his only son, was one of the eighteen boys from Stockton parish to die in the Great War. The family moved away; perhaps the rector wanted God to explain to him privately why so many had been sacrificed.

The veterans stand in line remembering village lads that did not return. Arthur Foster stands next to the rector and be-medalled Arthur Garbett stands next to the scout master.

"A fine body of men."

The pale stone of the memorial cross at Stockton, fresh cut by the mason's chisel, would weather and darken over the years. On the day of the unveiling it appeared clean and crisp through the folds of the union flag draped around it. The instruments of the Jackfield Silver Band gleamed and glinted as the musicians wet their lips and prepared to blow. This would be a day to remember, a day that required a permanent record.

The photographer set up his tripod and dashed about trying to arrange the crowd that filled the churchyard. The bandsmen, choirboys and Scouts were all well disciplined. By contrast the veterans seemed to have forgotten how to stand on parade. Even Major Arthur Foster struck a casual pose. The ladies stood in the lane outside the cemetery, the posh ones wearing extravagant hats.

"Hold it!" The shutter clicked. "And again, thank you."

When the plates were developed and printed the scene was not at all sombre as might be expected. The bright sun picked out the brass fittings on the cars that were lined up in the field across the lane.

The band and the choir prepare to 'give it their all'. A curious scout peers at the camera.

Permission given by Roy Coles

"Can we remember the tune?"

The bandsmen, with dark tunics and bright buttons, looked cheery and many others were wearing faint smiles. The time for shedding tears had passed. In the front rank of the choir, Sam Coles, a serious little boy with blonde hair, stood out.

When Sam and Les Webb, a cheeky dark-haired lad, had learned all they could at the village school they went on to learn a trade from estate craftsmen. Sam 'the chippy' and Les 'the bricky' followed their trades until the outbreak of the Second World War. Then both spent dangerous years with bomb disposal teams. Sam returned and practised his old skills with chisel and plane. In the estate workshop the carpenters crafted a memorial seat for Allan Brooks and Leslie Webb.

Lieutenant Allan Ivo Brooks of the Queen's Bays, son of the Honourable Herbert Brooks, and Corporal Les Webb of the Royal Engineers had very little in common. Nonetheless, the grief at their loss was felt equally by their respective families; the Brooks in the manor house at Ewdness and Charlie and Annie Webb at the bottom end of Village Road. Their boys had shared the same fate and they shared the same memorial. Both wars did something to change the order of things; the gentry and ordinary folk were united in grief.

Chapter 8

A Military Career

ETON AND SANDHURST

A whole generation of young men had been in uniform; the army had not been their chosen career. For the Goulburn brothers, Eddie and Cuthie, it seemed the obvious choice. Their father had served in the South African War with distinction. As a major in charge of the 42nd Battery of the Royal Field Artillery he had held out at Caesar's Camp and fought at the Battle of Ladysmith. If his sons were to follow in his footsteps they had to have suitable schooling. Eddie was packed off to Eton.

It is unlikely that the Duke of Wellington did actually say that 'The Battle of Waterloo was won on the playing fields of Eton', but it was a useful quotation to inspire lads expected to take up a career in the army. They got some of the best training in the backstreets of Eton and Slough. Outside the college gates battles were arranged with local ruffians. 'The 'Cads', street fighters of distinction, were tough opponents for the privileged young 'Swells'. With wide white collars and tall top hats, the 'Toffs' were easy targets for the catapults of the enemy. "Let's see if we can crack their chimney pots."

The local guerrillas also used camouflage. In their grimy jackets and tattered jerseys they concealed themselves against the peeling doors and crumbling brickwork of the back alleys. The sides were more evenly matched when it came to 'close combat' with sticks and bare knuckles. This was excellent training for all. The day would come when they would all wear the same tunic. Junior officers would look along the ranks of their company and misquote Wellington again. "I don't know what they do to the enemy, but by God they frighten me."

With sandstone cliffs to climb, the river and streams to ford, woodland and thicket for concealment, open parkland to charge across and an armoury in the hall there was plenty of opportunity at Apley for Eddie and Cuthie Goulburn to practise more war games before they went on to the Royal Military Academy.

When they graduated from Sandhurst, a decision had to be made. It may have been a disappointment to Eddie's father that he did not choose the Royal Artillery. Instead he was commissioned into the Grenadier Guards, the most senior regiment of infantry. Perhaps he was influenced by Uncle Henry who had spent twenty years with the Grenadier Guards. In 1898 he served under Lord Kitchener in the Sudan, and was with him at the Battle of Omdurman.

Cuthie Goulburn didn't want the Brigade of Guards; he might have to take orders from his elder brother. The 8th Hussars had plenty of dash and daring about them and that suited his style much better. Both brothers embarked on what would be very successful careers.

In the 1930s the British Army began to mechanise; tanks would play a key role in the war to come. Until then the cavalry were still expected to charge into battle on horseback. Cuthbert Goulburn senior, Master of the Albrighton Hunt, and William Foster were hunting mad. It was astonishing that there were any foxes left alive in the district. Eddie and Cuthbert junior spent a lot of time improving their horsemanship and got plenty of advice from the older generation.

The 43rd Regiment of Foot

In the course of his twenty-three years service with the 43rd Regiment of Foot, Tom Dovey rose through the ranks from private to regimental sergeant major. His early life had prepared him well for the competitive world of the professional soldier. Tom was born in the Black Country. Heavy industry, forges, foundries and factories had worked night and day to produce the weapons of war. Every item of equipment the troops carried into battle, down to the buttons on their tunic, was made in the workshops of the Midlands. When peace came the factories fell silent. Long queues stretched along the pavements; skilled tradesmen shuffled about waiting for the door of the labour exchange to open. There was no work.

Tom's father was in Flanders when he began his apprenticeship as a shoemaker. Father was away but there was still plenty of company at home. Tom was the sixth of ten children. Father came home and the whole family pulled together to support each other. Those in work handed over their meagre pay packets to their mother every Friday night. She did her very best working tirelessly in the home. Life was hard indeed, but the Doveys survived and the key to their survival was mother.

Cleaning a bedroom window, one dreadful afternoon, she fell onto iron railings in front of the house. Her injuries proved to be fatal; it was a year before she died. With mother gone her children dispersed to 'shift for themselves'.

In September 1922 William Thomas Dovey took the 'King's Shilling' and joined the 1st Battalion of the Oxford and Buckinghamshire Light Infantry, the old 43rd Regiment of Foot. Tom Dovey did not have the benefit of a public school education, nor did his family have distinguished soldiers in the background. He attended the 'School of Hard Knocks' and this was to serve him well in the troubled times ahead.

ONE OF THE BOYS IN BLUE

When agriculture collapsed in Victorian England some estates were split up; not so at Apley where the money from industry subsidised a rural way of life. Men returning from the Great War who were lucky enough to be offered work on the estate found a 'safe haven'. The Home Farm was not a profitable enterprise, principally because of over manning. The same applied to the hall and the gardens. Both farm and gardens provided fresh produce for the hall, and very little was sold on the open market. Gardeners and farmhands all had a share; free milk, potatoes from the fields and anything spare from the gardens. The Fosters' philosophy, unspoken but evident in what they did, was founded on a sense of duty they felt they had for the welfare of their workers and servants.

It was downhill almost all the way from Newton to Worfield. Every Sunday the Ward family walked this way, two and a half miles to church, and after the service two and a half miles uphill back home. It was no hardship. It was their Christian duty, and they were all very fit, especially young Bert Ward.

He made the same journey every day to school. When he left

school at fourteen he wanted to work in the open air; he wanted to be a gamekeeper. A fine suit of clothes came with the job and a pair of strong boots. Unfortunately there were no vacancies on the estate, and so for ten years he laboured on the farm.

Bert Ward's passion was football. He worked hard in the week and played hard for a Bridgnorth team at the weekend. In 1936 he decided to join the Royal Air Force and went to Edward Foster for a reference. This farmer didn't want to see good men leave the land nor did he want to lose a man who had worked for him so well for ten years, but he was generous. He gave a glowing reference. "I won't stand in your way. Good luck to you, Bert."

Aircraftsman Ward became a member of the team responsible for the development of equipment and the training of airborne troops. He progressed through the ranks. His skill and energy on the football field was recognised; he represented the Royal Air Force in inter-service matches. Bert served on a number of stations in England until the outbreak of war, and then he was posted to the Middle East to an airbase near Cairo. The Middle East Air Force was there in support of Montgomery's Desert Army, moving on from one desert airfield to the next until the job was done.

CALL FOR THE CAVALRY

Those who could not find work when the war was over went on 'the dole'. The Treasury had to account for this; they had to know exactly how many men were receiving 'dole money'. The government began to record unemployment insurance statistics in 1921. For hundreds of thousands there seemed to be no way out of the unemployment trap. There were 'lock outs' and strikes. Resentment built up until it boiled over into the General Strike of 1926. The strike was called by the Trades Union Congress in support of the miners.

Mine owners threatened to reduce wages and lengthen the working day. Understandably, the miners reacted. The government agreed to give the mine owners a subsidy to maintain miners' pay. This in effect gave them time to prepare for the inevitable dispute. The government had the popular press on their side led by the *Daily Mail*; strikers were labelled 'revolutionaries'. The monarch normally keeps out of politics but King George V was reported to have said, "Try living on their wages before you judge them."

The General Strike lasted nine days. Then the miners were 'on their own'. They held out for a few months but were forced back to work before the winter. To survive they had to accept lower wages and longer hours. The situation did not improve.

In 1929 the American stock market crashed. The effects were felt worldwide. Industry in Europe suffered. Prospects were bleak for anyone looking for work. Government statistics, published in January 1931, made depressing reading. More that two and a half million were unemployed.

Fred Todd was a powerful athletic lad; he wanted an active life with some security. He had Christmas at home in 1932; a fortnight later he went into a recruiting office and signed on for six years regular service and six years in the Army Reserve. He gave his trade as 'horseman', just the man they were looking for to be a trooper in the 3rd Hussars, the King's Own. Sent for initial training at Catterick Camp in Yorkshire he learned quickly, remarkably quickly.

So confident was he in the saddle that after only a year in uniform he was promoted. Lance Corporal Fred Todd carried away the trophy for First Skill at Arms at Aldershot in 1934. 'Tent pegging' was a skill that was no longer required on the battlefield. This sport involved riding at the gallop and picking up a small ground target using a sword or lance. It was popular with cavalrymen of all nations: Bengal Lancers, German Uhlans or Polish Hussars making preparations for war.

In the decades following the Great War military strategists recognised that in any future conflict air power and tanks would be decisive. The development of these weapons began in earnest in the 1930s. There was opposition from old cavalry officers; Field Marshal Earl Haig who believed there would always be a place for 'the well-bred horse on the battlefield'.

The 3rd Hussars were selected 'to carry out an experiment in mechanisation to replace horsed cavalry'. The decision was made in 1934. Three years later there was still only one squadron fully equipped; the rest of the regiment had to train with flags and trucks. Corporal Todd and his troop enjoyed themselves sweeping over the low hills around Tidworth. It was a rattling ride in the Vickers Light Tank with blue smoke from the exhaust blowing around them. It could not compare with the exhilaration of manoeuvres on horseback, but this was the future.

Hussars could always be relied upon to put on a good display for the public. Tournaments around the country helped to recruit fresh blood into their ranks. There was never any mention of blood that might be spilt. Dismounted and striding about the streets of Wolverhampton, Fred had an encounter with a girl who came to see the show. Miss Rowlands was bowled over by the uniform and the man inside it. They were married in 1939 at Pocklington, at the foot of the Yorkshire Wolds, between York and the sea. Fred was about to complete his six-year engagement with the army.

The climate in Europe was very unhealthy at the time; war clouds were gathering. Fred's civilian life was brief; he was almost immediately recalled to the regiment. Two days before war broke out he was back in Jellalabad Barracks, Tidworth, and back in uniform for another six years.

THE MATRUH MOBILE FORCE

There are those who live mundane lives and their achievements can be summed up in a few lines. Others have eventful lives that would fill a book and still the story would be incomplete. "The Old Brig, they don't make them like that any more."

Even out of uniform, in county tweeds, he was every inch a brigadier. 'Tall, handsome and much admired' was how he was described in the final paragraph of his obituary in the *Daily Telegraph*.

Like thousands before and since, Cuthie Goulburn began his soldiering at Aldershot. Apart from learning how to command a squad of wily old troopers he could also indulge his passion for polo and shooting. He was self-effacing and described his skill at both sports as 'good average'. Hussars were expected to be good horsemen; their forbears had taken part in the Charge of the Light Brigade. The days of the cavalry charge were over; the Great War had demonstrated that very clearly. After the opening skirmishes, Lifeguards, Horse Guards, Hussars and Lancers were all dismounted.

In 1929 the 8th Hussars received their first motorised transport, sufficient to form a machine gun squadron. The 'old hands' were not convinced and certainly did not intend to leave their mounts behind when they sailed for Egypt in 1934. The heat and the dust at the barracks at Abassia reminded Cuthie of stories he had heard as a boy from Major Henry Goulburn who had served in the Sudan, and talked of Kitchener and Khartoum.

For the 8th Hussars the Armistice Day Parade in 1935 was a particularly sad event. The officer commanding the Army of the Nile took the salute at Coombe Hill in the desert near Cairo. This was to be the last mounted parade. Three sabre squadrons of the 8th Hussars and the mounted band trotted past, wheeled and galloped away into the history books.

Equipped with armoured cars the 8th Hussars became part of the Matruh Mobile Force. New tactics were devised for the motorised Hussars and practised in the desert. This would stand them in good stead in the war to come.

Hitler's antics were watched with alarm by politicians in England. Troopers in Egypt were more concerned with daily routine, drill, sport and exploring the 'flesh pots' of Cairo. In the officers' mess once the latest infidelity of one of the wives had been debated and dismissed the conversation might turn to 'The Palestine Question'.

Jews and Arabs had been squabbling for years. Jews, persecuted in Russia in the 1880s, began to arrive in Palestine. Anti-Semitism spread throughout Europe and the number of immigrants increased.

During the Great War the Turks and the Germans were allies. Jews who had settled in the region joined forces with the British and with local knowledge provided useful intelligence. As a reward the British Foreign Secretary, Balfour, promised them 'a national homeland in Palestine'. The Balfour Declaration of 1917 was a document that would be quoted many times in the troubled history of Palestine.

After the Great War the British were given the thankless task of governing Palestine. Negotiations between Jews and Arabs led initially to an agreement. The Arabs accepted the immigration of Jews as long as they could remain independent. Declarations and agreements were soon forgotten when territorial disputes flared up. The flow of Jewish immigrants, particularly from Germany, increased when persecution by Hitler's Nazis became intolerable.

The Arabs wanted an independent state and no more Jewish immigrants. The Jews wanted unlimited immigration. The result was the Arab Uprising in 1936. To keep the peace British troops were drafted in from Egypt. With other members of the Matruh Mobile Force, the 8th Hussars set off by train from Cairo. They left their horses behind in stables in Cairo, and instead rode out in their spanking new Ford V8 pickup trucks mounted with Vicker's machine guns. There was considerable excitement; all ranks were eager to 'get stuck in'.

The Hussars set up camp near Talpioth. At the entrance they nailed up a sign, 'Balaclava Camp', to honour the achievements of the regiment in the Crimean War. This was going to be a less glorious campaign and probably best forgotten. Cuthie Goulburn was about to experience active service for the first time. He was an inquisitive young man and compulsive recorder of events throughout his lifetime. He kept a diary and made notes of incidents and encounters, and took 'snaps' wherever he went. Photographs of roadside bomb craters and damaged vehicles in Palestine were carefully preserved. The eventful years ahead would be similarly recorded.

Some of the tactics of the British Army were questionable. At the height of the troubles, in October 1938, Bernard Montgomery arrived to command a division of ten thousand men. Emergency powers were enacted that allowed collective punishment. Hundreds of Arabs were sent to overcrowded detention camps without trial. Palestinian villagers suffered most. If they were thought to be harbouring rebels their livestock and property was destroyed.

Many lost their lives in this bitter uprising. There were assassinations, intimidations, abductions, bombings and murders. Jews, Arabs and the British spent more than three years killing each other. As so often happens, troops sent to keep the peace did not endear themselves to either side. There was no answer to the 'Palestine Question'. The revolt petered out as the Second World War approached only to resume when that conflict was over.

Troopers of the 8th Hussars pulled up the tent pegs at Talpioth, the Balaclava Camp sign came down and the Matruh Mobile Force took the train back to Cairo. Preparations were made for the next conflict. New vehicles were tried out, cars for scouting, armoured cars fitted with machine guns and tanks for serious warfare.

The 8th Hussars testing their new American M3 Stuart tanks in the Western Desert, August 1941.

"Tally Ho!"

The King's Royal Irish Hussars prepared to do battle alongside 'colonials', Royal Canadian Hussars and the 8th Australian Light Horse, all founder members of 'The Desert Rats'.

Chapter 9

Playing Politics

BETWEEN THE WARS

The 1920s and 1930s were remarkable times; times of social change. When 'The land fit for heroes to live in' did not materialise, there was a reaction not just in Britain, but throughout Europe. The politicians who had promised so much could not find an answer. In Russia, a bloody revolution replaced the rule of the Tsar with the rule of communism. There was a fear that this might spread. There was strong support for it in France and Germany. Communism was suppressed in Germany and replaced by an equally dangerous ideology – Fascism.

This turmoil had little impact in the tranquil world of Apley. William Foster, who was mindful of the sacrifices that had been made, could afford to be generous and felt a responsibility for his tenants and the estate workers who had given so much during the Great War. He welcomed back the returning soldiers.

In 1924 William Foster died. Major Jimmy Foster inherited the estate and carried on the family commitment to 'old soldiers'. He appointed one of them as head gamekeeper. Norman Sharpe was charged with maintaining Apley Park as the place where country sports could be enjoyed to the full. This was achieved within a decade. For those who were part of it this was a 'Golden Age'.

The parkland, landscaped and planted in the previous century, was now mature – a perfect paradise. With shooting and fishing, tennis courts and a billiard room, there were plenty of distractions for guests at the Hall. No one was going to refuse an invitation to stay. Generals, politicians, men of letters and royalty were all entertained. Queen Mary and her son Edward, Prince of Wales, made private visits.

The 'guns' that made up the shooting parties came from far and wide from the stately homes of England, to the castles of Bavaria. There were parties made up of officers who had served in the most prestigious regiments of the British army, and Austrian aristocrats who had gone out to 'bat for the other side'.

The American Ambassador, Joe Kennedy, accepted the invitation and came to stay at Apley for a day or two and brought along his little boy, JFK. He played about in the corridors of the Hall and explored the winding pathways, grotto and fountain in the remarkable gardens. The house guests played billiards and tennis, and lay on the poolside amazed that the Major swam so well with only one leg. In the evenings, with a plentiful supply of drinks, the conversation may have turned to politics and the state of the nation. "Enough of that, we're here to enjoy ourselves!"

The guests retired to bed, and not necessarily to the one they had been allocated on arrival. If the 'goings on at the Hall' had been documented it might have been very revealing. None of the guests were ordinary; they had many and varied interests and appetites.

BLANDINGS CASTLE

One of the guests at Apley was the author Evelyn Waugh. He published his best known work, *Brideshead Revisited,* in 1945. Some of his material was gleaned at country house parties. Surrounded by 'toffs', socialising, with a glass in his hand, this was what Waugh enjoyed. Even so, he wasn't the perfect house-guest. He satirised his own class in his first really successful novel, *Vile Bodies.* It was to have been titled 'Bright Young Things', a phrase used to describe frivolous young socialites with more money than sense, and a fondness for fast cars and free love.

Not to be taken seriously were the tales of another guest, P G Wodehouse. The Hall can lay fair claim to being Blandings Castle, the scene of some of Bertie Woosters' misadventures. His childish behaviour got him into all sorts of difficulties. Jeeves, his faithful servant, with his superior manner and superior intelligence, was always able to solve Woosters' problems. The stories Wodehouse told of Jeeves and Wooster were best-sellers, they were very entertaining. Was this really the way the 'upper crust' behaved? Out in the real world things were not so funny.

Everyone was 'feeling the pinch', some more than others. Fortunately, the Foster's family fortune was large enough to enable the Major to entertain his friends, and still have funds left over to subsidise the way of life of the cottagers.

Politics Left Right and Centre

Lenin became the leader of the first communist country and this gave encouragement to socialists worldwide. Even in Britain, communism had its supporters but they were few. In Britain, the Labour Movement was gathering strength. To some even this seemed dangerous. Articles in the *Bridgnorth Journal* before the General Election of 1929 express the views of some local landowners. They feared that left-wing politicians would use Soviet Russia as a model for Britain, and their lands would be confiscated. This was scaremongering, but around Ludlow, in the south of the county, it was believed. No communists would be standing for election and there would be no revolution.

Politics was largely a question of class. There were intellectual socialists, trade unionists and well-off idealists in the Labour Party, but the rank and file were largely from the labouring classes. Neither capitalism nor communism appeared to have the answer to the ills of the world. Fascism offered an alternative. In Italy and Germany, Mussolini and Hitler were directing a vigorous programme of industrialisation, and that included rearmament. They had their admirers even in Britain.

Oswald Mosley certainly knew about politics, and he made a name for himself as the youngest MP in the House of Commons in 1918. He fell out with the Tories, sat as an Independent and then joined the Labour Party. Mosley thought he had developed a 'cosy relationship' with the Labour leader, Ramsay McDonald, and was expecting a place in the cabinet. When he didn't get it he stormed off and formed his own party.

Ramsay Macdonald was more relaxed in the company of Edith Picton-Turberville as they strolled round the Castle Walk in Bridgnorth. He was staying at the Crown and came to support the prospective Labour candidate for the Wrekin constituency. He admired the view, High Rock, Apley Terrace and the rich farmland below. He did not expect any support from that quarter. He went on to Madeley to preach to the converted, the men who worked in the pits and the foundries.

The Fosters understood the ways of heavy industry; they had made their fortune in the cradle of the Industrial Revolution. They were well aware of what went on nearby. Miners from Madeley poached on their land. Smoke from the factories and foundries, and the dust from the spoil heaps of the coal mines drifted across the corn fields of Old Park Farm when the wind was in the north.

The village school was closed for the day. Housewives came in and cast their vote on the way to the village shop. On the way home in the evening, men who had been labouring in the fields propped their bikes against the school wall and went in to vote. It came as something of a surprise that the winning candidate was Edith Picton-Turberville, the first Labour MP in the county. She was obviously a toff, a typical old fashioned do-gooder who devoted her whole life to the poor. She was a very good MP, spoke well and often in Parliament for the farming community and country people. She was Member of Parliament for the Wrekin for just two years. At the next election a Tory regained the seat.

Neville Chamberlain, the Conservative Prime Minister, made every effort to keep the peace in Europe, but to no avail.

ALL OVER AGAIN

The Second World War came; young men were called up and everyone seemed to be in uniform. The Major and other veterans of the Great War formed the Home Guard, and village lads joined them – all in khaki. Ted Lewis who kept the village shop was a special constable in dark blue, and Harry Williams was a fireman.

At the Hall there were lots of boys in uniforms of khaki and blue, and girls in starched white uniforms; it was a convalescent home. British boys, Poles, Czechs, lads from the Dominions were all patients at Apley. Many of them were young airmen who had suffered head injuries. They were patched up, cheered up by the nurses and, when they were well enough, sent back to do battle again.

There was still merriment at the Hall, with concerts and film shows and regular dances. It was the last fling. By the time the war ended the Major was over sixty and all the 'bright young things' he had known had lost their sparkle. Life at Apley Park was never the same again; wounded airmen and pretty nurses all left the Hall. The deer, culled before the war, did not return.

Shooting parties were revived by Norman Sharpe, the head gamekeeper. Broody hens from the village hatched out pheasant chicks.

Keepers reared them and protected them from predators, and then Norman arranged for them to be shot – the pheasants that is! The shoots were more modest than before the war; the Golden Days were gone. It could have been worse. If Hitler had won the war he might have invited himself to Apley.

An Unwelcome Guest

Hitler had made plans. His war machine brought France to her knees. British troops retreated to Dunkirk and across the Channel. His planned invasion and occupation of Britain was thwarted when the RAF drove the Luftwaffe from the skies over Kent. Hitler turned his attention to Russia, but he did not entirely abandon his dream of setting up headquarters in England in the heart of Shropshire.

A British soldier scouting around in Belgium for a souvenir to take home at the end of the war picked up a packet of documents in a deserted German Army post. No one showed any interest in his find for sixty years, then his family put the bundle of maps and 'secret' papers up for sale, and Hitler's plans were revealed. Detailed drawings showed lines of communication radiating from Bridgnorth to surrounding towns and villages. There were good reasons to choose the town as a base: it was central, there were airfields nearby, it was isolated and there were a number of comfortable country houses in the area where the Fuhrer could relax. Apley did fit the bill.

Perhaps the Prince of Wales had mentioned it in conversation with Hitler. Against the advice of friends and diplomats, Edward, Duke of Windsor, arranged a visit to Germany in 1937. He met Adolf Hitler and high-ranking Nazis. This only added to the suspicion that he and his wife, Wallis Simpson, did have some sympathy for the Fascist cause.

Another man of doubtful judgement was P G Wodehouse, a silly man, a bit like Bertie Wooster. He spent the war in Germany. He had taken up residence in France in the 1930s to avoid tax and was taken prisoner by the Germans at the outbreak of war. Classed as an 'enemy alien', he was held at camps in Belgium and Poland. Under the Geneva Convention he was released when he was sixty but did not return to Britain. Instead he worked briefly for the German Ministry of Propaganda and broadcast what he thought were humorous commentaries. The British public did not find his antics at all funny. He was investigated by MI5 at the end of the war. He denied being a traitor. Anthony Eden, a future prime minister, thought he was and so did the children's author A A Milne. The official verdict was that *he was stupid and naïve, but not a traitor.*

This was an official photograph approved by Hitler. Despite the best efforts of the studio staff they failed to make him look attractive and his style of moustache went out of fashion very quickly in 1945.

© Imperial War Museums (MH4919)

"That's a nice place you've got there."

Pre-war shooting parties often included English peers and Austrian aristocrats. Corporal Hitler would not have been welcome; he had little in common with the officer classes. With a reputation for good hospitality perhaps a visitor from Austria had recommended Apley as a country retreat.

Whatever connections there may have been between Adolf Hitler and Apley there was certainly only one way he could ever have been admitted to the Hall and that was over Major Jimmy Foster's dead body.

Chapter 10

The Day War Broke Out

Rob Wilton had a catchphrase to start some of his comic monologues:

> **The day war broke out...**
> *The day war broke out my missus said to me, 'There's been a major catastrophe.'*
> *'Major Catastrophe? Who's he?' I said.*
> *'The Major; him that lives at the Hall,' she said.*
> *'What's wrong with that?' I said.*
> *'He's been on his holidays in Austria,' she said.*
> *'Good for him,' I said. 'Wish I'd been there with him.'*
> *'No you DO NOT,' she said. 'Not on the day war broke out.'*

It was true. Major Jimmy Foster with 'his man' Tom Gray and chauffeur Steve Jackson were sunning themselves at Worther See in Austria in the week before the Second World War broke out. They had made the same trip several times throughout the 1930s. The Major made off when the spring cleaning ritual disrupted life at the Hall. "Mother, does every single carpet have to be taken up and beaten?"

The Major was well acquainted with Princes, Counts and the Austrian aristocracy. Over the years Jackson and Gray had enjoyed the company of the 'downstairs' staff, they were 'all pals together' now. In their youth they had faced each other across the battlefields of Flanders.

It was said that the Treaty of Versailles had been too harsh and that some of the German grievances were genuine. Hitler used this very effectively and once he had absolute power Germany began to build up her forces and conflict seemed inevitable. Czechoslovakia was one of the problems. In September 1938 this problem was solved to the apparent satisfaction of Der Fuehrer. Czechoslovak territory, inhabited by three million German-speakers, was transferred to Germany. Hitler was not satisfied, within a year there was war. Everyone saw it coming. The telephone rang in the Post Office at Norton. "Hello, put me through to the Hall, please. Grace Goulburn to speak to Major Foster."

"Jimmy, you're not going to Austria?"

"I am, it's arranged, we're off at the end of the week."

"There's going to be a war, you realise that."

"All talk, politicians will sort it out; in any case it's been arranged."

Jimmy ignored the advice of his sister. The Rolls, as if running on rails, sped down the park, out through the lodge gates and took the familiar route to London to 'pick up a few things'. The Dover road wasn't very busy and there was plenty of room on the ferry. Not much was said, they had made the same crossing many times, for the first time in 1914. That had not been a happy experience.

On the other side of the Channel the landscape had changed. Nature was reclaiming it. Many of the trenches remained as reminders of the conflict; rusting barbed wire and twisted metal stakes were concealed by weeds, and young rabbits played in the grassy hollows of old shell craters. Canals, roads and public buildings had been repaired with 'reparation money'. The Germans had been made to pay.

"We'll stop at 'Wipers'; have another look at the Gate."

They approached the town from the north across 'Flanders Fields' where poppies had grown in such profusion. In the distance were the low wooded hills surrounding Ypres. The trees were all in leaf. At the height of the war every one had been stripped and shattered by shell and shrapnel. Gliding past the canal the Rolls slid sedately into the town square and drew up opposite the Cloth Hall. This fine building had been raised from the rubble and restored to its former splendour. The Major walked stiffly into a nearby hotel, greeted the doorman in precise French and was directed to the restaurant.

"Shan't be long, Gray. You know the drill."

Trooper Gray and Driver Jackson settled into wicker chairs outside a pavement café. The young waiter and the two old soldiers chatted in 'franglais' for a few minutes. Steve ordered another bottle of wine, 'just to moisten that crusty bread'. Tom said, "They gave this place a pasting didn't they? By the end it was flat; they said a man on horseback might see across the town."

After the largely 'liquid' lunch they strolled around the square and back to the car. Steve put the bonnet up and sniffed the engine. The Major appeared, Tom Gray opened the door, Steve started the motor and they moved off without a word. In less than two minutes they stopped again just beyond the Menin Gate.

This memorial was built into the old town walls. On numerous panels were carved the names of fifty thousand soldiers. They looked around them. Royal Artillery, Lancashire Fusiliers, Black Watch, they were all there.

"Gray, see if you can find Captain Bowlby again, fine chap."

Bowlby and Phillips, fellow officers in the Royal Horse Guards, were both killed on the 13th of May 1915, the same day Jimmy Foster had received the terrible wound that ended his war.

They left and drove on. Steve Jackson glanced in the mirror as they set off on the perfectly straight road to Menin. He saw that the Major was leaning forward and staring intently at the surrounding countryside. The Memorial Gate, framed in the rear window, shrank steadily until it was only a blur. Steve relaxed, his hands resting lightly on the wheel. Just for a moment he tightened his grip when memories of war flashed into his mind. Along rutted tracks he had driven trucks laden with shells to artillery batteries on the front line. It was all over now. The road ahead was clear and he eased back into the comfortable leather of the Rolls.

In the past the holiday route had taken them through Germany where they broke the journey at Nuremberg staying at the best hotel. It was decided that this year they would travel through France and make for Basel in Switzerland. There seemed to be an unusual amount of traffic on the road south. Perhaps there was something in the air. Family cars appeared to be full of baggage; the middle-classes were on the move. The French had 'bled white' in the Great War and they certainly didn't want to repeat the experience.

Crossing the border from Switzerland to Austria was a formality. The Major took charge handing over all three passports. It was clear from the several visa stamps that they were regular visitors. The officials were all very polite. The Rolls drew smoothly away from the border post. "Tom, they've put the flags out for us," Steve remarked.

Driver Steve Jackson, the pipe was not part of the uniform.

Permission given by Glen Jackson

"Mother told me to wrap up warm."

Bold banners flapped and fluttered, black swastikas set in white circles, strong red borders around the edge. Union with Germany had been established in July 1938 when German troops marched into Austria. Within ten days ninety thousand Austrians, Jews, Communists and anti-Nazis were rounded up and sent to forced labour camps.

There may have been some who approved of Hitler's action, at least those actions that restored national pride. If there was one thing that united the English and German-speaking aristocracy it was fear of communism. Arthur Foster was not persuaded that fascism was the answer; this was discussed but like religion it was a topic to be avoided. They were here to enjoy themselves.

Friends of the Major, aristocratic remnants of the old empire, remained aloof. They were officers and gentlemen with little regard for Corporal Hitler. One might imagine that they were rather like Captain von Trapp, the lead character in *The Sound of Music*. Some officers even had socialist leanings. When they were required to put on uniform again and placed under Hitler's command their loyalty was not guaranteed.

A postcard from Worter See that Arthur Foster preserved in the family album.

Apley Estate Archives

"Peace and tranquillity, not for long!"

The English guests were given a warm welcome. In July and August the water temperature was the same as the Mediterranean. In the wooded alpine foothills there were trails to explore on foot or on horseback. No postcard could do justice to the view across the clear blue lake with the dark greens of the pine forest on the far shore and snow-capped mountains in the distance. If Julie Andrews had been there she would have burst into song.

Looking after the Major was routine; make sure his shoes were polished and make sure the Rolls was polished. Their Austrian hosts made sure they were all well fed and entertained. Off duty, Tom and Steve could enjoy swimming on warm days, boating on windy days, lolling in deckchairs, strolling in the woods, chatting and flirting with the housemaids. "We don't want anyone to spoil the party, do we?"

Meanwhile the British Prime Minister, Neville Chamberlain, was doing his best to preserve the peace. Diplomacy depended on negotiations between reasonable men. Hitler was clearly mad and bent on war. His generals made preparations to invade Poland. Britain and France had pledged to defend Poland. Hitler delayed the invasion for a few days.

"Bad news Gray, better pack. Pity, but there it is. Tell Jackson to give the motor the once over."

"Sir."

The party at Worther See was over. The final exchanges between hosts and guests were brief.

"So sorry, let's hope they all see sense. Have a safe journey. Goodbye."

They didn't waste any time on the way to the Channel retracing the route through Switzerland, and turning north through France.

"Not Calais, try Boulogne."

At the harbour there was feverish activity. The Major couldn't help recalling the painful events of 1915. He spent an agonising three weeks in No. 7 Base Hospital before being shipped home to Blighty from the same dock. Now there was another difficulty. "Sorry, sir, can't take the car. We're overloaded. Foot passengers only."

"Right, can't be helped. Jackson, get the bags. Gray, come on, lets get on board." The Rolls was left on the quayside.

The mood of the ferry passengers was strained. Those travelling alone made little effort to converse with strangers. Family groups and friends spoke in short sentences. There were long silences; it seemed the whole company was thinking, *whatever next?* The White Cliffs of Dover were a welcome sight. Disembarking was something of a scramble. Steve went ahead without the luggage and claimed a taxi. They were out of the harbour gates ahead of the crowd and swiftly settled the Major into first class on the London-bound train. Tom and Steve retired to third class. Once in the capital the major went straight to the Cavalry Club.

Steve and Tom retired to one of their old haunts at the end of the Strand. They bought copies of the *Evening Standard*. War, War, War was the word over all the papers and on everyone's lips. They had an extra pint and 'sat over' it for a while.

"Come on, Tom, we'll get a bed at my sister's place. See what the Major's up to tomorrow."

The Major slept well. It was surprisingly quiet at the Cavalry Club. Serving officers 'had things to do', and retired officers had gone to the country. In the morning, after a leisurely breakfast, he made a brief phone call to the Hall.

"Nothing to worry about, coming up by train."

He settled into a plush armchair and took in the view framed by one of the very tall windows. Below, traffic, cabs and buses moved steadily along Piccadilly. On the pavement opposite clerks in bowler hats and shop girls, some still in summer dresses, strode briskly in front of the railings surrounding Green Park; in the background, Buckingham Palace. The Major allowed himself some angry thoughts. *It's madness. Some blighter has gone off with* The Times! *Now, what does The* Guardian *have to say?*

'*The British people have never been so united in accepting a challenge as they are today in determining to resist the tyranny with which all free peoples are threatened*'.

"Well put."

A steward came over. "Can I get you something, sir?"

"Not just now, thank you. Ah,…steward, what do you make of all this?"

The Major prodded the front of The *Guardian*.

"Don't rightly know, sir. Hope it's not like the last one." The Major nodded.

When Tom Gray turned up at the tradesman's entrance there was a note from the Major; a detailed list, another bag to be packed with items from Chapel Street and the time of the train they were expected to catch in the morning. The Major would 'stay put'; they would all leave from the Cavalry Club together.

It took eight hours from the London main line station to Linley Halt. The time passed; there was a lot to think about. Their spirits were lifted when they set off on the last stretch from Bewdley up the Severn Valley. A few miles up the line there was picture-postcard Arley on the far bank and the parish church standing above outlined against the sky. Further on were the pit villages of Highley and Alveley. There was nothing picture-postcard about them. The black spoil heaps from the mines spread out until they ran into hedgerows and green fields. Near journey's end the train drew into the station at Bridgnorth. It was all so familiar, the town and the faces of the townsfolk. High above the station stood the ruined castle with the memorial to the fallen of the Great War in its grounds.

Tom and Steve moved to window seats as the carriage emptied and watched the activity on the platform. Greetings were unusually warm. It seemed there was a great sense of relief at being back in the arms of friends.

The crowd moved away towards the ticket hall. A whistle blew and a green flag waved and the train pulled away from the platform. Within seconds it plunged into the black tunnel that ran under the town. The passengers were silent. The rattle of the carriages and the streams of smoke and steam that rushed past the windows made conversation impossible. They had just got used to the dim carriage lights when the train burst out into open country.

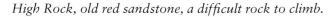

High Rock, old red sandstone, a difficult rock to climb.

Photograph by the author

"The stuff that fortresses are made of."

When the smuts and steam had cleared, there across the river was High Rock, part of Apley. It was solid, old red sandstone and cathedral-like. War? Surely not here; well out of harm's way.

Rob Wilton went on:

My missus said to me, 'We're not in harm's way are we?'
'Harm's Way,' I said, 'Isn't that where your mother lives.'
'You want to be careful what you say,' she said.
I agreed, my missus can be very sharp. So I said,
'Anything to keep the Peace.'

115

Chapter 11

The Expeditionary Force

BACKS TO THE WALL

The British Prime Minister spoke of 'Peace for Evermore' but no one really believed it. For years the nation had been making elaborate preparations for war. The civilian population were prepared for it; the armed forces had been training for it and were poised to put all that training into practise.

In late August 1939, Sergeant Tom Dovey and his company were at Billy Butlin's Holiday Camp at Clacton-on-Sea. It had been a fine summer with lots of sunshine; holidaymakers made the most of it.

The boys of the Ox and Bucks, working under the keen eye of Sergeant Dovey, were making alterations to the accommodation at Butlin's. It was being quietly changed from a holiday camp 'to provide secure accommodation for non-British personnel'. In Hitler's Germany there were some lucky lads who would put their hands up, walk off the battlefield and come over to Clacton to enjoy a long seaside holiday.

Boredom was the enemy of the professional soldier in peacetime. Tom was not bored; he had commitments. He had a promising career and was committed to the regiment which was like a family. Tom also had a real family; wife Alice and children Betty and John. When regimental duties were done for the day he went home to comfortable quarters. All this was about to change.

The 'Butlin's Squad' did not return to Hyderabad Barracks in Colchester, but went instead to a tented camp set up in Berechurch Park three miles outside the town. This was a precaution. Raids by German bombers were expected and they didn't have to wait long. The nation was mobilised and that included families in married quarters. They

116

were scattered across the country and expected to find accommodation with family or friends or wherever they could. Alice Dovey considered herself lucky to be welcomed into her sister's home at Sutton Maddock. Within a week of the outbreak of war air raid sirens were sounding over Colchester.

There had been a garrison at Colchester since Roman times. It was important at the time of the Napoleonic Wars and all wars since. At the outbreak of the Second World War it was the base of the 4th Infantry Division. The Lancashire Fusiliers, the East Surreys and the Ox and Bucks were all going to be part of the British Expeditionary Force; these professional soldiers were now joined by reservists.

On arrival they were treated to trench digging, route marches and small-arms instruction, just to remind them what life was like in the army. The weather changed in mid-September. It was cold and miserable in the tented camp; the warm, dry days of summer were gone. There were rumours of a move to more comfortable billets and rumours of forty-eight hour passes for everyone, but they were only rumours.

The battalion went first to Aldershot then they were loaded into troop trains at Farnborough Station and shunted off to the docks at Southampton. If any of the troops assembling there thought that this was just another military exercise they were sadly mistaken. They were off to war. If there was a 'grand plan' the men of the 43rd Regiment of Foot were unaware of it. They spent the first day on French soil 'awaiting orders'.

"C Company will now entrain!" They steamed slowly away from the port of Cherbourg, and one hundred and fifty miles later they were in the Loire Valley approaching the town of Sable. They crawled out, scratched themselves, gathered their kit together and marched awkwardly for another five miles to billets in barns and farm buildings.

Once settled in and fed they could prepare for battle. Route marches were organised and withdrawal exercises arranged. They hadn't advanced at this stage. The RSM and the padre went fishing. By some miracle of organisation the regimental transport, last seen at Aldershot, arrived but this was not to transport foot soldiers. They tramped back to the train station and embarked on another cramped journey through the dead of night, and then trudged in 'full service marching order' to new billets in a disused cinema.

117

As a change from route marches and practised retreats, the lads were kept busy building anti-tank obstacles and digging trenches. To get to this new location the train had passed across some of the old battlefields of the Great War where outlines of trenches could still be seen. This may have reminded the officers that trenches were an important feature of any war, and in any case digging was good and better for the men than 'hanging around'. During the seven-month-long 'Phoney War', senior officers pored over maps of the region the British Army were expected to defend against the old enemy. Some of the strategists recognised place names, tiny details of villages, streams and tracks, places they had not visited for twenty years when they were lowly lieutenants in the Great War. This would be a different war.

At the Ox and Bucks base there were regular hot meals, hot baths at the local colliery and concerts in the old cinema. Sergeant Dovey and 'C' Company were nicely settled in when orders came to move out to Tourcoing. The routine was the same, digging trenches and preparing tank traps.

The Duke of Gloucester arrived. He was a great events organiser and when he saw how smart the 1st Battalion of the Ox and Bucks were he included them in a march past for the king. This really was a 'Phoney War'. The king was perfectly safe; there was no action on this battle front – yet.

Christmas came. It was a white one with thick ice everywhere to top it off. The Ox and Bucks made the best of it; they gave a party for four hundred local children. The regimental band played, carols were sung and there was plenty of local pork and local wine to warm the troops.

There was no home leave although one or two lucky officers and senior NCOs were promoted and posted back to England. A new officer was welcomed into 'C' Company, Lieutenant Clutterbuck, a name no one was likely to forget.

A tour of the Maginot Line was arranged by the French who were proud to show off what they believed were impregnable defences they had built along their border from Switzerland to the edge of the Ardennes Forest. Harsh weather persisted into the New Year; the regiment moved again to a suburb of Lille and were billeted in an abandoned school. This was not the last move. Warning of an imminent invasion was given. Nothing happened. Preparations to resist the attack continued although planned exercises were abandoned because of the harsh weather. In mid-January the regiment marched five miles through deep snow to new quarters, and at the end of the month marched off again to very poor billets at Roost Warendin.

Anticipating a German offensive in the spring, construction of an underground bunker was begun. The work was supposed to be secret, but the earth spoil that littered the surrounding snow-covered countryside was obvious to the German reconnaissance aircraft that flew over dropping propaganda leaflets.

In early May, a sports day and tea party was organised for local children, an event enjoyed by all. The party was well and truly over on the 10th of May. The events that followed were recorded by Company Sergeant Major Dovey in his diary. In less than three weeks the Battle for France would be lost, and in less than a fortnight the British Military Chiefs of Staff would decide to abandon their allies and order the evacuation of the Expeditionary Force from the beaches of Dunkirk.

Throughout the winter Sergeant Dovey, Lieutenant Clutterbuck and 'C' Company had been shoring up defences around Lille, plodding from one billet to another and trying to keep warm and cheerful. It would prove to be a complete waste of time. If any one man could be blamed for this it was General Heinz Guderian.

Guderian devised a strategy of fast mobile warfare that became known as 'Blitzkrieg'; a co-ordinated attack with bombers, artillery and tanks which thrust through lines of defence and moved on to the next objective. Hitler had spent the Great War in the trenches going nowhere, and Guderian's strategy found favour with the Fuhrer. The 19th Panzer Corps had shown what could be achieved during the invasion of Poland. When plans were drawn up by the German High Command for their campaign in the west, Guderian told them he could be on the French coast within a week. His superiors thought this was an idle boast.

A lot happened on the 10th of May 1940. Churchill became prime minister and British troops occupied Iceland to prevent the Germans using the port facilities as a base to attack convoys. On the same day German paratroopers dropped on Dutch soil; over the border in Belgium a key fortress was also taken. The sky seemed full of low-flying enemy aircraft. Fortunately the Ox and Bucks were not a target on this occasion. The regiment 'stood to', and when transport arrived they moved on, crossed the border into Belgium and took over a forward position on the River Dyle.

Tom Dovey wrote in his diary:

News received that Germany invaded Belgium – Holland. Bombers raided Douai and passed over billets...I am moved...crossed Belgian frontier, arrived at 01.40 hours. Bivouacked on the square.

Along the way the roads were clogged with vehicles and progress was slow. As attempts were made to sort out the traffic jam a German bomber appeared and circled overhead. From nowhere a British fighter appeared and shot it down. The German pilot baled out into the arms of the Ox and Bucks who promptly handed him over to the Belgians.

Bombing of the Expeditionary Force continued the next day and as they consolidated their positions on the River Dyle one low-flying aircraft was brought down with small-arms fire from 'A' Company. Friendly fire brought down Private Ward who died of his wounds.

Staff Officers in a chateau nearby pored over maps and moved little coloured blocks which caused whole regiments to move. Tom and 'C' Company were treated to a tour of the countryside south of Brussels. The weather was pleasant and they enjoyed a cold lunch under beech trees near the historic site of the Battle of Waterloo. The following morning a full English breakfast was served; this was only spoiled by the dog fights overhead and the persistent anti-aircraft fire all around.

The Battle for France was well and truly underway and it was not going well for the French. They believed that the wooded hills of the Ardennes would shield them from any attack by German heavy armour. They were wrong. Plans drawn up meticulously during the winter months by the German High Command were put into operation. Supported by bombers General Guderian and his Panzers swept out of the forest. Others followed encircling the French Divisions.

An air raid on Rotterdam was the final straw for the Dutch and on the 14th of May they capitulated. In less than a week Guderian's tanks reached the Channel coast and the decision was made to withdraw the

British Expeditionary Force. The regiment was on the move again with the pounding of heavy artillery in the background and the screaming of Stuka dive bombers overhead. They certainly didn't like it but this was something the infantry were beginning to get used to.

WITHDRAWING IN GOOD ORDER

Bridges were demolished or mined in an attempt to hold back the enemy. Following repeated bomber raids, plumes of black smoke could be seen rising over Brussels. Refugees from the city and other stricken towns clogged every road and byway making the withdrawal operation very difficult. 'C' Company controlled a level crossing and did what they could to clear the way for the harassed families.

From now until they reached the safe shores of England there would be no rest for the Ox and Bucks. It was not possible to keep the whole regiment together; they moved in company formation. Communications were difficult after Headquarters Company lost all their kit. The whereabouts of 'A' Company was unknown and only half of 'B' Company could be located. Tom, Lieutenant Clutterbuck and 'C' Company lost touch with HQ so they did what soldiers were expected to do: 'obey the last order' which was 'to engage the enemy'.

German infantry, guided by spotter planes, was bearing down on them. On Monday 20th of May two more men were added to the casualty list. Heavy shelling the following day killed nine more and wounded seventeen. The only incident that cheered the retreating troops was when the Luftwaffe shot down one of their own planes.

There was no respite for anyone. The Gloucester Regiment had been holding back the German advance and now the Ox and Bucks were called on to cover their retreat. Three companies passed through the Gloucester's lines with Bren gun carriers preparing for battle, but found the whole area quiet. Exhausted after days without sleep the lads 'got their heads down', but not for long. Germans, well established in woodland nearby, opened fire. Training exercises to 'clear the enemy' had been rehearsed over and over again in parkland in Essex. Now the time had come to put what they had learned in peacetime into practise. Covered by gunners of the Royal Artillery and members of their own mortar platoon, 'B' Company crossed the open ground without incident, dodging shell craters as they advanced. 'C' Company were not so lucky.

A salvo of shells exploded close to the last platoon.

Tom Dovey wrote later:

10.00 hrs: Moved up to counter-attack wood. Company went in with bayonets north of Hollain. 2 Lt. Ingham along with Cpl Roper and Pte Wheeler were all killed and Sgt Grey was wounded.

21.00 hrs: Withdrew and platoons took up positions in houses north of Hollain.

From ten o'clock in the morning until nightfall the regiment was in close contact with the enemy. When German infantry supported by artillery pressed forward there were more casualties. No one, not even Lieutenant Colonel Whitfield, had the complete picture. The main objective of Sergeant Dovey and his company was to 'hold the line' as the Gloucesters and the Warwicks fell back.

They had no way of knowing that even Lord Gort, commander of the British Expeditionary Force, was fed up. He had to take orders from the French who he thought made some curious decisions. Had they been more decisive they might have turned the tables on the Panzers who, with no protection on their flanks, were charging towards the French coast. Gort felt let down by the French and withdrew British troops and, anticipating the collapse of the Belgian Army, made the decision to retreat to the coast. This decision saved the British Expeditionary Force from near certain destruction.

On the 22nd of May, Tom made a brief entry in his diary:

Still in position with spasmodic shelling from the enemy.

In just over a week he would be in sand dunes near Dunkirk, but getting there was not going to be easy. Patrols went out to collect dead and wounded comrades and arrange hasty burials. Supply lines had broken down and everyone was scavenging for food, ammunition, fuel and spares for the vehicles. There was much confusion; men from other regiments appeared and disappeared. The Ox and Bucks at least were operating as a unit. At nightfall they began to withdraw, and in the early hours crossed the border and found billets in French farms. They were able to keep out of sight of the spotter planes and had a quiet day and hot food. The French took over responsibility for manning the anti-tank ditches on the border and once again, under cover of darkness, the 43rd melted away. In the morning, at Vert Bois, there was just time to catch up on sleep, have a clean up, another hot meal and make ready to move on. Marching in companies they made good progress and regrouped in the evening. The whole of the BEF was on the move. Supplies of ammunition and food could not be maintained and rations were halved.

They moved away from Vert Bois in fine weather in a north-westerly direction towards the coast, and before they left slaughtered most of the farm animals. The owner was pleased to see this happen; he was evacuating his farm and didn't want any of his stock to fall into the hands of the Germans. These 'extra rations' kept the 43rd well fed. Orders were issued and changed repeatedly. The 43rd were given the task of defending a section of canal near Ypres, part of the border between France and Belgium, and taking over a section held by the Gordon Highlanders. Everywhere troops were on the move making their way to the coast. Columns of troops, convoys of trucks, bands of dejected refugees were all on the move along congested roads and tracks. Attacked from the air, there were casualties. Middle-aged locals were reliving the horrors of their teens when they had witnessed the chaos of the Great War in the same 'killing fields'.

The Expeditionary Force continued to fall back in an orderly fashion. Regiments interchanged on the front line to allow their comrades to withdraw as safely as possible. German infantry were never far away probing the lines of defence; everyone was tense and 'trigger-happy'. Colonel Whitfield was shot in the shoulder by one of his own men as he inspected a forward position after dark. Headquarters Company lost a Bren gun to mortar fire and a dozen men were injured. They were forced to move away to a position that could be more easily defended. No clear orders were received from 'on high' so the CO decided that the 43rd would 'hold their ground' at Wareton.

The 27th of May was a day of intense fighting for the boys of the Ox and Bucks. 'C' Company had taken up a strong position in farm buildings near Wareton and they were able to repel a determined attack by the Germans. There were casualties on both sides. Major Richards, commanding 'C' Company, was himself slightly wounded in the exchange. Lieutenant Clutterbuck was missing. He was last seen by the major at the upstairs windows of the farmhouse firing his revolver in all directions. He may have been attempting to hold back the enemy to allow his men to move out of the danger area, or he may simply have lost his head. Tom Dovey requested permission to go forward to help the young Lieutenant; permission was refused.

The next day the situation was worse. Counter-attacks were mounted by Hussars and Grenadier Guards to allow the 43rd to fall back to Messines. They withdrew. Shelled from a distance and shot at by snipers they maintained good discipline. They had done their bit and lost many good men. Even their commanding officer who had been severely wounded had been evacuated to the coast. What was left of the regiment regrouped and waited for transport to take them to Dunkirk. All equipment was abandoned to allow as many as possible to be crammed into the trucks. At midnight they set off.

Throughout the night and the following day (29th of May) they made their way through the chaos of fleeing civilians, dispirited French and Belgian troops and other men of the British Expeditionary Force. All were harassed by German artillery and attacks from the air. By evening the regiment rested in the relative safety of woodland, with sand dunes in front and the sea beyond, knowing that across the water was 'dear old England'. Here they destroyed their trucks and abandoned all but the most basic equipment. Under cover of darkness the regiment marched as one body along the coast until they were within the defensive perimeter of Dunkirk, and there set up defences of their own. They dug in and waited.

At last orders were received from General Headquarters. The regiment would be taken off the beaches in small boats and transferred to larger vessels at sea. The order was cancelled. They waited and watched as casualties were inflicted on troops nearby. Bombers of the Luftwaffe roamed above the beaches; occasionally a solitary Spitfire swooped across the clear blue sky spitting fire at the enemy to ward them off. Good management and good discipline had kept the 43rd together. New orders were received: 'Dunkirk, Eastern Mole'.

They marched as a column past crowds of confused troops all desperate to find a safe passage away from Dunkirk. Dive bombers and enemy artillery continued to pound the beaches as the Ox and Bucks plodded doggedly towards the Mole where rescue vessels were queuing up to take the troops home.

Vessels of every description crossed the Channel to evacuate the troops from Dunkirk. Among the cruisers and frigates of the Royal Navy were fishing boats, barges, dinghies, ferries and pleasure boats sailed by their owners.

© Imperial War Museums (H1645)

"Any more for the Skylark?"

As they arrived, a bomb hit the Mole. There were casualties; some in agony on the quayside, some dead in the water. Good order was maintained. The 43rd were to sail on the *Maid of Orleans*. Departure was delayed; she had to act as a floating stage for three other ships. The *Maid* docked at three in the morning and stayed moored to the jetty for six hours as troops crossed her decks. At last, with Tom and his company safely aboard, the *Maid* cast off and made her way out to sea. As they crossed the Channel, Navy gunners kept the German dive bombers at bay until they docked at Dover.

A tourist today looking down on the harbour from the white cliffs above would have difficulty imagining the scene in June 1940. In a little over a week over three hundred thousand British troops were rescued. A good number of these disembarked in Dover Harbour. The wounded had to be treated, the hungry had to be fed and the congestion on the quayside had to be sorted out. Troop trains and convoys of trucks carried the weary warriors away to temporary billets all over the country. The sense of relief was overwhelming; everyone was in a daze.

Tom Dovey could not say how he got from the docks at Dover to a tented camp in the Devonshire countryside. Along the way he must have eaten something and been offered a mug of hot, sweet tea that he clasped gratefully in his grubby hands. He slept the sleep of the dead. He woke up slowly. Above him the khaki fabric of the tent flapped gently. It was a comforting sound like waves lapping on a sandy shore. He closed his eyes and listened; there was birdsong. Perhaps he was in paradise. Alarmed, he woke up with a start. He had seen so much death in recent weeks that he thought he too was one of the dead.

Tom thought back. Lieutenant Clutterbuck was almost certainly dead, last seen at the upstairs window of a Belgian farmhouse. In the yard below Tom had come face to face with a young German soldier, his rifle slung over his shoulder. He fumbled desperately to unhitch it. Sergeant Tom Dovey drew his service revolver and fired; the unfortunate lad fell in front of him. He was just another casualty on the day and would be mourned by his mother for years to come.

The remnants of the regiment regrouped at Hereford and counted the cost of being part of the expeditionary force. Over seven hundred of the Ox and Bucks set off for France in 1939. They lost nearly three hundred; some killed, others wounded or taken prisoner. Nevertheless, they were still a fighting unit. Others would join their ranks; they would learn from their experience and go forward into battle again.

The response of the Ministry of Information to this military disaster was to print and distribute more posters with a simple message to the people: 'Keep Calm and Carry On'.

Chapter 12

The Desert War

WITH FRIENDS LIKE THIS

It's hard to feel any sympathy for Adolf Hitler. There was no excuse for what he did. It didn't help getting into bad company. He signed a non-aggression pact with Joe Stalin, and then decided to invade Russia because he didn't like communists. Joe was very angry. The Russian Bear turned ugly and mauled thousands of poor German lads Adolf sent off to the Eastern Front.

Benito Mussolini was a fascist dictator, the sort of man Adolf should have got on well with, but he was erratic and unreliable. Benito fantasised about being an emperor, so before the war he invaded Abyssinia and added that poor country to other African colonies. In 1940, Italian troops stationed in Libya heavily outnumbered British and Commonwealth forces in neighbouring Egypt.

MORE THAN JUST MANOEUVRES

In 2011, during the operation to help the Libyan people rid themselves of the dictatorial Colonel Gaddafi, the public became familiar with the map of Libya and many of the place names. News of the actions in Benghazi and Tripoli appeared daily. They had been on the front pages before, in the 1940s together with Mersa Matruh, Sidi Barrani, Beda Fomm and El Alamein. The battle front between the British 8th Army and the Axis forces swung back and forth along the coast of North Africa.

Cuthie Goulburn and the 8th Hussars had tried out their armoured cars in Palestine. Fred Todd and the 3rd Hussars had been charging around Salisbury Plain. It was time to put theory into practise. In preparation for the coming conflict the King's Royal Irish Hussars were given light tanks which were an improvement on the 15 cwt. pick-up trucks they had used in Palestine in 1936. The 'new' tanks were actually cast offs from another regiment. To add insult to injury the King's Hussars were ordered to replace their distinctive 'side hats' with the black berets of the Royal Armoured Corps. They were no longer Cavalry of the Line; so ended nearly two hundred and fifty years of tradition. Just a few weeks before war was declared the 8th Hussars were in the desert south of Mersa Matruh digging holes and burying cans of petrol. In the past, large supplies of hay had always been necessary to keep the cavalry mobile. Times had changed.

War was declared. Troops stationed in Egypt got news from home. An expeditionary force was sent to France and sat about for months. Back in England children were evacuated to the countryside. Nothing much seemed to happen and parents brought many of them home for Christmas. By the end of May the following year, everyone knew the 'phoney war' was over when news came through that the Royal Navy and a fleet of 'little ships' were sailing back and forth across the Channel to evacuate troops from Dunkirk. The Germans were having it all their own way; the Dutch, the Belgians and the Norwegians had all surrendered.

This made Benito Mussolini very brave. He imagined that because the British had retreated to Dunkirk and limped back to England they had no more fight left in them. Now was the time, he thought, to charge out of Libya and attack the British in Egypt. So, against the advice of Marshal Graziani, he ordered his troops to cross the border and attack the British in Egypt. This was a huge mistake. Benito had not reckoned with the newly formed 7th Armoured Division, the Desert Rats, and the Australians and Indians who fought alongside them.

The opening round went to the Italians; they penetrated sixty miles into Egyptian territory and set up a line of defence at Sidi Barrani. The Italians 'dug in' in September 1940. Before Christmas they were ready to leave.

Although there were risks, 'Operation Compass' was launched by Commonwealth forces. The Italian tanks were known to be of poor quality but they had twice as many artillery pieces as the British. The counter-attack began cautiously. Indian troops infiltrated Italian positions. This was most unnerving for troops experiencing battle for the first time. The Italians began to fall back, and the retreat became a rout. They were sent reeling back four hundred miles from Sidi Barrani to Bedda Fomm. Troops of the old British Empire captured a string of coastal towns along the way including Tobruk, Gazala, Benghazi, and they halted their advance at El Agheila. The retreating Italian 10th Army were overtaken by the 7th Armoured Division and trapped between the Desert Rats and Australian Infantry. In this operation more than thirteen thousand Italians were taken prisoner.

It seemed Italian soldiers did not want to lay down their lives for Benito Mussolini. They laid down their arms instead. Italy had fought with Britain and against Germany in the Great War. Many Italians in the officer classes had strong links with Britain and a low opinion of Mussolini. Peasants and the working class were admirers of the American way of life, and thousands emigrated there in the 1930s alarmed by Mussolini's politics. At the time of the mass surrender one tank commander came to a halt and remarked, "I'm stopped in the middle of two hundred, no, five hundred men with their hands up. Send for the bloody infantry!"

Most of the prisoners were shipped to England; some lucky ones were billeted in Apley Park and spent the rest of the war working on the estate farms. When the war was over a few stayed on.

Meanwhile, back in the desert Cuthie Goulburn's Hussars saw plenty of action. They captured a series of forts, witnessed the mass surrender of the Italians at Bardia and did battle at Bedda Fomm. They also took the airfield at El Adem. If that wasn't enough they were then packed off to Greece for a few weeks.

Mussolini had sent his unfortunate troops off on another campaign. They had some success in Albania and made plans to conquer Greece. He did not consult his ally, Adolf Hitler, but announced at the end of October 1939 that, "Victorious Italian troops crossed the Albanian frontier at dawn today." Der Fuhrer was furious. He knew that sooner or later Germans would have to step in to back up the Italians. Invading Greece was indeed a disaster. Within less than a fortnight the Greeks had taken five thousand prisoners, forced the Italians back to the border and then went on to inflict more casualties. They also captured a number of towns and a naval base. Winter saved Benito from further humiliation.

The Italians strengthened their forces in Albania until they had twice as many troops on the ground as the Greeks. In early March 1941 the conflict resumed and the Greeks held their position. To back them up small groups of British and Commonwealth troops began to arrive at the port of Piraeus. Cuthie and the 8th Hussars arrived. It was a brief campaign because Hitler's planners had been at work and they were now ready to rescue the Italians. The Germans did not intend to fight alongside the Italians but strike at Greece through Bulgaria. The planning was masterful; the Greeks were overwhelmed.

Commonwealth troops retreated to the beaches; some went to Crete others went back to Egypt. Fifty thousand got away, but thousands more went into captivity. Cuthie and the King's Hussars made it back to Cairo.

Troops diverted to the campaign in Greece had weakened the defences of the Allies in North Africa. This was the opportunity to turn the tide in favour of the Axis powers. Hitler sent one of his most able generals to Tripoli. Erwin Rommel's presence had an almost immediate effect on the conduct of the campaign and on the lives of everyone involved from generals to private soldiers. Even Churchill had words of praise for the legendary 'Desert Fox'.

"We have a very daring and skilful opponent against us and, may I say, a great general."

The war in the Western Desert swung back and forth along a strip of coast more than a thousand miles long. Commonwealth forces were pushed back towards the Egyptian border once again, but they did manage to hang on to Tobruk. The port was completely isolated and had to be supplied by sea. It could not be allowed to fall into enemy hands. The first attempt to raise the siege of Tobruk failed, and a second operation was planned.

'Operation Crusader' was a costly action for the 8th Hussars. As part of the 4th Armoured Brigade they were first in the order of battle. The airfield at Sidi Rezegh was a place best forgotten. As dusk approached during the three-day battle both sides withdrew. The Hussars formed a box leaguer for protection. They believed they were well hidden but German night patrols discovered their position, and in the morning all hell let loose. When the dust settled the Irish Hussars were left with only four Stuart tanks fit for battle. In all, thirty-five had been destroyed or captured. Many good men were lost.

The garrison at Tobruk, largely Australian infantry, managed to hold out for two hundred and forty days until relieved. Rommel and his Afrika Korps fell back and the 8th Army with its Desert Rats licked their wounds. Thirty-two new Stuart tanks were issued to the 8th Hussars, and they had a new commander, Lieutenant Colonel 'Smash' Kilkelly. They had lost none of their will to fight but within weeks Kilkelly was dead, killed in action at the Battle of Knightsbridge. The campaign swung again in favour of Rommel; the 8th Army withdrew in some disarray towards El Alamein.

General Neil Richie wanted to make a do-or-die stand at Mersa Matruh, but he was overruled. Claude Auchinleck managed to shepherd the forces under his command through the forty-mile-wide gap south of Alamein and set up defensive positions. His reward for this was 'the sack'. His replacement should have been General William Gott but he was killed, shot down over the desert. General Bernard Montgomery got the job of preparing defences and planning the defeat of Field Marshal Rommel's Afrika Korps.

No More Swanning About in the Blue

A new commanding officer was appointed to lead the Royal Irish Hussars, Lieutenant Colonel Cuthie Goulburn. He would lead them to victory in the desert, and after D-Day across Normandy and beyond.

A training exercise for the Desert Rats, June 1942. An officer of the Royal Tank Regiment giving instructions from his Daimler scout car to the commander of a Stuart tank.

© Imperial War Museums (E13537)

"Show me the way to go home."

The battles they played a part in have gone down in military history and are used by armchair soldiers fond of war games. For those on the ground it was no game.

General Montgomery put a stop to unauthorised patrols that brought back very little useful intelligence and wasted precious fuel. Monty decided there would be no more 'swanning about in the blue' for the cavalry. All efforts were to be concentrated on defending territory and preparing a knock-out blow against the enemy.

The Germans and Italians struck first. They were desperately short of everything; fuel, tanks, men and air cover, but if they had broken through and taken Suez the outcome of the war would have been very different. Rommel's move was predictable. He attempted to swing south and attack Montgomery's flank. 'Ultra' intelligence warned Monty of Rommel's intentions and he planned accordingly. The battleground favoured the defenders on the Alam Halfa Ridge. The tanks stood their ground and acted as artillery. Cuthie's Hussars withstood the first battering from German Panzers. Rommel was also receiving a battering from the RAF. He decided to withdraw. Steadily, the Germans and their half-hearted allies were pushed back across Libya to the Tunisian border.

THE CROSS OF WAR

The Honourable Artillery Company, founded in the reign of Henry VIII, was the oldest regiment in the British Army. This was Harry Russell's regiment. At the outbreak of war he was twenty-eight and left behind a young wife and a toddling son to fight in the desert.

The fort at Bir Hakeim, built by the Turks on the furthest border of their empire, had been there a long time. That empire withered away and was finally dismantled at the end of the Great War. Bir Hakeim was the last place on earth anyone wanted to go. Similar garrisons were set up in Tunisia, Algeria, Morocco and the French colonies in North Africa. They were all miserable dusty places on the edge of the Sahara manned by the French Foreign Legion. A series of *Beau Geste* films glamorised the life of the legionnaires, but there was nothing romantic about these locations.

The Free French Army was formed from men in France's Overseas Territories who would not accept the surrender in Europe, and the Vichy government. The French General Koenig had command at Bir Hakeim.

His men came from the ends of the earth, and some from paradise islands in the Pacific: Tahiti, Polynesia, New Caledonia. Native people and expatriate Frenchmen formed the *Battalion du Pacifique*. They assembled in Australia, boarded a Cunard liner and sailed for Palestine. After training they were ready to face Rommel in the desert. Captain Colley, Gunner Harry Russell and the rest of 'E' Battery of the Royal Horse Artillery took up positions beside them.

There had once been a reliable water supply at the oasis at Bir Hakeim which had since dried up. Water, fuel, ammunition, food, all things necessary to supply the garrison, was brought in on convoys of trucks; it was a crucial hub. If Rommel's men could overrun the fort the whole defensive line would collapse. In the end it did.

A serious attack was mounted on the 16th of March 1942. Captain Colley and his battery responded with 'all guns blazing'. Lieutenant Venning, Sergeant Banbury and Sergeant Stevenson were all killed. There were more casualties as Rommel's Panzers approached to within a hundred yards of the battery; the gunners could only reply with small-arms fire. It was a 'last ditch stand' to no avail. The Germans took nineteen prisoners including Captain Colley and returned to their lines. Nine men still lay on the battlefield. Harry Russell was one of them. The following day Lieutenant Sewell and a French priest returned to the position; the dead were buried where they had fallen. How these men died was plain to see – facing the enemy and out of ammunition.

Margery Russell received official news of her husband's death and tried to explain to her little boy that his soldier father would not be coming home. Harry's commanding officer wrote and gave some details of the battle; the heroic sacrifice men of the Honourable Artillery Company had made fighting alongside the Free French. At school little Johnny Russell retold the story to boys in the playground. His father had been killed in action. He was brave, a hero and he was going to get a medal. The lads listened. They were sorry his dad was dead, but there was nothing special about getting medals. Lots of blokes had them, even old blokes.

"My dad's getting a special medal from a French General." His schoolmates listened more intently when he told them this. Everyone agreed Harry Russell was a real hero. The medal never came.

Talk of the war faded; no one wanted to be reminded of it.

Then nearly forty years later a letter arrived in Church Lane from the headquarters of the Honourable Artillery Company. The action of 'E' Battery at Bir Hakeim had been recognised. Koenig, the French General, had indeed recommended the entire troop collectively for the *Croix de Guerre*. The French government accepted the recommendation and arrangements were made for Margery Russell to receive the 'Cross of War' from their ambassador in London.

COMBINED OPERATIONS

The campaign in North Africa ended when the Afrika Korps withdrew from Tunis in May 1943. The cavalry had led the charge in the major battles. Cuthie Goulburn, Harry Russell and Fred Todd had certainly been at the sharp end but they could not have taken on Rommel's Panzers without back-up from other Apley men. Arthur Lewis came with the Staffordshire Regiment, and Royal Marine Eric Timson helped out the Aussies at Tobruk. Bert Ward and Harold Evans, the village blacksmith, kept the Desert Air Force flying, while Sid Speke patrolled the coast on board HMS *Bermuda*. On guard at the entrance to the Mediterranean, Nick Davis manned the guns that protected the Straits of Gibraltar.

Monty's victories in the desert owed much to the efforts of cavalrymen, infantrymen and airmen flying from dusty airstrips. Sailors dodging U-boats brought in essential supplies. In the background, crossword fanatics at a country house in Bedfordshire played their part. Eccentric academics broke the German code; they intercepted and deciphered messages and provided vital intelligence to commanders in the field. In their spare time they played rounders on the lawns at Bletchley Park, and breathed not a word for fifty years. In retirement Natalie Hodgson tended her lavender garden at Astley Abbots and cared for her bees. In her nineties she spoke of summer days in Bedfordshire and her work for the Political Warfare Executive.

Chapter 13

Everyone Joined In

A HEAD FOR HEIGHTS

Anyone planning to spend their working life up a ladder must have a good head for heights. Young Arthur Evans was never troubled by vertigo. He could apply a fresh coat of paint to the top floor windows at the Hall, or the weather vane on the parish church with a steady hand. The real test came when he was called on to jump out of a basket over Ringway Airfield.

Arthur was a Territorial soldier at the outbreak of war but instead of joining the county regiment he was drafted into the Royal Welch Fusiliers.

When Churchill took over as prime minister in May 1940 he issued a directive, "Raise a battalion of parachute troops."

Volunteers came forward from all formations of the British Army. Then in August 1942 a whole battalion 'volunteered'. Arthur was 'invited' to join the 6th Battalion (Royal Welch) Parachute Battalion.

Fusilier Evans enjoyed the training and only once did he hesitate. Six 'squaddies' were sent up in a basket slung under a balloon and tethered to a winch below. It was dusk and one by one they dropped through the floor and floated to the ground. The instructor jumped leaving Arthur alone. It was remarkably quiet with just a light breeze to sway the basket. Arthur considered his position. In the fading light he could just make out tiny khaki figures below moving briskly from their billets towards the cookhouse. He was ready for a good feed and there was only one way to get it. He jumped. The training was over and this meant another change of badge and beret. Members of the Parachute Regiment were easily recognisable with their red berets and 'wings' on their shoulder.

The Germans and their Italian allies had controlled much of the Mediterranean. Now they were in retreat. The British held Cairo and kept the Suez Canal open. Malta stubbornly refused to submit to repeated attacks from sea and air. Montgomery had been victorious at the Battle of El Alamein and Rommel seemed to have lost his touch. German forces regrouped at the Mareth Line on the border between Libya and Tunisia. The Americans mobilised their forces preparing to land on the coast of Morocco and Algeria. This was to be a combined operation. British paratroopers sailed to Gibraltar where the planners for 'Operation Torch' had set up their headquarters.

General Eisenhower was the overall commander who decided what part Arthur Evans would play in the operation. Parachute troops were to be dropped ahead of the advancing tanks and infantry and hold their positions until they were relieved. Operation Torch was a success. Hitler was furious; he was a very bad loser. In future he decided commandos and the 'Red Devils' of the Parachute Regiment were to be given the same treatment if captured. They would not be made prisoners of war like other troops. They would be shot.

The Allies prepared to cross the Mediterranean and attack Italy, the 'soft underbelly of Europe' as Churchill called it. Arthur was not involved in this operation. He was back in England suffering from serious neck and shoulder injuries. He recovered and landed the job of driver for Major General 'Roy' Urquhart, Commander of the 1st Airborne Division.

WHEN THE BALLOON GOES UP

Troops in the trenches of the Great War always knew that they were going to be asked to do something dangerous when they saw 'the balloon go up'. In the basket under the balloon a young officer with compass, map case and notepad would gather information to hand on to staff officers so that they could decide where weak points in the enemy defences might be, and plan accordingly. They could also estimate how many casualties there were going to be. It was never nil or even single figures.

In the early days of the Second World War, even more balloons, at least four hundred, went up over London this time to protect the citizens against attack by low-flying enemy aircraft. The barrage balloon was a

136

great fat silver sausage with three floppy 'fins' at the back, and a cable that tethered it to the ground. The responsibility for operating these rubbery giants fell to the Royal Air Force. Balloon Command was set up in 1938, anticipating the trouble ahead. To keep a balloon flying round the clock required a 'flight' of about twenty airmen and WAAFs.

Bill Jones was in the RAFVR (volunteer reserve). He had no idea what he was volunteering for. He thought it might be something big when he arrived at RAF Cardington and saw the size of the old airship hangars which were colossal structures two hundred metres long.

Training balloon operators at RAF Cardington. Very few enemy aircraft were 'snared' by barrage balloons but they certainly did act as a deterrent and were a comforting sight to those on the ground.

"Don't let go the string!"

At the No 1 Balloon Training Unit he learned how to operate the winch to raise and lower the balloon on its steel cable. Some cables carried explosive charges; 'handle with care'. Hydrogen, the gas that lifted the balloon off the ground, slowly leaked through the canvas and had to be topped up regularly – definitely 'no smoking' when this was taking place. Often the winch was mounted on the back of a truck so that they could be moved around whenever the Luftwaffe changed their tactics, or attacked new targets.

Percy Price, the village postmaster at Norton, received a postcard, one of many. This one was addressed to him personally. It was official, authorised by the Royal Air Force. The black and white print of the Forth Bridge looked grim especially with barrage balloons hovering over it. On the end of one of the balloon cables was Percy's son-in-law, Bill Jones. He was sitting uncomfortably on a barge. Even though he was an airman Bill was a good sailor which was just as well. The barge bobbed about in the Firth of Forth tugged by the balloon on its flapping cable and buffeted by wind and waves. A strong stomach was needed to cope with this for eight hours at a stretch.

The Forth Bridge was a vital link to the north of Scotland and the base of the home fleet at Scapa Flow. It had to be protected. Percy's postcard wasn't top secret; quite the opposite. The RAF wanted the Luftwaffe to know that if they were planning an attack they would have to dodge the barrage balloons.

In May 1940, British warships made for Iceland and steamed into Reykyavik harbour at the same time as British troops were retreating to Dunkirk. If Britain was to survive the supply route from America and Canada had to be protected, and the German High Seas Fleet denied a base in Iceland. Sitting on a barge in the Firth of Forth wasn't comfortable, and Reykjavik harbour and the sea lanes around Iceland were even less inviting. "Never mind, Bill, at least Iceland has hot springs."

Leading Aircraftsman Jones' billet on the outskirts of Rejkavik.

Permission given by Bill's daughter, Tina.

"Now I know why they call it Iceland."

138

Bill sat it out in a Nissen hut with just a single sheet of corrugated iron overhead to protect him from the snows of winter. This was better than being out at sea where U-boats lurked below the waves intent on doing harm. Bill Jones and his flight of balloonists got into hot water, the sort that welled up out of the ground in Iceland. Immersed for twenty minutes they came out warmed right to the core. The sulphurous fumes from the geysers were similar to those that came from the coke stove in the billet, but that only warmed their knees.

Why Tell a Lie?

Not everyone has the ability or temperament for clerical work. Although trained as a plasterer, Len Dunn ran the office at the estate yard; sorting, filing, cataloguing, ordering. Dealing with all the paperwork that crossed his desk required an orderly mind. Len did not appear to be impetuous or dishonest but in 1939 he was.

He slipped out of the family home in Marvels Lane, walked confidently into a recruiting office in south London and told the RAF Sergeant behind the desk that he was born in 1921. It was a lie. He was only seventeen, he was impetuous and he wanted to be in from the start. No one ever asked for proof of his date of birth. The false date was copied from one document to the next for six years. This was not the first time in history that this had happened; hundreds of lads had been just as deceitful at the start of the Great War. At the outbreak of the Second World War a new generation of young men repeated the folly of their fathers.

Len, a cockney lad from Lewisham, took the train to Warrington and in six weeks was transformed from a plasterer in white overalls to one of the 'boys in blue'. His first posting was to the Flying Training School at Tern Hill. Until then he had never heard of Shropshire. Little did he know that this was going to be his adopted homeland, and Bridgnorth and Apley would become more familiar to him than Piccadilly Circus or Leicester Square.

In November 1939, RAF Bridgnorth was no more than a collection of about twenty huts surrounding the NAAFI. Len was posted from Tern Hill and with others formed the advanced party bringing what skills they had to help in the construction of the billets that would house new recruits. Many of the construction team were given accommodation in the town. There were no complaints; Bridgnorth had more pubs per head of population than London, and the natives were friendly.

The first winter on the camp was unpleasantly severe and progress on the site was slow. Czech, Polish and Dutch troops were among the first to fill the billets intended for RAF recruits. These foreign troops had been taken off the beaches at Dunkirk when British forces withdrew from the Continent. They would all regroup and one day return to help finish the job. In June 1940 N° 4 Recruit Centre began the work of training a generation of young airmen, then after a year there was a sex change. RAF Bridgnorth became the N° 1 WAAF Depot. Young airmen, permanent staff on the station, were outnumbered probably twenty to one by young women.

There must have been something about putting on a uniform that made every young man dash to the nearest photographer.

Permission given by Christine Lewis

"Len Dunn, one of the Brylcreem Boys."

The airmen must have been spoilt for choice. From his post at station headquarters, Leading Aircraftsman Dunn must have watched thousands of young girls pass through the main gate. Tempting indeed, but Len had already made his choice.

Charlie Lloyd's daughter, Ethel, was one of the friendly natives living in a farm cottage close to the camp. She worked in a factory on the riverside. Southwell's Carpet Factory had been taken over by Rootes Group to produce aero engine parts and other materials of war. It was mid-April, there was early blossom in the hedgerows and gardens, and daffodils everywhere. Romance was in the air. Len and Ethel made a decision. Come what may, they were going to spend the rest of their days together. In the Bridgnorth Registry Office the young couple signed the register and sealed the bond. They gave their occupations as 'munitions worker' and 'gunner', an explosive combination. The newlyweds were typical of many at the time. They had been born worlds apart and had it not been for the war they would never have met.

The RAF Regiment was formed to take responsibility for airfield security; they were trained as infantry. Len was a founding member of 2702 Squadron RAF Regiment. He was posted to Bentley Priory where Len's main concern was how to avoid bumping into 'Stuffy' Dowding in the corridors.

From the library windows at Bentley Priory there was a fine view across the gardens to Harrow-on-the-Hill marked by the spire of St. Mary's church. It was a very English scene; something worth defending, something worth fighting for. Air Chief Marshal Hugh Dowding thought so. Here he planned and schemed *to stop the possibility of an invasion, and thus give the country a breathing spell.* Dowding's operations room was moved to an underground bunker, and from here he directed operations during the Battle of Britain. Stuffy Dowding really was a dreary man but he did a fine job. The Luftwaffe would never have command of the skies over Britain and Air Chief Marshal Hugh Dowding could take the credit for that. Hitler cancelled the planned invasion of Britain and turned his attention to Russia.

Len went to Whitehall to man an anti-aircraft battery just to be on the safe side.

ROUGH SEA IN THE MEDITERRANEAN

In the early part of the twentieth century the cottages at the bottom of Railway Street housed the Speke clan, 'the Fighting Spekes'. They had

141

been soldiers of the Queen and could trace their commitment to empire back to the Indian Mutiny in 1857. Sid broke with tradition and joined the Royal Navy.

It was a while before Sid went to sea. HMS *Raleigh* was commissioned in 1940; she occupied several acres of land at Torpoint, Plymouth. Her ability to withstand an aerial bombardment was tested early the following year when a German bomb hit the air-raid shelter killing forty-four sailors and twenty-one Royal Engineers. Five months later, Sid arrived.

During the six weeks of basic training the recruits were barked at on the drill square, given small-arms training and lectured on naval history. The most important part of the training, without a doubt, was the ironing of the pleats in bell-bottom trousers. This had to be mastered even if this particular skill had no earthly use outside the Royal Navy. Bell-bottoms were part of naval tradition. Nelson's crew found climbing in the rigging and swabbing the decks easier with their trousers rolled up. When not being worn they were carefully folded to pack into a kit bag; to do this they were turned inside out and ironed with horizontal pleats, usually seven.

Sid mastered the technique but he didn't practise it for long; soon he would exchange his 'square rig' for something more practical. He was selected for training as an electrical mechanic and posted to HMS *Victory*. This was not actually Nelson's flagship but the South Western Hotel at Southampton. The final phase of the training course was on board HMS *Defiance*, a stirring title for three old ships anchored together on the River Tamar. They were within rowing distance of the shore and incapable of sailing anywhere.

Electrical Mechanic Speke finally stepped on board an ocean-going vessel, HMS *Bermuda,* based at Greenock on the frequently foggy Clyde. His 'life on the ocean wave' was about to begin in earnest. The crew spent some weeks 'working up', testing the equipment and the systems, and conducting speed trials in the North Sea. Then *Bermuda* sailed to Plymouth. She took on more crew and set course for Gibraltar.

Under 'The Rock', Eisenhower, the American General, set up his headquarters and from here directed the invasion of North Africa, the massive combined operation codenamed 'Torch'. *Bermuda* was a member of 'H' Force which escorted the troopships assembled in the

Atlantic through the Straits of Gibraltar. She then covered the landings on the Algerian coast. No one expected that it would be all 'plain sailing'. *Bermuda* and other escort ships were attacked repeatedly by German and Italian aircraft with bombs and aerial-launched torpedoes. This was Sid's first experience of war and it was unforgettable.

In this action HMS *Martin* was lost. On the evening of the 10th of November 1942, she was silhouetted against the Sahara sky. In the morning she was gone, sunk by *U431* torpedoes. Of a ship's company of nearly two hundred, only 4 officers and fifty-nine ratings were picked up. The names of the rest were inscribed on the Portsmouth Memorial alongside others who have 'no other grave but the sea'.

Sid remembers a rather odd incident at the time. Some ships of the Royal Navy flew the 'Stars and Stripes', and carrier-borne aircraft were painted with US markings. It was reasoned that the Americans might be welcome on the shores of an old French colony, but not the British. The French government had capitulated in 1940. The northern half of the country was occupied by the Germans. In the south a puppet government was set up, the Vichy government. A large proportion of the French fleet was in the Mediterranean and Churchill feared they might be used against the Royal Navy. In July 1940 two battleships, a battle cruiser and a carrier were dispatched to neutralise French vessels at Oran and Mers-el-Kebir in Algeria. There were negotiations, but no agreement. The Royal Navy sank a battleship and damaged two others.

Operation Torch was the largest Allied amphibious operation of the war so far with a hundred thousand men and one hundred and twenty ships involved. The operation was a success thanks to Sid and a few others.

TAIL-END CHARLIE

The dances on the camp at RAF Bridgnorth were very popular with local girls. They looked forward to being surrounded by boys in blue and finding a partner for the quickstep, or for life. "He looks nice, the tall one."

Bert Groves stood out in the crowd with his shock of dark hair and sergeant's stripes. Up close an inquisitive girl prodded his chest.

"You're an air gunner I see, and what's that pretty little blue and white ribbon for?"

"Never you mind, let's dance."

Sergeant Groves was grounded. He had flown his last mission and now he was a gunnery instructor inspiring new recruits to carry on the fight against Nazi Germany.

Bert had travelled a hard road from the Isle of Wight to the Severn Valley. His father died when he was twelve and his mother left to care for eight children. Three of her sons were taken into a care home. At fourteen Bert went out into the world and found work on farms in Kent and Oxfordshire. When war came he did not hesitate. Bert was ready to spread his wings.

The aircrew selection process revealed a problem that dated back to childhood. Surgeons attempted to correct a bone defect by fixing a steel pin in Bert's thigh. It was later removed and left two untidy scars on leg and hip. The medical officer remarked, "I see you've been in the wars already. Been working on the farm?"

"Yes, sir."

"It looks as if you've been caught up in barbed wire."

Bert was not going to disagree with the medical officer. He was passed fit for flying.

Much of the training for air gunners was in Scotland. It might have been reasoned that they could do less damage up there. Bert spent two months near Stranraer training on Whitley bombers. Everyone was fired with enthusiasm. Polish airmen were particularly keen to return to Europe. In the meantime they flew across the water and harassed flocks of sheep in Northern Ireland. Targets towed across the sky were the most realistic form of training. This could be dangerous. Although air gunners believed they were immortal Bert remembers when two aircraft collided and both crews were lost.

At Leeming, Sergeant Groves joined 10 Squadron and flew his first mission over enemy territory. Sergeant Lane, the Canadian pilot, was a memorable character. Today he would be described as a member of the first nation. Bert said, "He was a Red Indian."

Inevitably there were losses. In January 1942 a Halifax returning from a raid on Hamburg crashed in a snowstorm at Northallerton. Only the pilot survived. In March a whole crew was lost on the coast of Norway attacking the German battleship, *Tirpitz*.

At the end of May, 'Bomber' Harris scraped together every available aircraft and the RAF mounted the first thousand-bomber raid on Cologne. This number of aircraft overwhelmed the German anti-aircraft batteries. The inner city was almost totally destroyed. Miraculously, the twin towers of the cathedral were still left standing. The city was targeted repeatedly until the end of the war. It was on a bombing raid over Cologne that Bert Groves received the wounds that ended his flying career.

Halifax Q, piloted by Tony Ennis, took off from Leeming and flew steadily south over the Humber estuary and the flat lands of Lincolnshire and Norfolk where many fellow airmen were preparing for another night raid. They crossed the Channel; all knew what to expect when they reached the coast of Holland. Exploding shells fired from below sent lethal splinters of metal flying into the path of the advancing aircraft. This was 'flak' and there was no way of avoiding it. As they approached Cologne the bomb aimer took over directing the pilot over the intercom. The rest of the crew, navigator and gunners listened in. No one interrupted but they were all thinking, 'for Christ's sake get on with it and let's get out of here'!

Aerial photographs were taken to assess the accuracy of the bombing raids. The lone Halifax flying low over the Rhine at Cologne is very close to the action.

"Bombs away!"

Tony Ennis banked the aircraft and turned for home. The spires of Cologne Cathedral were clear to see lit by the flames of the shattered city. The Halifax was caught in the glare of searchlights. Flak burst around them. Two of the engines were damaged and Bert, in the rear gun turret, was hit. They lost height but Bert carried on firing to take out the searchlights and target the anti-aircraft batteries. They limped back low over the Ruhr.

With the Channel below them the pilot sent out a call to Manston to prepare for an emergency landing. The rest of the crew were silent. In the rear turret, cramped and cold, Bert did not know what had hit him. His flying suit was ripped apart, and there was blood everywhere from wounds to chest, arm, head and hand. He didn't want to distract the skipper so he kept quiet. Fred Simpson knew something was wrong. Bert was pulled from his turret and given a shot of morphine. They landed at Manston in the early hours and he was whisked off to Margate Hospital. This should have been a place of safety but sirens were wailing to warn the townsfolk of another Luftwaffe raid.

Sergeant Groves was 'patched up' at the RAF Hospital at Halton. The broken arm and broken ribs mended, but his left hand would never be the same again and he had lost an eye. For his troubles he was awarded the Distinguished Flying Medal with its 'pretty little blue and white ribbon'. At Buckingham Palace the king congratulated Bert and pinned on the medal. An inscription, in Latin, around the head of King George reminded his subjects that he was the King Emperor and Defender of the Faith. The inscription on the back for Bert Groves was simpler – FOR COURAGE.

Stationed at Bridgnorth as a gunnery instructor until the war's end, Bert had time to put his life in order and plan for the future. Demobbed in 1945, Bert considered going back to the land and opening a market garden on the Isle of Wight, but he had married a local girl. She loved her home town and they decided to stay.

Bert took up a new trade as a plasterer. He was skilful and he was tall; where others might need a ladder Bert kept his feet on the ground. In the course of his working life he smoothed over the cracks in town houses and country cottages for miles around. His skill and enthusiasm for his work was only matched by his enthusiasm for bowls and his skill on the greens.

Bert and his good friend Tony Bennett straightened up on the Norton Green and looked up into the sky. The Red Arrows swept overhead making for Cosford to put on a thrilling display above the waiting crowd at the air show. Historic aircraft of the Memorial Flight passed overhead; Spitfire, Hurricane, Dakota and a Lancaster bomber.

"You should be up there with 'em, Bert."

Sir Francis Drake had steadied his nerve with a game of bowls before he sailed out to take on the Spanish Armada. Bert Groves had flown out to take on another invader and played many a game of bowls when he returned. Bert bowled his last 'wood' in April 2013. He watched it roll away towards the 'jack', straightened up to see if it was on target and died there on the green. He was ninety-two.

Chapter 14

The Home Front

Don't You Know there's a War On?

Sitting comfortably in front of the TV, we watched with 'shock and awe' as American missiles burst in the streets of Baghdad. This is how we experience modern conflicts and then, after another episode of *EastEnders*, walk out into the garden for 'a bit of peace'. There is nothing there to remind us of war in the world beyond.

How the British viewed the war in the 1940s was not like that. There was no TV. The Ministry of Information had control of the media and made sure that the worst incidents of *Blitzkrieg* were not shown in flickering black and white in the cinemas. Photographs in the daily papers were also in black and white; no gory red to alarm the population.

In the evening after a hard day's work, farm labourers in cottages along Village Road would put down the paper, stretch and go out into the garden to 'see how the beans are getting on'. They knew there was a war on. All day long they had been working in the fields with 'Land Girls' and Italian youths. The prisoners of war had been taken back to their billets and the girls cycled away to a hostel or lodgings. Out on Village Road local urchins and evacuees from Liverpool were picking sides for a game of cricket in the dusty gravel. Overhead bombers were droning away to the east, and on the main road a convoy of trucks full of 'Yanks' rattled out of the village heading south for the Channel coast. They knew there was a war on all right.

Back into Uniform

Apley Hall and the Park was no longer a playground for the gentry. The deer were culled, parkland ploughed up, a pillbox built at the end of the suspension bridge and a searchlight battery put up near Home Farm.

The kitchens at the Hall were 'under new management' to cater for convalescing officers and the nursing staff that cared for them. The Major was not inconvenienced; he was comfortable enough in his bachelor flat on the top floor. He was back in uniform and promoted to Lieutenant Colonel to command the Home Guard. The whole nation responded to the 'call to arms'.

After the fall of France, in 1940, Britain stood alone. The Local Defence Volunteers (LDVs) were formed in May that year. Churchill referred to them as the Home Guard and the name was changed. Many young men were already in uniform serving in 'foreign parts'. However, there were still plenty of experienced soldiers left behind to man the defences on the home front.

Veterans of the Great War formed the backbone of the Home Guard. They shared their expertise with eager boys and farmhands exempt from military service. The Major called a meeting in the village hall. All able-bodied men were expected to attend. He would have noticed if anyone was absent. Trooper Tom Gray was the oldest man on parade. The youngest lad to get an LDV armband was probably John Nicholls, apprentice carpenter. His father brought him along. Albert Nicholls was a man who had 'seen some action'. Collectively, the Apley Company had a lot of battlefield experience.

Within a few months the farmhands, apprentices and the over forties were issued with khaki battledress, and stitched on various badges of rank. Deciding who would give the orders seemed a haphazard affair. In general, those with some position of authority got promotion. The rector, a lieutenant in the Great War, stitched his 'pips' on again and added a couple more. The Major's second in command was Stan Hibbert, retired gent, and then came Lieutenant Joe Dyas, tenant farmer and Lieutenant Norman Sharpe, head gamekeeper. Other old soldiers showed little ambition.

"It don't mean nuthin', 'avin' a stripe or two."

Ern Lane was given three stripes. He was Len Dalton's farm foreman. During the day Len told him what had to be done about the farm. On parade in the evening Private Dalton had to listen to what Sergeant Lane had to say.

The troops had to be armed. Farmers, gamekeepers and poachers all had shotguns and knew how to use them. Reconditioned Lee Enfields were issued. The old soldiers needed no instruction on how to handle these weapons. The Major opened up his 'armoury' at the Hall; weapons in it included hunting rifles capable of felling a tiger, or even a rhino. To bond this rag-tag company together a training programme was devised.

It was difficult to take some of the training exercises seriously. Tom Gray had learned semaphore drill at the time of the Boer War and he never made a mistake. It was his mission to hand on this skill to a new generation.

Semaphore, signalling with flags, had been a very useful way to send messages across the dusty plains of Africa. The signallers could be seen for miles on hilltops under blue skies. Signallers waving flags over the trenches of the Great War did not last long so other methods of communication were devised. Trooper Tom Gray took it all very seriously and could not understand why those under instruction did not share his enthusiasm for flag-waving.

The Apley Company set up defences. The only river bridge into the estate was guarded by the pillbox. There were trenches on one side of the approach road and barbed wire on the other. Sandbagged posts were set up in the hedgerows to the east of the village and a more substantial 'headquarters emplacement' at the crossroads below the church.

If anyone should have been injured in the line of duty then Private Harry Malin was there to stretcher them away. For this purpose he was issued with a brand new canvas stretcher, neatly rolled and tied up firmly with tapes. He turned up regularly on parade with his stretcher. When Victory in Europe was declared he handed it in. The tapes had never been untied.

DON'T TAKE IT TOO SERIOUSLY

A key part of the defences for Norton and Sutton Maddock was the lookout post on 'Windy Hill'. This had been built by tradesmen in the estate workshop. The design was unique; it was octagonal in form and sat on a platform which could be rotated through three hundred and sixty degrees. With windows on all sides the whole of the surrounding countryside could be surveyed. A team of observers sat in this elaborate 'conservatory' throughout the night.

There was plenty to see. Over the blacked-out villages and dark shadowy woodland, the bomber squadrons of the RAF and the Luftwaffe ploughed across the sky. In the evening, from airfields in the north of the county, Lancasters carried their deadly payloads across the Channel and returned – most of them – at dawn. The Luftwaffe circled the Black Country targeting factories producing the materials of war. On the horizon the undersides of clouds were lit by bursting bombs. Enemy airmen used the silvery Severn, lit by moonlight, to guide them further north to the docks at Liverpool. Occasionally, they were caught in the beam of the searchlight battery in the Park.

Home Guards, young and old, had day jobs and they needed sleep; a few hours at least. In the council yard across the road from the lookout post was the 'dormitory'. The sleeping quarters for the off-duty members of the observation team were housed inside a 'tin box'. It was a caravan made of sheet steel designed as a mobile command post to be towed around battlefields. It was a very secure piece of kit with grills at the windows and a snap-shut lock on the door.

In the early hours of one particularly sultry summer morning, a boy soldier got up off his sweaty bed and scampered outside. Nature called and he didn't want to wet his bed; he was very hot, and he was naked. He relieved himself. Now he could relax and go back to bed. Was it a sudden gust of wind or was it a playful comrade? The steel door swung shut with a solid clunk.

"Hey! Let me in!"

No reply, just a snigger.

"Hey! (thump, thump on the door) Let me in!"

No reply.

"You bastards!"

The naked youth streaked off across the road and up the hill. What a vision appeared before the nightwatchmen.

"Those bastards have locked me out!"

They were speechless, and they gurgled and spluttered. Almost paralysed with mirth they could only manage, "Sorry, can't help. Still on duty."

"You bastards!"

He streaked off again down the hill, his bare feet and ankles scratched by the stubble. He dodged in and out of the sheaves lying in the newly-cut cornfield, then across the road, around the caravan (thump, thump) and back again. On nearby farms, in steamy sheds, cows were being milked by patient cowmen. Other farmhands, in twos and threes, were pedalling steadily out of the village. Glancing over the hedge top something caught their eye. "What was that strange white figure flitting about between the sheaves on Windy Hill?"

It might have been a German parachutist who had shed his shameful uniform or was it some ghostly figure from the past, or just the victim of a childish prank?

There were other incidents, false alarms and comic events that could certainly have been used in episodes of *Dad's Army*.

NORMAN'S SHARPSHOOTERS

Norman Sharpe, a sniper in the Great War, trained his platoon on the range in the Park. So well did the Apley Company perform that in competition they swept aside all comers, even regulars of the Grenadier Guards. They were no match for farmers, under-keepers, seasoned poachers and an apprentice carpenter, who had followed Captain Sharpe's instructions to the letter. John Nicholls was a marksman, it would be his undoing.

Two years passed and there were signs that the tide was turning in favour of the Allies. It was time for John Nicholls to change from part-time soldier to full-time soldier. He was drafted into the Royal West Kent Regiment; many of the recruits were East Enders who might have liked to stay at home.

"Wish I 'ad your luck, Johnny, you'll be near my mum."

'Johnny Nic' was off to the East End. Private Nicholls was promoted to Sergeant. This meant more responsibility. Almost overnight he became the 'commandant' of a hostel housing 30 German prisoners of war. Around the Docks the Luftwaffe were busy converting dwellings into rubble. Who better to tidy up the bomb sites than German soldiers? In total there were about 700 of them. They were fed and housed, devised their own work schedule, made no attempt to escape and as long as they kept the creases sharp in Sgt Nicholls' battledress and his boots well polished everyone was happy. The working parties were directed from Shoreditch Town Hall where the kindly Colonel Astwell, had an office.

He was John's commanding officer, and they got on rather well. Then one day he announced, "I'm being retired, Nicholls. There's a new man taking over; his name escapes me. He wants to get to know the men. He's asked me arrange a little get together; a chat, a few drinks and a shooting competition, officers v sergeants. You're a good shot. I'll leave that to you."

John picked his team and they proved to be easy winners. When John reported to headquarters the following morning the company clerk greeted him.

"The new CO wants to see you, Sarge. He doesn't look pleased."

"Sergeant Nicholls."

"Sir."

There was no 'stand at ease'.

"You're posted to Dingwall."

"Sir, Dingwall? Where's that, sir?"

"Scotland of course. Be a change for you."

Sergeant Nicholls didn't want a change; he was happy where he was. Colonel Astwell said his last goodbyes.

"Goodbye, Nicholls, thanks for keeping everything in order."

"Thank you, sir...Sir, I've been posted to Dingwall. Why?"

"Why? You won, Nicholls, the shooting. Sergeants aren't supposed to win; officers win. I thought you knew that. Never mind. Best of luck in 'Bonny Scotland'."

When it was all over John took up his carpenter's tools again. A lasting memorial to his craftsmanship was the rather lavish bus shelter with solid oak pillars built to commemorate the Coronation, and as a memorial to the Fallen of the Second World War.

COSMETIC TREATMENT

Saint Chad's, the parish church at Stockton, stood on high ground above the village. The rectory nearby was a truly impressive building overshadowing the church, and a very suitable dwelling for a most important member of the community, the Reverend Prebendary Thomas Openshaw Coupe, MA (Cantab) and his wife, Eve. She was certainly 'a cut above the rest'. Careful grooming was most important; this was certainly the view of the rector's wife. For her ablutions only the purest water would do. It had to be heaven-sent. She used only rainwater on her tender skin, and to shampoo her carefully groomed hair.

Enemy bombers murmuring above with evil intent had to be watched. There was very little the Home Guard could do except watch, but they did it all the same. Down in the village at the Hundred House, the troops fortified themselves for the task ahead. The 'old sweats' supped quietly. The youngsters would not be outdone, downing an extra pint before they all turned out and trooped up the hill. They waved to their comrades manning the sandbagged post at the bottom of Church Lane, exchanged childish remarks and handed over large cider bottles filled with beer.

Perhaps because it was sacred, the church tower was not considered a suitable place to station men dressed for war. The watch for enemy aircraft was from the roof of the rectory. This was a job for young men full of vigour and beer. Up they went with sporting binoculars, a pack of sandwiches and two large bottles of mild beer. The old boys pulled two battered armchairs from an outhouse and settled down in the yard below.

It was June. For farmers and gardeners it had been a good spring. Crops were well advanced but now rain was badly needed. The river was down and water levels were low in ponds, wells and water butts.

The noisy boys above could be seen and heard capering about, waving the binoculars around the sky and arguing over the names of the constellations. When they settled down all was peace; no drone of aero engine, sweep of searchlight or crunch of distant bomb. The only anxiety for the young troops was the lack of toilet facilities. Two pints of beer and a pint of cider were dribbling through the system. The guttering that ran around the rectory roof was the obvious place to find relief. "That's better. I needed that."

The liquid frothed in a satisfying fashion as it swirled along the lead gutter and down a cast-iron pipe. Just audible, echoing out of the near-dry wooden barrel below, was the splashing and dribbling sound of...not water!

"What a relief!"

Now they could relax and get on with the serious matter of defending the homeland. The night passed without incident, and friendly bombers passed over on their way back to base. The young stargazers and the old hands assembled in the yard then pedalled down Church Lane together, and at the crossroads went their separate ways.

The rector was both an academic and a practical man. He kept the walled garden of the rectory in good order; an example to his parishioners. Husband and wife often worked together in the garden, the rector 'digging for victory', his wife deadheading the roses. She began to 'glow' and went indoors to freshen up. They sat down to a modest lunch of a boiled egg each. The rector blessed the eggs, then the toasted soldiers and dipped them into the yolk.

Eve Coupe spoke. "Tom, do you think my hair's all right?"

Without looking up the rector replied, "Yes, of course, perfectly all right."

His wife went on, "It feels like straw, prickly, not really clean." The rector studied his egg. She continued, "I think it's the water, you know, off the roof."

The rector made a brisk reply, "Quite likely, everything is tainted by war."

Captain Tom Coupe, padre and quartermaster to the Apley Company of the Home Guard, knew when to keep his head down. He knew something of the unsavoury habits of men in uniform.

WE DID OUR BIT

There must have been many at the time who did not take the Home Guard seriously. They could not imagine these part-time troops manning a roadblock in the Park, or blowing up the charming white suspension bridge below the Hall to prevent Hitler's storm troopers crossing the Severn.

"Surely before they get to Wenlock the Government'll throw in the towel."

Just in case there should be a call to arms 'D' Company were given Mustering Instructions. They were to report to Stockton Rectory in uniform, with rifle and thirty rounds of ammunition, steel helmet, respirator, rations for 24 hours and of course a bar of soap and shaving kit. What they were supposed to do next was not clear, find water and shave perhaps. It seems comical now but what the Home Guard did do was to give every community the feeling that they were doing something for the war effort.

"Do you remember the end of the war?" Seventy years later the little girl in the bonnet could say, "Yes, indeed I do!"

Reproduced from the Bridgnorth Journal

"We're going to hang up our boots."

At war's end they stuck out their chests and marched proudly into history along Bridgnorth High Street.

Chapter 15

The Soft Underbelly

THE DODGERS

The annual dinner of the Apley Legion was something to look forward to. The sparkle of Christmas was over, and then there were two months of cold nights before signs of spring would appear. The village hall was full. All three services and all ranks were represented. Most of the men at the top table were those who had held a commission: a captain, a brigadier, a couple of generals, the occasional wing commander and, guest of honour, Sir Oliver Leese. He was the National President of the British Legion, but he didn't have far to travel for this event; just a few miles from his home in Worfield, the neighbouring parish.

The menu was much the same every year; roast beef from Home Farm and apple pie from the Jubilee Orchard. There was free beer and 'fags' from the General followed by speeches and entertainment. The script for the speeches hardly varied. Each speaker ended with one or two well-known jokes. Members of the audience sometimes began to snigger even before the punch line was delivered. This was not a talent show and anyone could stand up and entertain the gathering.

"Come on, Harry, give us a song."

Before Harry Shepherd had even cleared his throat the legionnaires started to hum, 'Lily Marlene', and murmur the chorus, "We are the D-Day dodgers, in sunny It...al...ee."

Harry warmed to the occasion one verse after another. If he faltered there was always someone to help him out and join in with the chorus. Lieutenant General Sir Oliver Leese followed it all, smirked and nodded encouragement. He was one of the D-Day dodgers and there was no shame in that.

Lady Nancy Astor was held responsible for accusing the troops in Italy of dodging D-Day. She denied making the remark. Nevertheless, it prompted Harry Pynn, a Lance Sergeant in the Tank Rescue Section, to write a few verses set to the tune of a German love song. Many versions were added by unknown songwriters. Advancing into Europe from North Africa through Italy was supposed to be easy. Churchill called it, 'The Soft Underbelly of Europe'.

Oliver Leese and Harry Shepherd were not the only 'dodgers' in the room. There was Fred Todd, Harold Evans and Jack Lyth.

PLAYING FOR ENGLAND

Jack Lyth had a steady job before the war in a hardware shop in Hanley. There wasn't much spare time except on early closing days, usually Wednesday. Then shop boys had the afternoon off and games of football could be arranged. Clubs that originated in this way were easy to spot, like Sheffield Wednesday. It was every lad's dream to play for England. Young Jack would have settled for Port Vale. He had a trial for the club; he certainly had the skill but he didn't have the stature. The 'scout' was sympathetic. "He might fill out in a year or two."

At the outbreak of war Jack Lyth was twenty-three years of age. He was fit and athletic, and was whisked away into the army in a matter of weeks. After an unpleasant winter in France, the 2nd Battalion of the North Staffordshire Regiment was evacuated from Dunkirk much to Jack's relief.

For the next two years the 2nd Battalion trained, exercised and prepared for battle. Mixed in with the war games were ball games. There was plenty of opportunity for Jack to lace up his boots and take to the football field. Playing soldiers didn't last forever. Jack and the North Staffordshire Regiment were ordered out of the green fields of the Midlands and packed off to North Africa to finish off Rommel and his Italian friends. When the battles in Tunisia were over and tens of thousands of Italians had been shepherded into POW camps the 'top-brass' could then plan the next move in detail.

Lance Corporal Lyth was not consulted; he was not master of his own destiny. If he had been he would not have tagged along as Allied forces pushed back the enemy across Sicily over the Straits of Messina and north towards Rome. Field Marshal Kesselring and his generals were proving to be a considerable nuisance. They would not accept defeat unlike the Italians who had already thrown in the towel. There was no obvious weakness in the Gustav Line, stretching across the leg of Italy from east to west. There was no way round it except by sea.

Landing a large force on a hostile shore was hazardous; the Americans had learned that at Salerno. A more ambitious scheme was now planned for Anzio. Leadership was poor and planning confused but luck was on their side initially, and a large force of US and British infantry was put ashore on the 22nd of January 1944. First in the order of battle for the Anzio landings was the 2nd Infantry Brigade, comprising the Loyal (North Lancashire) Regiment, Gordon Highlanders and the North Staffordshire Regiment. The time had come for the young left-winger, Jack Lyth, to take to the field, or more precisely 'Peter Beach', six miles north of Anzio. Guiding the troops ashore was Major Denis Healy, a future Chancellor of the Exchequer.

A narrow beachhead was soon established. With little opposition this could have been rapidly expanded. Instead the infantry were ordered to 'dig in'. The US General, John Lucas, was criticised for being overcautious and giving the Germans time to prepare defences in the surrounding hills. Months of bitter fighting followed with some of Germany's finest troops doing everything possible to push the invaders back into the sea. Churchill and Mark Clark, the American General in overall command, wanted progress. More troops were landed and German positions pounded from the sea and from the air. This battle of attrition went on for three months.

Panzer Grenadiers and seasoned German paratroopers probed the Allied positions. In close combat both sides took prisoners. British infantrymen who had been there from day one were stuck in shallow trenches with the sea at their backs. The only way was forward. At the headquarters of the North Staffordshire Regiment, the colonel gave a pep talk to junior officers. The keen young lieutenant in charge of Lance Corporal Lyth's platoon was inspired. He had been told to 'lead from the front' and he did, leading his unhappy band straight into the arms of a German patrol. They were all 'in the bag'. Officers were separated from 'the men' so Jack didn't have time to give the young lieutenant a piece of his mind.

The journey from south of Naples to Mulberg, south of Dresden, took days. The Germans were handling not only Allied prisoners but also hundreds of Italians; whole battalions had now switched sides. The prisoners were transported in boxcars meant for cattle. Whenever the train stopped at stations along the way they had a glimpse, through the slatted sides, of the effects war was having on the ordinary folk of Austria and Germany. On the platforms rows of anxious faces, women and children laden with baggage were looking for a safe haven from bombed-out cities like Dresden. There was no boastful arrogance about them; they wanted an end to it all just as much as the troops who had lost their freedom.

Stalag 4B was no place to spend over a year of your youth. In the surrounding countryside, compounds had been put up to house the different nationalities: British, Americans, French, Poles and Russians. Working parties were forced to labour on a variety of projects in the region. Jack was sent down a coal mine providing the raw material for a new process devised by German scientists. More than seven thousand POWs were working on the construction of a huge plant capable of making fuel oil out of coal. This was a target for US and RAF bombers; it was attacked several times while Jack was there.

The Germans did discriminate. If there was any particularly dirty or dangerous work to be done then it was the Russians who had to do it. 'Ivan' was ill treated as a matter of routine; the 'Tommies' and the 'Yanks' were favoured. They received Red Cross parcels and visits from Swiss officials who sometimes gave news of the progress of the war. When the rumour spread that a foothold had been secured in Normandy in June 1944, everyone hoped that it would be over by Christmas. They waited and hoped for the best and whenever possible tried to stay cheerful.

In any group of men there are always those with talent; singers, chess players, actors, sportsmen, musicians. Tournaments, competitions, concerts and sporting events were organised as a distraction from the daily misery. Everyone lost weight and Jack hadn't much to lose, but he was still fit enough to kick a ball. When Jack took to the field it was before an international crowd. He would rather have been on Wembley turf instead of gravel and scrub behind the wire of a Stalag. He still put on a good performance.

The Christmas concert did little to cheer the war-weary. Everyone was on short rations, even the camp guards. Some who came back from home leave spoke openly and bitterly of the misery war had brought to their country. They feared it would be overrun and what they feared most were the Russians.

Winter gave way to spring and blossom and buds appeared in May as usual. Then one day, "Where have they all gone?"

The guards had gone, the compound gates were open and horsemen were trotting and wheeling among the confused prisoners. The cavalry had arrived, the liberators, the Russians. There was great rejoicing in the Russian's compound. The other nationalities were left to fend for themselves. Some were helped by local civilians who hoped that by sheltering American or British servicemen they would have some protection from the Russians who were unforgiving. Within days American GIs appeared and arranged repatriation. Victory in Europe had been achieved and Corporal Jack Lyth came home.

He had no experience of farm work but after some basic instruction he was offered work in the Corvedale and then at Apley Home Farm. The cottage where Jack and Agnes lived, with their son and daughter, was close enough to the football pitch for cheers to be heard across the fields when the home side scored. Team photographs were taken regularly. They turned up from time to time at village jumble sales.

"Anybody remember who these were?" Written faintly in pencil on the back the team members were named, Jack Lyth, Bill Beck, Fritz Platt…"Fritz, was that his real name?"

"Course it was, he was a German, a prisoner like Billy Beck and Jack Lyth."

All three had been captured; imprisoned on opposite sides. When it was over they were all on the same side.

A YOUNG DRAGOON

Sitting comfortably at home in the Manor House at Ewdness, the Honourable Herbert Brooks and his wife followed with pride the progress of their son, Allan, a lieutenant in the Queen's Bays, as he and his regiment fought their way up the length of Italy. The end was in sight it seemed. The Germans had been dogged in retreat setting up one line of defence after another, and using the mountainous terrain and fast-flowing rivers to their advantage. The Allies now faced the Gothic Line; they also faced the prospect of another winter and were keen to see an end to the campaign and the end of the war.

After a spell of front-line duty, the Queen's Bays, Lieutenant Brooks and 'B' Squadron were moved back for a month's rest around Perugia. Had the weather been kinder they might have found their stay there quite enjoyable. Perugia was an ancient town with attractive monuments and fine views over the surrounding hills. The weather was atrocious and there was no sign of any improvement. On the 13th of November 1944, they moved to the Adriatic coast and north to the Po valley. The battleground was waterlogged by the recent heavy rain. Despite this, the Queen's Bays together with lancers, Canadian infantry and sappers of the Royal Engineers made good progress. The Germans were pushed back, mines cleared, prisoners taken and bridges built to allow the armoured vehicles to advance still further.

Continuous heavy rain held them up again; they had to wait until the water levels in the rivers fell. Then they pressed on. There was fierce opposition, the infantry advanced, where possible, protected by the tanks. The Lincolnshire Regiment worked with 'B' Squadron. The next river to cross was the Cosina. The main body of the enemy had withdrawn to positions on the riverbank and clearly intended to make a stand. With difficulty, 'A' and 'B' Squadrons of 'The Bays' finally established a fire group and brought their guns to bear on houses sheltering the German defenders. After two days the enemy were forced back across the river and a bridgehead was established.

Infantry and armour faced fierce resistance. The bridgehead expanded slowly. 'A' Squadron advanced seven miles and crossed another river. In support was 'B' Squadron with Lieutenant Allan Brooks and Trooper Marsh riding together ahead of the rest. They moved cautiously under heavy shellfire. Trooper Marsh was killed together with his tank commander, Lieutenant Allan William Ivo Brooks. It was the 25th of November.

Life went on. The stockman fed the cattle in the yard at Ewdness Farm and Mrs Brooks looked on. The scene across the lawn at the Manor House had changed as winter approached. It was chill and less colourful. Although the sun did shine on the peaceful fields that stretched out to the horizon, the prospect for the family was bleak. Their son was dead. It was the time of year when Christmas cards were written. Friends and neighbours sent letters of condolence.

Fred Todd had been married less than three months when war broke out. The day before that happened he marched back into Jellalabad Barracks at Tidworth to rejoin his old regiment, the 3rd King's Own Hussars. With six years experience pre-war, Fred was promoted to sergeant and joined the training staff. He handed on his 'skill at arms' to new recruits and learned something himself of modern warfare, including chemical warfare.

Sergeant Todd was transferred to the Hampshire Regiment and then to the 9th Battalion Manchester Regiment. He sailed with them to North Africa in December 1943 and arrived off the coast of Tripoli just before Christmas. By the time Fred arrived, Allied forces had already crossed the Mediterranean and clawed their way up the leg of Italy. Fred followed at a safe distance. In February 1944, he was in Syracuse on the island of Sicily.

Allied forces were stalled on the Gustav Line south of Rome. The dominant feature at the centre of the German defences was the monastery at Monte Cassino. New Zealanders and Indian troops launched an attack in February 1944. Nothing was achieved. The New Zealanders made a second attempt to take Monte Cassino, but hampered by the appalling weather the attack was called off after they had taken four thousand casualties. Oliver Leese, in command of the 8th Army, looked on with concern.

Finally in May the Gustav Line collapsed, and on the 4th of June the Americans entered Rome in triumph, two days before the Allied landings on the Normandy beaches. Good news for the Allies, bad news for Field Marshal Albert Kesselring, but he was a determined man and he intended to contest every yard of territory. Using the mountainous terrain of the Apennines to their advantage, his generals set up a series of defensive lines to obstruct the Allied advance. Rivers that flowed from the spine of Italy to the Mediterranean in the west or to the Adriatic in the east were a key part to the German strategy. Bridges were blown up as they retreated to hinder the advance of the Allies. None the less the Germans were steadily pushed back until they made a stand on the Gothic Line.

Fresh formations were moved to the battle front. Sergeant Todd serving with Manchester Regiment was transferred back to the

'Hampshires' in July 1944. Oliver Leese's 8th Army attacked along the east coast pursuing the retreating Germans. The Gothic Line was breached, rivers crossed and by the 4th of September they were on the outskirts of Rimini; the defenders held out for a fortnight. Kesselring moved forces to halt the advance of the 8th Army. There was a lull in the fighting while both sides licked their wounds.

Fred Todd was patched up at a casualty clearing station. After a brief stay he returned to duty. The Hampshires were poised to advance north of Forli. Continuous heavy rain made everything very difficult as they moved up to the front line. Even behind the lines there were casualties. Mines laid by the retreating Germans and shelling by their artillery took a toll. Six officers were killed and dozens of men wounded.

Forli was taken early on a foggy morning in November; mines were cleared and snipers silenced. The battalion took stock. Heavy shelling made their stay in Forli uncomfortable. On the 14th of November they moved on to capture Villafranca. When patrols went out to investigate the next river crossing they came under heavy mortar fire. All the rivers were swollen by heavy rain. The battalion withdrew to Forli and waited a week until the water level went down. In the face of fierce opposition five small bridgeheads were secured across the Cosina River. The infantry were supported by tanks and aircraft, but life in the front line was still very unhealthy.

There was a turning point in Sergeant Fred Todd's military career on the 22nd of November. The Hampshires crossed the Cosina and passed through the lines of the Somersets to capture objectives beyond. In the evening 'A' and 'D' companies were preparing to advance when they came under heavy mortar attack. There was some confusion. Fred could not recall if it was a mortar or something delivered by a dive bomber that 'bit' him. He was on his way to a standpipe with a bucket in hand when the Stuka swooped on the camp. He threw himself on the ground, arms extended. There was a 'ping' in the bucket when a bit of shrapnel landed in it. Shrapnel was flying everywhere, but this particular piece had just passed through Fred's forearm. He hardly felt it at the time. He was treated at the casualty clearing station and the next day whisked away to the south to a field hospital.

If you were going to have a war wound this was the sort to have; a flesh wound with no pieces of shrapnel left in it. Recovering at the seaside he wrote home to tell the family that he was fine and well out of harm's way. He enclosed a postcard of Trani. The ancient port was most attractive with many historic monuments and blue sea all around. Fred was back with the regiment before Christmas, but no longer in the front line. The New Year celebrations were genuine. This year, 1945, would surely be the last of the war. The war was over in Italy on the 2nd of May and in the rest of Europe two days later. There was rejoicing. Fred celebrated in Salerno, then quite unexpectedly he was bitten again, but not by shrapnel this time. He spent nearly a month in hospital recovering from the attack by a mosquito, one that lurked in the swampy ground near the port no doubt. Malaria was common in southern Europe at the time.

THE DODGERS DISPERSE

After the war Lieutenant General Sir Oliver Leese soldiered on for a couple of years then retired to his garden in Worfield, and interested himself in cacti and cricket.

Corporal Jack Lyth was pleased to be out of uniform of any sort whether it was German POW or British khaki. He made a name for himself, away from the field of battle, on football pitches in all the surrounding villages.

Sergeant Fred Todd had crossed the Cosina River and run into trouble on the 22nd of November. Two days later Lieutenant Allan Brooks had crossed the Cosina River and was killed in action. He was buried in the military cemetery at Forli. A bright new headstone was erected over his grave in Italy, and he was remembered less grandly on a bench outside Norton School. Before Fred Todd came home Churchill sent him off to Greece for one final campaign.

THE FIERY GREEKS

When the Nazis invaded Greece in 1941, the king and leading politicians escaped to Egypt and set up a government in exile. The 'royalist' politicians had little influence on events in Greece. Resistance to the German occupation was largely directed by communist militias. They waged a very successful campaign, and by the time the country was liberated they were already in control of most of it. Allied liberators arrived in Athens in October 1944.

Stalin had agreed with Churchill that post-war Greece would be within the British sphere of influence, and did not intervene to consolidate the communist position. Even so, Churchill did not want the Greek monarchy to be replaced by a communist government. British troops were sent to keep the peace until elections could be arranged.

Ioaninna was a most attractive place set in wild countryside on the shores of a lake with a castle and many historic buildings. Fred and the Hampshires were in billets and tents. During his two-month stay, Fred learned that his brother-in-law, Corporal Tom Rowlands of the Somerset Light Infantry, was also in Greece. He made the two hundred mile journey south to Athens to meet him. They stood together, as tourists do, to be photographed in front of the Parthenon.

Things moved quickly. In October 1945 Sergeant Todd was back in Italy, in November he took the train from Milan to the Channel coast, in December he was back in Colemore Green and in January 1946 he was transferred to the Army Reserve after twelve years in uniform.

He had begun his working life as a horseman, and now began a new career as a woodman on Apley Estate.

Chapter 16

All At Sea

GLOBE AND LAUREL

In wartime Britain basic foodstuffs were rationed. If a bag of sugar fell off a shelf and burst on a shop floor in Melton Mobray this was an event, and someone had to take responsibility. Seventeen-year-old Eric Timson couldn't take it seriously. His days as a shop assistant were numbered. Eric spent a day in Leicester. He walked briskly back along Doctor's Lane and into the family home. "I've passed the medical, Mother."

A month later, in May 1942, he reported to the Royal Marine Depot at Lympstone and the first entry was made, in black ink, on Form R138, his Certificate of Service. The clerk changed his pen and wrote in red ink in block capitals, VOLUNTEER.

Eric lost count of the number of times the train stopped on the journey between Leicester and Exeter. The carriages were full of men in uniform. Many left the train at Exeter. The city was still in a state of shock. Ten days earlier, on the 4th of May, thirty acres of the city had been destroyed by the Luftwaffe. The night raid killed one hundred and fifty-six citizens.

Four miles down the line at Topsham, Eric and a number of lads in sports jackets and flannels got off and looked around nervously. Before they had time to think, a marine sergeant gathered them up and packed them into the back of a truck. At Lympstone Depot they were herded in through the back gate. For six weeks they were pummelled by training staff until they were judged fit enough to be seen in public and pass out through the front gate. Lympstone had been hard, Dalditch was harder. The new recruits were now in the hands of men who had faced much danger, and they were determined that after the seven-week course the new recruits would be well prepared for anything, anywhere. The globe on their cap badge was an indication that they were expected to fight in every corner of the world, *Per Mare – Per Terram* (by sea – by land).

The service records of sailors and marines usually contained a list of all the ships on which they served. It seemed that Marine Timson only sailed on one, HMS *Odyssey*. For two years he served with the 2nd Royal Marine Group, part of the MNBDO. Until they learned otherwise some young marines believed that MNBDO meant 'Men Not Being Drafted Overseas'. They were wrong. This was the Mobile Naval Base Defence Organisation. Mobile meant they were everywhere; sailing on convoys to the Mediterranean or Artic Russia, or setting up shore bases on hostile coasts or distant islands. A record of Eric's travels, and more importantly a record of his pay, was kept in the HBL (Home Base Ledger) on board HMS Odyssey – a hotel in Ilfracombe.

Some of the operations of the MNBDO were small scale involving only a handful of men; others involved hundreds of marines. Not every operation was a success. The first attempt to relieve troops trapped at Tobruk failed.

Eventually they were successful, and Eric appeared very pleased with himself when he posed, fag in hand, with his mates under a desert palm in North Africa. After a long tussle in the sand dunes the Germans retreated to Italy pursued by the Allies. Marines were the first to go ashore on the coast of Sicily; useful practise for the invasion of mainland Europe. Marine Timson missed the boat as he was in hospital at the time. Eric came back to Home Base.

Much of the rigorous training for the Royal Marines was undertaken in Scotland. Eric's posting to the Bell's Hill Camp was a life-changing experience. Nearby was the naval base at Faslane and the open sea. Closer at hand was his wife-to-be. Who could resist the glamour of walking out with a Royal Marine? Like so many other couples they had to wait until hostilities were over before they could marry.

Training on the rugged coastline and in the Highlands of Scotland prepared the marines for operations even closer to the North Pole. Naval Parties (NPs) were often detached to do specific tasks; some dangerous and secretive. Often they had no idea of the purpose of the mission. In June 1943, Eric, in a party of marines, along with Norwegian commandos boarded HMS *Bermuda*. She sailed north, visited Iceland and sailed on across the Arctic Circle towards Spitsbergen. Before they reached their destination the only land they may have glimpsed was Bear Island, home to an uncountable number of seabirds, and a few dozen big white bears. Sailors knew that bears in this part of the world were to be avoided; one had made a mess of Nelson's arm.

Eric Timson, leaning second on the right. This quartet of Royal Marines learned how to laugh in the face of danger.

Permission given by Alan Timson

"This palm tree needs support."

Although the Germans had occupied Norway they had not, at that time, interfered with the weather station on Spitzbergen which continued to supply useful information to Allied ships. HMS *Bermuda* approached the coast of Svalbard, entered Isfjorden and steamed purposefully towards Longyearbyen. Officers on the bridge scanned the waters and the surrounding mountains. There were plenty of seabirds, a few seals, no walrus, no whales or bears, and no sign of human activity. On the slopes above the town, coal tubs hung on cables between a line of pylons. All was still. The Russian miners had all gone home when mainland

Norway fell to the Germans. Somewhere in the collection of huts that lined the single muddy street leading from the dock were the 'met men', transmitting their weather reports. *Bermuda* did not dock.

Boats were lowered, the commandos and marines clambered into them, stowed their gear and made for the shore. This was not the place for a British warship to be trapped at the end of a forty-mile-long inlet. The crew was watchful, and eyes and binoculars swept the waters and the coastline constantly. Royal Marines returned, the Norwegian commandos did not. Who knows where they went or what the purpose of the mission was. After just two hours the engine room got the signal from the bridge, "Slow ahead." *Bermuda* made for the open sea and her base at Greenock.

The date for D-Day must have been set by someone, though Eric was kept in the dark. He suspected that something was going to happen when 'C' Company were introduced to the 'pom-pom' and trained to man an anti-aircraft battery. After a month's practise they were ready to fend off the Luftwaffe in the Channel. The pom-pom was not as soft and innocent as the name suggested. The QF2 was quick firing and spat two-pound shells into the sky at an alarming rate.

The gun crew of a Vickers Mark VIII pom-pom.

© Imperial War Museum (A 11760)

"What we need now is something to shoot at."

Throughout the summer of 1944, as Allied forces drove the Germans back to the Dutch border 'C' Company sailed back and forth from Plymouth. As ports on the French coast were freed the Royal Marines secured them and opened them up so that vital supplies could be delivered to the advancing armies as they pushed on to Berlin and victory.

To tidy up his affairs Marine Timson marched past the neglected flowerbeds in front of the Collingwood Hotel, up the 'gang plank' and onto the threadbare carpets of HMS Odyssey. Now he knew where the Home Base Ledger was kept and met the clerks responsible for working out his weekly pay. Finally, Eric went back to Dalditch. With two years of active service behind him he was no longer the raw recruit. Eric had volunteered to serve for the duration of the war; when the victory celebrations were over he could prepare for a new life.

Kay and Eric were married. Just for the record, Marine Timson dressed up in his best tunic with bright buttons and a colourful row of medal ribbons, and smiled at the camera. The newlyweds might have settled in Leicestershire or Lanarkshire, but they chose Shropshire instead. In July 1946 Eric was out of uniform and serving behind the counter of Mason's grocers shop in Bridgnorth. As manager he was responsible for checking the stock; counting bags of sugar. This could not compare with the outdoor life of a Royal Marine. Eric was fed up. The young couple made a move from the flat on Waterloo Terrace to a thatched cottage next to the blacksmith's shop in Village Road, Norton.

Eric was the sort of man prepared to turn his hand to anything. Almost immediately he made a name for himself when a row of new houses were built along Windmill Lane. All trades were involved – bricklayers, carpenters, plumbers, painters, but before they could begin foundations had to be dug. Call for the Royal Marines! Nobody could dig a trench like Eric Timson.

If all goes well life is a series of happy accidents. Eric and Kay were uprooted by war; this was not a happy event. They were adopted by the village community and found lifelong happiness together with never a thought of moving to Melton Mowbray or north of the Border.

DODGING THE WOLF PACKS

Operation Torch, the invasion of North Africa, had been a warm experience for Sid Speke, what with bombs from Stukas, shells from shore batteries and scorching winds blowing from the Sahara. It was a relief when the duties of 'H' Force were done and most of them could sail back to Scapa Flow in the Orkney Islands. It was much cooler there and cooler still where Sid was going. Iceland for a start!

From Hval Fjiord on the west coast of Iceland, HMS *Bermuda* joined a convoy bound for Vaenga carrying vital supplies to the Russians.

If there was one thing that surprised Sid Speke when Bermuda docked at a Russian port it was the number of women who were doing 'a man's job', operating cranes or at the helm of a tug boat.

Permission given by Sid Speke

"Cheeky boy, I'll deal with you later."

At this desperate stage of the war the Russians were grateful for anything they could get. The round trip through cold and savage seas beyond the North Cape could take weeks. The crews were always relieved to be back at their berth in Scapa Flow.

In June 1943, *Bermuda* ferried Norwegian commandos to Spitzbergen. This was the nearest Sid got to the North Pole; within 15 degrees, about six hundred miles. Three months later the Germans sent an invasion force to Spitzbergen including the pride of the German Navy, the *Tirpitz*. This was heavy-handed. They overran the Norwegian garrison in less than four hours. They were punished for this. The Royal

Air Force hounded the *Tirpitz* until they disabled her in a Norwegian fjord with twelve thousand pound 'Tall Boy' bombs.

HMS *Bermuda* seemed to have a roving commission on escort duty all over the North Atlantic. It was dangerous work. Wolf packs of U-boats roamed the seas, prepared to strike at anytime. In 1943 *Bermuda* took part in an historic mission.

During the course of the war, Winston Churchill crossed the Atlantic five times. His first visit was in December 1941 immediately after the bombing of Pearl Harbour by the Japanese, the action which brought America into the war. In the summer of 1943 he sailed for the States again. His safety was a concern but he was a man who brushed aside danger. *RMS Queen Mary*, with Churchill on board, sailed from the Clyde and out into the Atlantic escorted by three destroyers. They ran into a storm which handicapped the escort vessels. They simply could not keep up with the liner. Churchill ordered the captain of the *Queen Mary* to press on unescorted; she could, in fact, outrun any U-boat. The *Bermuda*, already at sea off the coast of Iceland, was alerted and shadowed the liner until she reached the safety of Halifax harbour on the coast of Nova Scotia. The prime minister disembarked and was escorted to Quebec where he met with President Roosevelt and Mackenzie King, the Canadian Prime Minister. At the conference they discussed the conduct of the war, and planned for the future.

In the meantime, for Sid and his shipmates it was 'business as usual'. They were in the North Atlantic until December 1943 when they made one last trip to Russia, and then into dry dock in the Govan shipyard. Sid came home on leave for three whole days. On Boxing Day he was posted to dry land, HMS Drake near Dover.

The south coast of England was a very busy place. Something big was being planned.

ATTACKER AND CHASER

A lot of lads were disappointed when they were called up; they couldn't follow their trade. Clerks had to dig trenches and gardeners became cooks. Bert Powell got just what he wanted. He had worked on aircraft at Cosford since leaving school and volunteered for the Fleet Air Arm. After brief training at HMS Gosling near Warrington, he stitched a propeller on his sleeve to show he was an air fitter and joined the crew of HMS *Chaser*.

173

On the badge of Bert's training ship, *Gosling*, there was what appeared to be a lame duck. HMS *Chaser* had a dashing greyhound. This was very appropriate because Bert Powell was going to have a very lively time for the next two years. The Fleet Air Arm's 816 Squadron came on board *Chaser* in January 1944 with eleven Swordfish and eleven Wildcats.

These Fairey Swordfish are about to take off over a calm sea, with no ice. It wasn't always that easy.

"We may look harmless but U-boats beware!"

If the aircraft names were anything to go by they meant business. Trials and repairs completed, they were ready for operational service and given the task of providing air cover for a convoy to Russia.

The convoy set off from Loch Ewe. The merchant ships were escorted by frigates and destroyers of the Royal Navy. HMS *Chaser* sailed out of Scapa Flow and joined convoy JW 57 making its way across the North Sea. The Germans were fully aware of all this activity. On the 23rd of February, Focke-Wolf 'Condors' were sighted shadowing the convoy. Swordfish and Wildcats chased them away but they still kept watch. Several U-boats were spotted and attacked the convoy. HMS

Kessel joined in and sank *U-713* with depth charges. Two days later an RAF 'Catalina', based in the Shetlands, sank *U-601* that was tracking HMS *Mahratta*. What they failed to spot was *U-990*. The U-boat launched two deadly torpedoes. Of a crew of two hundred and thirty-six only seventeen were rescued and brought on board *Chaser*. These lucky few were wrapped in blankets and warmed with mugs of hot cocoa. The crew dressed them in whatever spare clothing they could find. "These socks might need darning."

The convoy stayed on course. The heavy escort and the air cover kept the U-boats at bay, and they arrived at Kola Inlet near Murmansk without further incident. JW 57 was the largest convoy ever to sail to Russia.

Airframe fitters like Bert Powell and the rest of the ground crew of 816 Squadron had done their job. They kept the Swordfish flying, marshalling and refuelling the aircraft in all weathers. One of their hardest chores in the Arctic was, without a doubt, de-icing the aircraft. Hot breath froze instantly; beards and moustaches were caked with ice as they worked. A word of warning from Bert to anyone doing this job, "If your nose runs don't wipe it, unless you want to lose some skin."

Bert and *Chaser* cruised off the coast near Murmansk for a week then joined anther convoy to give some protection on the return voyage to Loch Ewe. The German wolf pack attacked again off Bear Island. HMS *Onslaught* and *Chaser* retaliated; *U-472* was spotted from the air and attacked with shells and depth charges. The U-boat crew abandoned ship, and twenty-seven German submariners were rescued and taken on board HMS *Onslaught*. The following day Swordfish 'F' spotted another U-boat (*U-366*) and attacked with rockets. There were no survivors. Swordfish 'X' was equally successful, launching rocket projectiles at *U-973*. HMS *Boadicea* rescued fifteen lucky-to-be-alive German submariners.

Pilots and air gunners were rewarded with a handful of medals; the ground crew organised a raffle. The prize was a little bronze oak leaf to stitch on the ribbon of the Atlantic Star to recognise that one of them had been mentioned in dispatches, and had avenged the sinking of the *Mahratta*. Bert was unlucky in the draw and got no reward.

Back in Scapa Flow, *Chaser* dropped anchor near her sister ship HMS *Attacker*, and the crews swapped yarns and prepared for the next mission. Plans had to be revised when the weather changed. Gale force winds swept across Scapa Flow and battered the fleet. *Chaser* dragged her anchor, collided with *Attacker* and was grounded. This was a sorry sight. Tugs towed her clear, and in less than a week she was passing under the Forth Bridge on her way to the dockyard at Rosyth. March 1944 had been a memorable month.

SWINGING THE LANTERN

Politics and religion are topics best avoided. It is sometimes difficult to pick a topic that is of interest to everyone. Babies, family disputes and changing fashions are for the ladies. Sport, cars, work or recalling drunken pranks of their youth are for men only. The same applies to military matters. Some old sailors spend time swapping yarns or 'swing the lantern' when they get together. Sid, Bert and Eric, the marine, had all sailed in Arctic waters and had tales to tell.

"What's the proper name for that place with all the glaciers? Is it Spitsbergen or Svalbard?" No one knew for certain. Sid went on, "We sailed up there on *Bermuda* and landed a party of marines."

Eric looked surprised. "When was that?"

"On my mother's birthday in June 1943."

"That was me. I was in that party."

In the confusion of war with men sailing, flying and marching all over the world, it was inevitable that paths would cross and brothers and old friends would share the same experience, and would say, "I remember that. I was there."

Chapter 17

Preparing the Armada

THE PARISH PRIEST

To invade England and bring the country under Catholic rule, Phillip II of Spain sent an armada of one hundred and fifty ships up the Channel. It was then the largest fleet ever seen in Europe. A combination of stormy weather and Francis Drake caused havoc. The invasion failed and only sixty-five Spanish ships returned to port.

Three hundred and fifty years later, Adolf Hitler had the idea of sending an armada of river barges across the Channel to bring the British under Nazi rule. Before 'Operation Sea lion' could be given the go-ahead the Germans had to have control of the skies. In the Battle of Britain the RAF were victorious and the invaders never left port.

No sooner than the Americans had entered the war in 1941 plans were made to assemble an Allied armada for the invasion of mainland Europe. There would be six thousand vessels involved including four thousand specially designed landing ships and landing craft. The Reverend Melly was going to witness an historic event; just as important as the one Sir Francis Drake had played a part in.

Aleck Melly wasn't a 'reverend' in 1942. He was a clerk by day and a part-time private in the Home Guard. He could not remember getting a card for his eighteenth birthday, but he could remember getting a letter in a brown envelope 'inviting' him to join one of the armed forces. Changing from Home Guard khaki to navy blue seemed the right thing to do. His elder brother, Peter, was already a naval officer. They both had a lot to live up to. Their father had distinguished himself in the Great War, and was awarded the Military Cross twice. Young Aleck had all the background and education to be selected for officer training; he had an excellent School Certificate.

"Rather flattering actually. I stayed on an extra year. Mother said I was a late developer."

Most of his contemporaries with similar backgrounds sailed through the selection process and became commissioned officers. The Royal Navy decided that Aleck was best suited to a career on the lower deck.

Every three weeks a thousand new recruits arrived at HMS Collingwood to start ten weeks of basic training. Aleck walked through the gates on the 12th of May 1942. He remembers it very clearly. Everyone who went through this process remembers it, and what they remember most was that no matter where they went it was 'at the double'. No one was quite sure why, but it was best not to question the authority of the instructors at this 'stone frigate' moored on solid ground somewhere between Gosport and Fareham. The torment eventually came to an end and the recruits 'passed out' into the watery world of the Royal Navy; not Aleck Melly.

Vehicle mechanics were trained at Fulham Technical College and this was going to be Aleck's trade. Even here there was some danger from bombing raids by the Luftwaffe. One evening Ordinary Seaman Melly was rendered unconscious but not by enemy action. Riding home on his bike in the blackout, the front wheel collapsed and he fell into the road. He was hospitalised and had to repeat part of the mechanics course. In the end it made little difference. He assessed his own performance: "I was hopeless, a parasite, protected by the competent tradesmen around me."

The war was not going well. The fight had to be taken to the enemy but a large-scale invasion across the Channel was not possible at this stage. Canadian troops had been mobilised at the beginning of the war and sent to England to help out 'the old country'. They had been playing war games for two years; 'overtrained and underused'. Under some pressure from the Canadian government, Churchill agreed to use them to mount a raid on the port of Dieppe. It was hastily planned, overambitious and a disaster. The cost of this failed raid was staggering. The Canadians were cut to pieces when they landed. Thousands were lost and thousands taken prisoner. All the vehicles and equipment were lost. In an attempt to provide air cover the Royal Air Force lost over a hundred aircraft. At least Aleck couldn't be blamed for this. He was billeted in luxury flats at Hove at the time undergoing more training before he, at last, went to sea on board an LBE (Landing Barge Engineering).

Special-purpose landing craft were being designed and built to land troops on hostile beaches. There were LCIs and LCTs (Landing Craft Infantry and Landing Craft Tank) and there were LSs and LBs (Landing Ships and Landing Barges). Having learned lessons at Dieppe the next raid on the coast of North Africa was a complete success. The Germans withdrew from Tunisia and the Allies then chased them across the Mediterranean and up the leg of Italy.

Plans were well advanced for D-Day. To transport, supply and support the invading troops the Royal Navy used almost anything that would float. Many of the Thames river barges were lying idle because much of Britain's shipping had been diverted to the west coast ports; the Royal Navy requisitioned around a thousand of them. They were refitted to do a variety of jobs. The LBF (Landing Barge Flak) produced flak to deter enemy aircraft and LBKs (Landing Barge Kitchen) could produce sixteen hundred hot meals every day. The LBE had all the facilities of an engineering workshop including a forge and anvil. The rear of the barge was fitted with a ramp so that a workshop truck or a mobile crane could be landed when needed.

It was as a member of Landing Craft Recovery Unit 209 that Aleck Melly went to sea. Their task was to patch up and make seaworthy any landing craft disabled by the enemy. They didn't have to wait until D-Day to practise their skills. For months the twenty-strong team sailed up and down the south coast of England. Elaborate rehearsals for the landing were undertaken by infantry and tank regiments. The exercises were made more realistic by using live ammunition and explosive charges. There were accidents, some tragic. LC Recovery Unit 209 had plenty of work to do but no amount of practise could fully prepare them for what lay ahead.

FROM SANDY DESERT TO GREEN FIELDS

The Desert Rats were better prepared than most for the battles in Normandy. When Rommel's Afrika Korps withdrew from Tunisia some of the armoured regiments that had chased him across North Africa came home to prepare for the invasion of Europe. The 8th King's Royal

Irish Hussars, now under the command of Lieutenant Colonel Cuthie Goulburn, set up camp near Thetford in Norfolk.

Centuries earlier in the surrounding countryside, the formidable Celtic Queen, Boudicca, put her troops through rigorous training to prepare them for battle against the occupying forces of the Roman Empire. Cast in bronze, she stands in her chariot, wielding a sword and threatening to charge across Westminster Bridge. Today the defiant spirit of the British is commemorated in Thetford (Walmington-on-Sea in *Dad's Army*) with a statue of Captain George Mainwaring sitting on a park bench. Tourists who enjoyed the series on TV can sit beside Arthur Lowe and smile for the camera.

Equipped with Cromwell and Stuart tanks the 8th Hussars made preparations for D-Day. They were designated as an armoured reconnaissance regiment which meant they were expected to scout ahead of the main battle force. The reputation the Desert Rats had earned in North Africa allowed them to be eccentric, even reckless, and this worried the High Command. On training exercise in 1944, it was noted that they were 'assing about generally'. Questions were asked about their fitness for battle. The generals now had serious doubts about their ability to lead the charge. To force a way through enemy lines in Normandy would require good discipline. Perhaps the Desert Rats were too experienced; they knew how bloody war was and had become 'devil-may-care'. Unblooded formations might be steadier.

On another occasion the colonel entertained a Russian general. Naturally they both had an interest in military history. At dinner they examined the cloth embroidered with the battle honours of the 8th Hussars dating back to the Crimean War. "Balaclava, General, a great British victory."

The interpreters conferred and the Russian replied, "Indeed, Colonel. Balaclava was a great victory for us also."

Both commanders now had their sights set on Berlin and victory over a common enemy. In preparation for the invasion of mainland Europe, 8th Hussars moved nearer to the coast. At Gosport tanks and support vehicles were waterproofed. They were ready for 'the off'.

Mindful that they were about to take part in an historic event, arrangements were made for an official photograph. In the shade of a chestnut tree over forty officers of the regiment arranged themselves carefully in four ranks. They looked rather serious, and only about half a dozen managed a smile. Within a year a quarter of them were dead.

To boost morale, VIPs visited the troops. Churchill, Montgomery and Eisenhower inspected the 7th Armoured Division. Colonel Cuthie Goulburn met the King at Sandringham and again at West Tofts Camp to show off the gleaming tanks of the 8th Hussars.

Apley Estate Archives

"May I ask who polishes your boots, sir?"

LEAVING A DESK JOB

A truly professional soldier, Eddie Goulburn had served fifteen years with the Grenadier Guards before the outbreak of war. In September 1939 he was appointed adjutant at Sandhurst, a particular honour for any officer. He was well remembered by many young officers who passed through the gates of Sandhurst in the early years of the war including Lord Carrington who went on to serve with him in battles from Normandy to the Rhine.

Major Goulburn was promoted in 1942 and took command of the 1st (Motor) Battalion Grenadier Guards, a founding member of the Guards Armoured Division. The Guards had by tradition always been at the top in the 'order of battle', and they expected to be there in the battles to come.

181

For protection in modern warfare it was decided to cram guardsmen into tanks, a controversial decision. This was a particular problem for the King's Company Grenadier Guards, some of the tallest men in the British Army.

This is 'man's talk' between Colonel Eddie and HM King. The Queen just smiles and looks gracious.

Apley Estate Archives

"Sir, I didn't realise Her Majesty had an interest in tanks."

The 2nd Battalion Grenadier Guards trained in Sherman tanks named after an American general. Thousands were supplied to the Allies under the Lend/Lease Scheme. The King's Company of Eddie Goulburn's 1st Battalion were spared the discomfort of squeezing into the Shermans. Companies were split into eight-man sections and initially trained in 15 cwt. trucks. Later they were issued with half-track vehicles designed to carry twelve men.

The role of the Motor Battalion was to provide infantry support to the tanks; they were more mobile and expected to be 'everywhere at once'. Final manoeuvres took place on Salisbury Plain. The beaches in Normandy were secured and the invaders pressed forward. Eddie's Guards crossed the Channel. They landed ready for battle and went straight to the front to spearhead 'Operation Goodwood'.

AUCTO SPLENDORE RESURGO

He was not a Latin scholar, but from time to time officers of the King's Shropshire Light Infantry must have reminded Reg Glaze and others in the ranks of their regimental motto: *I rise again with increased splendour.* Reg had never been accustomed to great comfort so he accepted sleeping rough as the lot of the common soldier. The 1st Battalion KSLI was dispatched to France at the outbreak of war and came back from Dunkirk with their tails between their legs. Reg had lain in ditches and under hedgerows in Belgium, and shaken sand out of his blanket in North Africa and on the beach at Anzio. As D-Day approached he was snatching a few hours sleep on the stony ground of northern Italy. *I rise again with increased splendour* hardly applied to Private Glaze.

In the meantime another Apley youth, Private Charlie Oliver of the 2nd Battalion KSLI, had been sunning himself in the Caribbean. In 1942 he came home with the rest of the battalion to prepare for serious warfare. They might have hoped for a posting within the borders of Shropshire. They were disappointed. The new location for the 2nd Battalion was Berwick-on-Tweed, three miles from the Scottish border.

Charlie was two hundred miles away from home but still pleased to be back on English soil – just. Time passed, the summer and autumn of 1943 were pleasant enough even at Berwick-on-Tweed, and then during the winter months the training intensified. A rumour spread that when the invasion of mainland Europe did take place it would be the 3rd British Infantry Division that would spearhead the assault.

Clearly foot soldiers could not do it alone. The Royal Navy would ferry them ashore and shell the German positions ahead of them. The RAF had control of the skies and intended to keep it that way. In the depths of winter Charlie Oliver and the 2nd Battalion went further north and practised landings on the shores of the Moray Firth and Cromarty Firth with the snow-covered Black Isle in between. Surely after this landing on French soil would be 'a piece of cake'.

The LCAs (Landing Craft Assault) were not the most comfortable vessels to sail in; flat-bottomed with no cover overhead, they pitched and rolled even in relatively calm seas. By the time troops were landed they were usually soaked to the skin. To add realism to the exercises and more misery to the troops, live shells fired from the support vessels exploded on the shore and small-arms fire sprayed the beaches as they landed. Predictably, there were casualties from 'friendly fire'. In the spring of 1944, two large-scale exercises were staged back in Cromarty Firth. There were more fatal casualties. Men drowned when 'swimming tanks' sank in rough waters whipped up by gale force winds.

In May the order was given to move south. Charlie Oliver parted company with the 2nd Battalion in Yorkshire. He was one of the casualties. One of the training exercises had been a bit too realistic. A piece of his shoulder was blown off and an eardrum perforated. It might have been worse. The lad on his left lost an eye, and the one on his right lost a hand. The inquiry decided that they had been 'mishandling explosives'.

Private Oliver was left behind when the battalion journeyed south on a bright sunny day. At Haywards Heath, just over ten miles from the Channel coast, they moved into a tented camp set up by another regiment. It was camouflaged and sealed off with barbed wire from the outside world. Letters were censored and no phone calls were allowed. Everyone knew where they would be going next and this was confirmed when French phrasebooks and French francs were issued.

FUNNY, PECULIAR

The raid on Dieppe had been a disaster. Just over five thousand troops had landed near the French port. Well over three thousand failed to return. D-Day planners had to think hard if the mistakes at Dieppe were not to be repeated in Normandy.

Major General Percy C S Hobart was recalled from the Home Guard to command the 79th Armoured Division. He was an eccentric; he had funny ideas. He inspired a team of boffins and craftsmen who transformed tanks from simple mobile guns to machines capable of a variety of tasks. The most successful was probably 'The Flail', a rotating drum with chains that thrashed the ground ahead exploding landmines and clearing the way for the infantry. 'The Bobbin' had a spool mounted on top that held a hundred yards of matting which it laid under its own tracks to advance over soft or slippery ground.

These and other similar contraptions were collectively referred to as 'Hobart's Funnies', designed to entertain the Germans. Built by the British and offered to the Canadians and the Americans, they were not all taken seriously. General Eisenhower admitted later that lives would have been saved on Omaha Beach on D-Day if they had been used.

Spickernell is an ancient surname; it dates back to the Norman Conquest. Spickernells were the 'Keepers of the King's Seal'. When a monarch signed a document a Spickernell had to be on hand with hot wax and a seal to make it legal. The *Magna Carta* is the best example. Graham Spickernell was a charming man and when he arrived in Bridgnorth from the south coast he lost no time in charming a local girl, Freda Dorrington. They married in 1939. Just before the outbreak of war, he made a sentimental journey with his young wife, to the coast near Bournemouth. They looked over his boat, *Moonraker,* and Graham made sure everything was secure before leaving. He grew up sailing. He knew the tides and currents of the Channel, and these were skills he thought would be useful in the Royal Navy, so he volunteered.

Driving home over Salisbury Plain they could see rows of parked tanks.

"Tanks, that's not for me. I'm glad I chose the Navy."

He was in for a disappointment. In no time at all Graham was in khaki battledress, a private in the Tank Corps. At the end of training at Bovington Camp, his squad was kitted out for service in a warm climate. There were a few possibilities: India, Singapore, Hong Kong maybe the West Indies. Graham and five others went first, picked out in the middle of the night and whisked away. They were dispatched to Lowther Castle in the Lake District. This was their base for the rest of the war.

In the early days workshop and living conditions were primitive. Before Nissen huts were put up to accommodate the men, they were housed in 'bell tents' of the type issued in the Boer War. To give extra protection they were pitched inside marquees. Just before the first Christmas, gales blew down the marquees and the tents inside them, not once but twice. What went on at Lowther Castle was 'hush, hush', Top Secret. At home in Bridgnorth, Graham's young wife was kept in the dark. To begin with she assumed he was in the tropics. Eventually postcards arrived, heavily censored, but from where? Freda complained that the correspondence she did receive was far too brief. When it was all over Graham said, "I knew the letters were read by censors and I didn't like it."

In the meantime Freda was doing war work of her own. The carpet looms at Southwell's factory on the riverside were 'mothballed'. American machine tools were shipped in. The factory was extended and camouflaged. Rootes Group from Coventry was relocated, and aircraft parts were produced 'round the clock'.

Secrecy was such that no one company was given the contract to produce the tank components. Orders were placed with engineering firms all over Britain. One afternoon Graham arrived home unannounced. He stayed in Bridgnorth overnight. He was on his way to Coventry to 'collect parts'; that was all he could say. Government propaganda reminded everyone that *careless words cost lives* and *tell her you love her, that's all she needs to know*. The full story could not be told for thirty years.

Graham, disappointed that the Royal Navy had rejected him, was given the opportunity to demonstrate his sailing skills on Loch Striven in front of an audience of army officers and anxious craftsmen. The designers called it Duplex Drive. The men who rode in the DD tanks called them Donald Ducks. If they were lucky the canvas skirt raised around the tank stayed waterproof and the linkage from the engine to the screws at the back drove them steadily through the water. From a vessel moored offshore, Sergeant Spickernell drove the second tank to be launched into Loch Striven. The first Sherman dipped its tracks nervously into the chilly waters of the Clyde, slid gracefully into the water and disappeared into the depths. The driver was left spluttering on the surface. Next off was Graham Spickernell. His DD bobbed about a bit and then chugged off confidently to the shore. How would they perform on the Normandy beaches?

Graham's particular baby was the Canal Defence Light. It was intended as a defence for the Suez Canal to illuminate the landscape and reveal enemy positions. Improvements to the design were intended to change the CDL from defence to a weapon of attack. In the modified turret a carbon-arc searchlight was mounted. The light was intensified by an optical system and directed through a narrow slit. As it advanced over the battlefield, enemy infantry would be blinded by the brilliant beam of light. If it had been widely used this secret weapon might have shortened the war. It should have been deployed in North Africa. With rapid tank manoeuvres and wide open spaces this was ideal terrain, but strategists were reluctant to play what they believed was a trump card.

The CDL was not used on D-Day because this was essentially a daylight operation. In November 1944, Graham's tank did at last go into action at Geilenkirken together with 'flail' and 'flame-throwing' tanks. The following year they were used during the crossing of the Rhine. When at last Victory in Europe was declared, CDLs lit up the battlements of Lowther Castle.

Today the tracks over Askham Fell are busy at weekends when mountain bikers arrive in all weathers to test their machines – and themselves – over the rugged terrain. Man and machine were tested over the same tracks when Sergeant Spickernell was resident at Lowther Castle. Then 'Crocodiles' spitting flames crawled over the backs of other tanks to ford streams, and the 'DDs' lifted their skirts to take a dip in Ullswater.

CRAFTSMEN AND SAPPERS

In bygone battles the glory often went to the cavalry plunging into Napoleon's ragged lines, or the infantry standing firm in the face of withering fire. The Great War changed all that. Famous regiments began to lose their mounts in the 1930s; hussars, lancers and dragoons were mechanised. Fine horses of the Queen's Bays were replaced by 'Crusader' tanks. The Royal Scots Greys made their last charge on horseback in Palestine in 1940 before they too were mechanised. No more feeding and grooming for the troopers. Making sure that 'Crusaders', 'Shermans' and 'Churchills' were fit for battle was now the responsibility of craftsmen of the Royal Electrical and Mechanical Engineers.

It was clear from aerial photographs and military intelligence gathered by commandos that the beaches of Normandy were covered with tank traps and obstacles of every sort, and there were minefields to be cleared. Before the infantry could advance, sappers of the Royal Engineers went ahead making the mines safe and clearing the way for the armoured regiments.

The Apley Legion was well represented in Normandy by Bill Roberts, Bill Dyke, Sam Coles and Les Webb, all Royal Engineers. In the first week of June 1944, they too were 'ready for the off'.

Chapter 18

The Longest Day

Going to 'the pictures' was very popular in the 1950s. The Majestic in Bridgnorth was full when *The Longest Day* was shown for the first time. Reluctant fathers were dragged out of the High Street pubs and badgered by teenage boys to take them to 'see what it was like'. Filmed in black and white and viewed through a fog of fag smoke, *The Longest Day* could not possibly convey the whole picture of the events and incidents of D-Day.

GOING ASHORE

Hundreds of photographs were taken on D-Day. One of the most famous was taken by Sergeant Jimmy Mapham on Sword Beach at eight thirty in the morning on that fateful day. Although the scene is captured in black and white and the men frozen in time, it is so vivid that it is as if, at any minute, they may take another step forward, pass you by and carry on with the task they were given. In the background we see Lord Lovat's commandos wading ashore. In the shallows men of the Suffolk Regiment, laden with equipment, are helping wounded comrades. Closest to the camera are Jimmy Leask and Cyril Hawkins, of the Royal Engineers.

The task of the Royal Engineers was to disarm mines and clear obstructions in front of the advancing infantry. The commandos 'pressed on regardless'. They had very specific instructions to silence a gun battery on the Orne Canal, east of the port town of Ouistreham. One after another troops of commandos arrived on the scene. 'E' Troop and 'F' Troop prepared for the assault. Barbed wire and an anti-tank ditch protected the battery. One man carried a special ladder to bridge the ditch but he didn't arrive to do the job. Sid Smallman lay back on the beach. He left a widow in Bridgnorth. He was one of the first local men to die on D-Day morning.

This photograph has been called 'The Greatest Picture of the War'. As Sergeant Jim Mapham's camera shutter clicked the beach came under heavy artillery and mortar fire from German batteries inland.

© National Army Museum (107304)

"A fine time to be taking snap shots!"

CALL FOR THE CARPENTER

When Sam Coles left school at fourteen he was apprenticed to Jim Norris, an estate carpenter. What could be better? He was 'working in the dry' a mile away from the house he was born in. There was going to be a war so Sam volunteered hoping to follow his trade. The army had other ideas. His new trade was not one he could return to when the war was over. He joined a bomb disposal squad made up largely of Black Countrymen; they were all dispatched to London. Unlike the Guards outside the Palace there were no ceremonial duties so there was no need to get dressed up every day. The lads of No 5 BD Company were billeted with local families in Acton near their depot.

No one knew who picked the site for the depot but it must have been someone with very little imagination. The bomb disposal team operated out of the sports ground of the Acton Gas and Light Company in the shadow of gas tanks the size of a block of flats. What would happen if a high explosive bomb punched its way through the top of one of the gas tanks?

It was the bombs that failed to explode that Sam and his mates had to worry about. Somebody had to make them safe. Really big ones were never just lying about conveniently in some open space. When they hit the ground they went down and down. That meant digging a big hole – carefully. No two problems were the same; there were always complications with gas mains, water mains, electricity cables, sewers and the weather. The sides of the holes had to be shored up. "Come on, Sam, you're the 'chippy'. Get down there, while we brew up."

There must have been many anxious moments for the bomb squad. On this occasion Sapper Sam Coles and his mates seem very pleased with themselves.

Permission given by Roy Coles

"Put that fag out, Sam!"

Doing dangerous work, often in the dark and in all weathers, 5 BD Company had been on the battle front since the outbreak of war. They deserved a holiday at the seaside. When Sam saw Churchill, Eisenhower and Montgomery prowling about the quayside at Portsmouth he suspected that what they had in mind was not going to be any picnic. What were they up to? Were they just counting the days D-Day minus three...minus two...minus one? Everyone was left 'hanging about', while Eisenhower talked to the 'weathermen'. Low cloud and rough seas delayed the invasion by a day.

The equipment of 5 BD Company was checked yet again on board one of the LCILs (Landing Craft Infantry, Large). These vessels were capable of carrying up to one hundred and eighty troops accommodated below decks with support vehicles and equipment on deck. They were escorted by a Royal Navy frigate. In the chaos of the invasion things went badly wrong for Sam and his squad. Sam had decided to stay on deck in the fresh air; this may have saved his life. The LCIL was holed by a mine below the waterline and began to sink. Some men below decks were drowned. The frigate took them in tow and began to take off Royal Engineers. As they scrambled to safety they witnessed an unpleasant incident, a shouting match between a Royal Navy officer and one of their officers, "Get back with your men! The commanding officer is always the last man off!"

That was the way it was done in the Royal Navy, and the same was expected of an army officer. The frigate returned the 'Sappers' to port. Within a week Sam was on French soil camped in a field near Arromanches watching thousands of men and machines pass through and push on to engage the enemy. Overhead, Allied bombers droned towards the enemy lines to make life uncomfortable for the Germans. In a hurry to return to base one American 'Flying Fortress' dropped a bomb in Sam's field.

"Whose side is he on?"

MOPPING UP OPERATIONS

The Canadians of the 3rd Infantry Division and Royal Marine Commandos may have been raring to go, Aleck Melly of Landing Craft Recovery Unit 209 was less enthusiastic, but like thousands of others caught up in events they waited to carry out whatever duties the D-Day planners had in mind. The invaders were already at sea, and it was still rough following the storms of the previous day. Admiral Ramsay was in the Channel on his flagship directing operations. Recently promoted Leading Seaman Melly was up a creek near Southampton.

In the early hours of the 6th of June, all the invasion beaches, Utah, Omaha, Gold, Juno and Sword were pounded by Allied air and naval forces. Just after 6 o'clock the Canadians began to transfer from the escort vessels to their landing craft. The whole operation was timed to the minute. All the landing beaches had been carefully surveyed. The invaders of 'Juno' knew what to expect. Rocky outcrops were a natural hazard, the beaches were mined and the German defenders had erected steel and wooden obstacles in the shallows. The invaders had intended to go ashore at low tide when the German defences were exposed, and the demolition teams of the Royal Engineers could clear a passage for the infantry. They missed the tide and many landing craft in the first wave were lost, snared on steel girders hidden by the sea. Troops could not be landed on the sand and had to wade ashore. They walked into a 'killing zone'. There were heavy casualties.

Specialist armour, some of Hobart's Funnies, went into action for the first time. Rough seas hampered the 'swimming tanks' that should have arrived to support the infantry. Canadians of the Regina Rifles pressed on and overwhelmed the defenders of Courseulles. Despite the fact that the pre-invasion bombardment had failed to destroy all of the German defences, by midday the Canadians were well established along a six-mile stretch of the coast. At the seaside village of St Aubin, the defenders in their bunkers got a shock when Churchill tanks opened up with 'flying dustbin' mortar bombs about a foot in diameter.

Two thousand Canadians had landed on 'Juno' on D-Day. The beaches were littered with abandoned equipment, burnt-out vehicles and bodies. To maintain the momentum of the assault more men and machines were piled onto the beach to take on the Germans and drive them back inland. A vital part of the operation was keeping the beaches clear of obstacles, mines, wrecked tanks and unseaworthy landing craft.

At their base near Southampton the men of Landing Craft Recovery Unit 209 were still 'awaiting orders'. They had been confined to camp for days. They wrote letters home that were censored by unseen officials before dispatch. Equipment was checked and checked again. The exercise was off, and then it was on again.

Aleck Melly's Landing Barge didn't have an official name; the crew didn't belong to any one of His Majesty's Ships. They were just 'attached to Gosport'. This sort of anonymity suited Aleck very well; he wanted no part in the affair. When the order was given the barge was made ready, cast off her moorings and sailed down Southampton Water to join with a dozen more Landing Barges assembling off Langstone. Sealed orders, marked SECRET, were opened and then they knew the chart reference of their destination for the day.

The map and aerial photographs of Juno Beach were clear enough. The off-shore rocks, exposed at low tide were something to be avoided. The coxswain steered the landing barge cautiously towards the mouth of the Seulles River and sailed in towards the lock gates. The crew came ashore exactly according to plan. They set about establishing their base, surrounding themselves with sandbags and planting the White Ensign in the sand.

This is D-Day but there does not appear to be any threat to the troops coming ashore here. They are moving steadily up the beach past two members of a Royal Navy 'shore party' sitting beside their White Ensign.

© Imperial War Museums (2401)

"Call this a shore party, it isn't much fun!"

The scale and complexity of the D-Day operation was beyond belief, almost beyond description. A man with a way with words was sent by the Admiralty to record events. Neville Shute, an officer in the RNVR, was the ideal man for the job. He was already an established author. In 1940 he published *Landfall*, the story of an RAF pilot patrolling the Channel. Neville Shute arrived on Juno beach on D-Day +1 and made his way towards Courseulles. "I walked delicately ashore from the wrecked

LCT, treading carefully in the wheel tracks of vehicles until I could find out a little more about the situation regarding mines."

He had landed near the hamlet of Graye, separated from Courseulles by a sluggish little river. Houses on the seafront had suffered severely from shelling. The church tower had also been hit, a feature Aleck Melly also noted. A sniper in the tower took pot shots at the boys in navy blue from time to time. Neville Shute remarked, "I wished very much that I had been wearing khaki and not blue." Lieutenant Shute moved on briskly passing the dock and the lock gates where Leading Seaman Melly and recovery unit personnel were busy unloading their equipment. More and more vessels came ashore to discharge men and materials.

The German troops were a mixed bunch, among them old men, veterans of an earlier war, and boy soldiers. There were slave labourers, Poles and Russians, all of them only too pleased to put their hands up. One of the snipers left behind to give the invaders a reason to keep their heads down turned out to be a sixteen-year-old boy. Two German prostitutes with nothing better to do after their customers left the town lobbed a few mortar bombs onto the beach before they too fell into the arms of the Canadians, and normal service was then resumed.

The Royal Navy was responsible for most of the explosions that day. Battleships and cruisers continued to bombard enemy positions inland ahead of the advancing troops. Aleck can recall only one shell coming in the opposite direction. There was brief excitement when German aircraft dived out of the clouds, dropped bombs at random on the beach, disappeared back into the clouds and were never seen again.

The recovery unit had plenty to do. The once even surface of the beach was pitted with great saucer-shaped depressions made by the wash of propellers. Added to this there were mines and beach obstacles everywhere, wrecked landing craft, burnt-out tanks, abandoned equipment and the dead of both sides. It was surprising that the landing operation went as smoothly as it did. They had to be adaptable. Every job was different and some decidedly unpleasant. In one of the abandoned landing craft they found the body of a German soldier. They said he was a good German because he was a dead German. Perhaps he ran forward to surrender, was wounded and died in the abandoned landing craft. No one would ever know the true nature of the man. He was just another casualty.

Neville Shute spent another few days on the beach chatting to troops and French townsfolk. He finished gathering material for his report before hopping on one of the Landing Ships, into the captain's hot shower and back to London. Leading Seaman Melly and his shipmates made themselves at home in a hole surrounded by sandbags.

For the next three months LCRU 209 was very busy trundling around with their mobile crane, patching up the landing craft and whenever possible making them seaworthy. They operated as far west as the Mulberry Harbour at Arromanches with their 'terrapin'. This amphibious vehicle was the British equivalent of the American DUKW, a superior craft and the envy of the recovery unit.

Mulberry Harbour had been essential to the success of 'Operation Overlord'. The planners knew that any attempt to take a port on the Normandy coast would be costly and so decided to take their own harbour with them. Assembly of the pre-fabricated sections began as soon as troops landed, and two separate harbours were operating within a week. Unfortunately, the harbour set up for the Americans was damaged by storms and was never fully operational which meant that the British harbour had to handle twice as much cargo. Once Cherbourg, Honfleur and Le Havre had fallen into the hands of the Allies, ocean-going ships could dock. The beach landing craft had done their job, the recovery units had salvaged what they could and Aleck Melly sailed away on 'HMS Landing Barge Engineering'.

GOOD INTELLIGENCE AND FALSE INFORMATION

To land the Allied invaders on the beaches required an incredible amount of hardware and supplies. Men travelling in trucks to the coast to take ship to France were astonished at the sheer volume and variety of material stacked at the roadside; tanks, jeeps and artillery pieces in every field. Surely German reconnaissance aircraft and spies on the ground must have seen all this and warned the High Command of the build up in preparation for the invasion. They were completely deceived. Even when forty miles of the Normandy coast was swarming with Allied troops there were still German generals who believed that this was a sideshow and held back their troops to defend the Pas de Calais. They had also been led to believe that the British and the Russians were planning a joint invasion of Norway.

'Garbo' and his network of spies gave them all the details. Garbo was a double agent handled by storytellers from MI5. They created fictitious armies, airfields and naval bases, and even fictitious spies to provide more false information. To back up their stories rubber tanks were inflated in fields in East Anglia and dummy landing craft were moored in creeks nearby waiting for ghost regiments to come on board. On roadside verges near the coast flat-pack plywood field guns were parked, all as harmless as a nursery toy.

It was nice to know that the deception was working. Messages sent from German intelligence to the generals were all deciphered and translated by teams of backroom boys and girls in England. Mathematicians, linguists and crossword fanatics at Bletchley Park had penetrated the German ciphers; they could intercept and decode all their signals. These confirmed that the Germans did believe the main invasion force was preparing to sail across the Straits of Dover and they told their friends the Japanese. Their code had also been broken.

The Allies had excellent intelligence. In the opposite camp top men of 'the master race' could not believe that the brash Americans and the bumbling British were capable of such cleverness. Counter-intelligence required a huge team of people with many talents.

Who would have thought that a white-haired old lady tending her bee hives in a lavender garden at Astley Abbots had once lied for a living? Natalie Hodgson was twenty-seven at the outbreak of war. She had been educated in Paris at the Sorbonne and had made several trips to Germany. She had just the sort of background the Foreign Office was looking for. Based at Woburn Abbey close to the code-breaking centre at Bletchley Park, she spent the war writing 'black propaganda' to deceive the Germans. She admitted that by the end of the war she had difficulty distinguishing fact from fiction.

STATION X

The Germans had faith in their 'Enigma' machine. They did not believe that coded messages transmitted by Enigma could possibly be read. They were wrong, machines designed and developed by the brilliant mathematician Alan Turing and his team did just that. At Bletchley Park and 'outstations' worldwide thousands of servicemen and women toiled with one aim, to bring about the downfall of Hitler and the Japanese

Emperor. Daisy Bailey from Worfield played a part.

Eighteen-year-old Daisy became a 'Wren', a member of the Women's Royal Naval Service. They weren't expected to go to sea but some may have hoped at least to get a glimpse of it, at Portsmouth or Plymouth. Daisy went off to Eastcote in Middlesex to meet young Americans eager to show her how to operate a Bombe. These code-cracking machines had been developed at the Government Code and Cypher School at Bletchley Park and this was where she was posted when her training was complete.

Daisy began work in the Japanese Section. She could not know then how valuable this work would be not only in the campaign in the Far East by in the planning for D-Day. The Japanese Military Attaché in Berlin had been given a guided tour of the Atlantic Wall, the system of defences built by the Germans on the French coast. He made detailed notes, wrote a report and sent a long series of messages back to Tokyo. These messages were intercepted, read by the code-breakers at Bletchley Park and provided vital information for the Allies.

'Colossus' was a mighty machine, the first true computer. A number were installed at Bletchley, one in the Japanese Section. The Wrens who operated Colossus and the Bombes worked in eight-hour shifts around the clock. By working extra hours they might accumulate time off for a weekend break, there was no question of leave at this stage in the war.

Colossus could be temperamental. It read information from punched tapes that whizzed at high speed around flimsy spools mounted on a frame in front of the machine. Things could easily go wrong. The operators, the Wrens, had to be alert at all times ready to step in and 'sort things out'. The day to day maintenance was the responsibility of RAF boys, those that had a badge with a 'fistful of sparks' on their arm. In the heart of the machine fifteen hundred thermionic valves glowed. The heat generated was such that at times the Wrens stripped off their uniforms to the delight of the RAF technicians always on hand to make adjustments to the equipment!

The most remarkable thing was that no one talked. Everyone was sworn to secrecy. For more than thirty years nothing was said of the part they played in battles worldwide. All the Bombes were dismantled; the house and grounds at Bletchley neglected. Then when the secrets were revealed the public wanted to know more and came to visit in droves. The huts and the house were opened up. Replicas of Colossus and Turing's Bombe were built.

In 2007 the Duke of Kent came to perform a ceremony. Daisy was invited to attend.

At the gathering she met others who had spent time at Bletchley. They swapped war-time stories and told of how their lives had change in the years that followed. They came from all walks of life: posh ladies who spoke perfect German, university dons, clever men in tweed jackets, technicians in white coats and girls in white blouses and navy blue skirts. They had all played a part.

Chapter 19

Good Hunting

PERSONAL MESSAGE FROM THE C-IN-C
To be read out to all troops

There were five numbered paragraphs in the document. It was signed,
B L Montgomery. Although General Bernard Montgomery must have
thought about it very carefully, the message didn't sound very personal
except for a little touch at the end.

> *5. Good luck to each one of you. And good hunting on the*
> *mainland of Europe.*

This at least was the sort of language that Eddie and Cuthie Goulburn
understood. They had enjoyed good hunting with the Albrighton Hunt
chasing foxes around the Shropshire countryside. In June 1944 they were
joining another hunt – in Normandy.

Even in pursuit of a fox the huntsmen needed back-up; the 'whipper-
in', stable lads, saddlers, farriers, kennel maids and carters to bring in the
hay. The cavalry and front-line infantry needed sailors to land them on
the beaches, air support to soften up the enemy, fitters to keep the wheels
turning and cooks to keep up morale. In the war diary of the 8th Hussars
was praise for the 'excellent catering arrangements' provided at a tented
camp on the eve of D-Day. Dash and daring alone would not win the day.

THE GAMBLERS

The Americans were the big providers. Without the Liberty ships and
landing craft from the shipyards of the USA the invasion of Europe would

199

not have been possible. Two hundred and sixteen thousand six hundred and ninety-nine is a big number. This was the number of American troops, the GIs, that landed in Britain in April 1944.

They staggered down the gangplank at the docks carrying heavy packs. They couldn't carry everything they would need; trucks and tanks and artillery pieces. Going into battle they would need stretchers, bandages and blankets, medals to pin on the wounded and chewing gum to calm frayed nerves. Somehow all this had to be transported to the south coast. The village folk of Norton and Sutton Maddock must have thought most of it was being driven past their front doors. From the docks at Liverpool the main road south passed through Whitchurch, Wellington and Bridgnorth. Convoys rumbled past the pub and the village school day and night in the weeks before D-Day, and for months after.

The schoolchildren were delighted, especially the boys. They pored over pictures in comic books or photographs in the daily papers but here, moving before their eyes, were all the weapons of war in colour and with real soldiers waving. Girls stood apart as the convoys trundled past, interested in the young men not the machines. They waved and giggled. "See him, the black man, he waved."

Everyone knew the chant, "Give us some gum, chum!" they all sang out. Sometimes the call was answered and packets were scattered across the road. Big boys charged, snatched and kicked, and shared it out amongst themselves. Small boys waited. If they were lucky they might be given a soggy portion when all the flavour had been chewed out. They pressed it under the desk lid to dry out.

These were dangerous times for workmen pedalling from the village to the farms along the Bridgnorth Road. "These Yanks are wild and some of 'em are 'alf asleep."

Veterans of the Great War must have thought they were back at 'the front' when they swung out of Village Road. Once in a while the convoy would be at a standstill. Maybe up ahead a dreaming driver had run off the road; easy to do on the downhill stretch to Rindleford Bridge. Then the cyclists, farm boys, 'old codgers' and Land Girls could safely weave through the line of trucks. The girls were greeted warmly by the soldiers but refused all offers. Men and boys gave the troops words of encouragement, "Give the Jerries what for, lads"

It was smiles all round except for those GIs who had an addiction – the gamblers. They did not look up to acknowledge the passing cyclists. They showed no emotion; 'deadpan' you had to be to win at poker. In tight groups crouched on the roadside the players clutched their precious cards. In turn, they examined their 'hand' and made a bid. Then they focused on 'the pot', a 'tin hat' full of dollar bills. No matter where, no matter what time of day or night, the gamblers had to play. Some were lucky. They gambled all the way from the sandy lane below the Manor House at Ewdness to the gates of Berlin. Others diced with Death and lost.

EVER HEARD OF VILLERS-BOCAGE?

'Operation Perch' had been planned well before the 7th Armoured Division left the shores of England. The details were not disclosed at the time. Lieutenant Colonel Goulburn did not know what part his Hussars were expected to play. In preparation for the battles ahead, tanks and trucks of the 8th Hussars were painted with brilliant white stars; this was to protect them from friendly fire. Colonel Goulburn wasn't happy about it because it was a break with tradition, and tradition was important to the Royal Irish Hussars. Some of the officers wore their 'tent hats' instead of steel helmets when they came ashore at Sommervieu on the 9th of June.

It was a very busy place with landing ships offshore, landing craft ferrying troops and weapons to the shore and barrage balloons flying overhead. This was no place for ceremony. Bill Bellamy parked fifteen vehicles on the beach only to be told by the beach marshal, "Not on my beach, sonny!" The regiment found comfortable quarters to leaguer their tanks in an orchard and around the edges of a hay field. Cuthie Goulburn sent Lieutenant Bellamy off on an errand. "Tell the GOC the 8th Hussars have landed, and are ready for battle."

He thought this would be well received. After all, the Desert Rats had a fine reputation. Bellamy saluted, offered Major General 'Bobbie' Erskine greetings from his commanding officer and reported the arrival of the Irish Hussars. "Good God, man, I don't want any more bloody tanks. Give me 131 Brigade!"

That wasn't very civil. General Erskine got his infantry brigade, and for the time being the Irish Hussars were brushed aside. On the road to Bayeux, Bellamy's fuel and ammunition trucks were forced into a ditch. German shells were arriving from the opposite direction. Bill Bellamy found himself sheltering next to his CO. "Ah, John, you're here. Well done."

Cuthie got his name wrong. It didn't matter, he made a name for himself soon after.

British and Canadian forces were held up on the outskirts of Caen. With more armoured support the KSLI might have entered the town on D-Day. Now the town was held by an SS Panzer Division, formidable opponents. They were pounded daily by artillery on the ground and Allied bombers from the air. Most of the casualties were French civilians. In the west the Americans seemed to have the upper hand. Fresh troops and supplies landed on Utah and Omaha beaches, and they pushed the enemy steadily back from the coast.

Responding to pressure from General Eisenhower, Montgomery decided to act. The plans drafted for Operation Perch assumed that Caen had already fallen. New plans were drawn up. If the operation was successful and the German defences were breached the Desert Rats could then swing south and attack the town from the rear.

Key positions on the battle plan handed to Cuthie Goulburn were Villers-Bocage and point 213. Before his Hussars left England no one had heard of Villers-Bocage. When it was over it would be a place best forgotten. Reputations were lost here.

The Battle of Villers-Bocage got off to a slow start partly because Brigadier W R N 'Looney' Hinde was still working from the original plans. The role of the 8th Hussars hadn't changed. They were a reconnaissance regiment and set off first to investigate the route on the morning of the 12th of June. They penetrated six miles into enemy territory, and then they ran into trouble. The troop sergeant's tank was hit; one of the crew escaped four others were missing. First blood to the opposition. There was some 'dithering' higher up in the chain of command. Cuthie Goulburn stepped up and 'issued verbal orders'. His Hussars pressed on with the mission. All went well until they reached Livry where they lost another tank to a 'bazooka'. Two more troopers were killed and others wounded.

The County of London Yeomanry took over the lead and with infantry support cleared the village of enemy troops. By the end of the first day of the Battle of Villers-Bocage, Cuthie's regiment had lost nine men – six troopers, a lance corporal, Sergeant Haylock and Lieutenant 'Bill' Hervey-Talbot.

The next morning 'Looney' Hinde directed Cuthie's men to move on towards Villers-Bocage. They received a mixed welcome. Before they reached a vital crossroads at the entrance to the town the two lead tanks were hit. One young officer and six of his men were missing. The war diary often listed men as 'missing' because sometimes they did turn up. The German defenders melted away leaving only snipers to sting the invaders. Jubilant French residents came out to greet the tank crews who hopped out to embrace local beauties.

In the meantime the County of London Yeomanry and supporting infantry were making their way towards Hill 213 through typical 'bocage' country. The patchwork of small fields and woodland, and narrow lanes with high hedges favoured the defenders, particularly those who held the high ground. Cottagers waved them on.

From his vantage point on Hill 213, SS Captain Michael Wittmann watched the British yeomanry and infantry as they moved in his direction, nose to tail, up a sunken road. He made a snap decision. Leaving two 'Tigers' on the high ground he went forward alone to meet the advancing column. Within minutes he had disabled tanks, half-tracks, troop carriers and scout cars. Numbers are disputed but certainly at least a score of vehicles were put out of action. Leaving a trail of destruction in his wake he entered Villers-Bocage.

The joy of the locals and British liberators was short-lived. Wittmann arrived and created havoc in the high street. Six-pound anti-tank shells simply bounced off his tank. The Tiger tank had acquired a fearsome reputation against the Desert Rats in North Africa and against the Red Army on Russian soil. Wittmann was already credited with over a hundred 'kills' on the Eastern Front. He added at least a dozen more to his tally in Villers-Bocage. His rampage came to an end when a 'Firefly' stung one of his tracks and immobilised his Tiger. He left the scene and made his way back to Hill 213 to watch the final episode of the battle.

The Royal Horse Artillery and the rest of 22nd Armoured Brigade withdrew and formed a defensive box on the same road they had travelled less than twenty-four hours earlier. Cuthie's Hussars were lucky not to have been involved in the skirmish in the town. On the flank of the main force they fought their way through one village and set up an observation post near Tracy-Bocage. They beat off an attack by infantry and a Tiger tank, losing three of their own. Fortunately there were no fatal casualties. At nightfall the curtain came down on another grim day.

A hasty burial service beside the road to Lesieux. Tanks of the 8th Hussars pass by to continue the advance.

© Imperial War Museums (B 9365)

"He wasn't a casualty, he was our mate."

Retreat had not been part of the plan for Operation Perch; now it was clear that this was the only option. 'B' Squadron of the King's Royal Hussars moved out at five thirty in the morning, 'A' Squadron remained attached to 131 Brigade as they 'advanced to the rear'. Everyone was involved in one more battle at Briquessard. Throughout the day German forces attacked on all sides what became known as the 'Briquessard Box'. Royal Horse Artillery within 'the box' and American gunners in Caumont, miles away, shelled the invaders. On the perimeter 'B' Squadron knocked out two Tiger tanks.

Complete withdrawal was timed for just before midnight, a tricky operation in the dark. The Germans made a final effort to break down the British defences. The attack was beaten off at a cost. Major Dunne and Lieutenant De May were killed by a mortar shell. The withdrawal was delayed by about an hour. The 8th Hussars war diary describes the event.

> *When it did commence it was not interfered with by the enemy and all units drove out without interference. Last to leave were B Squadron and one company of 1/5th Queens, riding on the back of their tanks. They had held the roads and tracks leading into the east side of the village from the south, until the whole force was out of the village.*

The following day there was still work to be done. 'C' Squadron supported infantrymen holding back the Panzers that were still in pursuit. Repeated attacks were beaten off during the hours of daylight. When it seemed that the toe-to-toe fighting was over for the day Lieutenant Pegler was killed. From the middle of June to the end of October hardly a week went by when Cuthie Goulburn's regiment did not lose men, and 'Bert' Pegler was the sort of man they could ill afford to lose. Commissioned from the ranks he had been awarded the Military Medal and the Distinguished Conduct Medal for acts of bravery in North Africa.

The man best remembered for his exploits in the Battle of Villers-Bocage was undoubtedly SS Captain Michael Wittman. His daring on the battlefield was recognised once again. He already held the Knight's Cross, Germany's second highest award for gallantry; swords and oak leaves were added to it after Villers-Bocage. Today the battle is fought repeatedly by war game fanatics.

Sifting Through the Rubble

The Americans swung west from their landing beaches and took the port of Cherbourg before the end of June. They then turned their attention to the east. St-Lo was a particularly hard nut to crack. Bombing raids on the town must have demoralised the defenders. An RAF pilot, strafing a convoy of trucks, unwittingly struck another blow to German morale. He wounded Field Marshal Rommel putting him out of action for a while. After three weeks of supreme effort St-Lo fell to the Americans.

In the meantime British and Canadian forces were still hammering on the gates of Caen. The town was pounded by surrounding artillery, bombed from the air and shelled by warships off the coast. When the time came to move in the invaders found the streets blocked by fallen masonry. The infantry fought through the shattered town, house to house, street by street. As the Germans fell back they left behind ingenious booby traps wherever they could. This was a job for the Royal Engineers, men like Sapper Sam Coles and Corporal Les Webb.

Troops preparing for D-Day were given 'live firing' exercises. Sam and Les had been defusing bombs dropped by the Luftwaffe for more than three years. Now on French soil there were mines and booby traps to be made safe. They were 'learning on the job'; in the first weeks of the Normandy campaign new techniques had to be tried out. Things could go dangerously wrong.

Visitors to the St Charles de Percy War Cemetery are advised to take the N175 south-west from Villers-Bocage. This was a similar route to that taken by the 11th Armoured Division when they drove the Germans back. As they retreated they laid land mines and booby traps. The job of defusing these devices fell to Sappers of the Royal Engineers.

Watchful Frenchmen knew where the mines were placed and could warn the British troops. On a Monday morning in August, Corporal Les Webb and a truckload of Sappers pulled up on the road near Viessoix. About half of them took out a pack of cards and started another 'pontoon session'. The rest scratched about on the roadside and soon discovered 'a dreaded Reigel mine'. This was a difficult customer to handle. It was primed by pulling slender metal bars from the side; spring-loaded shutters closed the holes. To make the bar-mine safe a nail might be prised back through the holes, but this was not always possible. The cover of the mine was held in place by wire. Les Webb sat with the mine across his knees; he wanted to take the lid off and get at the mechanism. A couple of lads looked over his shoulder. "Give us the pliers will you."

The explosion shook the truck. Hearts, clubs, diamonds and spades flew in all directions. There was a mess in the road. Two men dead and two wounded. Les Webb was found in a field nearby, taken to a dressing station and buried later that day.

Corporal Leslie Webb of the Royal Engineers, killed 21ˢᵗ of August 1944, buried in the St Charles de Percy Cemetery, south-west of Caen.

Permission given by Sid Speke

"Corporal Webb, a determined man."

This was the last time anyone would attempt to defuse a mine of this type. From then on the mines would be scooped up and set off with a controlled explosion. This was little comfort to Annie Webb and Charlie. They had lost their only son.

RUNNING ON EMPTY

Jerry cans and 'Pluto' were designed to keep the wheels of war turning and troops mobile. Without fuel jeeps, trucks, troop carriers and tanks were going nowhere. The problem was considered as early as 1939 when Britain sent her expeditionary force to France. There was always the possibility that supplies might be disrupted on the Continent and an undersea pipeline was considered. France fell and British forces were forced back home. To defeat Germany they knew that one day they must return.

When planning for the invasion of Normandy began in earnest a team was assembled to design a harbour that could be transported across the Channel, and a pipeline to supply Allied forces with fuel. When the tanks of Cuthie's Hussars and the half-tracks of Eddie's Grenadiers went ashore, they were topped up with fuel from the jerry cans strapped to each vehicle. They carried with them as many as they could. As they moved inland, tankers followed along the coast to keep them supplied.

Handling fuel was a dangerous business. Oil installations on the south coast of England, tankers at sea and fuel trucks were all vulnerable to attack from the air. The safest way to transport this vital fuel was though a pipeline network. The pipeline had its beginnings on Merseyside and stretched across English farmland to Avonmouth and on to the Isle of Wight. One long section ran the length of Shropshire.

As the Allies swept across France to the German border the pipeline was extended. American combat engineers and Royal Engineers bolted together one length of pipe after another. They laboured night and day to keep pace with the advance from Cherbourg to St-Lo through Chatres and on to Luxembourg. Pluto was a top secret project but once the secret was out it became a prime target for enemy aircraft. Royal Engineers like Bill Dyke did not need to be told 'no smoking'. Had the Luftwaffe been told 'no bombing'? The engineers did not stop coupling the pipes together until they reached the Rhine.

When it was all over, if Bill Dyke, from Sutton Maddock, wanted to remind himself of the part he had played in the downfall of Hitler, he had only to walk down Church Lane and follow the narrow road towards Harrington and look for the markers in the hedgerows. There he would find an enamel plate mounted on concrete pillars. Under the Apley fields of corn and potatoes still ran the pipeline that fuelled our tanks on their way to Berlin.

OFF TO THE RACES

The race meetings at Epsom and Goodwood attract thousands. They appeal to all sorts: Arab sheiks, peers of the realm, professional gamblers there to risk a fortune and casual punters having a flutter. When the weather is kind the meetings at Epsom and Goodwood are enjoyed by all, especially the girls who sport extravagant hats on Ladies' Day.

Bad weather delayed the D-Day landings and more storms in the Channel damaged the Mulberry Harbours, and slowed down the build up of Allied troops. This allowed the Germans some time to move extra troops up to the battle front. In an attempt to break through the enemy lines east of Caen, 'Operation Epsom' was set in motion. The weather was so bad that flying was out of the question, and ground forces pressed on without air support. A racing commentator would have described the going as 'soft'. 'Epsom' was only partially successful. Monty's men only managed to dent the German armour.

General Eisenhower, the supreme commander, put more pressure on General Montgomery. He arranged another 'race meeting' for his men, 'Operation Goodwood'. Claimed to be the most beautiful racecourse in the world, 'Glorious'Goodwood was the place where fashionable socialites feasted on strawberries and champagne. Monty had a real treat in store for his troops. He outlined his plans to senior officers in the second week in July.

Rommel had fortified a number of villages south of Caen, and some of his finest troops held the ridge on both sides of the road south to Falaise. Montgomery imagined that he could use the same tactics he had employed in the deserts of North Africa to the cornfields of Normandy. The operation would involve over sixty thousand men and over eighteen hundred tanks and armoured vehicles. To reach the German positions they all had to cross a river and canal using three modest bridges. They also had to pass through minefields within range of enemy artillery. The Luftwaffe also had to be taken into account.

Few if any of his senior officers came away from the briefing with anything other than a feeling of deep gloom. It seemed that many were not convinced by Monty's bluster and bravado, but they were military men and trained to follow orders. Certainly Colonel Rankin of the 4th County of London Yeomanry was one who questioned the wisdom of the plan. His regiment had been on the receiving end of Michael Wittmann's rampage only weeks earlier.

Early on the morning of the 18th of July, tank crews waiting in a traffic jam were encouraged by the sight of two thousand RAF and American bombers streaming towards the German lines. Things did not go well. Brigadier 'Looney' Hinde lived up to his nickname by exhibiting some remarkable behaviour, dashing about in a scout car and seemingly unwilling to commit his Desert Rats. General Roberts was not impressed.

Monty had won a famous victory in North Africa. In the eyes of ordinary soldiers he could do no wrong. Senior officers who came in contact with him found him a very difficult man to get on with. One of the kinder words used to describe his character was 'opinionated'. His battle plan was clearly flawed and General Eisenhower was reported to be 'blue with rage'.

At least the 8th Hussars were living up to their reputation. Having spent a fairly comfortable night harboured in a large open field near Demouville, they moved forward to take a small village called Fours. They made good progress on both sides of the main road south to Falaise. They cleared three strongly held villages only to be held up at Verrieres by tanks of the 1st SS Panzer Division.

The Guards Armoured Division, the 11th Armoured Division and the Desert Rats were the key formation in Operation Goodwood. When Cuthie and his troopers were called up from the reserve on the 20th of June, he was then fighting shoulder to shoulder with his elder brother, Eddie, commanding the Motor Battalion of the Grenadier Guards. 11th Armoured Division led the charge into the carefully prepared defences on the slopes of Bourgebus Ridge. In two days of fighting they lost two hundred tanks. The Guards suffered over a hundred casualties on the first day.

Despite supreme efforts by all, the German line could not be broken and the road to Falaise remained in enemy hands. 'Epsom' and 'Goodwood' had both been disappointing. There were no winners. The big gamblers, General Montgomery and Brigadier Hinde, had lost some of their reputation. The lads in the ranks with little to lose were lucky if they came away without a scratch.

BREAKOUT

British and Canadian forces withdrew and regrouped. Goodwood had failed but they had at least drawn most of the Panzers away from the Americans who were manoeuvring through the difficult countryside of the Cherbourg peninsular, and attempting to circle south of Caen.

Montgomery planned a new offensive, 'Operation Bluecoat'. His plan was approved by Eisenhower. Carpet-bombing preceded the operation but was not as effective as hoped for. Bad weather again hampered the Allied airmen. On the ground the advance was also hampered by mines laid by the Americans!

Infantry divisions supported by tanks set off towards the German lines early on a Sunday morning. Despite stiff opposition there was steady progress, and armour and infantry poured forward to take up new positions. Men of the Monmouthshire Regiment, the Rifle Brigade and two companies of the KSLI took the fight to the Germans supported by the Royal Tank Regiment and Hussars. Lives were lost including that of Alan Ainsworth, a twenty-year-old lad from Bridgnorth. Eddie Goulburn led the Grenadier battalions in to defend the sector. The following day they went forward again, and together with the Welsh Guards attacked the German positions on the ridge over the Catheolles Valley. "The fighting was furious, the hamlet (Drouet) was finally captured."

They fought off a German counter-attack. The Grenadiers were shelled by SS artillery for most of the following day but they held their ground against repeated counter-attacks. Elsewhere, the Grenadiers had the upper hand and German units began to withdraw allowing the Grenadiers to go on the offensive once again.

On the 17th of June a Panzer regiment attacked the Northumberland Fusiliers, and Cuthie's Hussars came to their aid. They lost five Cromwell tanks and suffered twenty casualties as a result. This meant rapid promotion for some young officers who became squadron leaders in their teens. After a week of fighting and casualties on all sides the operation ground to a halt.

The German forces were in danger of being surrounded. They withdrew and moved back to Falaise. This was a turning point for the Allies. Trapped in the 'Falaise Pocket' the Germans suffered terrible casualties. On the 13th of August Hitler realised that the game was up and gave the order to disengage.

Allied forces gathered their strength and set off across France with their sights set on Berlin. Months of bitter fighting lay ahead but at long last there was hope that within a year at most it would all be over. Eddie's Grenadiers played their part in Operation Bluecoat. Cuthie's Hussars helped them out.

After suffering casualties and loss of armour it was expected that the Hussars would be taken out of the line. This did not happen. There was a tense atmosphere; all ranks were feeling the strain.

Brigadier 'Looney' Hinde visited the front line. In company with Cuthie Goulburn he sauntered across the fields in front of the Hussars. This was not the first time he had behaved in this way. Lieutenant Bill Bellamy ran over to them and gave them a piece of his mind for giving away their position. This was 'out of order'. Colonel Goulburn didn't reprimand him he just said, "That's enough, Bill."

This time he managed to get his name right. Later, when the events that followed D-Day could be considered, the conduct of the Desert Rats and in particular the bizarre behaviour of 'Looney' Hinde were questioned. "Desert Rats spent some time looking over their shoulder and appeared to obey only orders that suited them."

Major General Verney believed that some of the criticism was well deserved. There were casualties not just on the battlefield but in the 'management team'. Montgomery sent a number of commanders back to England before the next phase of the campaign. Lieutenant Colonel Goulburn remained firmly in command of the 8th King's Royal Hussars, and in the months to come the reputation of the Desert Rats would be restored.

Chapter 20

Mixed Fortunes

THE WORLD TURNED UPSIDE DOWN

The Second War affected folk worldwide. Laplanders herding reindeer, Arab tribesmen riding camels, South Sea islanders spearing fish over coral reefs, it touched the lives of all. Ordinary folk were asked to do extraordinary things. Shropshire schoolboys who watched swallows and swifts swooping over still pools on a summer's evening learned to fly. Lads who couldn't swim a stroke sailed halfway round the world. Young men who had never crossed the border into Wales visited lands they'd never heard of and battlegrounds they wish they'd never seen.

At home they left gaps in the workforce that had to be filled. Girls from the towns came to work on the farms and in the forests. The Land Girls and Lumber Jills loved the open air. Bevin Boys worked in a different atmosphere. They had no choice. Lads who would gladly have worn the king's uniform emerged from the mines at the end of each shift in shirts stained with sweat and black with coal dust.

No matter who you were or where you came from, everyone was expected to play a part. In munitions factories young ladies from private schools worked alongside girls from the 'school of hard knocks'. Nervous girls frightened of mice and spiders assembled bombs that could knock a house down. They all spoke the same language but not necessarily with the same accent. "We're all in the same boat."

Then others climbed into the same boat. The Yanks arrived in their thousands. There were Australians, New Zealanders, South Africans; they arrived from every corner of the Empire. Poles, Norwegians, Dutchmen and the Free French arrived from the Continent to join in on our side. These were fighting men, not here to help in the fields or factories.

Old farmhands and the Land Girls were given some help by boys who had laid down their arms. Boys from Germany, boys from Italy – the prisoners of war. Languages, lifestyles, political points of view, every card in the pack, they were all shuffled and thrown up into the air by the Second World War. It was a silly game.

Bringing Home the Bacon

He must have been a brave lad, Stan Fox. His courage was recognised with little brass oak leaves to stitch on his medal ribbons to show that he had been mentioned in dispatches – twice. After the chaos and clamour of trench warfare he looked forward to a peaceful future in green pastures. He took over Church Farm at Rushbury in partnership with his brother. The association ended badly. Stan did the practical work and Humphrey looked after the 'financial side'. In short, Stan worked from dawn to dusk and didn't see much of the money.

It wasn't all gloom. He married Audrey Williams in 1930 and the following year their son was born. It was time for a change. The family moved from the rolling hills of Rushbury to Kensal Rise in the London Borough of Paddington. The surroundings could not have been more different; the cramped rows of smoke-blackened Victorian houses compared with the lush greenery and open spaces of Shropshire. Stan was working for United Dairies. If he closed his eyes the milky smell of the distribution depot reminded him of distant cowsheds.

Their daughter, Ann, was born three years before the outbreak of the Second World War. She remembered how it began. It was very troubling. "It's out there. It's the size of an elephant."

It wasn't a bad description of the barrage balloon swaying above the rooftops. It was fat and rubbery, and about the size of an elephant. They were all over London to serve as a defence against low-flying enemy aircraft, but they could not stop the bombers. When the bombs began to fall Audrey Fox lost no time in taking her children away from the smouldering capital to a place of safety.

With 'what they stood up in', they crossed London and boarded a blacked-out train for the Black Country. All the way Ann clung on to her battered teddy. From Wolverhampton station they made their way to Village Road, Norton. In the clean air and sunshine things looked brighter; they knew they would be well cared for. 'District Nurse' had been carefully painted on the sign in the privet hedge outside the house of Nurse Morgan. Stan's cousin welcomed them in.

At the village school across the road, Ann and her brother shared desks with other evacuees, mostly from Liverpool, and children who had never travelled more than ten miles from home. The Fox children didn't see much of their father. He had served with the Royal Artillery during the Great War. He was back in uniform once again but this time he was not expected to fight in the front line. Newly commissioned, he was sent to a miserable place on Dartmoor near the prison at Princetown.

A lot of wicked men were behind bars on Dartmoor. Those that Lieutenant Fox took charge of had done very little wrong. They had just been caught wearing the wrong uniform. Some of the German POWs did have farming skills, if they didn't Stan taught them. Dartmoor was not the ideal spot for arable farming and an uncomfortable place for livestock. Only the local ponies seemed to enjoy being there.

Above all else the task Stan relished most was putting bacon on the breakfast plates of British troops. The herd of pigs grew larger and the number of German prisoners increased. The prisoners made such a difference that their contribution to the war effort was reported in the national press.

Captain Stan Fox taught prisoners of war how to look after a herd of pigs on Dartmoor. He carried on after the war and taught animal husbandry to British soldiers hoping to find work on the land.

Permission given by Ann Fox

"She's a lovely girl this one."

215

Just before war was declared, Bill Snow was enjoying a spot of camping with the Territorials. This little holiday should have lasted a fortnight. Bill and his whole company were suddenly whisked away, and he didn't see wife or family for the next three years.

In London, Camden Council, responsible for organising the evacuees, gave Ethel Snow detailed instructions. They told her what to pack, where Peter, Shirley and their classmates would assemble and what time the train would leave to take them away to Dorking. "The 'ole school went, teachers an' all."

Baby Tony stayed with his mum. For months the British Expeditionary Force sat on the Belgian border. Apparently the Germans were in no hurry to start the war. Everything seemed to go quiet so Peter and Shirley came back to Camden Green. Then all hell let loose. The Blitz started and Ethel decided that London was no place to bring up a family. She knew the perfect place, a cottage on the banks of the Severn, where her brother Bert lived with his wife Gwen.

Winscote Hills, the Park and surrounding woodland was another world, and the children liked it. Peter knew that some lucky children went on day trips to London Zoo; the animals there were all kept in cages. In his new surroundings the animals were free. There were rabbits everywhere, foxes, badgers, deer and birds of every size and plumage from wrens to buzzards. The important thing was that he could also roam free in this magic land. He learned to fish. Equipped with a two-pound jam jar success was guaranteed. Sticklebacks could be snared by the score. Gamekeeper, George Cook, taught Peter the ways of the countryside; how to land bigger fish, to shoot and to trap.

Book learning was done at Worfield School. The village children were sharing their classroom with 'cocky' boys from the town and the Davenport Girls. They were marched down from Davenport House in the morning and marched back up the hill at night. It was said that they all came from an 'approved school' in Liverpool. Certainly they needed a firm hand.

For Peter and Shirley Snow the most direct route to school was over the fields. In winter they were sometimes allowed out early to trudge home through the snow. That was when they were grateful for the school dinners, hot and substantial. Mrs Fincher's menu hardly varied. Monday, Wednesday and Friday it was stew, with a lot of swede, a few potatoes, fragments of meat from farm animals and some from the wild; rabbits and pigeons. Tuesday and Thursday there was rice pudding. Both dishes were ladled out of a cast-iron boiler into white enamel mugs. The price was the same for both – 'tuppence'.

At the weekends Peter went hunting with Tom Botley. Tom had a title, 'Pest Control Officer'. He ranged over a wide 'patch' from Apley Estate and the neighbouring farms to the slopes of the Wrekin. During the week, one of Tom's duties was to ferry prisoners of war to the surrounding farms to do their bit for the war effort. All this was a life-changing experience for a boy from Camden Green. The wild woods of Shropshire cast a spell. He returned time and time again for more than sixty years.

FINDING A NEW MUM

Hundreds of Italians surrendered to Cuthie Goulburn's Hussars in North Africa and thousands more in Italy when the Allies fought their way up from 'the toe to the top'. They had never been 'wholehearted', and never shared Mussolini's enthusiasm for the war. Lounging about in a comfortable prison camp in Britain and waiting for the war to end seemed a sensible alternative to fighting.

Even in the Shropshire countryside there was some danger. Bombs fell everywhere, on docks, railways, factories and homes. Bombs, probably intended for Birmingham, fell on Bridgnorth and lives were lost. Half a dozen that fell near Apley Home Farm frightened a few cattle and rattled the windows of army huts nearby.

Sheffield was famous for steelmaking and an obvious target for the Luftwaffe. They mounted repeated raids on the town and on nearby Chesterfield. More lives were lost including Mrs Brown, Fred's wife. Corporal Fred Brown of the Pioneer Corps was the 'camp commandant' in charge of a hut full of POWs in Apley Park. The Brown children were cared for by family in Chesterfield until arrangements could be made for them to live with their father.

Two new boys and a little girl arrived at Norton School; they were quiet and well behaved. Everyone knew their mum had been killed but little was said. Arthur and Joe stayed; their sister went back to Chesterfield.

Being a prisoner of war was no hardship at Apley. Security at the camp was very relaxed. The Italian boys could wander about the lanes in the evening happy to be out of the war. They were equally relaxed

217

during the day. Local farmers would have preferred Germans to help in the fields, "They've got more work in 'em."

The national pastime in Italy was flirting with girls. Even as prisoners of war they practised the sport. Some of this must have rubbed off on Corporal Fred Brown. He found romance with a village girl, Nesta Richards. At war's end they married and set up home in the village. Fred's boys, Joe and Arthur, had a new mum.

THE JERSEY GARRISON

It was a perfect day for harvesting. Not a cloud in the sky. A light breeze rustled the standing corn on the gently sloping hillside above the church. He loved the open air, farm and garden. Fritz Platt was now at rest. His old friends stood casually around at the graveside, offered their condolences and quietly left in twos and threes. The distant hum of a combine harvester was heard somewhere in the direction of the Uplands. The view from Chelmarsh church across the Severn Valley seemed timeless. Over the years things had changed, even the way the corn was harvested.

Sixty year earlier at Ewdness Farm they were using a 'binder' not a 'combine'. With steadily turning 'sails' to stroke the standing wheat onto the vibrating blade, the binder moved purposefully around the field below the Manor House. Fritz and Billy Beck, another German lad, housewives, farmhands and children watched. As the day wore on the sheaves tossed out from the side of the simple machine were set upright in 'stooks' of six by this mixed band of village folk. Labourers in baggy corduroys, wide braces and collarless shirts of blue and white, wives in kitchen smocks, girls with billowing cotton frocks, boys with scarred knees and lace-up boots all moved about methodically chatting as they worked.

Rabbits and the odd hare bolted out of the corn; they were chased and mostly scampered back in again. As the binder cut into their safe haven they grew more agitated and desperate to escape. Before the final cuts were made the 'guns' arrived. A gamekeeper, a neighbouring farmer and 'a gent' took up position. The children were given stern warnings. "Don't get runnin' about, you'll get shot."

With the last cut of the binder, terror-stricken rabbits fled in all directions. Some were checked in their flight; arched and stiffened when the shot hit them. Some were missed and dashed towards the safety of the hedge bank. They had to pass through the surrounding cordon of villagers. Arms were waved and little boys dashed after them. They were never quick enough.

Fritz was so swift and agile he could run and dive onto the stubble and snatch-up the scampering rabbit as cleanly as an English cricketer might save a boundary. Fritz was no cricketer, he had been a soldier and a prisoner of war, and everyone knew that. It didn't matter now the war was over.

One Thursday night in July 1943, thirty thousand died in Hamburg when RAF bombers set the city alight. In nearby Oberhausen, eighteen-year-old Fritz Platt dressed in his new field-grey uniform was preparing to leave. He was going to spend a year or more on British soil.

Jersey had been under German occupation for nearly three years already.

> *There had to be at least a working relationship between the islanders of Jersey and the occupying German forces. Shoppers are going about their business as his Luftwaffe officer and a British bobby pass the time of day.*

© Imperial War Museums (HU 1761)

"Have you lost your way, sir?"

219

With slave labour from all over Europe the Germans had changed the island into one of the most heavily defended parts of Hitler's Atlantic Wall. No attempt was ever made to invade and take back this piece of Britain.

After the invasion of Normandy, Jersey was isolated. The islanders and the German garrison had to fend for themselves. Churchill decided to, "Let them rot."

For nearly a year they survived until British forces sailed in. Fritz was 'in the bag', along with all the other garrison troops. His stay in captivity was brief.

Fritz went home to be reunited with his family. Oberhausen, Hamburg, Cologne, the whole area, bombed day and night for three years, was devastated.

There was no work. He turned his back on Germany and began a new life on the land in England. It was surprising how well old enemies got on so soon after the war. The fascists and their fanatical followers were the real enemy. Ordinary blokes got along perfectly well. It helped that Fritz and Billy Beck were footballers, heroes when their skill and enthusiasm won the match for the village team. "They're fine lads those two."

Fritz stood out in a crowd. Joan Lewis spotted him at the bus stop in Bridgnorth High Street. They didn't waste any time getting to know each other. They married in 1948, set up home in Village Road and started a family. Other young mums peered into the pram and admired Carla. She was a girl who could break down barriers.

In time they moved away, south of the town, to The Uplands. There was no better place to view the district than from the pasture in front of the farm. The cows looked up when they heard Fritz open the gate, and without any word of encouragement made their way to the milking parlour. Before he turned to follow them in he looked up and down the Severn Valley. Up over the market town with High Rock and Apley Terrace in the distance, and down onto Chelmarsh Reservoir where sailing dinghies bobbed about, their tiny sails like handkerchiefs waving farewell. The river flowed on to the Bristol Channel. Fritz did not linger to reflect on the unhappy months he spent in the Channel Islands

Fritz Platt was laid to rest in 2009. The young parson spoke well. He addressed most of his remarks to Joan and her girls. He talked of sixty years of happy marriage. He mentioned Hamburg and Jersey. That was in the distant past and no one in the church that day had known him then. He had been a Shropshire farmhand all his working life. It was easy to pick out of the congregation those who had shared his trade. They were the ones that held the white service sheets in powerful stout-fingered hands. Fritz was one of them.

LAST RESTING PLACE FOR THE DPS

Joe Stalin, the Russian dictator, was a man to be feared. It didn't matter whether you were an army general or an ordinary soldier he was capable of destroying your life. Adolf Hitler thought he had a friend when the two tyrants joined forces and agreed to attack Poland together. Russians, Latvians, Estonians and Germans were all on the same side for a while. Then Adolf decided to walk all over Russia. That was unforgiveable, and Hitler lived to regret it.

Even though he thought it was a good idea at the time, Joe Stalin never forgave troops who had fought alongside the Germans, and that included lads from Latvia. The lucky ones were those taken prisoner and brought to Britain. These were Displaced Persons, the DPs.

In The Park, the huts put up for the troops to man the searchlight battery were moved nearer the road, and filled with Italian prisoners. When peace came they went home. Some returned but they couldn't go back into their old billets because the DPs were there. Some worked in Apley Woods, some found work in factories in the Black Country and some went 'Down Under'. For ten pounds they could buy a passage to Australia and start a new life.

Bill and Alfred had nowhere to go; they could not return to Latvia. For a while they had worn the wrong uniform and fought for the German. Mrs Rowley carried on cooking for them and they carried on working in Apley Woods. Alfred had a few letters from home from his wife. He never knew if she simply stopped writing or if the authorities were destroying her letters. Of course he wanted to see her, but he knew that he would face a firing squad if he ever returned.

Alfred and Bill were regular customers in The Hundred House. They propped up the bar and were part of the furniture. Always amiable, they never 'cried in their beer'. They accepted the poor hand that Fate had dealt them, they never left the Estate. Alfred Berzins and Vilis Ozols were finally laid to rest, far from home, in friendly English soil.

The census of 1910 showed that the staff at the Hall came from every corner of the country. Professional servants, footmen and lady's maids moved from one grand estate to another. They worked alongside the gardeners and the 'maids of all work', but they rarely mixed with the villagers. Workmen out in the fields and surrounding woods came from families that had lived nearby for decades, even centuries. This state of affairs survived the Great War but not the Second World War.

There was still gaiety and laughter at the Hall during the war years when it served as a convalescent home. Wounded officers and the nurses who cared for them were able to laugh in the face of tragedy. Light-hearted fun that houseguests had experienced before the war went on. There were weekly film shows and acts put on by West End entertainers. Charlie Chester, a cheeky comedian, danced with the head gardener's wife, and 'Dolly' Coombes never quite got over it.

When peace came the laughter died away. There were no more dashing young officers and nurses to flirt with. The liveried staff did not return. There were no more gala balls. Major Jimmy Foster's old dancing partners were, like him, feeling their age. He lived simply with just a few faithful companions. Everywhere about the estate there were new faces and strange accents. Nothing would ever be the same again. For centuries farm boys had looked no further than the next parish for a partner. Landowners arranged marriages with families who shared the same interest in keeping their estates intact.

The whole country was 'shaken and stirred' by war. British and American servicemen billeted nearby captivated local girls. Some stayed, and some went. Land Girls from Manchester married local lads and stayed. Old enemies from Germany and Italy became good friends and made good husbands. There had been much bloodshed during the war. Perhaps new blood was no bad thing.

Chapter 21

The End Game

TALLY HO!

A 'pocket' was created around Falaise by Canadian, Polish and British forces advancing steadily to the north, and the Americans swarming across country to the south. The embattled Germans were harassed on all sides and from the air, strafed and bombed during the hours of daylight and constantly shelled by artillery. Some made their escape through a three-mile gap. Even Eisenhower was shocked when he saw the scale of the devastation that the Allies had inflicted on the Germans. "It was difficult to walk without treading on human flesh."

In the ten weeks since D-Day, at least fifty thousand Germans had died, and two hundred thousand were prisoners. On the 25th of August 1945, the Americans marched into Paris alongside Free French forces.

In the meantime Montgomery's men were making for the Belgian border, eager to finish the job. The advance of the Guards Armoured Division across France was spectacular. They covered thirty-four miles in less than six days, sweeping north of Paris, across the Seine, through Arras and the battlefields of the Great War, over the Somme and across the border into Belgium.

THE PERSONAL TOUCH

The people of Belgium suffered occupation twice in thirty years. Reminders of the Great War were everywhere. Buried there were tens of thousands of British soldiers including Private Edwin Hill, a married man from Claverley. On the morning of 13th of November 1916 he was killed when the KSLI advanced across no mans land. He never saw his baby son. 'Little Ted' grew up to be a fine lad, and very smart he was in the tunic of a guardsman.

He first met Eddie Goulburn at Kasr el Nil Barracks in Egypt in the 1930s, where they served together for three years. A good officer knows his men, understands their background and gains their respect. Guardsman Hill shared his own sad story with Captain Goulburn.

Edwin Hill's young widow, traumatised by the death of her husband, could not cope. One Sunday morning she walked up the garden path of her sister-in-law's cottage and offered her 'Little Ted'. "He's yours now. Look after him, please."

She didn't come into the house. She walked away, never looked back and never came back. Will and Elizabeth Elkes already had six children. One more made little difference and he was brought up as one of their own. He had a happy childhood, surrounded by three older sisters he was petted and spoiled. From an early age he knew his father had died in the war. That did not deter him. As soon as he was old enough he too became a soldier, a Grenadier.

Ted Hill spent all his working life in uniform either as a Grenadier guardsman or as a police officer with the Wolverhampton force.

Family photograph

"One of Colonel Eddie's men."

224

Advancing to the German border Lieutenant Colonel Goulburn and Guardsman Hill were serving together again as the Guards Armoured Division swept triumphantly into Belgium. Just over the border the Motor Battalion rested overnight. Ted Hill spoke to Colonel 'Eddie'. He had a request to make.

"What is it, Hill?"

"It's my father, sir. He's buried not far away, near Serre."

"You want to visit his grave?"

"Yes, sir, I do."

"Of course, you must go, Hill. Get a move on, we'll be off again in a couple of hours. Catch us up, soon as you can."

"Thank you, sir."

Eddie Goulburn knew his men; in some ways they were more closely knit than many families.

The fields around the cemetery were lush and green. As Ted Hill made his way along the Serre Road, cottagers waved. There was the joy of liberation in the air. It was a very different scene here in November 1916 when the 7th Kings Shropshire Light Infantry emerged from their freezing trenches and trudged through mire and mist, many to die. When Ted Hill stood before his father's white headstone, among the many set in orderly rank and file, it made him an even more determined soldier. He lost no time in getting back to the battalion. Colonel Eddie just nodded acknowledgement when he saw him arrive.

THE GREAT SWAN

With Caen and Falaise behind them the Desert Rats were now asked to fight in country more favourable to tank warfare. As they advanced there were dangers to face not only ahead but overhead. The 8th Hussars suffered air attacks from the Luftwaffe and friendly fire from the RAF. The white stars painted on every vehicle at Bognor did nothing to protect them. Norfolk Yeomanry and the Hussars suffered twenty casualties.

Their spirits were lifted when the townsfolk of Livarot greeted them as liberators with flags, flowers and wine. They went on to take Liseux, the birthplace of Saint Teresa. The fighting here was bitter, many beautiful old buildings were destroyed and there were more casualties. The town was in ruins but at least the reputation of the Desert Rats was restored.

After a faltering start at the opening of the Normandy campaign the

Allied armies rolled on from one town to the next. The Americans swept south through Sedan and Verdun under the command of General Patton. Allied morale was high. There was some talk of 'Berlin by Christmas'. This optimism was misplaced, although the Germans were in retreat and they did manage to preserve some of their battle groups.

Eddie and Cuthie Goulburn were both heading in the same direction once again. The only thing that hampered them as they cantered across French fields was the weather. The logistics of supplying the advancing armies with food, fuel and ammunition was extremely challenging. Nevertheless, on the first day of what was described as 'The Great Swan' the Hussars covered over seventy miles. They were swanning along at such speed that they ran out of route maps. Some formations used tourist guide books. Members of the French Resistance could now reveal themselves; they had local knowledge and were invaluable as interpreters. A pretty schoolmistress was the ideal travelling companion for Colonel Cuthie Goulburn.

The 8th Hussars crossed the Seine and pressed on. Now there was a real sense that victory was within their grasp. Helped by the Free French and 1/5th Queens Regiment, Cuthie's men took St. Pol and then drove on in the direction of Lille. At a mining village on the outskirts of Bethume, the Hussars rested for a week; the officers in the Chateau des Pres.

NIJMEGEN COMPANY

At ceremonial events today the colours of the 2nd Battalion Grenadier Guards are carried by Nijmegen Company. After basic training guardsmen are posted to Wellington Barracks, and given extra training to prepare them for life in the 1st Battalion. They learn something of the glorious history of the Grenadier Guards, and the reason why the Nijmegen Company is so called. "Way back in 1944…"

As the Guards Armoured Division pressed on across Northern Europe, the liberators were greeted enthusiastically by all. When they crossed the Belgian border the reception was overwhelming. In every town and village on the road to the capital there were flags and banners to greet them. Bands played and they were showered with flowers and kisses.

The column regrouped on the outskirts of Brussels; they did not know what to expect. The last act of the retreating Germans was to set fire to the Palace of Justice in the main square, and leave a few snipers behind to make a nuisance of themselves. It took three hours for the Guards to force their way to the centre of Brussels, their progress slowed by the crowds of well-wishers climbing on to tanks and armoured vehicles. There were more cakes and kisses, fruit and wine, all the ingredients for an orgy. No time for that. The Germans were falling back but still a dangerous enemy. They had to be pursued. The troops who saw the liberation of Brussels knew they were witnessing an historic event. The Grenadiers were going to make their own regimental history very soon.

The end was in sight. The question was how best to bring it to a speedy conclusion. The strong personalities of the British and American commanders meant there were often serious disagreements. Eisenhower had overall command and he wanted to approach the German border on a broad front. Montgomery devised a bolder plan which he believed would shorten the war. Reluctantly Eisenhower agreed and 'Operation Market Garden' was given the go-ahead.

Thousands of airborne troops would be involved. The British 1st Airborne Division was commanded by General 'Boy' Browning, his American counterpart was 'Jumping Jim' Gavin whose style was quite different. The ultimate objective of Operation Market Garden was the bridge at Arnhem. A number of bridges had to be taken en route including the bridges at Nijmegen over the River Waal. The 'market' element of Operation Market Garden was the responsibility of airborne forces. The 'garden' troops formed an armoured column intended to force a way through enemy lines to reinforce the paratroopers.

Browning landed by glider near Nijmegen with his entire headquarters staff. Gavin with his Parachute Infantry Regiment dropped nearby. At the time the road bridge was only lightly defended, and if they had acted decisively they would have taken the bridge. German reinforcements arrived and held it. At Arnhem, British paratroopers, led by Lieutenant Colonel John Frost, had some early success. Despite communication problems they battled their way to the bridge. Heroic efforts to take it failed. They hung on confident that once reinforcements arrived they would take the bridge.

Thirty Corps set off on the road to Arnhem. Almost immediately they were attacked on their flanks. The opposition was brushed aside by supporting artillery and RAF Typhoons. Bad weather hindered the advance and progress was slow. Colonel Eddie and his Grenadiers pressed on. They first made contact with American paratroopers at Grave on Day 3 of the operation. By this time they should have been at Arnhem to relieve John Frost's 'Paras' who were hanging on by their fingertips.

Colonel Cuthie couldn't help. The 8th Hussars were held up at Herenthals.

For two days the division watched the myriad Dakotas, Stirlings, Albermales and glider-tugs crammed with paratroopers swooping and wheeling like great birds over Eindhoven towards Arnhem dropping their precious cargo.

The Hussars moved slowly across the Dutch border and joined the queue of vehicles of every type. They stalled again, their spirits dampened by pouring rain. Up ahead plans were being made for the assault on the road and rail bridges at Nijmegen.

Browning, Gavin and Eddie Goulburn met to plan a joint operation. Wherever possible British Grenadiers and American Parachute Infantry would be shielded and supported by the tanks and armoured vehicles of the Guards as they fought their way through the town. The tanks would make the final assault on the road bridge. Gavin wanted troops on the opposite bank. "We need boats!"

"We have canvas boats, they're on their way."

Things were going badly all along 'Hell's Highway'. The supply line was threatened by German counter-attacks. The boats were delayed. The scheduled strategy had to go ahead 'come what may'.

The day dawned when Nijmegen would become a name to set alongside Waterloo and the Crimea in the annals of the Grenadier Guards. At eight thirty on the morning of Wednesday the 20th of September 1944, Grenadier Guards and companies of the Parachute Infantry Regiment advanced in two columns through the town. The Germans had strengthened their defences and two tanks were disabled in the opening exchange of fire. Helped by Dutch guides they fought on, house to house. By the afternoon it was clear that they were not going to overrun the German defences easily. At the rail bridge the Guards lost two more tanks in a frontal assault. There was nothing for it but to hold their positions and regroup.

The boats arrived at three o'clock in the afternoon. Downstream from the rail bridge the first 'guinea pigs' set off. They were short of paddles; some used their rifle butts. This was a bold venture but, despite casualties, enough men were landed on the opposite bank to distract the Germans.

In the town the Guards and American infantry fought on. At dusk they were in a position to attempt an assault on the road bridge. Outside the Nijmegen Hotel, Eddie Goulburn briefed the men who were going to lead the assault. First in the line of fire was Sergeant Peter Robinson, a professional soldier, one of his most experienced troop commanders. The tanks that backed him up were to be led by Captain Lord Peter Carrington. Between the Sherman tanks of the Guards was a light armoured car, in it 2nd Lieutenant Tony Jones and his Sappers. They were not expected to dash about doing daring things, just quietly snip through any wires that might detonate the charges hidden by the Germans in the girders of the bridge.

They set off and came under fire immediately. The advance faltered when Robinson's radio was disabled. He transferred to another Sherman, and contact with his commanding officer was restored. "Get on with it, Robinson."

Troop carriers and lorries moving freely over the bridge at Nijmegen. In the foreground is the body of a German soldier.

© Imperial War Museums (B 10175)

"There's still a hard road ahead."

229

With engines roaring and guns blazing he led his troop into a storm of small-arms fire from snipers and anti-tank grenades launched from Panzerfaust, a crude but effective weapon. They reached the great steel arch of the centre section of the bridge, the explosive charges laid by SS engineers failed to detonate. They raced on and slid through the roadblock on the far side. It had not been a 'walkover'.

Captain Lord Carrington remembers well the warm greeting they received from the Americans who had crossed the river by boat that afternoon, and were now eager to push on through Lent and on to Arnhem. Fired with the same enthusiasm, Robinson set off. By now it was dark. Undeterred, Grenadiers and Parachute Infantry together fought their way through Lent until they hit a roadblock and a German 88 anti-tank gun, a formidable weapon. The tanks withdrew to safe positions. The Grenadiers emerged from their vehicles, took out the kettle and began to 'brew up'. "Nice cup-a-tea is what we need."

There then followed a bitter exchange between Captain Carrington and his counterpart Captain Burriss. The American could not understand why the British had stopped for a cup of tea ten miles from Arnhem, and why they did not take on the German 88. To advance would have been futile. At Arnhem the paratroopers were surrendering. Colonel Frost was taken prisoner and could not give full vent to his anger for another year. Operation Market Garden had failed and someone had to take the blame.

Aerial surveillance and messages from the Dutch Resistance warned of the presence of battle-hardened German forces building up in the area. Montgomery chose to ignore this piece of intelligence and dismissed General Browning's famous warning: "Monty, we may be going a 'bridge too far'."

Captain Burris blamed Captain Carrington. The man who should have taken the blame was Bernard Montgomery. 'Boy' Browning took the blame instead.

Eddie Goulburn and his men had done everything that had been asked of them. They had taken the Bridge at Nijmegen intact. This proved to be crucial as the Allies advanced to the Rhine and on to Berlin. The efforts of the Grenadiers were recognised. Sergeant Peter Robinson was awarded a Distinguished Conduct Medal and Lord Carrington a Military Cross. Eddie Goulburn received the Distinguished Service Order and was promoted to brigadier. He took command of the 8th Infantry Brigade, and led them across the Rhine. Following this action he was awarded a second DSO.

DON'T HANG ABOUT

The Allies put Market Garden behind them and moved on. The 8th Hussars were soon in action again at Doornhoek. They did well and Colonel Cuthie recommended Bill Bellamy for a Military Cross. They rested for two days until Brigadier Wingfield came on the scene. He was doing the rounds of field commanders making bad-tempered demands for more effort.

The 11th Hussars were stalled on the road and the 8th Hussars were held up behind them. On either side there were drainage ditches full of water. Junior officers were enjoying a leisurely breakfast in the middle of the road. Seated at the head of the table was their CO wearing his favourite headgear – tent hat of green and gold. The irate Brigadier Wingfield arrived. There was an exchange of words.

Wingfield – "What the bloody hell do you think you are doing here?"

Goulburn – "Breakfast, care to join us?"

Wingfield – "Move off!"

Goulburn – "We will bloody well move off certainly, even if we sink into the polders!"

Brigadier Wingfield went away. The 11th Hussars moved on. The 8th Hussars followed without getting their feet wet.

All were soon engaged in full-scale battle using tactics little changed since the Peninsular War. An artillery barrage opened proceedings. Highlanders marched forward in extended order to the sound of bagpipes, and to finish off the enemy the cavalry swept in. Dongen was taken by the 8th Hussars and 1/5th Queen's. They were welcomed with open arms by the grateful Dutch. This was the sort of welcome Cuthie enjoyed. The mayor of Tilberg arranged a dance in the town hall. The colonel, as usual, led from the front, swooping around the dance floor with the prettiest girls.

They rested on their laurels for ten weeks which took them into what was to be the last year of the war. Over the Christmas period all sides attempted some festivities, but there were casualties even on Christmas Day when the Germans launched an attack on Gebroek village. They were repulsed on Boxing Day.

In the New Year, from their position in the front line, the Hussars watched V1 and V2 rockets pass overhead. Even this latest technology did not turn the tide for the Germans. Defeat was inevitable. The winter weather was atrocious adding to the misery of all the troops at the battle front. The surrounding countryside was depressing; coal mines and spoil heaps everywhere. It was difficult to plan an advance with the obstacles of dykes and canals in the way. The 8th Hussars were given the task of securing Panheel Lock on the Wessem Canal, very difficult terrain for tanks to operate in. It was decided that they would leave their tanks in the rear and fight as infantry. New tactics had to be learned quickly, and an officer of the Rifle Brigade arrived to advise them. After the Hussars had successfully completed their task they were pleased to be back in their tanks. The push to Berlin continued.

'Operation Blackcock' was devised in an attempt to break through the German lines. The 8th Hussars now encountered some of Germany's toughest troops, Parachute Regiment Hubner. This was Cuthie Goulburn's last battle in Europe. His tanks supported the Durham Light Infantry in bitter house to house fighting against a determined enemy. 'Blackcock' was a bloody affair for all concerned. By early February the operation was over to the satisfaction of the Allied High Command. There followed a lull.

Active service done, Cuthie handed over command of his Hussars. For his courage in the recent battle and his service with the Desert Rats, since their creation, he was awarded the Distinguished Service Order.

COME ON, ADMIRAL. HAND IT OVER

The 4th Battalion the King's Shropshire Light Infantry crossed the Rhine on the 28th of March 1944, and advanced into Germany. The seat of government for what remained of the Nazi regime was at Flensburg. Grand Admiral Doenitz was the man in charge. To mark his promotion to Grand Admiral in 1943, Hitler presented him with a baton. He hung on to it for two years. Lads of the KSLI came along and he had to hand over his baton to them. The war was over.

Before the war, Germany had some fine athletes and the Olympic Games of 1936 was an opportunity for Hitler to show them off and demonstrate the superiority of the 'master race'. A grand stadium was built in Berlin.

Germany topped the medal table, the USA came second and Britain just scraped into the top ten. This was just as Adolf Hitler would have predicted. The British simply didn't have the necessary drive and determination. They were a nation of bumbling eccentrics who allowed Jews to occupy positions of influence.

The Slavic people were another race despised by Hitler. He called them the *Untermenchen*, sub-human. Russian peasants formed the backbone of the Red Army. When they fought their way, street by street, house to house, into Berlin, they proved to be superhuman. Adolf Hitler took the easy way out and committed suicide. This was a pity because he should have been taken back to the Olympic Stadium to watch the preparations for the victory parade.

The Victory Parade in Berlin, 21st of July 1945. Winston Churchill and Field Marshalls Montgomery and Brooke pay tribute to the Desert Rats.

© Imperial War Museums (BU 9078)

"Well done lads, it's been a long road from the Western Desert."

233

Colonel Cuthie Goulbrun rejoined his regiment in Berlin. They camped in the Olympic Stadium and prepared for the victory parade. The 8th Hussars had posed for a group photograph at Bognor a few days before they sailed for France. Sadly many were lost along the way to Berlin. They posed again for more photographs in the Olympic Stadium. The images would have been too much for Adolf Hitler. There they were, a bunch of coarse ruffians led by casual toffs and part-time amateurs all smirking at the camera. How could they have triumphed over 'the master race'?

To review the troops Churchill, Montgomery and Brooke rode together in a half-track vehicle. It had been 'spruced-up' for the occasion. The paintwork shone and the serial number was picked out in black. There was something special about their 'carriage'. This half-track belonged to the Motor Battalion of the Grenadier Guards. It was the one Eddie Goulburn rode in when he crossed over the River Maal by the Bridge at Nijmegen.

Chapter 22

Out in the Far East

VE DAY

When Victory in Europe was declared wild scenes were captured on film in Trafalgar Square and Times Square. The citizens of London and New York 'let their hair down' in an orgy of celebration.

There does not seem to be any record of the scene in Village Road, Norton, although it was said that within the adult community only the rector remained sober. Twenty-four hours later, when heads were clearer, it dawned on everyone. "It's not over yet. The Japs are still at it."

In September 1945, after nearly another four months of fighting in the Far East, the Japanese did surrender. Only then could the troops come home and be reunited with their families. Eddie Smout had been in Burma for over two years and Arthur Lewis and Reg Powell were out there somewhere. Len Dunn, Nigel Evans and Aleck Melly set sail for the Far East as soon as Victory in Europe was won.

MOUNTBATTEN'S MAN

It was a 'good step' from Upper Forge to the school at Astley Abbots. Mary Smout walked there with her little lad, Peter, to introduce him to Miss Teece on his first day at school. He already knew the way; down the track to Linley Station, along the railway past Rookery Coppice, through Colemore Green and along the lane to school. All the lanes were narrow but there was no traffic, and he could safely make the trip twice daily and collect a can of milk on the way home. He was never alone. There were children everywhere, sauntering or scampering through the fields, or along the woodland tracks. One or two, like him, had never known their father. Children sometimes asked personal questions. "Where's your dad?"

Peter didn't know exactly where he was. "He's in the war."

Every child knew there was a war on because 'grown ups' talked about it every day. They said it was a world war and they were right.

From the south coast of England, American, Canadian and British Forces invaded Normandy. The skies over Germany were darkened daily by bombers and fighter aircraft, some piloted by Poles and South Africans. Australians and New Zealanders who helped to defeat Rommel's Afrika Korps marched on through the olive groves of Italy. Russian tanks were moving through marshland across Poland. On the other side of the world, at sea and on the tropical islands of the Pacific, men were dying in the desperate struggle against the Japanese. The 'Japs' had swarmed over South-East Asia, humiliating the garrisons in Hong Kong and Singapore. They came so close to Australia that they bombed Darwin. It truly was a world war.

Eddie Smout had been a part-time soldier before the war; at the outbreak the Territorials were all turned into regulars. The first job for 1st Battalion the South Staffordshire Regiment was to 'see off the Italians' in the desert. More than half a million Italian troops were stationed in Libya. They were mobilised and a powerful force crossed the border into Egypt. The Italian advance was brought to a halt at Mersa Matruh. This was Eddie Smout's first taste of battle.

Then the South Staffordshire Regiment were given another job against an altogether different enemy – the Japanese. They invaded Burma even before the fall of Singapore in February 1942. British and Indian forces tried to hold them back, but to no avail. Airfields were abandoned and RAF Units moved to India. The Japanese then dominated the skies. They had achieved their objective.

Mountain ranges with their roots in the Himalayas ran north to south across Burma. The Chindwin and Irrawaddy rivers flowed in great valleys to the sea. This was difficult country to fight in. Adding to the misery of the troops were the monsoons. In the hot and damp conditions, biting insects, leeches and tiny bacteria all thrived. Malaria, typhus, dysentery and cholera took a heavy toll killing more men than the enemy.

General Bill Slim of the Indian Army led 'Burcorps' on the longest retreat in British military history. The bedraggled troops crossed the Chindwin River and made a stand at Imphal. This was a very long way from Upper Forge on the banks of the River Severn. Slim had faith in his men and believed that with proper training and effective air cover they could succeed. A special force was trained in India to operate behind enemy lines.

General Orde Wingate began training his Long Range Penetration Force in 1942. He gave them a shorter title, the 'Chindits'. Their emblem was the Chinthe, a mythical figure, half-lion half-dragon, that guarded the temples of Burma. The men selected for this task were a mixed bunch, Hong Kong Chinese, Nepalese, Indians, West Africans together with the Burmese and the British. Many of them were used to hot climates and jungle conditions. Eddie Smout was a woodman. At home in the woods, he moved easily through the jungle scrub and teak plantations, but even for him staying alive in the jungle was not easy.

Here the Chindits are on a training exercise, practising a skill essential to the whole operation against the Japanese. Using damp leaves and sticks they are preparing to brew some tea.

© Imperial War Museums (IND 2289)

"Put the kettle on somebody."

Far away in England his little lad was playing soldiers, scampering in the woodland tracks, fording streams and limping home scratched and bruised. He was 'kept in order' by his granddad, a gardener at Apley Hall.

General Wingate's Long Range Penetration was not a small-scale operation. His brigade was organised into columns that marched into enemy-held territory and relied entirely on the RAF to supply them. In 1943 the first military expedition into Burma was launched from Imphal. It was successful but at a cost. Almost a third of the Chindit force of three thousand was lost. The great benefit of this operation was the boost to morale. Commonwealth forces had proved that they were more than a match for the Japanese in jungle warfare.

Special Force 3rd Indian Infantry Division was formed and the second Chindit expedition planned. In this formation were two columns of the South Staffordshire Regiment, Eddie Smout's 'mob'. Each column was made up of about four hundred men and fifty mules. They had to be self-contained. In addition to platoons of infantry there were demolition specialists, a Burmese reconnaissance platoon, medics, signallers and RAF personnel.

In March 1944, the force landed behind the Japanese lines in gliders towed by Dakotas. Airfields were established to bring in supplies and reinforcements, and to evacuate the casualties. 'Operation Thursday' went well. When the first stage was complete, Wingate issued an 'order of the day' congratulating his men. A stirring message that Eddie and his comrades would long remember.

One outstanding Chindit was Mike Calvert. He led by example leading the charge with a bayonet if necessary. He was only thirty-one when he took his men behind the enemy lines, and for three months they harassed the Japanese. Operating in daytime temperatures of 40° C and living on a diet of 'K' rations, and very little water was not easy. Every man had been give training in survival skills. In addition to their personal weapon, each man was issued with emergency rations, field dressings and a map. It was a simple map; rivers, (flowing south), roads (to be avoided), mountains, (where are the passes?). It saved the lives of one or two who walked out of the jungle to the amazement of their comrades. It was printed on silk. Eddie brought his home. "It might make Mary a headscarf!"

March to June 1944 must have been the most dangerous months of Eddie Smout's life. He must have longed to be back in Apley Woods. He dreamed of peace and a settled home life. He imagined how it would be, stepping onto the platform by the single track at Linley Halt, passing the flowerbeds full of colour and the gleaming red fire buckets hanging on black hooks.

His dream came true. He pushed back the five-bar-gate at the bottom of the track that led to Upper Forge and let it swing shut behind him. He looked back. The train had gone. Across the river the Hall was still standing, solid and reassuring. Mary had heard the train whistle as it left the station, wiped her hands on her apron and went out into the garden. Peter followed her. As Mary skipped forward to greet her husband, so long away, the little boy stood back and looked on. So this soldier was his father.

Eddie Smout, Bill Ellingham and Louis Mountbatten survived the war. Eddie and Bill died peacefully in Shropshire. Lord Louis died a violent death, assassinated by the IRA. They planted a bomb on his fishing boat off the west coast of Ireland.

Permission given by Peter Smout

"The woodman, the publican, and the commander-in-chief."

The Burma Star Association was formed and Eddie attended the reunions to keep in touch with old comrades. There was a lot of banter and backslapping to go along with more solemn ceremonies. The Chindits laid up the old standard and received a new one at Lichfield Cathedral. Eddie Smout was one of the escorts. Dinner followed, speeches were made and yarns were retold. A cameraman went round to capture the scene. Bill Ellingham, the landlord of the Hundred House was toastmaster for the day, he posed behind Eddie Smout and Lord Louis Mountbatten.

As a souvenir of the occasion, two of Eddie's old commanders, Orde Wingate and Michael Calvert, signed the menu. George Cairns was remembered.

A combined force of Ghurkhas and South Staffs managed to disrupt road and rail communication to the Japanese front line. The Japanese counter-attacked. The South Staffs mounted an assault on one of their strong points. Attached to the regiment was a thirty-year-old Lieutenant from the Somerset Light Infantry, George Cairns. He led the attack. In the fierce hand-to-hand fighting a Japanese officer hacked off Cairns's left arm with his sword. Undeterred, Cairns killed his enemy, picked up the sword and continued to lead the attack. The Japanese fled. Lieutenant Cairns subsequently died of his wounds. For this act of outstanding heroism he was posthumously awarded the Victoria Cross. His young widow had campaigned for five years until, at last, George Cairns's bravery was recognised. The full story appeared on the front page of the *Daily Mail* in May 1949. Eddie kept a copy.

When Eddie Smout was laid to rest in Stockton Churchyard, family and friends reflected on his life. It had been good and long and happy; they were proud of him.

When Eddie was far from home and the first stage of Operation Thursday was successfully completed, General Orde Wingate issued his 'Order of the Day'. He concluded:

This is not the moment, when such an advantage has been gained, to count the cost. This is a moment to live in history. It is an enterprise in which every man who takes part may feel proud one day to say, 'I WAS THERE'.

Eddie Smout was there. He did take part and had every reason to feel proud.

Private Arthur Lewis of the South Staffordshire Regiment. He is wearing a slouch hat of the type issued to Australian infantry. The brim was pinned up on the left to allow a rifle to be slung over the shoulder.

Permission given by Charlie Lewis

"I'm thinking it's a long way from home."

A quiet and reliable man who can be depended upon to put his back into any job *he takes on,* was how Colonel Pike, commanding the 2nd Battalion South Staffordshire Regiment, described Arthur Lewis on his release certificate. He was handed this in Germany in the depths of winter, a very different climate compared with countries he had 'wintered' in during the previous four years. He had followed the same trail as Eddie Smout, to North Africa and on to India and Burma, and then back to join the British Army of the Rhine.

Germany was devastated. In the months that followed the surrender, all the occupying forces could do was keep order and help to organise food and shelter for the thousands of refugees. Field Marshal Montgomery sent Private Arthur Lewis, and everyone else in uniform, a little brown card which told them how to behave in occupied Germany.

In streets, houses, cafes, cinemas etc. you must keep clear of Germans, man, woman and child. You must not walk out with them or shake hands with them, or visit their homes, or make them gifts or take gifts from them. You must not play games with them or share social events with them. In short you must not fraternise with Germans at all.

Monty himself would have found all this very easy to do. He was not very good at playing games and sharing social events. He even had difficulty fraternising with military men like General Eisenhower and Air Chief Marshal Tedder.

Arthur didn't have to worry about this for long. At No 8 Military Dispersal Unit in Hereford, on the 13th of February 1946, a clerk stamped his leave pass. He was home again and could fraternise with anyone he liked, Germans included.

INFANTRYMAN IN BLUE

Reg Powell was among the first to undergo training as a gunner when the Royal Air Force Regiment was formed. The role of the regiment was to defend airfields and other RAF installations.

When the Chindits set out to harass the Japs they needed plenty of support, and Reg was one of the lads called on to help out. The columns, fighting miles behind enemy lines, relied on the RAF to supply them with food and ammunition, to bring in fresh troops by glider, to drop paratroopers and bring out casualties. As the column advanced, airstrips were established behind enemy lines and defended by men like Reg Powell. There were times when they had more difficult and harrowing duties.

If aircraft were lost in the jungle, patrols were sent out to locate them and bring in any survivors. They were often too late. The enemy got there first. The would-be rescuers witnessed many a gruesome scene; the crew hanging in trees near their stricken aircraft, their bodies mutilated. Next of kin would be told that they were 'killed in action'. It was best that they never knew how their loved ones had died. It was impossible to explain why the Japanese committed such acts. The way they behaved during the war was beyond belief.

On the home front, Leading Aircraftsman Dunn had been busy since the early days of the war. From the comfortable grounds of Bentley Priory where Air Marshal Hugh Dowding directed operations during the Battle of Britain, Len was dispatched to the roof of the Air Ministry in Whitehall. A Londoner born and bred, he felt very much at home, but must have missed his new bride, miles away in Shropshire. The RAF put more miles between them when they sent Len off into the wilds of Lincolnshire.

Bombers from Waddington and the many airfields in East Anglia were in action over German cities almost daily. Len's contribution was to ride a motorbike between the bomber bases. The surest way to convey information between the station commanders was in a briefcase on the back of Len's bike. He enjoyed his work. If he was told 'this is urgent', it gave him the excuse to weave through traffic, dodge military policemen or ride along the top of the sea wall.

At Ludford Magna, Len got his first taste of 'FIDO', and the smell lingered in his memory for years. The airfield was built in the peaceful pastures of High Fields Farm on the Lincolnshire Wolds. Below in the fens, damp conditions created fog and the bombers were often grounded. Fog, Intensive Dispersal Of was supposed to solve the problem. FIDO involved burning huge quantities of fuel in petrol heaters, just another unpleasant duty for those with responsibility for airfield defence.

As the war in Europe came to an end, Leading Aircraftsman Dunn took to the skies flying back and forth to the Low Countries with supplies of food and medicines for Dutch civilians. With the war in Europe at an end, Len could relax for a little while as he sailed to Calcutta to join in with the rest, and finish off the job in the Far East.

FALLING ON THEIR SWORDS

The politicians in Tokyo had believed that if they could get a foothold in Assam, Indian troops might turn against the British, their imperial masters. They were wrong. British and Indian forces held firm at Imphal and the weary Japanese troops withdrew across the Chindwin River. This was a humiliation and the Japanese High Command invited General Soto to commit *hara-kiri* – ritual suicide – to fall on his sword.

The ship carrying Leading Aircraftsman Dunn from England sailed into the Bay of Bengal and docked at Calcutta. Len flew on to Burma. On the ground the Chindits forced the Japs out of the jungle and onto the plains north of Mandalay. Len was in the air making supply drops to the 14th Army until Rangoon was taken. Even though some Japanese units fought on and refused to surrender, Mountbatten knew he had the upper hand and arranged a victory parade in June 1944.

Thousands of Japanese troops died of starvation and disease, hundreds were killed in battle fighting to the last round and some may have committed suicide rather than surrender. Surrender they did after 'The Bomb' was dropped on Nagasaki.

Len flew south to Butterworth in Penang. Malaya was back under British administration. Another big parade was organised. Rank on rank of the 94th Division of the Japanese Army lined up at Sungai to lay down their arms. Ordinary soldiers handed in their rifles, their officers surrendered their swords. Len picked one up. "Can I keep this?"

"Of course you can. I'll give you a chit."

Len kept the slip of paper that allowed him to pack the sword in his kitbag and bring it home.

Some units had to wait a long time before a passage home could be arranged. Len was lucky. He sailed away from Singapore on the *Winchester Castle* and was back in England on the 26th of January 1946. Len kept his RAF blue greatcoat and wore it when he started work in Apley Woods. His sword went into the garden shed because Ethel wouldn't have it in the house.

SAVED BY THE BOMB

For Leading Seaman Melley the end of the war couldn't come soon enough. He was very grateful to Allied soldiers when French ports were opened up and Landing Craft Recovery Unit 209 could sail away from Normandy and tie up in Devon. With a mild climate and attractive beaches this was the ideal place to while away the winter. It was not to be.

Aleck Melly and his shipmates spent a miserable Christmas at Greenock, on the Firth of Clyde. The New Year was celebrated with 'wee drams' of Scotch and an extra 'tot' of Navy rum. When heads cleared they considered the future. Surely, with German forces retreating on every front, this year would be the last of the war.

The tide was turning in favour of the Allies in the Far East and the Pacific. Much to Aleck Melly's dismay, his Landing Recovery Unit was expected to join in. As land forces plodded determinedly towards Berlin, Aleck Melly's team set off for Bombay.

Before the war an imposing structure had been built at the entrance to the great natural harbour to welcome King George V and Queen Mary to India. When the king and queen arrived at 'The Gateway to India' they walked up carpeted steps. Other dignitaries followed. Troops arriving with Aleck Melly sailed past and docked in less grand surroundings. They were welcomed by local girls. This was no surprise; sailors were supposed to have a girl in every port. Aleck Melly was cautious.

"It was a shock to me. Young women in saris offered themselves and older women offered their daughters. Our surgeon lieutenant had warned us that any intimate contact could have unpleasant consequences. He even handed round photographs to make the point. I didn't accept any offers."

The recovery barge stayed moored in the harbour, and the crew were billeted on the outskirts of Bombay. For decades troops waiting to be shipped home after their tour of duty in India whiled away the time at the transit camp at Doelali. They sometimes waited for months. If they couldn't stand the wait they 'went doolally' and were locked up in the lunatic block until they came to their senses. Treatment for the mentally ill was rather crude. Black humour and comradeship sometimes helped. Aleck Melly remained sane and sensible. He didn't go 'doolally'.

The Royal Navy Recovery team stayed put while the American General MacArthur was 'leapfrogging' across Pacific islands, bypassing some of the islands and leaving the Japanese defenders isolated. Brave men were lost every time. As they moved ever closer to the Japanese mainland they encountered increasingly fanatical opposition. Once in control of the Marianas Islands the Americans could mount repeated bombing raids on Japanese cities. A hundred thousand were killed in a single raid on Tokyo in March 1945.

The Americans had more experience of beach landings than anyone. They made landings on the islands of Iwo Jima and Okinawa that made history. The scale of the operation to capture the island of Okinawa was comparable to the D-Day landings in Normandy. Certainly the Japanese were going to be defeated but at what cost to the invaders? Iwo Jima and Okinawa had demonstrated the scale of the assault that would be called for to land troops on the Japanese mainland. It was estimated that at least half a million lives would be lost. Members of Aleck Melly's recovery unit feared they might be invited to join in. They were not looking forward to it. "We should leave it all to the Yanks."

The Americans intensified the bombing campaign hoping that this would bring the Japanese government to its knees. Despite the devastation there was no sign of surrender. The decision was taken to use The Bomb.

On the 6th of August, the *Enola Gay* took off from her base and dropped 'Little Boy' on Hiroshima killing seventy thousand people instantly. Three days later 'Fat Man' was dropped on Nagasaki and fifty thousand more Japanese died. In less than a week the emperor, Hirohito, broadcast to his people and called on them to lay down their arms. The news was joyfully received all over the world.

The Melly family were great letter writers and Aleck had been receiving news from home every week since he first put on uniform. Now there was no news and no letters arrived for him at the transit camp near Bombay for six weeks. He never understood why, but this was certainly a blow to morale. He still didn't go 'doolally'.

In due course he sailed home. The whole process of demobilisation seemed frustratingly long. During this period he was unexpectedly promoted. He was never sure what he had done to deserve it. Normal life resumed in May 1946 when Petty Officer Melly changed into his 'city suit' and went back to 'clerking' in the Cunard offices overlooking Trafalgar Square. Visitors to the capital looked up in awe at Admiral Nelson on top of his column. Petty Officer Melly was not impressed. He was probably the least enthusiastic sailor ever to put to sea. He declared that he had been, "Saved by the Bomb!"

Free from Evil

Nigel Evans, the village bobby, sometimes pondered over an unsolved mystery. How did he, a young stoker, find himself on the slopes of Table Mountain in the care of a black lady twice his size? Many police reports in cases such as this used the phrase 'alcohol was involved', and this was probably the explanation. Nigel was on his way to the Far East aboard the *Aquitania*.

The young stoker was led astray by Australian soldiers and airmen returning home. The war in Europe was over and they had very good reason to celebrate. The officer responsible for discipline on board was a British colonel.

"We take on oil and water at The Cape. No one will go ashore. That's an order!"

The war was over and back pay was burning a hole in the pockets of those who had not already gambled it away. When the water bowsers, brought alongside to replenish the tanks, had completed the task they took on extra crew. Frustrated soldiers, sailors and airmen 'jumped ship'. They were welcomed into the dockside bars and afterwards reeled out to explore the town.

Nigel got into trouble. He blamed 'the Aussies'. It wasn't his fault that he misunderstood the notice that said OUT of BOUNDS and woke up hours later in a dimly lit hut. Even in this poor light the broad grin of the dark girl was clear to see. Back on board, and with the coastline fading into the distance, Nigel looked back at Table Mountain for the last time, still unable to explain his abduction.

In Sydney Harbour Nigel joined the crew of the Golden Hind, not Sir Francis Drake's old ship, but brick-built barracks that served the whole of the Pacific Fleet. There was no stoking to be done here and he was soon transferred to a battleship, HMS *King George V*. With battles over she was being used as accommodation for recently released prisoners of war.

What Nigel witnessed on board *King George* was horrifying. Ships of every class were bringing away broken men from Burma, Malaya, Indonesia, China, and Japan. Men so changed that family members would hardly have recognised them. They had been beaten, starved and driven to the point of exhaustion. On board *King George*, the crew did their best to make these men as comfortable as possible. The sailors were most moved by the prisoners who had lost their minds. Nightmare images flashed back repeatedly. Some of those who were unable to put these scenes into the past stumbled aimlessly about the decks. Others raved like animals and were locked up in specially adapted cells. This was the final humiliation for men who had been locked up for years by the Japs. If any of those who witnessed this had ever doubted the righteousness of the cause to which they had given their youth, they knew now that it had been a just cause.

Petty Officer Evans sailed home via Singapore, Suez, Malta and Gibraltar. He stayed in uniform and was given a job training new recruits. He married a local girl and decided to leave the Navy rather than be separated from her. Within a year he was back in uniform, this time as a police constable.

Constable Evans arrived in Norton in 1951 and he stayed for twenty years. He kept the peace in the village and surrounding district on foot, on bicycle and astride the 350cc BSA motorcycle. Lads who couldn't resist the rosy apples in neighbours' gardens were given a warning. He kept a watchful eye on generations of bikers without lights, school truants, amateur and professional poachers and the occasional drunk. He made them all into good citizens.

Even in the quiet of the countryside there were unpleasant incidents. Fatal accidents, suicides and family tragedies all had to be dealt with. Nigel did so with tact and sympathy which earned him great respect. He received the Police Good Conduct Medal in 1972, and five years later he was rewarded with the Queen's Jubilee Medal. Probably the award he treasured most was The Pacific Star.

WELCOME HOME

The long voyage home helped some of the prisoners of war to adjust. Blue skies, the sound of the sea, fresh air and warm food all helped. They were comforted by the knowledge that soon they would be in the arms of loved ones. There was time to chat. Talk of the horrors of the camps was replaced by hopeful visions of the future. Sometimes there were doubts.

"She never heard anything from me."

"She might have found somebody else."

"Look at me now."

On arrival they had to be processed. The ship eased alongside the quay, the moorings secured, the gangplank lowered. Clipboard in hand, a smart young Royal Navy Lieutenant came on board to explain the arrangements for disembarkation. He watched as the men who had suffered so much filed past him down onto the quay and into the waiting transport. They were thin, but a little less drawn than a month before, cheery but apprehensive, unsure of the future. They would all remember this moment, when they set foot again on English soil, and so did Lieutenant Hill.

Fifty years later, at ease in his flower-filled garden at Brockton Barns, David Hill, very occasionally, recalled the scene he had witnessed at Southampton in his youth.

"What happened to those lads was unforgiveable."

Chapter 23

Trouble Spots, Old and New

THE FIELD KITCHEN

A quiet life, woodland shade, open skies, birdsong, peace and solitude; it didn't suit everyone. The work of a gamekeeper meant unsocial hours and out in all weathers all year round, yet George Farmer wouldn't have changed it for the world.

The Second World War was a year old, Margaret Farmer had just been born and her dad was about to leave her. George would have much preferred to stay at home instead of trekking off to Cark Camp in Lancashire to train as a gunner. He carried a shotgun every day of his working life, but the Royal Artillery decided he needed more training. When that was complete, he joined the 6th Light Anti-Aircraft Battery. Someone had to feed them and George volunteered. He knew nothing of the mysteries of the kitchen, but at the end of his training he knew how to prepare Muligatawny soup and Christmas pudding for a hundred men.

He returned to the battery to try out his new skills. There was one thing he was clear about. "I don't care where I go as long as it isn't by sea."

The *Dominion Monarch* was a luxury liner, built for travel to Australia and New Zealand. The 6th Light Anti-aircraft Battery together with other contingents of the Royal Artillery sailed from Liverpool Docks bound for Egypt. U-boats were active in the Atlantic; George saw nothing more dangerous than a few dolphins. The *Dominion Monarch* took the long way round Africa via Freetown and Cape Town, north passed Madagascar, round the Horn of Africa and in to the Red Sea.

Port Tewfic, at the southern entrance to the Suez Canal, was where

Private Farmer and the gunners of the Royal Artillery got off and set up their anti-aircraft battery. The Canal was vital as a supply route to build up the forces in Egypt that would drive the Germans from North Africa. The security of the Canal had to be maintained throughout the war to support troops fighting on the battlefields of the Far East.

On the waterfront at Tewfic there stood a memorial to four thousand men of the Indian Army who had died in the Great War fighting against the Turks in Sinai and Palestine, a reminder that this was a troubled region.

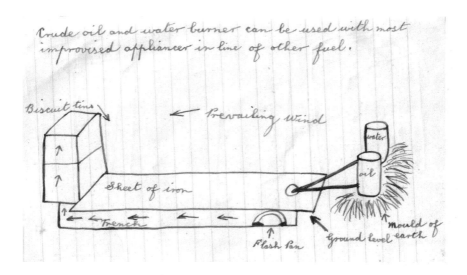

Permission given by Margaret Farmer

"Don't try this at home."

The battery moved to Haifa on the coast of Palestine; George had to wait almost a year after the end of the war before he was shipped back to England. He had time to travel to many of the sites mentioned in the Bible. The parables he had listened to at Sunday school came to life. To walk the same roads as Jesus and his disciples gave him great pleasure. He would much rather have been at home in England, but he made the best of being a tourist and brought back souvenirs from Jerusalem, Damascus, Beirut and Cairo.

Gamekeeping was what George Farmer knew best, and in the

autumn of 1946 he went back to it. In khaki drill he had travelled, visited historic places and learned much. He had even learned how to cook.

In the woodland around the keeper's lodge he knew where there were several suitable sites to set up a field kitchen. There was plenty of fresh meat around. George could always find 'something for the pot'. He had been trained to produce hot meals daily under difficult conditions, not now. The war was over, something best forgotten. He never claimed his medals, rarely commented on his days in uniform and he didn't do any more cooking.

READY FOR ANYTHING

The girls tucked their frocks into their knickers and did handstands against the wall of the school yard. Bill Rowley and Jim Jackson looked on. It was all very interesting but it wasn't a war game. These two 'cowboys' had lost count of the number of Red Indians they had killed in the Park. There was talk of German paratroopers, dressed as nuns, dropping in fields nearby. With Sten guns fashioned from bits of wood, Bill and Jim were ready to face the threat. Alf Rowley and Steve Jackson told their boys about the old enemy, the one they had faced in the Great War. Village lads in uniform confirmed that the Germans were still behaving badly.

Bill and Jim grew up, left school and started work. Shortly, both lads would be made aware of a campaign that had been put on hold for six years. No sooner was peace declared in Europe than trouble flared up again in Palestine.

ONE OF THE KING'S COMPANY

Career choices for teenagers were once simple. They might qualify for one of the professions, or be a white-collar worker, a clerk, or be apprenticed to a tradesman. The safest bet was to follow a trade. Men who had been labourers all their lives counselled their sons, "With a trade you'll never be out of work, my lad."

Bill Rowley began his apprenticeship as a plumber. To be the best meant working hard with the best, evening classes, trade tests and written examinations. For Bill it also meant hours of pedalling to Horne and Meredith's yard in Bridgnorth and, on Monday evenings, peddling on to 'The Tech' in Wolverhampton. With the City and Guilds Certificate, he came back to work at Apley and waited for 'the call-up'.

For a man with a trade, the Royal Engineers sounded just right. There was a bewildering choice of regiments and other outfits from the Black Watch to the Catering Corps. The sergeant in the recruiting office made a decision. "You've got the look of a guardsman about you. The Grenadiers."

In eighteen weeks, drill instructors at Caterham Barracks had to produce guardsmen who would be on very public view, immaculate and capable of performing ceremonial duties without making a single mistake. Their feet hardly touched the ground. If they were not stamping about on the parade ground they were slogging along the surrounding roads on twenty-mile route marches. This was the only time they were given a glimpse of the outside world. They passed out fit for the parade ground, but not considered fit for the battlefield. After twenty weeks at Purbright, they were ready for anything.

Guardsman Rowley was outstanding, smart, one of the tallest and considered very suitable for the King's Company. On state occasions it was the King's Company that took the lead. Bill Rowley, in bearskin and red tunic, began his service on ceremonial duties at St James's Palace with the 1st Battalion Grenadier Guards.

It wasn't long before the battalion was on the move to Palestine to relieve the 3rd Battalion. The conflict between Jews and Arabs that British forces had tried to resolve before the war was now made more serious by mass migration. It was understandable that Jews of Europe should turn to what they believed was their God-given land. Britain had a responsibility to keep order; it was an impossible situation. It wasn't war, it was counter-terrorism. The enemy were all around them. Bill's father understood something of the dangers his son might face. During the Great War he had served in France and in Ireland, and preferred the trenches to the backstreets of Dublin. "In France at least you knew where the bullets were coming from."

The advanced party, sixty men of the King's Troop, boarded the *Arundel Castle* and sailed from Southampton. This was what they had joined up for and trained for, to see the world and see some action. The atmosphere on board was one of excitement and anticipation.

Bill Rowley's company of Grenadier Guards disembarking, probably at Haifa.

"The only way is forward."

At Port Said, the Grenadiers disembarked and were swiftly transferred to the *Tripolitania*. The two-day voyage to Haifa was memorable and enjoyable – if you liked stew for every meal. With all their kit strapped about them the guardsmen stepped ashore in the problem state of Palestine.

Israel had not yet been created; this would become an even bigger problem. In the meantime, as usual, British troops were on the ground in the midst of it, trying to keep order. Infantrymen were deployed to every settlement. They set up road blocks and went about their business of 'stop and search'. There was trouble everywhere and there were casualties. Next of kin were informed, but often by the time the news of their lost son had reached them he was already buried in foreign soil. The death of a comrade bonded the guardsmen even more closely together. Being in uniform did not mean losing their identity.

Bill was surrounded by familiar faces. Even the Officer Commanding the Guard's Brigade was familiar, Brigadier 'Eddie' Goulburn. "Good to see you, Rowley. Stay out of trouble!"

British rule in Palestine came to an end in May 1948 when

David Ben-Gurion declared Israel an independent state. The last unit to withdraw was the 1ˢᵗ Battalion Grenadier Guards. They transferred by LST (Landing Ship Tank) to Libya, and barracks near Tripoli. Guardsman Rowley was going to team up with Captain Spowers, a man who spent a lot of time looking for trouble.

I Flew with the Aussie VC

Victory in the Battle of Britain made RAF pilots national heroes. Schoolboys in the Air Training Corps could only dream of such glory. Jim Jackson was kitted out with a scarlet blazer and rode off through the Park to the Grammar School in Bridgnorth. Twice a week he changed into blue. The Air Training Corps was formed at the school; he became one of the most enthusiastic cadets. At sixteen he had passed School Certificate and exchanged his bright blazer for a dark suit. Jim spent eighteen frustrating months as a trainee auctioneer before he could join the RAF. He was hoping to fly of course.

No one suspected that Jim had a hearing problem until he went through the selection process for aircrew. They failed him. He was never going to get his pilot's wings, or even the 'half-wing' of a navigator. All was not lost; his studies for the School Certificate paid off. Elementary facts knocked into him by the physics, chemistry and geography masters were enough to make him a suitable candidate for the meteorological branch of the RAF.

Preparations were made for the invasion of Normandy. Jim went to Blackpool to be kitted out for the Arctic. There was a change of plan, if there was ever any plan at all. Tropical kit was issued and Jim sailed away from Liverpool, destination unknown. As the troopship passed the coast of Portugal, there was an announcement, "Allied troops have successfully landed on the coast of Normandy." By the time Jim and his shipmates had reached Alexandria, lads of the 2ⁿᵈ Battalion King's Shropshire Light Infantry were pushing inland.

One of the daily duties of the junior ranks in the RAF 'Met Service' was to nip out of the office behind the control tower to check the instruments that recorded temperature, pressure, humidity, wind speed and direction, and examine the empty rain gauge. Jim gathered and recorded data on the ground, but the weather was made in the clouds, and luckily he was given every opportunity to study them at close quarters.

Leading Aircraftsman Jackson flew in every type of aircraft. From Cairo he flew to Beirut, Baghdad, Basra, Jerusalem and a place few people had ever heard of, Sultanabad. This town near Karachi was famous for rugs and carpets woven in similar style to the flying carpets Arab wizards were supposed to use.

Jim made many flights; two were particularly memorable, one in the cabin of a flying boat, the other in the belly of a Mosquito. The Short 'C' Class Flying Boat was a remarkable machine. Imperial Airways used them to fly posh passengers from the British Isles to the outposts of the Empire. Some of these aircraft were taken into service by the RAF during the war. Flying in this machine was an entirely new experience for Jim; he could only imagine how it would be.

He knew the ways of swans. As a boy he had watched them gliding effortlessly among the willows, or ploughing confidently across the sky in formation, necks outstretched. They always seemed less self-assured when they came in to land, wings out to slow the descent, feet stretched forward awkwardly as if feeling for the river. Skating, splashing and flapping as the yellow webs sank into the water the lovely bird regained its dignity as the curve of the white breast settled onto the surface. He had witnessed this so many times on the Severn below Stone Cottage.

Jim examined the craft as he boarded. He could see that the fuselage was built for the job, shaped like the prow of a speed boat, under the wings two substantial floats and, set into the wings, four reassuringly powerful engines. They roared at full throttle, choppy waves at take-off caused a few judders. Passengers gripped their armrests then relaxed as the great seabird took flight. Leading Aircraftsman Jackson made the necessary meteorological observations. As usual there were plenty of clouds over the coastal waters of the British Isles. As they came in to land he looked out at the floats. He wondered what sort of landing this bird would make. It was splendid, exhilarating. Arches of spray rose up under her and streamed past the cabin windows. Lucky lads on the sunny side glimpsed flashing rainbows in the spray before she settled gently into the water, and taxied to her berth. How could this compare with a ride in the belly of a Mosquito?

Home leave was precious. Too much of that precious time was taken up with travelling; a lift was always welcome. You had to be in the know to get a 'gash' flight. "Groupie's off to Cosford. That's up your way, you might get a ride."

Group Captain Hughie Edwards was an Australian, an approachable man.

"Jackson, is it? Want a lift? Jump in, down there." Group Captain Edwards was one of the most decorated airmen in the RAF. Following raids on The Hague and Bremen he was awarded first the Distinguished Flying Cross and then the Victoria Cross. A year later, for another act of heroism, he received the Distinguished Service Order.

As an ATC cadet, Jim had learned to recognise the various types of Mosquito. The bomber variant had a clear Perspex nose with a bombsight in it. The bomb aimer lay on the cushioned floor below the pilot. Jim took up this position for his flight from North Weald. For a good part of the journey they followed Watling Street, the old Roman road. It was a wild ride to Cosford, but safely home again Jim had something to tell his mates, "I flew with Hughie Edwards, the Aussie VC."

When Jim came out of uniform he got a job for life. S E & A Ridley was the oldest established firm of seedsmen in the whole of the British Isles. They had seeded and shaped the landscape around Bridgnorth for over three hundred years.

He had seen the Shropshire countryside from the air and could compare it with other lands – Libya, Egypt, Palestine, Jordon, Iraq – not all of it sand and scrub. There was the green fertile delta of the Nile, and the lush marshlands on the banks of the Tigris and Euphrates, north of Basra. For Jim there was no place like the Severn Valley and the Shropshire Hills. His love of the land and his attachment to Apley was so strong that in the last years of his life he came back time and time again to wander the woodland paths, the riverbank and the fields of his youth.

History Can Teach Us a Lot

The Battle of Tel-el-Kebir, in 1882, lasted about an hour; some of those who fought in it carried on talking about it for years. In the drawing room at Apley Hall, little Arthur Foster wanted more details. "Uncle Jimmy, tell me about the battle again, and about the Pyramids, please." Arthur was so impressed by the tales he heard from Captain Foster that in adult life he preferred to be called 'Jimmy'.

Magazine artists produced numerous romantic pictures to illustrate the British victory at Tel-el-Kebir. Here General Sir Garnet Wolseley is being cheered on by his men as he trots into history.

"It was a walk over, chaps."

The construction of the Suez Canal proved to be of enormous benefit to Britain. It made the passage to India and to all the colonies and dominions in the east much swifter. In addition, it put a lot of 'shekels' in the pockets of French and British shareholders.

Discontented officers of the Egyptian Army thought they should have a bigger say in what was going on in their country. In 1882 they seized power from the government of Khedive Tawfiq. Britain and France were not going to stand for this. An Anglo-French fleet arrived off Alexandria and bombarded the coastal defences. It was hoped that this would be enough for the rebel commander, Ahmed Urabi, to 'see sense'. It wasn't.

General Garnet Wolseley gathered a force of over thirty thousand men from Malta, Cyprus and Aden, and went ashore intending to march across the Nile delta from Alexandria to Cairo. They failed to reach their objective. Wolseley tried a different approach. With forty warships and troops from Britain and India, he steamed into the Suez Canal. They disembarked at Ismailia and prepared for the march on Cairo. Wolseley followed the line of the railway track. Close by the Sweetwater Canal carried fresh water from the Nile to Ismailia, very useful for troops preparing for battle.

The Egyptians dug in at Tel-el-Kebir. Wolseley examined the defences personally, declared them flimsy and noted that the outposts were not manned at night. The surrounding area of desert was flat with no obstructions. It was like a huge parade ground. The plan was very simple: move into position under cover of darkness, mount a frontal attack and drive Urabi and his men off the field of battle.

With parade ground precision, Highlanders, Guards, infantry and cavalry arrived in front of the Egyptian positions overnight. At dawn they checked their dressing and marched on into battle. The Guards Brigade, led by one of Queen Victoria's sons, fixed bayonets and charged. Captain Jimmy Foster filled in the gory details when he retold the story to his nephew. About two thousand Egyptians died on that day, and fifty-seven British troops were killed.

Wolseley took the train to Cairo, and Khedive Tawfiq, Britain's man, was reinstated. Lieutenant James Foster of the Grenadier Guards received the Egypt Medal, with the head of Queen Victoria on it, and the Khedive's Star.

This was a different story to the one told by Corporals Garbett and Bryan seventy years later.

IN THE LAND OF THE PHARAOHS

In the heart of Norton village adjoining the stables of the pub were the cowsheds of Yew Tree Farm. On cold winter mornings the steamy breath of the beasts within mingled and drifted through the doorways, and even out between the roof tiles. This was the world Paul Garbett was born into. Before school began he was among the cows helping his father with the milking. Many of his schoolmates 'followed their father' to become carpenters, blacksmiths or labourers. Paul went to Home Farm.

He didn't learn anything new, he simply carried out the same tasks his father had taught him. George Griffin, the farm manager, was a distant, difficult man with a strange turn of phrase. He sounded as if he had just stepped off a pirate ship. "Do as I tell ee, Paul, me lad."

Being born to follow the plough did not mean that young men like Paul enjoyed the work. There was nothing romantic about this sort of drudgery. For boys in post-war Britain there was a way out, if they chose to take it. Time spent during the years of National Service could be used to prepare for a new trade. Coal miners and farmworkers were in reserved occupations. They could stay at home. Paul was a useful lad at Home Farm. Mr Griffin wanted to keep him. "I can get ee deferred."

259

George was not at all pleased when Paul refused the offer and accepted the invitation of Her Majesty to join the county regiment. In March 1953 he reported to Copthorne Barracks. The medical officer offered him a card covered in coloured spots, "What can you see on that?"

"Forty-five, sir."

"No, Forty-eight, you're colour-blind. Off you go, Ordnance Corps."

The list of postings, pinned up for the newly qualified clerks of the RAOC, informed Paul Garbett that when he left Blackdown Camp he would be shipped off to the Canal Zone. If Paul had known where he was going to spend over twelve months of his youth he may have read articles in the *News of the World* more carefully. There were reports of *Convoys ambushed along the Sweetwater Canal*; *Trains Derailed by Bombs*; *Bodies of British Servicemen Dragged through the Streets.*

A cruise from Liverpool on board *HMT Lancashire* across the Bay of Biscay and through the Mediterranean ended halfway along the Suez Canal at Ismailia. A short truck ride put Paul down in the compound at Tel-el-Kebir, (T.E.K) to the residents. They were a mixed bunch, Highland Light Infantry, the East Surrey Regiment, infantrymen who did the patrolling in dusty and dangerous areas. Then there were the Somalis who were not speaking to the British and the Mauritians whom the British were not allowed to speak to. Top of the pile, without any doubt, were the men of Royal Army Ordnance Corps. It was they who had the billets not the tents, and toilets not latrines dug down-wind near the perimeter fence.

Paul was particularly privileged because he was a clerk (general duties) in the company office, and as such was excused guard duty. He had little to worry about provided he could produce company orders daily without a typing error. Company commanders came and went, mostly unambitious Captains unlikely ever to be promoted to Major. One, a 'mad Scot', may have been removed to a mental institution. He was a practicing 'headbanger'. If anything disturbed him he would storm into his office, slam the door and bang his head against it repeatedly.

Apart from acts of terrorism outside the depot a serious problem inside was pilfering, apparently a national pastime in Egypt. There were at least ten miles of perimeter fence to guard; difficult to patrol. The 'Gipos' cut through the wire regularly and ran off with anything that was not tied down, and even tents that *were* tied down. Within the Ordnance Depot gangs of local labourers were employed to move stores. They were kept in order by one of their own who wielded a long cane, and chased them squealing along the gangways of the warehouses.

For squaddies who were sporty there were football tournaments, boxing matches and games of cricket. The NAAFI was for boozers and the Church of Scotland Centre was for teetotallers. For anyone wanting to escape to Hollywood there was the AKC Cinema.

Sometimes Paul's duties did take him down the road to Ismailia. With the rank of Corporal he was the man in charge, he had to draw a Sten gun from the armoury. He was a '1ˢᵗ class shot' with a Lee-Enfield rifle, but the Sten gun was a far more dangerous weapon, so erratic that it might kill anyone, friend or foe, standing nearby.

For decades the Egyptians had wanted to see the back of the British. Socialists, royalists, liberals and military men were all agreed on one thing: the British had to go. The situation was complicated by the Cold War. Concerned by the spread of communism, 'containment' was the policy of the West. The Canal Zone was an important part of this strategy. Arabs, Jews, Russians, Americans and the old colonialists, Britain and France, all had an interest.

Corporal Garbett also had an interest in turning the pages of the calendar and planning their return to the United Kingdom. In the meantime he needed to stay healthy in the Canal Zone where Egyptian youths were practising guerrilla warfare, and Egyptian flies were crawling over his breakfast porridge. The threat of terrorism didn't stop Paul doing some sightseeing in Cairo. In the National Museum there were no tourists, only academics, archaeologists and students. He examined the treasures of Tutankhamen at his leisure. At Giza he crawled into a burial chamber in the very heart of a pyramid. On a repeat visit forty years later, he was jostled by the crowds.

During his tour of duty, Corporal Garbett accumulated three weeks leave. He could have flown home but knew that returning at the end of leave would be a wrench and chose to fly to Cyprus instead.

261

At Famagusta, on the north coast, there was sun, sand, a cooling sea breeze and time to do a bit more sightseeing.

One more cruise on the *Empire Orwell* brought him back to Southampton. The longest three weeks of his army career were spent waiting for demob at Feltham near Heathrow. The airport was on a heath then, surrounded by market gardens, not covered with transit hotels as it is today.

For the willing and well qualified there was plenty of work. Factories all over England had 'vacancy' signs at the gates. Paul went from company clerk at Tel-el-Kebir to costing clerk at Farmer Bros (Agricultural Engineers) in Shifnal. No more hoeing beet for George Griffin at Home Farm.

LET NO MAN PUT ASUNDER

Cliff Bryan had lost his father. The headmaster at the Grammar School gave him some advice. "Join the Army." Cliff did just that when he was fifteen. This proved to be a mistake. The boy soldier began three years training at Aldershot and all went well. He graduated into the regular army and he married the girl of his dreams. Things looked promising.

The Canal Zone was no place to begin married life. The wives of servicemen were intimidated when they went shopping. The situation worsened after five British servicemen were killed. More than a thousand families were moved out of Ismailia in 1951; some decided to fly home. The town was declared 'out of bounds' to British troops, and more lives were lost trying to maintain order along the Canal.

Corporal Bryan had been married for just a fortnight when his name appeared on company orders. He was posted to the Canal Zone for a three-year unaccompanied tour. He was numb, he could do nothing, the military machine took over; report there, sign here, check new issue of tropical kit, move out. Surrounded by dozens of lads waiting at Googe Street Underground Station for transport to Stansted, he still could not believe what was happening to him.

The RAF Hastings touched down in Malta, warm and sunny in August. The 'troops in transit' filed past a row of solemn cooks and had a lukewarm meal slopped onto a tray. They sat down and started to chat. There was some excitement. Lads with nothing to keep them in England were looking forward to a bit of 'active service'. Cliff Bryan was leaving behind everything he held dear. He recalled the words of the parson, "What therefore God hath joined together let no man put asunder." Was the British Army aware of this?

From the air, troops arriving at RAF Fayid could see rows of huts, rows of tents, all covered in dust and surrounded by wire. There was nothing attractive about this place. To reach his final destination Cliff boarded a windowless train. He sat squinting at the heat haze over the desert, sweating in a uniform better suited to the Yorkshire Moors. "What the hell am I doing here on a Bank Holiday Monday?"

At Ismailia, Corporal Bryan began his three-year unaccompanied tour. He counted the days and accumulated leave. Paul Garbett had opted for a holiday in Cyprus. Cliff flew home to see his wife; worse still he had to fly back. There had to be a way out.

Military morale was low everywhere. When the Korean War came to an end, dissatisfied servicemen were given the option to 'purchase discharge'. Corporal Cliff Bryan bought himself out. Life could now begin. The Canal Zone had been a miserable, and for many, dangerous place. Over forty years later the British Government recognised this by issuing veterans with the General Service Medal. This was small compensation.

THE BUTTON BOY

Fred Brown lost his wife to the Luftwaffe when they bombed his home in Chesterfield, and ten years later lost his two sons to the British Crown. Arthur and Joe both left the Grammar School at fifteen. Arthur went as a boy entrant to the RAF, and a year later Joe became a boy seaman.

Classroom studies continued, naval history was added to maths and English, and there was a lot of PT. Physical training, marching at double-time, cross-country running, boxing and swimming made boy seamen very fit. The men responsible for the training had a reputation; they were 'hard taskmasters', 'firm but fair', or just plain 'sadistic bastards'.

The most prominent feature at HMS *Ganges* was the mast taken from the deck of HMS *Cordelia* and fixed firmly in solid ground at Shotley. It was nearly as high as Nelson's column and played a big part in the passing-out ceremony for boy seamen. The chosen division manned the mast from bottom to top. At the very top, standing to attention was the 'button boy'. This boy had a lot of nerve or no imagination.

Standing on 'the button' the boy seaman did get some support from the lightning conductor gripped between his knees. Being struck by lightning was the least of his worries.

"What a lovely view from the top!"

While Joe Brown was learning seamanship at Ganges, trouble was brewing in the Middle East. An agreement was made with Colonel Nasser that British troops would be withdrawn from the Canal Zone by 1956, and indeed they were, but not before Anthony Eden, the British Prime Minister, had made a fool of himself. None of the main characters who played a part in the Suez Crisis came away with any credit.

Nasser claimed that Egyptians were neutral in the Cold War, which meant he could appeal to both sides for support in his plan to develop the country's resources. The Americans, who feared the spread of communism, agreed to finance the building of the Aswan Dam that would control the waters of the Nile, and greatly improve Egyptian agriculture. Support for this project was cancelled when Nasser bought arms from communist Czechoslovakia. He then had to find money to complete the dam. The Suez Canal Company was a very profitable business, and in July 1956 Nasser announced that it would be nationalised. For three months attempts were made to find a diplomatic solution. In the meantime Britain and France assembled a fleet in the Mediterranean and built up their forces in the region in preparation for an invasion.

Powerful outsiders, Canadians, New Zealanders and Australians who in the past had given Britain full support in any crisis, could see that Eden was making a mistake and told him so. In the House of Commons a score of Labour MPs voiced their opposition, and even the Tory cabinet was split over it. Despite widespread protests the build-up of forces for Operation Musketeer continued. Reservists were called up. They were probably the unhappiest of all those asked to take part in what proved to be a pointless exercise.

Joe Brown's division manned *Cordelia*'s mast for the passing-out parade. The button boy had swung safely down to earth and the boy seamen went on to learn a trade. When Joe had mastered the old skills of semaphore and the more efficient Morse code then he was ready to join the crew of a real ship. HMS *Eagle* was Britain's largest and fastest aircraft carrier. Joe once pored over a cut-away drawing of this mighty ship in the centre pages of the *Eagle*, a popular comic for boys. Other boy seaman must have done the same; it was their dream to serve on this famous ship.

Nelson went to sea when he was twelve, Joe and his classmates were seventeen, but still considered too young for active service. To man the invasion fleet for Suez naval regulations were changed. Boy seamen became ordinary seamen overnight and Joe got a chance to put his signalling skills into practise. Excitement mounted as Firework Night drew closer. 'Remember, remember the 5th of November'.

At five in the morning on the 5th of November 1956, men of the 3rd Battalion of the Parachute Regiment floated down onto El Gamil airfield, west of Port Said, and let off some fireworks. The RAF joined in and dropped a few 'bangers'. There were fierce skirmishes with the Egyptians, but by the end of the day British troops were in control of the area.

Mr Bulganin, the Russian Prime Minister, put a damper on Guy Fawkes Night celebrations. He sent a note to Anthony Eden threatening military action against any aggressors in Egypt. The American President also made it clear that he would not give support to Britain and France in this adventure.

Overnight the Royal Navy prepared for their big day. At four in the morning their guns began to pound the defences of Port Said. Before five o'clock Marine Commandos were swarming ashore; more arrived by helicopters. It was clear that the Egyptians could not hold out for long against the elite troops of Britain and France attacking from the Mediterranean, and the Israeli Army advancing in Sinai.

However, on the New York Stock Exchange, the British pound was taking a hammering. The Americans refused to prop up sterling until Britain and France agreed to withdraw their forces from Egypt. A ceasefire was ordered. Lives had been lost and nothing had been gained. Slowly British forces withdrew, and by Christmas most were on their way home.

Soldiers, sailors and airmen who had taken part in Operation Musketeer were rewarded with the General Service Medal (Near East). Joe Brown was among the youngest to receive it. His career in the Royal Navy was about to begin. The Prime Minister resigned, the political career of Anthony Eden was at an end.

Chapter 24

Keeping an Ear to the Ground

A RED MIST APPEARED BEFORE THEIR EYES

The first 'Red Scare' gripped America in 1917 following the Russian Revolution and the founding of a communist state. The second scare added another word to the dictionary, 'McCarthyism'. Senator Joe McCarthy inspired witch-hunters. Hollywood stars, union leaders and left-wing intellectuals were all asked to explain their 'un-American activities' in front of anti-Communist panels. Certainly a lot was revealed. There were Soviet spies working in government departments but Charlie Chaplin was not one of them.

In Europe communists had put themselves in the front line in the fight against fascism. The International Brigade fought hard against Franco in the Spanish Civil War. Many Austrian communists paid with their lives when Hitler took over their country. Communists formed the backbone of 'The Resistance' in France and Greece. The outcome of the war would have been very different had it not been for the mighty efforts of the Russians. Could they be trusted in peacetime?

Throughout the Cold War, British agents were sent out worldwide to gather intelligence. Most of it was of doubtful value but it did help Ian Fleming and the makers of James Bond films. Spy stories had always been popular. A favourite tale with a generation of schoolboys was *Kim* by Rudyard Kipling. Colonel Creighton, of the Indian Survey Department, trained Kim as a map-maker and spy and sent him off to gather information on India's North West Frontier. The Russians, the British and the French all had an interest in Afghanistan even then. Adventurous boys read about Kim and the survey department; they all wanted to play a part in the Great Game.

At Government House in Calcutta Lieutenant William Spowers was 'licking his wounds' received in Italy. He recovered sufficiently to take part in the assault on Mandalay and help drive the Japanese out of Burma. He was wounded again for his troubles. None of this put him off life in the Army; he soldiered on as a Captain in the Grenadier Guards. This was all true, not one of Kipling's stories.

From Crew to Baghdad

In May 1948, the State of Israel was born. It had been a difficult labour and British troops stationed there were glad it was over. From then on the Jews took on responsibility for their own security. Eddie Goulburn's Grenadiers were the last to leave. The guardsmen moved to Libya into Giallo Barracks, once used by Italian cavalry.

After active service in Palestine they now returned to routine soldiering; exercises, parades and inspections, but not Guardsman Rowley. He was introduced to a new officer.

This was not a 'cloak and dagger' operation. Captain Spowers and Guardsman Rowley drove around in a shiny Rolls Royce with a union jack on the front. Who would suspect they were gathering information for Military Intelligence?

Permission given by Bill Rowley

"Spick and span and ready for the road."

"This is Captain Spowers. He's looking for a driver." Bill Rowley had been behind the wheel of a variety of army vehicles, bouncing over rough terrain. He would have to be a bit more careful with the Rolls-Royce. He had some practise on tarmacked roads around Crewe. Mechanics at the Rolls-Royce factory gave him advice on how to keep the bodywork gleaming, and the engine purring efficiently. Motor and driver were then shipped off to North Africa.

Back in Tripoli Bill packed his kit and a toolbox in the boot of the 'Roller', and Captain Spowers checked his survey equipment. They were ready to follow in the tracks of Kim and the fictitious Colonel Creighton of the Indian Survey Department.

Rowley and Spowers were taken off the payroll of the 1st Battalion Grenadier Guards and paid by the War Office instead. This was where Captain Spowers filed his reports. Geographic survey was the responsibility of Military Intelligence, Section 3, when it was set up in the early part of the twentieth century. MI3 was absorbed into MI6 at the end of the Second World War and is now a department of SIS, the Secret Intelligence Service.

For the next three years Rowley and Spowers toured the Middle East from the border of Morocco to Baghdad. The Captain gathered intelligence, and his driver collected souvenirs and took pictures for his photo album. *This is the Mount of Olives, taken before the Jews took over*, and *The Italians put up this monument when they were in charge in Libya*. Bill had an impressive collection. *Emperor Haile Salassi, visit to Cairo*, also *The Bridge over the Tigris in Baghdad*.

On occasions when Captain Spowers flew back to England to file his reports at the War Office, Bill went back to the depot at Purbright, and on to 16 Cheswardine Lane, Norton. One leave was cut short by a telegram. "It just says, report to barracks."

No questions asked; this was the nature of the work. Officer and driver spent a lot of time in each other's company. They became friends for life. They drove together, dined together, swam together and jumped together. Spowers had been a platoon commander with the Parachute Regiment in Italy. Every year he liked to renew his 'wings'. He encouraged Bill Rowley to jump out of a Dakota over the Egyptian desert. This did not appear on his military record but a lot of what they did was not recorded.

Just before Rowley and Spowers teamed up, the Foreign Office appointed a new First Secretary at the British Consulate in Istanbul. His work involved overseeing British agents in the region. There were many strange men in the shadowy world of British Intelligence, men like Colonel David Smiley, an aristocratic cavalry officer. The First Secretary set him the task of changing the regime in Albania, and he was well qualified to do this. He had helped guerrillas establish the communist state there in 1943, and now he was going to plot its downfall. Changing sides was just part of the job. Smiley found recruits, some former Nazi collaborators, and gave them commando training in Libya. Several groups were dispatched to Albania to undermine the communist government. Most of the infiltrators were caught; about three hundred were shot. It was suspected that details of Operation Valuable had been leaked. The First Secretary was a suspect.

Spowers and Philby, the First Secretary, did have things in common. They both knew North Africa and Italy and India, and as boys had probably both read *Kim*. That was how Harold Philby got his nickname. 'Kim' Philby defected to Russia in 1963, and died in Moscow in 1988, a disillusioned double agent.

The Grenadier Guards' tour of duty in Libya came to an end. Captain Spowers was planning an overland trip to the family home in Melbourne, Australia.

"Rowley, you must come. I'll have a word with Colonel Eddie."

The Colonel certainly knew Guardsman Rowley well enough. He had often passed the family home on the way down to Apley Hall. "Absolutely not! I cannot allow it." That was that. There had to be an explanation but none was given.

Back home on leave, Bill opened a letter with a Melbourne postmark and in it Bill Spowers set out the details of the trip he had just completed: Baghdad, Istanbul, Trabzon, Kabul. Then over the border to Islamabad, Calcutta, Bombay. Spower's old haunts in India had little changed since the days of Kipling and the background for *Kim* and the Great Game.

COLD WAR ON THE EQUATOR

The Special Operators of 'Y' Branch were subject to the Official Secrets Act; they didn't have any choice. They couldn't disclose the nature of their work to anyone. As far as Roy Coles was concerned there wasn't much to tell. The most interesting bits of his military service were the off-duty hours.

In the first week of January 1960, the administrators at Catterick Camp decided that they were going to convert a draftsman into

270

a signalman. Men of Corps of the Signals, Education Corps, Pay Corps, and Intelligence Corps were not expected to display great skill on the parade square. They had other talents. Nevertheless, they were barked at by drill corporals, stamped about for a few weeks, 'passed out' and went on to learn a new trade.

At Garats Hay Camp in Leicestershire, Signalman Coles became a Special Operator capable of receiving Morse code at thirty words a minute. 'Y' operators were not expected to send many messages. They were just going to 'listen in'. Station Y, at Beaumanor Hall nearby, was where messages transmitted by the Germans were intercepted during the war years. At Station X, Bletchley Park, the messages were decoded and translated. During the Cold War, Russian, German and Chinese linguists worked alongside the signallers listening in to military and diplomatic chatter.

From this lush green fox-hunting country, Roy was flown out to Cyprus to a sunny seaside town. There could not have been a better start to a package holiday than being flown out on a Bristol Britannia. The Queen's Flight used the same aircraft. The state of emergency in Cyprus was over, and for the time being the atmosphere more relaxed. After six sunny weeks with the 9th Signals Regiments at Famagusta, Roy broke the soldiers' golden rule. He volunteered. He agreed to a transfer to Kenya. After the beach holiday it was time to go on safari.

Roy then embarked on the most dangerous episode of his military service. He flew first to El Adem, a staging post in Libya. This RAF base was surrounded by sand and Second World War minefields, not a place to spend any time at all. Roy was there for about twelve hours. He was flying on an RAF Hastings. In the desert below was the wreck of one of these aircraft. This was not the only one of these aircraft to fall out of the sky. The Hastings chugged over the Sahara to Khartoum and after a brief stop headed south towards the equator. On the approach to Nairobi, Roy took a photograph over the wing. Black oil was streaming over the cowlings of all four engines. This was alarming but quite normal, and they landed safely.

Signalman Coles had landed on his feet; he had what soldiers describe as a 'cushy number'. With 637 Signals Troop, Roy practised his new trade and played all day with the latest communication equipment. Off duty he practised and played with something he really loved – bat and ball. His talents were spotted, particularly his dangerous spin bowling that had confused so many hopeful batsmen on cricket fields all around Bridgnorth. He was selected to play for the Combined Services Team. Corporal Roy Coles was the odd man out; all the other team members were officers. That didn't matter. He had a Land Rover and a driver at his disposal to take him to fixtures. He did wonder, *Was the British taxpayer aware of what was going on?*

Meanwhile, in Europe, lads in armoured cars were patrolling the barbed wire border separating East and West Germany. These were Cold War warriors. It was hard to imagine that signallers just south of the equator were part of the same team. The opposing ideologies of communism and capitalism played a dangerous game, constantly trying to outmanoeuvre each other. Information gathering was a vital part of the game.

All over Africa the European powers were granting independence to their old colonies, sometimes gracefully, sometimes after bloody conflict. Of all the colonial powers Belgium was the worst. The Congo had been poorly administered and was ill-prepared for independence. Within a week of the celebrations the army had mutinied. Patrice Lumumba, the Congolese Prime Minister, asked the Russians for military assistance. Fearing the spread of communism, the United States 'arranged' the assassination of Lumumba by Belgian paratroopers. A UN force was sent to restore law and order, and prevent other nations becoming involved. The Congo was a fine example of a country where everyone wanted to get involved. The Katanga province had a lot to offer including copper, uranium and industrial diamonds.

What would be the Soviets' next move? What could Corporal Coles and the rest of the 637 Signals Troop do about it? Over a thousand miles from the action, they couldn't keep an eye on the Russians so the signaller intercepted their messages, and the linguist tried to make some sense of them. Everyone was at it, the KGB, the CIA, British Military Intelligence and probably the South Africans as well. There was no solution to the problems in the Congo; fifty years of chaos followed.

Kenya had troubles of its own during the 1950s. The path to independence had been a bloody one. Mau Mau gangs mainly from the Kikuyu Tribe terrorised the population, targeting white farmers and their black workers. Thousands of Kenyans died and thousands were held in detention including Jomo Kenyatta. He was released in 1961 and became Kenya's first Prime Minister. He did recognise the contribution white settlers made to the economy and encouraged them to stay on in the country. Servicemen touring the country on local leave were always welcomed by the white farmers and their daughters.

Roy made the most of his local leave visiting some of the places that would be part of package tour itineraries of the future. Thomson's Falls spilling out of a gap in the forest plunged seventy metres onto craggy boulders below; spray rose up to keep the surrounding bush permanently drenched. Colourful birdlife was everywhere; downstream hippos snorted and squabbled in the river. For wildlife on a large scale he drove to the plains near the Longonot Crater where herds of wildebeest and zebra ran together. Giraffes cropped leaves from the acacia trees avoiding the one with the sleeping leopard. If all this was too exciting for a young signalman, there was always 'rest and recuperation' at the Silversands leave camp near Mombasa.

Stewards in starched white tunics carried cold beers out onto the terrace for thirsty young squaddies. They gazed out over the Indian Ocean at white coral sands, a shimmering sea and swaying palms. All this at government expense!

Lucky lads; few could enjoy safaris and beach holidays like this before the days of package tours.

Permission given by Roy Coles

"Another drink? No thanks, I'm not feeling too bright this morning."

273

In the morning, those with a sore head and troubled by the glare did not appreciate the beauty of the sunrise across Nyali Beach. It can be spectacular. It couldn't last.

In blazer and flannels, Roy boarded the Boeing 707 at Embakasi Airport. The homeward-bound flight was altogether more comfortable than the outward bound. There was still trouble in the Congo; there was fighting on the ground. Roy was above it all, even above the mountains of clouds piled up over the tropical forests, and the crackle of electric storms. Rainforests gave way to grassland over Nigeria, and by the time they touched down at Kano Airport there was little greenery to be seen.

After a refuelling stop and just enough time to take a black and white 'snap' to record his visit, the Boeing was airborne again over the Sahara. Not a cloud in the sky, below mile after mile of desert until they crossed the Mediterranean coast. There were signs of winter weather over France and Roy was reminded of how dismal it can be in Britain especially in North Yorkshire.

There must have been some local lads who had pleaded to stay at Catterick so that they could go home regularly to see their 'mam', and tuck into the Sunday roast with piles of Yorkshire pudding running with gravy. The alternative could have been an eighteen-month-long sightseeing holiday with warm sandy beaches and lots of cricket in the sun. Corporal Coles was 'processed'. That was the end of his military service and the end of National Service for everyone.

A CHARM OFFENSIVE

In the officers' mess of the 8th Hussars, broad grins, cheers and raised glasses greeted Colonel Cuthie when he returned to take command again. For four years he continued to inspire and entertain his men and then, in 1950, he was given a desk job. He didn't complain. He was back in Egypt as military attaché. An attaché might advise on education or agriculture and might help to set up a defence force. The Egyptians didn't need any advice on agriculture or defence. Diplomatic relations between Britain and Egypt had never been good. After the battle of Tel-el Kebir in 1822, Britain took over the administration of the country which was then part of the Ottoman Empire. The Turks fought with the Germans in the Great War. Britain made Egypt a protectorate and it became the base for operations in the Middle East. Egypt was granted independence in 1922. Britain still maintained a military presence and an atmosphere of resentment persisted.

In the opening stages of the Second World War, when Italian and German forces appeared to have the upper hand, King Farouk and his government would have been pleased to see British, Anzac and Indian forces pushed out of Egypt. The king was forced to replace his pro-German government with one more sympathetic to the allies. He never forgave Britain for their intervention. Egypt remained diplomatically neutral and only declared war on Germany in 1945 when it was clear that they were going to lose. It was hard to take King Farouk seriously. He was a gambler, a glutton and a womaniser.

The poem with the shortest title must be *If* by Rudyard Kipling. It begins:

If you can keep your head when all about you are losing theirs and blaming it on you

This certainly applied to Brigadier C Goulburn DSO. Kipling went on to describe the sort of qualities that made a man, an outstanding man.

If you can talk with crowds and keep your virtue, or walk with Kings – nor lose the common touch.

Cuthie Goulburn could do both.

King George VI met Colonel Goulburn a couple of times and seemed quite relaxed in his company. They strolled together between the tanks of the King's Hussars shortly before they sailed for Normandy.

Earlier, when the 8th Army was preparing to deliver the final blow to Hitler's Panzers, King Farouk was invited to inspect the Desert Rats. He was dressed up for the occasion. He must have felt uncomfortable. The uniform could not hide his bulging waistline neither could he disguise his displeasure. The British were winning.

When the war was over, Farouk spent a lot of time and a fortune in the casinos, restaurants and brothels of Europe. He was able to impress a succession of mistresses by showering them with jewellery. It wasn't only Brigadier Goulburn, military attaché at the British Embassy, who found this sort of behaviour distasteful. Officers of the Egyptian Army arranged a coup and Farouk went into exile in 1952. Colonel Nasser was now the man in charge, a very popular man with the Egyptian people and probably the sort of man that Cuthie could have rubbed along with. The diplomatic service had something else in mind.

The Brigadier spoke Spanish and he had plenty of opportunity to practise in Madrid. At receptions at the embassy he stood out in his full dress uniform. Ladies found him irresistible. Military men admired his bearing on parade. Away from public duties there were mountains to climb and horses to ride. This was a rightful reward for a man who had given his all in defence of the country he loved.

With parades and parties to attend Brigadier Goulburn must have thoroughly enjoyed is duties. He was even on the Christmas card list of the King of Spain.

Apley Estate Archives

"The 'Brig' in full fig."

Apley Estate Archives

"Just another admirer."

He kept a diary over the years and added to his collection of photographs and press cuttings; simple things like the menu for a regimental dinner, a 'snap' of his favourite dog or his German housekeeper. There were of course official regimental photographs and scenes of battle. He was captured chatting with King George. King Farouk was caught looking uncomfortable on parade. A memento from the King of Spain was carefully preserved. Brigadier Goulburn did indeed 'walk with kings' – nor did he lose the common touch, Sergeant Hopper made sure of that.

A LOT TO TALK ABOUT

The Hoppers had been miners and coal merchants for generations, but when young Tom left All Saint's School in the Black Country he was apprenticed to an engineer. The war came and he became a sapper in the Royal Engineers, and was rapidly promoted. He defused bombs, built bridges and destroyed bridges. When it was all over he set up shop in

Wolverhampton. The business supplied shotguns and ammunition, rods and fishing tackle to anyone interested in country sports. If the money was good Tom had no favourites. Peers of the realm or poachers were all treated alike.

The Brig was out of uniform but Tom knew by his bearing that this was a man of rank. Straight to the point he handed over his gun and said, "Can you do anything with this?"

"Yes, sir, I certainly can."

"Were you a sapper?"

"I was."

"In Normandy and on to Berlin?"

"We came to a halt at Hamelin on the Weser." This was the sort of man Cuthie could get on with.

The Foot and Mouth Epidemic of 1967 brought them together. Tens of thousands of cattle were slaughtered; farmers lost their livelihood. Vast areas of the countryside were quarantined and access severely restricted. Ramblers in the Lake District and elsewhere had to stay at home, so did fishermen. Shoots were cancelled, game birds were happy and the salmon too. Almost overnight Tom Hopper's business collapsed. The Brigadier solved the problem. "Not to worry, Tom. Move into 'The Station' until things pick up."

Tom and Rose took up the offer and moved into Linley Station. The line had been closed, the station master gone, the waiting room empty, the flowerbeds ran wild, grass grew between the lines and in cracks on the platform. Tom and his wife became part of estate life. For over thirty years Tom was 'the Brig's right-hand man'. They spent a lot of time in each other's company, debating current affairs and swopping tales of the past. Tom recalled an event at Hamelin. This was where he could have lost his stripes.

Hamelin was where the Pied Piper made a name for himself. He played a merry tune on his flute and charmed a plague of rats out of the town and into the river. The townsfolk were very pleased but the council wouldn't pay the piper's fee. He returned and took his revenge on the children of the town. While the parents were at church he lured the little ones away with his pipe. They were never found. They may have been entombed in a cave or, like the rats, drowned in the river.

The river certainly was a place where things might disappear unexpectedly; large objects, such as a pontoon bridge. Sergeant Tom Hopper and his team were responsible for bolting the bridge together and making sure it would do the job. They stood back and watched trucks trundle across the Weser. At dusk the bridge was closed. The engineers retired and a squad of infantrymen stood guard. In the morning they had some explaining to do. The bridge had disappeared. It might have been sabotage or just a childish prank.

The Pied Piper's rats were never found. However, unlike the children he charmed away, the bridge was found twenty miles downstream. Someone must have got into hot water, but not Sergeant Hopper. He had an exemplary service record with the Royal Engineers and a knack of avoiding trouble.

In his youth Tom did a bit of 'fish farming'. Taking fish from a reservoir in Wolverhampton wasn't poaching; the fish swam in waters publicly owned. Surely they belonged to anyone who could catch them. Tom looked after his fish especially in the winter. He slid a few sheep's heads out onto the ice so that when it melted, skull, skin, rotting flesh and maggots all sank to the bottom, a tasty snack for the fish waiting below. It worked well until during an unusually cold spell the ice stayed firm, firm enough for a bailiff to walk out and examine the 'fish food'. "I know who's responsible for this. I'll have him for polluting the public water supply."

Tom was charged and brought before the magistrate. He was guilty of course, but not to the charge on the sheet. He was not guilty of polluting a river. His solicitor pointed out an error in the charge. His client had polluted a reservoir and not a river. "Case dismissed!"

Tom and the Brig shared many stories during the years they spent together.

How Cuthie Goulburn managed to fit so much into his life out of uniform is remarkable. His obituary in the *Daily Telegraph* attempted to list his interests that ranged from chairman of the West Mercia Police Authority to supporter of the Scout Movement. He was equally at ease in the company of territorial officers of the Shropshire Yeomanry or chorus girls of the operatic society. His enthusiasm was boundless. No sooner had he retired from the army than he made a name for himself locally by setting up the Ironbridge Gorge Museum Trust. He was generous, giving freely of time and money. His lasting memorial is the *Spry*, a 70-foot sailing barge that once carried iron products from the foundries of his ancestors downriver through Apley and into the wider world. Farming at Harrington, he kept in touch with the land for thirty years.

The Brig had not been well but he still felt it was his duty to attend morning service at the parish church. Rosy Cox cleared away the breakfast plates and washed up. She put on coat and Sunday hat. Tom Hopper was waiting on the drive and the three of them drove to church. The congregation was small; at the end of the service Cuthie had a word with everyone. "We'll have a run out to Harrington, Tom."

It was April and the farming year was underway. As they drove through the lanes, the Brig commented on the crops and livestock in the fields along the way. "We won't stop at the farm just now."

Tom turned the car around and they made for home. There was a pause. Tom glanced at the Brigadier. There was nothing more to say. He was dead. Tom knew that. Not wishing to distress Rosy sitting on the back seat he said,

"He's not very well. I'll drive him to Bridgnorth, to the hospital."

In the days that followed there were tributes from lords and ladies, generals and private soldiers, landowners and labourers. Cuthie Goulburn certainly never lost the common touch.

Chapter 25

On the 38ᵗʰ Parallel

FIRST FOLLY OF THE COLD WAR

The empires of Britain and France were in decline. All over the world people wanted an end to colonial rule. Communism was not the ideological force behind the unrest in Arab lands. Egyptians simply wanted the British out of Egypt and the Syrians wanted the French out of Syria, it was as simple as that.

The Americans gave some encouragement to independence movements; they could not forget that America had once been a British colony. Hasty arrangements were made for Indian Independence. A bloodbath followed. A change in the system of government did not mean a change for the better.

In other parts of the world exchanging colonialism for communism may have seemed attractive to those with little to lose, but if they compared their lot with that of Russian peasants they would have seen that life under the Soviet system was just as hard. The main feature of American foreign policy was preventing the spread of communism, and this obsession clouded their judgement.

KOREA, WHERE'S THAT?

Korea had been a Japanese colony. After the war the administration of the Korean Peninsula was shared between the Americans and the Russians. A dividing line was drawn along the 38ᵗʰ Parallel. The occupying powers set about creating separate states modelled on their own. The superpowers withdrew their occupying forces; first the Russians and then the Americans in June 1949. Almost immediately the North Korean Army swept south until only the port of Pusan remained in the hands of the South Koreans, and would have fallen if the Americans had not intervened.

No amount of diplomatic pressure changed the situation. A United Nations force was assembled with the aim of restoring the boundary between the North and the South.

In May 1951, in Hong Kong harbour, cheeky boys not long out of school were only half listening when General Mansergh made his farewell speech on Holt's Wharf. It wasn't a great speech. He rambled on about regimental history and what a fine job the King's Shropshire Light Infantry had done over the last century, and how they could be relied on to do well again in Korea. There wasn't a big crowd to see them off; dock workers, a few senior officers, and a handful of soldiers' wives with toddlers. Bandsmen of the South Staffordshire Regiment played a selection of tunes from 'Annie Get Your Gun'. Those who could remember some of the words joined in as they climbed aboard the USS *Montrose*.

At four in the afternoon the *Montrose* cast off from the wharf. On board, the Shropshire's own band struck up with the regimental march, 'Old Towler', then both bands joined together to play 'Auld Lang Syne'. White handkerchiefs waved by the wives were lowered to wipe away tears. In the front rank a girl bent over a black pram to comfort a crying baby.

The Korean War was described by historians as the war neither side dared to win. The North Koreans came close to occupying the whole of the country. The Americans poured into the port of Pusan and held them off. Douglas McArthur, the US commander, landed a large force of UN troops at Inchon and pressed on north towards China. He prepared to cross the border. This would have been a disaster. President Truman intervened and recalled McArthur to Washington. Using nuclear weapons to bring the war swiftly to an end was considered. Invading China or dropping an atom bomb might well have triggered a Third World War.

After lengthy negotiations the conflict came to an end in 1953. The 1st Battalion KSLI served longer in Korea than any other infantry regiment.

SKITTLED OUT IN THE BOWLING ALLEY

Father and son worked side by side for John Foster on his farm at Newton. The pay was poor but the view was fine from the front garden of the

Smith's cottage. Shropshire fields stretched away to the Staffordshire border, and there was so much sky above, a beautiful place, peaceful and homely. The cottage gardens, neatly kept, supplied vegetables and fruit in season. When the many damson trees were in bloom, it was a perfect picture. Why leave a place like this and go to the ends of the Earth to fight in a war that no one understood?

Miners, merchant seamen and the criminally insane could claim exemption from National Service. The same applied to farmworkers. Alex Smith followed his father's example and chose to leave the land and wear khaki. Gordon Smith from Friar's Street in Bridgnorth and Alex Smith from Newton reported to Copthorne Barracks on the same day. They were both going to have a rough time.

Marching, handling weapons, spitting, polishing, cursing, painting stones white and then more marching at a hundred and forty steps a minute, this was called basic training. After Copthorne, the pick of the bunch went off to a foreign land, Yorkshire. After ten more weeks they were infantrymen. It would have been most fitting for Alex to join the county regiment. Instead he was drafted into the Durham Light Infantry and promptly shipped off to Korea.

The papers were full of reports of the battles in Korea, at places no one had ever heard of before 1950. The new recruits to the DLI were first given some idea of what life on the front line would be like at the Battle School at Fan Ling in the New Territories of Hong Kong. Instructors from the Royal Ulster Rifles left them in no doubt that serving in Korea was not going to be pleasant. The Durham privates put on a brave face. "Let's get on with it."

Underneath there was anxiety, but once the order was given there was no time to dwell on the situation. A boat ride to Japan, pick up more kit, boat to Pusan in South Korea, pile onto the train and off up country. There was hardly time to think. Sitting on the slatted wooden seats, surrounded by packs and rifles, those next to the windows looked out glumly across the dreary countryside. They jollied each other along. "Cheer up, mate, it might never happen."

It was different sitting alone at the end of the carriage, crouched over a hole in the floor, trousers round the ankles, watching the track flash past below.

"What the bloody 'ell am I doing 'ere."

Nothing had changed in nearly forty years. Conditions for troops in the trenches on the front line in Korea were just as dreadful as those experienced by their fathers in France during the Great War.

"Very good advice."

The new boys arrived at Company Headquarters and were greeted by 'old sweats' in their late teens. The company commander addressed them briefly and Alex was introduced to Lieutenant John Pearce, a National Service officer from Market Drayton, another Salopian. How different was the landscape John and Alex had grown up in compared with the scarred hills that surrounded them now?

John Pearce's training as a surveyor was very useful in the minefields in 'no man's land', where his Assault Pioneer Platoon spent many nervous hours. Their experience was little different from that of men who had been in Flanders well over thirty years before. In some ways it was worse. A white Christmas was guaranteed, with forty degrees of frost. Christmas came and went. John Pearce and his platoon went in and out of the line. They were tasked with demolition work, minefield maintenance and wiring; always in danger.

Maps of the area were redrawn by Army Intelligence and the main features given names that made sense to the troops. Lieutenant Pearce explained, "We are on Hill 159...The line of contact is called 'The Bowling Alley'...The opposition are sitting on that row of hills across the valley, the four apostles, Matthew, Mark, Luke and John...John is Hill 227 on the map."

The King died in February 1952. The following June his daughter,

284

Elizabeth, was crowned. The Queen's Coronation Honours List was published and John Pearce was on the list. Part of the citation for his Military Cross described how, 'on the second occasion, on the night of 26/27 Jan. 1953, near Pt.159 he again entered a minefield, without a detector and with skill and courage affected the dangerous task of getting out a wounded man.'

A youthful Lieutenant Pearce poses outside company headquarters sporting the bright new ribbon of his Military Cross.

"Cheerful Hero."

He didn't think twice about it. The wounded man was one of his platoon, a close companion, Alex Smith. A telegram arrived at the Smiths' door at Newton which told them that Alex had been wounded. It didn't say how seriously. He was evacuated to an American Military Hospital in Japan.

When his wound was first assessed by an American doctor, it was decided to amputate the leg. An Australian surgeon believed the limb could be saved and he took responsibility for the operation. Alex was the perfect patient and certainly enjoyed the attention of the Australian nurses in their starched white uniforms. He never said how the other patients reacted when he learned to play the bugle. "I can't do jigsaws all day long."

When he was fit to travel he was flown home in an RAF Hastings. The aircraft was fitted with racks to hold the stretchers for those unable to walk. At RAF Lyneham, medical orderlies and a nursing sister in a blue cape were there on the tarmac to receive yet another planeload of casualties. Green fields all around and fresh Wiltshire air, it was as good as a tonic.

The Smith family moved to Old Park Farm. Labouring on the farm was hard even for those in good health. Alex had some luck. He moved to lodgings in Bridgnorth and started to drive buses for Wolverhampton Corporation, and there he met his wife. Drawn back to the land he tried his hand at farm work again, but it was too much and he had to settle for a factory job. He never complained. "Plenty worse off than me."

He served the Apley Legion well as standard bearer and bugler. Veterans of all campaigns gathered around the memorial cross in Stockton churchyard on cold November mornings and listened as their president read the names of the fallen. In the silence that followed, faces and places appeared before them: jungle and bare mountain, sand and sea, places with no name like Point 159 on the battle map of Korea. Some had scars to remind them. 'Only a scratch' in their youth became a handicap in old age. Alex did not allow his wound to ruin his life; he remained cheerful to the end.

Lieutenant John Pearce MC, his old platoon commander, had the last word. Gathered in Worfield Church among the local mourners were men who were strangers to the parish. As John spoke there were smiles and chuckles. The congregation made their way to the cricket club after the ceremony. With beer and sandwiches inside them the 'strangers' revealed themselves. They were all old comrades, veterans of the Korean War. "Good lad he was, he would have enjoyed this."

BACK TO NORMAL – NOT QUITE THE SAME

Harry Richards examined his new medals; one with the head of the young Queen, the other from the United Nations, a globe with a wreath around it and a clasp that said KOREA. Harry was home, National Service done. He wandered up the lane from Home Farm and slipped into the pub.

"How do, 'arry, enjoy it out there did you?"

It wasn't worth making a reply.

"Give us a pint."

Harry had followed the same trail as Alex Smith. Copthorne Barracks , Hong Kong, Korea and back, except he was back in one piece. There were no wild celebrations. He had a few drinks in the Hundred House and put his feet up for a day or two.

One afternoon he took his bike and fishing rod from the shed and rode down to the river. He went to his favourite spot, a sandy bank near the remains of an old wharf. There were still mooring rings set at head height in the masonry. It was just the same as it always had been. The sandbank shelved off into deeper water, downstream there was the overhanging willow where his line might snag.

He cut a forked stick and rested his rod. He watched the float for a while. He didn't expect to catch anything at this time of day. He looked around taking in the familiar scenery and then he looked down at his knife. Folded on the side of it was a spike, the sort scouts used to stab holes in tins of condensed milk. Near one of the mooring rings in the sandstone wall behind him he started to scratch and then carve deeper. When he had finished he glanced at the float, nothing doing, then at his handiwork on the wall:

KOREA '53
What a place that was. I wish I'd never heard of it.

Chapter 26

They Couldn't Call it a War

MEREBIMUR: WE SHALL BE WORTHY

The regimental motto reminded troopers of the 15th/19th Hussars that they had something to live up to. During the Battle of Waterloo they had covered themselves in glory and gore, and they had been collecting battle honours ever since. Robin Nicholls didn't want gore or glory, he just wanted to see a bit of the world. Mrs Coupe was ready to show him the way.

The Nicholls family home at the Leavenhalls Farm was within sight of the rectory. The rector's wife was 'chatty' and knowledgeable, even on military matters. Her first husband had been killed in the Great War; he had won the Military Cross. Her son was an officer in the Hussars. Chatting to Robin one day she said, "Captain Smalley is taking his Hussars to Malaya to chase bandits. I'm sure it will be terribly exciting."

It seemed like a good idea at the time. In the winter of 1953, Robin left the comforts of home and took the train to Carlisle for basic training with the Royal Armoured Corps. The NCOs responsible for training were not normal human beings. It was rumoured that they had been produced in a breeding unit for unmarried mothers. Certainly they were all bastards. Robin learned to withstand the barking of the drill sergeant, how to apply Brasso and Blanco, paint stones white and handle small arms. Comradeship and a common enemy kept most of the lads cheerful and they passed out.

Useful skills Robin had learned in Reginald Tildsley's workshop in Shifnal were next applied in the workshops of the Hussars. The engine of a Saracen armoured car was not dissimilar to that of a Fordson tractor.

The Hussars were about to embark on a new campaign. If they were expecting a big send off to Malaya they were disappointed. Robin and his fellow troopers were told to report to an old air-raid shelter between Warren Street and Leicester Square. Lads brought up in the country were not familiar with the London Underground system. They could see from the map that the Northern line went right through the centre of the capital, and there were some noteworthy stops along it. There was Euston, where trains left for the Midlands, Waterloo where Hussars had made a name for themselves and Highgate with the cemetery nearby. The Goodge Street transit camp was a collection of tunnels that had been enlarged during the war, and this was where troops destined for sunny lands waited in the gloom. They waited for days and not a single train came along. Then, quite suddenly, the officers made a dash for the lifts and out into the fresh air and sunlight. The troopers trooped up the stairs. They piled into trucks and trundled out into the Hertfordshire countryside. Transport aircraft were waiting at Blackbushe airfield. Five hours later they were in Rome, another five hour flight took them to Cyprus, then Bahrain, Karachi, Delhi, Bangkok and finally Singapore. It wasn't a short flight. There were two overnight stops. When the young Hussars arrived they were weary and fed up, some airsick, some homesick. They didn't have time to feel sorry for themselves. The regimental headquarters was up country, at Ipoh.

Before they boarded the train they were kitted out for jungle warfare, issued with the short-barrelled Lee-Enfield rifles and fifty rounds of ammunition. The long, long ride on the narrow gauge railway seemed to stop at every kampong (village) on the way. From Ipoh Robin they went on to Raub. The Hussars with their armoured cars escorted convoys of food and supplies to other units in the Cameron Highlands, along a narrow treacherous road with forty miles of hairpin bends.

There was always an element of danger, the possibility of ambush, a landslip or a roadside bomb. They might also encounter a nitwit.

On Robin's first trip up Fraser's Hill to Raub, he was waiting in the back of the Saracen with another novice soldier. The floor was littered with various weapons. Trooper Senseless picked up a rifle. "Oh, this gun is cocked," he observed.

"Well, don't pull the trigger!"

Too late, the round hit the differential of a vehicle parked behind and splinters of metal flew everywhere. Robin was hit in the upper arm. His silly companion was hit in the hand and 'bled like a stuck pig'. There was an enquiry and Trooper Senseless had another big slap on the wrist.

Drying out after a dip on the dusty road to the Cameron Highlands. Robin Nicholls on the left.

"15th/19th Hussars Weight-Watchers Club."

In the topics it rains like nowhere else on Earth. If there are high winds to go with it, that's a typhoon. Anything that is not lashed down is blown away. Robin and his mates were in their billet relaxing, reading tattered copies of *Reveille,* filling in the demob chart and listening to the rain drumming on the roof. The walls of the hut shuddered; one or two of the lads got off their 'pits' to look out of the window. Everyone got wet. The roof and the sides of the hut just flew off. In all, fourteen huts were damaged. One lad had a broken arm and there were cuts and bruises, but no serious casualties. This was a lucky escape.

No matter what the weather or the state of the roads convoys had to be escorted along the tortuous road to the Highlands. On one return journey a Saracen was in the wrong place at the wrong time. A tropical downpour caused a landslip that swept the vehicle off the road. Two boys died. Robin had another lucky escape.

It wasn't all misery and mayhem; there was local entertainment and romance. In steamy bars around the camps there was Tiger beer and steamy girls. Under the influence impressionable lads might be led astray. 'Tiger Lil' or 'Suzy Wong', the name was not important, were there to charm the troops. They often appeared more charming when viewed through the bottom of a beer glass. They listened to lonely soldiers sob stories and offered private treatment.

Trooper Ward was charmed by Suzy Wong; he couldn't see enough of her. Corporal Nicholls and Trooper Ward were having a quiet drink with others of their company. 'Wardie' slipped away. They understood. He was besotted, poor lad. He left a gap around the bottle-cluttered table. When the rest of the party left they spotted another gap in the row of armoured vehicles parked outside. Trooper Ward had shot off in the 'Dingo' scout car fuelled by testosterone. "***kin* *ell, we all know where he's gone, don't we?"

Corporal Nicholls was in deep trouble. He was the man in charge, and he had to make sure that military hardware did not get into the wrong hands. They didn't know the exact location of Suzie's bungalow, just the street. The splintered gateposts were a clue. The Dingo, designed for 'jungle bashing', had left its mark on these obstructions that stood between Wardie and Suzie. There was trouble; an enquiry, a severe reprimand, but in the end complete happiness. Miss 'Wong' became Mrs Ward.

Tan is a simple little word. Fine leather; calf skin, for example, is tanned. This involves carefully removing the skin from a young beast, scraping off surplus flesh, stretching, drying and curing with tannin. Robin Nicholls went through a similar process. Soldiers serving in the tropics are expected to be tanned, and quickly. No one wants to be taunted with, "Hello, milk bottle. Get your knees brown."

Shortly after arriving at Raub, Robin was given the task of painting the Daimler armoured car. He took off his shirt. There wouldn't be a problem because the sky was overcast. The sun's harmful rays penetrated the clouds and Robin got a blister on his back. This was not the usual blister the size of a fingernail or a small coin; this was the size of a small dinner plate. The medical officers were all qualified doctors. Medical orderlies came from varied backgrounds; they might have been gardeners, postmen, gamekeepers or even butchers. Robin 'reported sick' and was treated by a man who had possibly treated farm animals. A comforting pad of lint was laid over the whole ruddy area and strapped in place with surgical tape. This is the sort of material that is now used to remove unsightly body hair. Robin had been patched up. His back went from tender, to raw, to unbearable. He went for a second opinion. The same orderly ushered him in to the medical officer. To examine the wound the dressing had to come off. A technique practised by conjurers was used. If all went well the magician gripped the tablecloth and removed it with one snatch leaving plates and cutlery on the table; magic. Robin didn't see this coming. He lost the skin off his back and lost consciousness. He came to on the floor. "Take him to hospital, not mine," said the MO.

Robin was given care in the community; he went into a local hospital. His grasp of the language was limited but within a day he understood, "No meals provided." The trusty orderly came and went with drinks and titbits, but his catering skills were no better than his medical skills. Miraculously, Robin survived. Six months later the scars began to fade, but the memory lingers on.

WHAT A DRAG

At least half the troops who served in Malaya were National Servicemen which meant they were not usually there longer than eighteen months. The Malayan emergency lasted twelve years from 1948 to 1960, at the time the longest campaign involving British servicemen.

They didn't call it a war because claims for damage to the tin mines or rubber plantations would not have been met by Lloyds insurers. The mines and plantations were vital to the economy of Malaya and targeted by the CTs (Communist Terrorists). They were almost exclusively Chinese, and had fought well against the Japanese when they swept through the country from the north, and occupied it during the Second World War. The CTs were experienced in guerrilla warfare and determined to establish a communist state. The British Government knew they meant business when they assassinated the British High Commissioner in 1951. Something had to be done about it.

A strategy was developed that in the end paid off. Workers in the countryside were particularly vulnerable to attack. To protect them their villages were fortified and guarded. Foot patrols were sent out to engage with the enemy. Contacts were few but mostly successful. The infantry called this 'jungle bashing'. Pictures of teenagers in floppy hats picking their way through tropical forests hung with creepers appeared regularly in the papers at home. From a distance this looked like a rather exciting game.

Five hundred British and Commonwealth troops were killed during the campaign. Several local lads took part. The Royal Engineers gave Stewart Jones some training and rapid promotion. Second Lieutenant Jones served with a Malaysian Regiment at Kluang, in Jahore. He worked on jungle airstrips, repaired roads, built bridges and disposed of bombs. Helicopters flew from jungle clearings, and Junior Technician Arthur Brown made sure they were airworthy. In 1960 responsibility for security was handed over to Malaysian forces. British and Commonwealth troops had fought a long campaign. The new nation was stable and democratic thanks to Jones, Brown and Nicholls.

STAY OUT OF TROUBLE IF YOU CAN

Within days of leaving school Brian Jones had a shotgun in his hands and was taught how to use it by head gamekeeper, Norman Sharpe. He could not have found a more experienced tutor. After three years of training as a keeper the 'call-up' came for National Service. Brian completed two years with the Pay Corps and then he had a change of heart. He didn't go back to the woods.

For better pay he went to Sankey's, a company that did 'metal bashing' on a large scale. They thumped out the chassis of heavy vehicles and anyone who experienced the racket in the press shop could confirm that they went at it 'hammer and tongs'. After three years he marched out of the factory gates in Wellington, and in through the gates of Copthorne Barracks to join the King's Shropshire Light Infantry. In July 1963 he passed out as best recruit.

An infantryman can expect a more active career than an army pay clerk, and Brian got it. After a year of Cold War duty in Germany he returned to the historic Plumer Barracks at Plymouth and prepared for training in jungle warfare. The RAF VC10 approached the coast of British Honduras over the Caribbean. The deep blue of the sea changed abruptly at the edge of the barrier reef to a paler sparkling blue, and then to a cloudy blue-grey that spread out from the coast around Belize City. The heat and humidity of the tropics hit them when they disembarked.

Pale-skinned soldiers piled into the waiting transport and drove off to Airport Camp. On the way they noticed something odd. The telephone posts along the roadside weren't straight or upright, and some of them were growing. This was the tropics with greenhouse conditions where almost anything would grow.

Brian, who knew about woodland trees, was surprised to see pine trees growing on the ridge around the School of Jungle Warfare. This was the base for training troops destined for hot spots in other parts of the world. The dangers here were from bacteria in the drinking water, biting insects, scorpions, poisonous snakes and shrubs with evil, needle-length thorns. They encountered all these as they crawled around playing hide and seek.

At weekends scratches and stings were soothed on the coral beaches and offshore islands, as yet undiscovered by package tourists. Brian flew home with a suntan for a bit more soldiering in Britain, and then back to Belize again. The battalion were off to Malaysia and needed appropriate training. The military planners had failed to spot that this had already been done.

The KSLI flew to Singapore and moved into Seralong Barracks near Changi. This had been a place of suffering for so many Commonwealth prisoners who had fallen into the hands of the Japanese during the Second World War. The war that occupied Commonwealth forces now was between North and South Vietnam.

Australian forces were fully committed. In New Zealand there was considerable public opposition. Nevertheless, they sent troops. The British Government, quite rightly, refused to commit any of her forces. History would show that we were right to stay out of the fight in Vietnam. The American Secretary of State, Robert McNamara, who had directed foreign policy at the time, admitted in 1995, "We were wrong, terribly wrong. We owe it to future generations to explain why."

Foot soldiers from Australia and New Zealand did not see it that way; it was black and white to them. "We're in and the Brits are out. What's the matter with them?" The King's Shropshire Light Infantry had nothing to be ashamed of. They had served on the front line throughout the Korean War, longer than any other unit.

A change of scenery was arranged for the 1st Battalion. They moved up country to Terendak on the Straits of Malacca. This was the home of the Commonwealth Infantry Brigade and the military hospitals that received casualties from the conflict in Vietnam. This was a reminder to the Aussies that war was not all glory.

British troops were called on to calm the troubles that flared up in Mauritius. Even on this paradise island Christians and Muslims could just not get along with each other. Coldstream Guards from Aden flew in and the hooligans behaved themselves for a while; the Guards flew off. The country was being granted independence, and rather than celebrate together rival gangs came onto the streets. The British Governor declared a state of emergency.

As the date for independence approached, the rival gangs, 'Istanbul' and 'Texas', got up to their old tricks. At short notice Corporal Jones and 'A' Company were deployed. They boarded RAF Hercules in Singapore and few direct to Mauritius. The KSLI stayed long enough to ensure that the independence celebrations went off peacefully. The Mauritians were joyful; Shropshire lads were sad.

The King's Shropshire Light Infantry went on parade on Vesting Day in July 1968 and marched off as just plain Light Infantry. They had lost some of their identity. The county regiments of Shropshire, Yorkshire, Somerset and Cornwall all disappeared. Attempts were made to preserve historic traditions but things could never be the same again.

The county regiment could trace its origins back to 1755 when the 53rd Regiment of Foot was raised by William Whitmore of Apley. In 1881 it merged with another regiment to form the King's Shropshire Light Infantry. Men from the estate had been in the ranks of the county regiment throughout its history, and they were there on the last parade.

Before the battalion came back to Europe, there was one last encounter with the Aussies. The battalion was sent on a six-week detachment to Enoggera Camp, in the suburbs of Brisbane. This time the atmosphere was different. The camp was one of the largest in the country and the scene of repeated anti-war protests. Inside the camp were many who had served in Vietnam and now acknowledged the futility of it all.

FOLLOWING THE DRUM

Agreeing to any proposal always comes with a risk. There's no telling where it might lead. Jim proposed and Rose agreed. Jim came home on leave for Christmas. Around the kitchen table at Stockton Farm, plans were made for a July wedding. Craftsman Keen and Rose White had known each other since childhood and wanted to be together always. Easter arrived and Jim came home again. Just to be sure he took Rose back to Germany at the end of his leave. She talked to soldiers' wives, and after ten days she was sure. In July Rose married Jim, and married the army.

They should have known it wouldn't be that easy. Army regulations covered everything, including matrimony. Army regulations stated that Jim and Rose were too young to live together. They were married but separated by the English Channel. Jim soldiered on in Dortmund and Rose carried on producing prize-winning cheeses at Stockton.

None of this would ever have happened if Jim had not decided to leave Frank Yates's farm. The work was fine but there had to be more to life than this. Old soldiers may have had an influence; they spun yarns of the campaigns of their youth. "There's all these little wars goin', but not like the one I was in."

Jim presented himself at the recruiting office. "Just the man for the Guards!"

Jim was not persuaded. He signed on for nine years with the Royal Electrical and Mechanical Engineers. First stop, Arborfield, the REME depot in Berkshire. The accommodation was typical of the time, wooden huts arranged in 'spiders' connected by corridors to a central block with ablutions. The recruits slept in three-bed bunks, snoring together in an atmosphere of body odours. After six weeks of 'square bashing' Jim moved on to Gosport for trade training, and then to Borden. Training complete, Craftsman Keen was off to Dortmund permanently attached to the 45th Field Regiment Royal Artillery.

After their honeymoon the British Army had put five hundred miles between Rose and Jim, and this was about to be extended. Gunners of the 45th Field Regiment RA were given their marching orders. They were off to Malaysia and so were the REME craftsmen attached to them.

Jim flew out in July 1963 and Rose followed in December, taking the same route from Stansted to Singapore. Once British Airways described itself as 'The World's Favourite Airline', Transport Command of the Royal Air Force was never a serious competitor. They couldn't offer the same level of service and comfort.

The ground crew went through the take-off routine. One after the other the engines barked out blue smoke, cowlings rattled and propellers whirled. Directed to the runway by a youth in oily overalls, the pilot held the Hastings on the brakes, revved up the engines and with a bounce and a sway they were airborne and climbing over Essex. A glimpse of the Thames Estuary and a corner of Kent was all they would see of England for well over two years. Germany and Austria slid away under the belly of the 'Hasty Bird'. After that no one knew exactly where they were.

Gently the aircraft slipped through the clouds, and there was Istanbul. Towers and domes of the mosques, ships ploughing through the Bosporus, the sprawling suburbs, all came into view. The railway track and the network of roads grew clearer. Almost without warning they were gliding over the rooftops and touching down on tacky Turkish tarmac. The air temperature was 90°F. Ground crew crawled on the wings and refuelled the aircraft. Passengers were ushered into a canteen and refuelled with 'wads' and tea.

Within seconds of take-off they were over Asia, still a long way to go. Turkey looked dry and rocky, Iraq a bit greener down the Gulf, the Arabian Sea unbelievably blue. They came in to land at RAF Kat (Katunayake), north of Colombo in old Ceylon. They knew they were in the tropics now; the airfield was surrounded by tens of thousands of coconut trees. This was the last opportunity Rose had to get spruced up before she met Jim at Changi Airport. She was greeted with heat and humidity when she stepped out of the plane. The tropics have that particular damp smell of rotting vegetation.

Husbands and army wives were reunited. Jim had hired a taxi to take his bride of many months all the way to Malacca, a journey of over a hundred miles. They hadn't gone far when Rose started to strip off. Of course she was pleased to see her husband but it wasn't passion this time. It was the heat of the tropics, and more particularly the nylon stockings and all the belts and buckles necessary to keep them in place that Rose wanted to be free of.

At last the army took the young couple under its wing and gave them a love nest. They moved into a three-bedroomed house on a smart new housing estate complete with an 'Amah' to do the chores. Rose needed free time to fit in coffee mornings and badminton practise. She was a lady of leisure; this was the sort of life Rose could get used to.

The couple spent over two years in 'quarters' near Terandak Camp, the centre of their social life. Corporal Keen drove back and forth, in his three-ton truck, to Singapore for supplies. There was never any serious incident. The only worrying part of the journey was the river crossing at Muir. The ferry boats, primitive tugs and the barges used to transport Jim's truck and three tons of stores across the river, should all have been taken to a boatyard, examined and converted into firewood.

The Malayan emergency came to an end officially in 1960. The new state of Malaysia included Singapore and part of the island of Borneo. The southern half of the island was Indonesian territory. Trouble flared up along this border almost immediately. Malaysian troops were backed up by Commonwealth forces. The Indonesians mounted attacks by land, sea and air. They had little success. British and Australian airmen quickly took command of the skies. Indonesian paratroopers did land on mainland Malaysia but they were soon rounded up.

A raiding party crossed the Straits of Malacca and came ashore at Sungei Kesang, south of Terendak. The insurgents numbered over fifty, half were killed and half were captured by Australian infantry. It was unlikely that the Indonesians would try this again. To be on the safe side British troops patrolled the beaches at night just in case any guerrillas, bearing a grudge, did land and take a pot shot at anyone. Jim often strolled along in the evening to give Sue, a little mongrel, some exercise.

When Jim and Rose wanted to get away from it all they tootled around the rough country roads in their Ford Popular. On local leave the happy couple drove up the tortuous road to the Cameron Highlands. This was a challenge for a little car with a three-speed speed gearbox and just a shade over 1000cc under the bonnet. They lost count of the number of hairpin bends on the climb up to the Highlands, but with a few stops and radiator top-ups she made it. The cool air of the Cameron Highlands was a welcome change after months on the steamy coast.

It was too good to last; the 45th Field Regiment and their REME team completed their tour of duty. Jim and Rose flew home together. At Stansted they picked up a brand new Vauxhall Viva and drove in style into the farmyard at Stockton. After three weeks of visiting and catching up on local gossip, it was back to Dortmund. The good times were behind them, baby Neil arrived, and it was time to put the expanding family first.

They set up home back at Apley. It was all so familiar, and the perfect place for toddlers to run free. A short walk out of the sheltered valley was granny's house in Hope's Lane. Their house at Winscote had a history. Sailing barges once carried all manner of products from the 'cradle of industry' at Coalbrookdale to the outside world. The crews of the Severn Trows and the men who hauled them through the narrows rested overnight in caves on the riverbank. In the evening the boatmen were offered home-brewed ale and, it was said, the ladies of the house offered a little extra to cheer them on their way.

After forty years of marriage, Rose and Jim celebrated with a sentimental journey to compare the Cameron Highlands with Winscote Hills. At Apley little had changed; more overgrown perhaps, and the new tenants didn't seem to have the same interest in the gardens or livestock. It was certainly tranquil, just birdsong, no clucking hens, grunting pigs or laughing children.

The road from Jahore Barhu to the Cameron Highlands was unrecognisable because in the 1960s it wasn't there. As they drove up the six-lane highway with its modern service stations, Rose and Jim recalled the trips they had made in their dusty Ford Popular along unmetalled roads passing through the kampongs. Children playing in the shade under the stilted houses scurried out and waved as they passed. It was a different world.

Chapter 27

The Big Bang

The striking statue of a soldier stands out above the flower beds and shrubberies of the Castle Gardens in Bridgnorth. Strangers to the town spot it as soon as they pass through the gates. Some hurry on, camera in hand, to get a closer look. The bronze figure is frozen, leaning forward arm extended. It seems that at any minute he may spring to life and stride on. They circle the plinth looking up to find the best angle for the photograph. The lucky ones capture the fine features and jutting jaw that catches the sunlight. On panels on the plinth below are the names, with regiments and ranks.

John Ealey was the only man on the town memorial to hold the rank of Donkeyman in the Merchant Navy. What did he do and why was he remembered on this memorial so far from the sea?

Mahogany, cut from the tropical forests of the Niger Delta, was hauled to the port. The huge baulks of timber swung on to the deck of SS *Nigerian*. The donkeymen were busy attending the fire and maintaining the steam that drove the donkey engine. This was the machine that powered the winch to lift the cargo on board. Oil seed was stowed below and the merchant ship pulled away from the dock at Port Harcourt into the open sea and set course for the Gold Coast. At Takoradi they loaded cocoa and sailed on across the Atlantic.

The donkeymen were busy all the time, they were responsible for the generators and pumps of every description. Steam and oil, clean water and foul water flowed through what appeared to be a tangle of pipework around the ship. The donkeymen were on call day and night to deal with any breakdown; they had to know the workings of every valve and pump. For centuries, when disaster struck, sailors were given the same order: "All hands to pumps!"

The *SS Nigerian* sailed through the doldrums, 10° north of the equator, and along the friendly coast of British Guiana. The crew were looking forward to a warm welcome in Trinidad. If the ship turned around quickly John Ealey might be home in Liverpool for Christmas. The Nigerian never reached safe harbour at Port of Spain. She was stopped in her tracks by *U-Boat 508*, and sank below the blue waters of the Caribbean.

Sarah Ealey, somehow, broke the news to her children. Little Johnny was eight years old. "Your Dad won't be coming home for Christmas." That he died is recorded in the garden of Trinity Square close to The Tower of London, and in the gardens next to Bridgnorth Castle. The Ealey family left Liverpool early in the war when the Liverpool docks were the target of German bombers, and they never returned.

Little Johnny grew up and took up a trade similar to that of his father; he became a plumber. He 'served his time' and at twenty-one he got 'the call to arms'. A letter from 29 Bagot Street in Birmingham left him in no doubt about how to proceed:

You are called up for service in the ROYAL NAVY and are required to present yourself on Monday 29 AUG 1955 between 9 a.m. and 4 p.m. at VICTORIA BARRACKS RN SOUTHSEA HANTS.

It was best to follow the instructions; anyone who failed to do so was given a reminder by the local constabulary.

Form-filling, medicals and kitting out did not take long. Within a fortnight he was off to Portsmouth to receive 'on-the-job' training in seamanship on board one of Her Majesty's ships. Aircraft carriers *Implacable* and *Theseus* were at their moorings. *Implacable* had last seen action against the Japanese. She looked rather forlorn. When the tides were favourable they both left harbour, *Theseus* to sail to the Mediterranean, *Implacable* to the Firth of Forth to be scrapped. John had the luck of the draw and a cap band, HMS *Theseus*.

The pilots kept up their flying hours buzzing around *Theseus* as she made her way under 'the Rock' and into 'the Med'. Trouble was brewing on the sunshine island of Cyprus. *Theseus* offloaded equipment and supplies for troops who were doing their best to keep Greeks and Turks apart.

On the way home *Theseus* put in to Tangier, a courtesy call by the Royal Navy and a chance for John to start his postcard collection. Returning to home waters he transferred to HMS Pembroke at Chatham, a shore establishment. He was hoping for another cruise. National Service wasn't so bad, he was home for Christmas, bronzed and ready to tell 'tales of the sea' to anyone prepared to listen. Leave nearly over, he ironed the pleats in his bell-bottom trousers and strode down Sydney Cottage Drive on his way to the tropics.

Ordinary Seaman Ealey did not know of anyone who had succumbed to cholera or yellow fever, and Surgeon Lieutenants of the Royal Navy made sure that John was given full protection from these terrible diseases. At regular intervals, for the next twelve months, they filled up his arm with vaccines.

He flew with Skyways to join his ship at Singapore. Flying with Skyways was not without hazard. One of their 'Yorks' was lost without trace over the Atlantic in 1953. This was not mentioned when the 'Hermes' took off from Stansted on the first leg of the flight. Miss Hepburn and Miss Osler handed out snacks over Italy and a card that informed the passengers that Crete was coming up on the starboard side. The sailors knew which way to look. They touched down at Nicosia in the early afternoon. Waiting three days for an onward flight meant there was time for a trip to Kyrenia on the north coast of Cyprus. They took off again. A month later a Skyways 'Hermes' was blown up by terrorists on the same stretch of tarmac.

There were two more stopovers, at Delhi and Bangkok, before Captain Cruston flew them south over Malaya to Singapore. The barrack blocks of HMS Terror were basic, nothing like the famous Raffles Hotel. John did not complain. He was seeing the world at government expense. Ordinary Seaman Ealey was issued with a new cap band, HMS *Alert*. She had already taken part in operations involving the test firing of nuclear weapons.

The decision to join the arms race had, to a large extent, been forced on the British Government by Guy Burgess and Donald Maclean, two senior officials at the Foreign Office. They had been spying for the

Soviet Union for years and defected in 1951. After that Britain had to develop her own atomic weapons because the Americans were no longer willing to share their nuclear secrets.

British scientists conducted tests in the Pacific and on the Montebello Islands off the coast of Western Australia. The arms race was on. The British, French, Americans and Russians all wanted to demonstrate the power of their own weapons to the rest of the world. Operation Mosaic was the codename for the next series of nuclear tests. HMS *Diana* was on her way to join the flotilla of ships waiting at Singapore to sail in support of the operation. Among the crew were men like John Ealey, National Servicemen who were pleased that the Royal Navy was giving them the chance to see the world. They did not know when they set off on this voyage that they were on their way to witness a truly awesome display of power, and an event that would change the course of their lives.

South across the equator, Royal Navy ships converged on the Montebello Islands. The RAF flew in the bombs. Technicians and scientists erected two thirty-metre high aluminium towers on separate islands in the group. The bombs positioned in black cages on top of the towers were detonated from a concrete bunker. Naval destroyers came no closer than twelve miles from the site. The second bomb was experimental, a 'trigger' for a more powerful H-bomb to be developed later. This went off with a real bang exceeding the calculations of the scientists. The flash was seen three hundred miles away.

The whole operation was reported in the press. Dramatic photographs appeared in British newspapers but could not capture the true scale of these explosions. Even eyewitnesses found these events hard to describe. After five seconds when observers at sea turned towards the island they saw a glowing cloud climbing into the sky, red and violet flames flashing at its heart. The mushroom shaped cloud began to lose its shape when it reached about twenty thousand feet. From the base toxic gasses billowed out across the sea. Within a minute a heatwave swept over the decks of the ships; the crews hosed them down to avoid contamination.

Two vessels, *Narvik* and *Diana,* were ordered into the cloud to measure radioactivity. It was claimed, at the time, that these ships were specially protected.

One of three tests conducted on the Montebello Islands. Photograph taken from the deck of HMS Narvik.

"This is close enough."

Top Secret documents made public fifty years later revealed that the crew of HMS *Diana* had been deceived and betrayed. They were treated as human guinea pigs, deliberately exposed to radioactive fallout, their only protection facemasks, overshoes and sunglasses. Within weeks, some of the crew had lost teeth, others had lost hair. Only one in five lived to enjoy old age; at least a hundred died with cancer.

Able Seaman Ealey and his shipmates sailed safely back to barracks in Singapore. John added press cuttings of this historic event to his collection of postcards.

In the very heart of this modern city of skyscrapers, a patch of green turf was preserved so that residents could enjoy a game of cricket and take on visitors. The sailors already had their 'whites', part of their tropical kit. John took to the field. His performance was reported in the *Straits Times*. It wasn't very impressive. He didn't take any wickets;

twenty-eight runs were scored off his eight overs. With the bat he managed just four runs, which was creditable as only three of *Alert*'s team reach double figures. The Navy lost to the locals.

From the balcony of the barrack block John took distressing pictures of sailors marching. They were not supposed to do that; sailors sail, airmen fly and soldiers do the marching. They were rehearsing for something every deckhand dreads, an inspection by the Commander-in-Chief. HMS *Alert* was spruced up and sailed off to Hong Kong to meet the Admiral. Sprucing up was not enough. Everything wooden was scrubbed, scraped and varnished, rusting steel scraped and painted, and anything that could be polished, polished.

Admiral Sir Alan K. Scott-Moncrieff was piped aboard HMS *Alert*. Covered in gold braid and medals, he inspected the guard of honour and made what he thought were humorous remarks to the lads in the galley. Surrounded by Commodores and Captains he prepared to review an assortment of vessels, all under his command. It was a noisy affair. Escorted by seven motor launches, *Alert* steamed across Hong Kong harbour and past Kowloon Point. HMS *Tamar* fired a seventeen-gun salute. HMS *Alert* replied with an eleven-gun salute. There must have been a reason for choosing these odd numbers, part of Royal Navy tradition no doubt.

The review in Hong Kong harbour was the last big event in the naval career of Admiral Scott-Moncrieff and Able Seaman Ealey; they both retired from the Royal Navy in 1957. The Admiral filled his diary with reunion dinners and John went back to plumbing on Apley Estate.

Photographs, postcards and press cuttings were all carefully preserved to remind John in later life of the two eventful years he had spent in Navy blue and Navy whites. He would open up the photo album and there he was, a youth in shorts surrounded by grinning shipmates, pipe in his mouth, camera round his neck. He had visited the market place in Tangier and the Taj Mahal at Agra, the Marble Palace in Bangkok and a Crusader Castle in northern Cyprus.

He had witnessed the mushroom cloud of an atomic bomb over the Montebello Islands and the review of the fleet off Kowloon Point. The Royal Navy had taught him nothing about plumbing but he had been places and learned a few new songs to entertain the guests at the Legion annual dinner.

With one hoof raised the blue bull half turned and glowered at the public through a circular frame with a crown on the top. Below there was inscribed a single word – DETER.

A new crest was designed for RAF Marham in 1957 when the Valiant bombers returned to base after service in the Middle East. They were a key part of our nuclear deterrent. Armed at times with the deadliest of weapons, the Valiants flew daily from the airfield across the Norfolk countryside and over the North Sea. This was no secret and they didn't seem to care who knew about it.

Mr Andrei Tupolev, the leading Russian aircraft designer, was shown round Marham one afternoon with Bulganin and Khruschev, the Soviet leaders. They probably didn't learn any more than they already knew. B and K did the usual things on their state visit to Britain – had lunch with the Queen, chatted with the Tory Prime Minister and fell out with members of the Labour Party. They didn't show much enthusiasm for the special performance put on for them at the Opera House in Covent Garden. The visit to RAF Marham was far more interesting.

No V-bombers left the ground until RAF Form 700 was complete. The tradesmen and technicians responsible for servicing the aircraft all signed the form, then the pilot added his signature and the aircraft was his. Engine mechanics, airframe and instrument fitters kept the bombers in the air. 'The Deterrent' was the responsibility of the armourers.

The best trained technicians of the Royal Air Force were Old Haltonians. The most famous 'Halton Brat' was Frank Whittle, 'father of the jet engine'. There was keen competition to enter Halton; a written examination, intelligence and aptitude tests, and the candidates had to be fit. Ray Evans was very fit and skilful at any sport that involved a ball. He was a competitive Grammar School boy, just the sort of lad the RAF was looking for.

He fitted well into N° 3 Squadron (Electrical & Armaments). For two years apprentices toiled away in the classroom, in the workshops, on the drill square and playing field. The learning experience in schools and university could not compare with RAF Halton. There was no slouching and shambling. Apprentices marched to the classrooms and workshops in columns, sometimes accompanied by the station band to wake them up.

In January 1958, proud parents gathered to watch the passing-out parade. The band played, the squadrons marched and counter-marched, they 'sloped' arms and 'presented' arms. It all went like clockwork. The commanding officer gave a speech, the usual stuff, "…well done…bright future…fine tradition."

For the benefit of parents he retold the story of the invention of the turbo jet engine by the most famous Old Haltonian, Air Commodore Sir Frank Whittle. Speeches over, a lone piper played 'Will ye no come back again?' and the graduating apprentices marched past the saluting dais for the last time, and marched off the square. It had been an inspiring day.

Junior Technician Ray Evans reported to the guardroom at RAF Upwood. This was not a very inspiring building. The off-white concrete pillars supporting the grey concrete roof were shabby compared with the brilliant white webbing and caps of the 'Snowdrops' who greeted him. The RAF Police had all been trained to be unpleasant, and they enjoyed their work. Ray was greeted more warmly in the station armoury.

During the war Upwood had been the home of a squadron of Pathfinders, the bravest of men. In 1956, 'Canberras' flew from Cyprus, bombed targets in Egypt and returned to Upwood. This was their last combat mission. However, shortly after Ray arrived, RAF strategists decided that they needed some more bombing practise so they arranged a 'jolly' for aircrew and ground crew, a five-week deployment to Malta.

Tourists on their way to Malta on Easy Jet have just enough time to read the in-flight magazine, have lunch on a tray, a drink and a doze before they arrive. Ray and his mates on board the RAF Beverley were in the air for eight hours, and it wasn't all that comfortable. The best seats were above the cargo deck. There was even a toilet up there. There was no cargo on this flight. The cargo space was filled with 'bods' crouched in canvas seats. After seven and a half draughty hours flying into the wind, everyone was looking forward to landing at Luqa, even if it was raining. On the approach the Beverley slid down through the clouds and into a thunderstorm. The first air pocket must have been twenty feet deep, the next felt deeper. The weary passengers were sick of this. Just because they were airmen didn't mean they were immune to airsickness. Vomit was everywhere; down uniforms, on kitbags and equipment, and all over the floor. Welcome to Malta.

Luftwaffe bombers gave Malta a pasting during the war; the population held out. No one wanted a reminder of this experience so the Canberra crews on their bombing runs were careful to target rocky outcrops well off the coast. While 'riggers' and 'fitters' were crawling over the aircraft to make sure nothing was going to fall off, 'plumbers'(armourers) were crawling underneath arranging clusters of twenty-five pound bombs that would definitely drop off.

Ray's tour of duty on Malta might have been more relaxed if it had not have been for Dom Mintoff. Negotiations for Maltese independence were taking a long time. British Government officials and Mintoff got bogged down in the small print of the agreement. While this was going on, frustrated Maltese youths started throwing things. They hurled stones over the perimeter fence of RAF Luqa and insults at young airmen in the streets. Neither caused much damage although sensitive lads might have been distressed if they had understood the Maltese dialect. *Firrah jaqbdek cancer fil bajd,* translates as, 'I wish you cancer in your testicles'.

Airmen visiting Valletta were ordered to go out in groups of three. The most serious threats of physical violence came not from the locals but from stokers of the Royal Navy. For months on end these men spent eight hours a day sweating below deck. Tensions built up. They looked forward eagerly to a 'run ashore' at Valletta. Some of their frustrations were relieved by professional Maltese ladies. Even so, there might still be some pent-up aggression. The sight of a British Army cap badge was enough to spark off a bare-knuckle brawl, and an Air Force blue uniform was like a red rag to a bull. The bars and the alleys around 'The Gut' were the scene of more than just inter-service rivalry.

A twenty-first birthday party should be a memorable event. A celebration was arranged for Ray at a bar in Luqa village. He has only a vague recollection of the evening's events. American servicemen joined the party. They were generous and turned it into a cocktail party. "Vodka and fresh orange juice, maybe a little lime-soda, that's a screwdriver."

It went down so easily. More followed. There was chatter and singing and backslapping, then things became hazy. The only thing Ray could remember clearly was the series of wide white lines that ran down the middle of the main runway. The lads who supported him on the shortcut back to the billet agreed. "This is a bad place, we should not be here."

The next morning Ray wasn't sure if a 'screwdriver' was something out of a tool box or an instrument that had been forced into the top of his skull.

Tour over it was time to return to base. Outward bound the Beverley had struggled to complete the journey in eight hours. "The trip home has to be quicker." The wind had changed. It took nine hours.

Back at Upwood, Ray could get on with the serious business of football practise. His skill on the field was in great demand playing for the station team, playing for the Command and playing for Norton FC. Bill Ellingham, publican of the Hundred House and manager of the village team, played a dangerous game. He did something that might have damaged Corporal Evans's RAF career. Norton FC had reached the final of the Bridgnorth Cup. This was the highlight of the season. Bill Ellingham badly wanted his team to win and he badly needed a striker. Ray was well over a hundred miles away and subject to military discipline. With a forty-eight hour pass he could be home, take to the field with the village team and be back on duty before the weekend. After a telephone conversation between Ray and the team manager arrangements were made. A telegram arrived at Upwood: MOTHER DANGEROUSLY ILL.

Shocked by the news (apparently), Ray went to see his CO. "Forty-eight hour pass? Not sure about that, Evans. Oh, alright."

The squadron leader was reluctant, but he signed the 'chit'. Norton FC won the cup. There were celebrations in the Hundred House, the publican was jubilant. Ray's mum was a picture of good health.

After two years at Upwood, Ray was posted to RAF Marham. This was a good move. The Canberra squadrons were being disbanded one by one to make way for V-bombers. The Valiants, Victors and Vulcans were all designed to carry nuclear weapons. Most of the Valiants were painted in camouflage colours; one or two were a conspicuous white. When a hydrogen bomb exploded there was a blinding flash followed by searing heat. The white paint was supposed to be anti-flash; its effectiveness was never tested. The airfield was protected by a score of Bloodhound surface-to-air missiles. These were not Ray's responsibility. He was a member of the team that handled the nuclear weapons and armed the Valiant bombers.

On the tarmac Handley Page Victor, on the trolley Yellow Sun Mk II nuclear weapon.

"Whatever you do don't drop it!"

The outer casing was code-named 'Yellow Sun', which sounded quite comforting. The warhead was 'Red Snow', something that would make a bloody mess. Some of the bombs were 'dummies'. Bombs with 'Red Snow' were brought under escort from US arms dumps; Bentwater Park was mentioned. The armourers knew they were handling the real thing because when it was trundled into the hanger it was accompanied by burly Americans wearing shiny helmets and carrying ugly-looking firearms. It was hard to imagine that anyone was going to carry one away under their arm. If, after fifty years, Ray needs to be reminded how to fix 'the bomb' into the belly of a Valiant there is one waiting for him in the RAF Museum at Cosford.

Sergeant Evans completed his service at RAF Stafford. His team serviced and refurbished a wide range of weapons: Sten guns, Bren guns and Lee-Enfield rifles, all designed to kill. A more complicated piece of equipment was the Martin-Baker ejector seat, designed to save lives. Whatever was put on the bench in front of them the armourers stripped it down, examined it, made good any repairs and tested it. When part of the mechanism of the ejector seat was redesigned dozens of stainless

310

steel rods were scraped. "I'll have a few of them, never know when they might be useful."

The time came for Sergeant Evans to make a decision: service life or family life. He lost his RAF identity when he handed in RAF Form 1250 and became a civilian. Ray had learned a lot at Halton. He put this knowledge into practice, handling the deadliest of weapons.

The skills and knowledge his father gave him were more durable, a life-long love of cricket and a love of gardening. In the spring when Ray prepares the seed drills for beetroot and carrots, he sets them out carefully with string stretched between slender metal rods. He thinks back to the days he spent at RAF Stafford servicing the ejector seats and says to himself, "Bright as ever, I knew they'd come in for something one day."

Chapter 28

The Army of the Rhine

ALLIES NO MORE

No sooner had the Second World War ended than there was talk of a Third World War. This would be a nuclear war against the Soviet Union.

In their final battle to take Berlin the Red Army lost at least seventy thousand men. A special unit sent in with the invaders raided the Kaiser Wilhelm Institute which housed the German nuclear research centre. The Russians knew the Americans had mastered the technology to produce an atom bomb and that the Germans were also at an advanced stage with their research. The Soviets own nuclear programme was lagging behind. The three tons of uranium oxide they carried off to Moscow gave a boost to their development programme.

The victorious allies divided Germany into occupation zones. Berlin itself, which was entirely within the Russian zone, was divided into sectors, American, French, British and the Russian sector. Movement in and out of the capital by road and rail was controlled by the Red Army.

The 'chummy' relationship between wartime allies soon turned sour; a chilly atmosphere developed. The Third World War was the Cold War and it lasted for the best part of fifty years. In October 1994, the Prince of Wales took the salute at a parade of dragoons and infantrymen to mark the disbandment of the British Army of the Rhine.

THE BERLIN AIRLIFT

Not content with victory over Germany, the USSR wanted to expand its influence to other neighbouring countries, Norway, Greece and Turkey. The most serious threat to the security of Western Europe came when the Soviets began their blockade of Berlin in June 1948. Road, rail and canal access was blocked; essential supplies had to be delivered by air. American, French, British and Commonwealth airmen were flying round the clock to supply Berliners with food, fuel and everything to make life tolerable. This was operation 'Plain Fare', very appropriate; milk, flour and medicines were the basics.

The RAF flew into Gatow with nearly a thousand tons of supplies every day. Trucks were leaving 431 Equipment Depot, near Hamburg, at the rate of one a minute. Military police were supposed to check every vehicle but this was an impossible task. Eighteen-year-old 'Tony' Taft did the best he could. He should have been counting 'pop' bottles in his father's soft drinks plant in Birmingham, but National Service interrupted his career.

Tony went from schoolboy to special investigator in just over a year. From the RAF Police Training School at Pershore he was posted to a transit camp in Yorkshire. RAF Police were disappearing to stations all over the world, and within weeks Tony was the most senior man. He left for Hamburg.

The whole area was devastated. The destruction was largely the result of allied bombing raids. Boys in blue were the target of abuse in the streets. Off-duty airmen were advised to wear civilian clothes.

Tony was shocked to see that families were living in bombed-out buildings, some under sheets of corrugated iron, cooking in the open using any scraps of wood they could find. This was a desperate situation that brought out the best and the worst in people. Everything was in short supply but almost anything could be obtained on the Black Market – at a price.

Checking trucks passing out of 431 Equipment Depot and catching petty pilferers was routine. Tony wanted something out of the ordinary so he volunteered for the Special Investigation Branch.

The SIB had unusual powers; no one was above the law no matter what their rank. An RAF Warrant Officer of the Provost Section was arrested for selling Jeeps. Aircrew officers grounded at the end of the war were given desk jobs. Relieved from the stress of combat, but missing the excitement some turned to drink, and this led to crime. Interviewing men like this and bringing them to book was particularly difficult.

Within one of the biggest equipment depots in Western Europe there was plenty of scope for crime on a large scale. To transport goods hundreds of packing cases were made in one section. Nearby another section was set up where they were sawn up, converted into firewood and driven off-site to be sold. When SIB uncovered this operation they discovered that tools used to build and dismantle the cases were also being shipped out with the 'scrap' wood.

Many frustrated young soldiers could not resist the pleasures on offer in the red-light districts. These were 'Out of Bounds' and had to be policed. Despite the health risks many could not resist the temptation. Every month units submitted reports on the number of men treated for VD (venereal disease). Military police examined the 'league table' so that they could target the worst offenders. Unfortunately, Royal Navy shore patrols and army 'Red Caps' were often the worst offenders. They obviously got 'up close and personal' when carrying out their duties.

The border between East and West Germany had been agreed and a line drawn on the map. The fence and guard posts had not yet been built. Where roads crossed the border there were signs to warn that the Russian zone was up ahead. Tony and a colleague strayed over on one occasion. They only realised this when they were stopped by a border patrol on the way back to base. Clearly there was very little to stop an invasion from the east. The plan, as Tony understood it, was that in the event of a Russian attack anyone capable of driving should jump in the nearest vehicle, make for the Channel coast and leave it to the Armoured Brigade.

THE SOVEREIGN'S ESCORT

It was anticipated that if the Russians did decide to break out of their zone of occupation they would advance across the North German Plain, an area well suited to tank warfare. Leading the charge on our side might have fallen to the most senior regiment in the British Army, the Lifeguards. They had been scouting about in Aden and Oman in the 1950s, and after a spell of ceremonial duties at Windsor they were sent to Germany. Wherever they went Corporal Roger Williams of the Royal Electrical and Mechanical Engineers went with them to keep them rolling along.

Roger Williams was never happier than when he was up to his elbows in engine oil. He got under his father's feet in the tractor shed, and it was a relief to Harry when his boy left school and began his apprenticeship with Reg Tildsley in Shifnal. When the time came for him to put on a uniform he followed his brother Ken's example and became a vehicle mechanic in the REME.

It was good to be back in barracks at Windsor after the heat and dust of Aden; everyone was happy. Nurses at the nearby hostel welcomed the troopers. Subalterns – who eighteen months earlier had been schoolboys at Eton – went back to their old school to swagger about and tell stories of 'scraps with the Arabs'. Corporal Williams and the REME mechanics kept out of the way. Not involved in ceremonial duties, they tuned up the Daimlers and gave them a run in Windsor Great Park.

Patrolling the Iron Curtain between East and West Germany, they had a lot more to do. To keep troops on their toes an endless series of 'schemes' was arranged. These war games were intended to prepare allied forces for a possible invasion from the east. Everyone who had ever been involved had a farcical story to tell. After at least ten years of practice, it should have been clear that real battles on German heathland could only end one way.

The real battle on German soil, especially for conscripts on low pay, was against boredom. If they were not sporty they lounged about and saved up for the next alcoholic binge. Fraternising with the old enemy was discouraged and, understandably, German fathers did not want to see their daughters on the arm of a lad in British uniform. As years went by attitudes changed and when his tour of duty in Germany was over Roger came home with Helga, his German bride.

THE RED CAP

John Dovey was one who did make the most of his service with the British Army of the Rhine. John was one who did look forward to doing his bit for his country, but when the letter arrived that told him to report to Inkerman Barracks his confidence began to seep away. It meant leaving home and leaving Margaret, his childhood sweetheart. His father, ex-Regimental Sergeant Major Tom Dovey, gave him a bit of advice, "Keep your head down, watch your back and get your hair cut."

John got on his bike and rode to Madeley. George Jones was not a hair stylist. He had a barber's shop, cut hair and talked; that didn't make him a barber. Most of his customers were miners; they were not fussy men. John went under the clippers and rode home. His mother greeted him. "What have you done to your hair?"

"Nothing, George Jones did it."

The journey from Wolverhampton to Woking was an education. It meant crossing London. John had been to Regent's Park Zoo on a school trip, and that was the nearest he had been to the centre of the capital. Now he had to cross London by Underground, from Paddington to Waterloo. He passed the map-reading test and boarded the train to Woking. He was greeted outside the station by a Sergeant of the military police with a waiting truck. He was not surprised. It was John Dovey's aim to qualify for the same Red Cap.

When the new squad was assembled another sergeant lined them up and spoke to each man personally. "Haircut...haircut...haircut... haircut...Are you trying to be funny?" Even he, who had seen it all before, was shocked when he saw what George Jones had done. When all the basic skills of soldiering had been mastered to the satisfaction of Sergeant Wood, the squad was rewarded with a thirty-six hour pass. These were precious hours and barely enough to travel across London, north to Birmingham, Wolverhampton and Sutton Maddock, and back before midnight on Sunday night.

MPs were expected to be mobile, capable of handling truck, jeep or motorbike. John began his training in a quarry, to master the art of double-declutching, before joining a convoy at Heathrow and driving on down the road to Brighton. Remarkably, some recruits who were assigned to the motorbike team couldn't even ride a pushbike. They were given a crash course. There only remained the formality of the passing-out parade, promotion for everyone to lance corporal and the 'green' Red Caps were ready to take up duties anywhere in the world.

Before they left the depot they were briefed on the special circumstances that applied to service in Germany, how to deal with the old enemy, with strict courtesy on duty and no socialising off duty. They were given 'jabs' to protect them from unpleasant diseases and warned about viruses that attacked young lads below the belt. The film, in flickering black and white, should have been vivid enough to put them off the red-light districts. The descriptions of the treatments for conditions resulting from 'the joy of sex' made celibacy seem a better option.

With a handful of others John was driven from Inkerman Barracks direct to Liverpool Street Station to join a troop train. It chugged out of the East End across the uninspiring Essex countryside, through the garrison town of Colchester, along the Stour estuary and right through the dock gates at Harwich, and on to Parkeston Quay. The Channel crossing was not good. The sea was calm enough when the *Empire Parkeston* pulled away on the evening tide and John watched the lights of Harwich fade. The ship pitched and rolled towards the Hook of Holland. John had an hours sleep in a canvas bunk.

At Krefeld there was more training to explain how the military police, the local Politzei and the Intelligence Corps worked together. With a sore head following the end-of-course booze-up, John took the train to Herford and began duties in pre-war German barracks that were now the Headquarters of the 11th Armoured Division. With newly-tailored battledress and distinctive shoulder flashes (black bull on a bright yellow ground) he looked the part. Throughout Lance Corporal Dovey's tour of duty hardly a week went by without incident. The MPs responded to incidents that were serious, tragic, mysterious, childish and entertaining. Above all they were reminded that the British Army of the Rhine were there to keep an eye on the artificial border created between the Russians and the Western Allies.

At Hildesheim John went on patrol in the backstreet that bordered the Russian zone. There was nothing discreet about it with white webbing, and Smith and Wesson revolver on a lanyard. The MPs were easy to spot, even in the dimly lit alley. The nearby Provost Section was housed in a large country house, a place of morbid interest for students of war. This was where Hermann Goering had committed suicide. Goering had been Commander-in-Chief of the Luftwaffe, and Hitler's deputy. The founder of the Gestapo, after the war he had a lot to answer for. At the end of a long trial he was sentenced to death by hanging. He asked to be shot. On the way to execution someone smuggled a cyanide pill into his cell. When John was shown into the room it was full of cardboard boxes, there was nothing left there as a memorial to Goering, nothing anywhere. His body was displayed at the execution ground to show that justice had been done, then cremated and the ashes scattered.

Saving squaddies from themselves was just one of the duties of the Royal Military Police. Stopping fights, raiding nightclubs, locking up drunks and picking up lads on the steps of brothels, this was all in a days work. Then there was traffic duty, out in all weathers.

The most unpopular schemes were those arranged in the winter months. A hard bed in a barrack block was bad enough but this was better than a tent or a barn on Luneburg Heath. Outside they dug a slit trench to jump into when warning of a nuclear attack was given. The planners always tried to include one warning in each exercise. On the stroke of the appointed hour everyone had to lie flat no matter where they were. This must have seemed odd behaviour to a child coming out of Kindergarten when the Red Cap directing traffic sudden fell in the road. *"Mutti, ist tot oder verrückt?"* (Is he dead or mad?)

Before John went home on leave for the first time he went with Sergeant Heron to a murder scene. "He had it coming to him." This was the view of some of the soldiers who had witnessed the killing. The taunting by the barrack-room bully drove one boy to breaking point; he stabbed his tormentor repeatedly in the chest as he lay on his bed. At the scene of the crime the MPs examined the bloodstained sheets, made notes, conducted interviews and filed a report. The unfortunate infantryman served five years for manslaughter in the military prison at Colchester when he should have served just two years of National Service.

Home on leave John and Margaret planned their wedding. He left the fine details to his bride-to-be. The treat waiting for him on his return to BAOR was yet another 'scheme'. Sergeant 'Paddy' Heron supervised the setting up of the camp that would be home base. He was meticulous, tents lined up, guy ropes lined up, the compound fenced off neatly and a large sign to tell everyone that this was 'RMP 3 Section'. Paddy had a tent of his own and the only table and chair. After a few days of inactivity some began to question Sergeant Heron's map-reading ability. They were in the middle of nowhere, not a tank or trooper in sight, just a few trees in the distance to break up the monotony of the landscape. An Auster spotter plane appeared, circled and flew off. "He must be lost as well."

The big event of the scheme was the trip to Hamburg. The lucky ones who had brought civvies with them filled up the truck, carefully buckled up the canvas at the back and tried to imagine what nightlife in the port city would be like as they bounced along the road. Hamburg with its U-boat pens, oil installations and armament factories had been the target of repeated bombing raids by the RAF and the USAAF.

Operation 'Gomorrah' killed over forty thousand civilians. Eight square miles of the city was destroyed in a firestorm.

When the talkative young lads jumped down from the back of their truck on the outskirts of the city they were shocked to see the extent of the destruction. Even after ten years there was rubble everywhere. Paddy Heron shepherded his squad into the nearest U-Bahn and they took the train to the Reeperbahn, a street every soldier had heard of, described locally as 'the sinful mile'. There was something there to suit all tastes.

A little unsure of themselves the group stayed together, slipped out of the glare of the neon signs and down into a cellar bar. Paddy settled them around a dingy corner table. Drinks arrived; they sipped their lager and looked around. Two of the company bursting with testosterone spied a pair of local beauties. Long shapely legs twisted around the bar stools looked inviting. They made a move; it was a brief encounter and they scurried back to the corner. "They're blokes, Sarge, with lipstick on, really they are!" Paddy nodded, they drank up and skipped out into the street.

Had it not been for the 'call-up' John might have carried on working in the builders yard at Sutton Maddock, and a whole cast of characters that he met on his tour of duty in Germany would have been unknown to him, men like Sergeant Paddy Heron or an American who called himself Pinkerton. Pinkerton was a man of mystery. Sergeant Heron's instructions were clear enough: "Pick up a US Army Investigator and take him wherever he wants to go."

John drove into the yard of the main railway station at Detmont and parked. Passengers poured out of the entrance and an unremarkable man walked straight to the MP vehicle. He got in without a word, then said, "I'm Pinkerton, Gutersloh." Nothing more was said until they reached the outskirts, then he gave directions to some army barracks, got out, thanked John and walked away.

Back at the Section Sergeant Heron spoke to John, "You are not to discuss any of this with anyone and that includes the Intelligence Corps, understood?" Pinkerton's agents had been operating as private investigators for a hundred years and they did have links with the CIA. It did not seem sensible for anyone who wanted to conceal his identity to call himself 'Pinkerton'. It was all very strange.

The Russian Military Mission made no secret of their presence.

Senior officers with big hats and lots of medals drove around the countryside in huge black limousines, similar in style to those favoured by the American mafia. This was allowed by the terms of the agreement between the victorious allies. Both sides were allowed to observe military manoeuvres and both sides did everything they could to be obstructive; changing road markings, boxing in vehicles, setting up roadblocks, all part of the game.

The Cold War warmed up considerably in 1956. British, French and Israeli forces were planning to invade Egypt. Colonel Nasser had nationalised the Suez Canal, Anthony Eden, the British Prime Minister, said this would threaten oil supplies from the Middle East. The situation was not that simple but in the event it was decided to take the Suez Canal by force.

Public opinion was against it and Class 'A' Army Reservists were definitely against it. They believed they had already done their bit. Some had served in Malaya and Korea and now had a steady job, and were enjoying family life. The brown envelope dropped on the doormat and within days they were off, first to collect basic kit and then to await transport to Germany. Many would have gone back home if the Channel had not been in their way.

Stewing away in barracks with no money and wives at home uncertain of their whereabouts, the mood of the reservists grew dark and ugly. The MPs of Section 3 knew nothing of this. They knew that trouble was brewing in the Middle East because all their vehicles had been painted to match the desert sand. Trouble was about to erupt on their own doorstep.

Everything was quiet at the section; Corporal Thompson was helping Prentice, a 'new boy', to settle in, Sergeant Heron was bedded down with his lady friend in Bad Oeynhausen and John was upstairs writing home. Thompson burst in. "Get your kit on, there's an emergency and there's only you, me and Prentice!"

The trio set off, John in the driving seat. On the way the Corporal explained that a disturbance had been reported at one of the barracks; the duty officer of the Manchester Regiment had phoned and requested back-up. As they approached the barracks they realised something was odd. The main gate, normally open, was closed and regimental police were prowling about on the road outside. The gates opened as the MPs arrived. They swept straight in and stopped at the edge of the barrack square. Ahead of them was a mob of angry men shouting and waving their arms about. "They're threatening to burn down the officers' mess!"

Spokesmen for the mob had made their position clear: they wanted to be paid and put in touch with their families, not unreasonable demands. Corporal Thompson and Lance Corporal Prentice disappeared in the direction of the officers' mess. The only remaining symbol of law and order was the Red Cap of Lance Corporal Dovey. Standing as tall as he possibly could, hands clasped behind his back, he stared ahead over the crowd. After perhaps five minutes – it seemed like an hour – there was silence and men began to drift away into the gloom. A knot of militants remained. The commanding officer arrived and repeated his warning that if they did not disperse, courts martial would deal with them and a prison sentence would follow.

The MPs, Thompson, Dovey and Prentice, handed the problem over to the regimental police and climbed back into their jeep. With a real sense of relief they sped away from the barracks. On the long straight approach road they were met by a convoy of trucks with headlights blazing. "Good God, it's the bloody Manchesters! I'd forgotten about them." The duty officer of the regiment had not just called up the Red Caps, he had rounded up as many men as he could find, armed them with pick-axe handles and fired them with enthusiasm. John dipped the headlights of the jeep as they slipped past and let them get on with it.

Anyone planning a career with the police had to be prepared to cope with tragic scenes. For years he could recall the smell of blood and booze in the car in which two young officers had lost their lives, and the bloody depression in the sand where the body of a young trooper had been crushed under the tracks of his own tank. John's tour of duty and his military career were coming to an end. His service with the military police had prepared him well for transfer to a civilian force. A training course was arranged at Hohne for men who had this in mind.

He took the train to Hamburg and changed there for Hohne. He had heard of it before. It was the place where the best mouth organs in the world were made. He seemed to be the only 'Brit' on board; he was surrounded by farm animals and sweaty yokels. Fortunately, the carriage was well ventilated; everyone except John seemed to enjoy the atmosphere of tobacco smoke and garlic. The train slowed and through the haze he made out the name of the station, Hohne and Bergen.

The camp was huge. All the comforts of home were provided for the American troops stationed there. "What is there to see outside?"

"Nothing, unless you want to visit Belsen."

Bergen-Belsen, this was another place he had heard of, the site of one of the notorious concentration camps. After Sunday lunch he set out on his quest. Finding the way was easy. Civilians in twos and threes were walking, downcast, in both directions. After half an hour the road narrowed and John found himself looking out across an area of flat land covered with numerous mounds, the mass graves of some of the victims of the Holocaust. Since the 1950s tens of thousands have visited the site.

It wasn't all gloom and danger. There were hilarious incidents like the case of the alsatian dog and the heating system. The handler tethered his pet to a radiator in the guardroom. When an unsavoury character was brought into the room for questioning, the dog decided he was guilty already and leapt forward to punish him. There was great confusion, the radiator was ripped off the wall, steam and scalding water was everywhere. "Sit, there's a good boy." Prisoner and pet both sat down.

Surrounded by khaki and the occasional dash of blue, John settled into his seat on the train heading for the coast. The lads seated nearby were cheerful and chatty; they were off on leave. John was thoughtful, thinking of his wedding day only weeks away. He looked out of the carriage window. The military train from Berlin approached the Dutch border; half-timbered farmhouses slid by, fir trees close to the track were a green blur, rolling hills beyond slowly fell away. Lance Corporal Dovey twisted round in his seat to take one last look at the German countryside. In years to come he would have time to consider all that had happened since he first crossed to the continent to join the British Army of the Rhine.

Dispatched by Air

When the 'call-up' letter arrived his first instinct was to ignore it, but that would have invited trouble. Mick Hockenhull had been dismembering sheep in Mr Higgs' butcher's shop for over two years. Perhaps two years in the army would be a nice change. "The Service Corps, they have butchers, that'll be your mob."

After his initial interview no more mention was made of butchering, and after the tedium of square bashing Mick went off to Driving

School. The Royal Army Service Corps had a long history; originally they were the Royal Wagoners. Horse-drawn transport was all gone; wagoners were replaced by drivers.

Driver Hockenhull waited in line to begin the drivers' course. The convoy of trucks was pointing in the direction of the camp gates and the public highway. Engines coughed into life. Every learner driver had his own instructor who explained the functions of the gearstick, clutch and accelerator pedal, handbrake and steering wheel. For the complete novice this was a lot to take in.

"See that gate up ahead? Go!"

The trucks were almost identical, same colour, same size, but they all reacted differently. Some jerked, juddered and stopped, some crept forwards at a snail's pace and others bounded away like kangaroos. "What are you waiting for, Hockenhull?"

"For them to make up their minds, Corporal."

After browbeating by the instructors and plenty of practice, all but the hopeless passed the driving test and could rightly hold the rank of Driver.

Pay was poor for the private soldier; even a few extra shillings every week would be welcome. It was rumoured that if you were an Air Dispatcher you would receive 'flying pay'. Mick and a squad of hopefuls arrived at Watchfield to begin the course. They drove packages to RAF Abingdon, loaded them on board 'Valettas' and threw them out over Watchfield. There was nothing difficult about that. They were taught to pack the parachutes that ensured a soft landing for the crates and bundles. Inevitably, mistakes were made.

They began to suspect that the rumour about flying pay was untrue, but they did know that the one sure way to get extra pay was to pack a parachute and jump out with it. The little squad were shown how to land and how to deal with tangled lines. When the required number of jumps had been made they would have wings on their shoulders and money in the pocket. On the last day of the course they had one more jump to make from a balloon over the airfield.

"Sorry, lads, too windy."

Mick picked up a bit of grass and let it drift to the ground. "Where's the wind?"

"Don't be cheeky, lad."

No wings no pay. Some were given a shoulder patch with an old Dakota on it to tell the world they were Air Dispatchers, but still no pocket money.

Before Mick and his mates were drafted to Germany they demonstrated their newly acquired skills at an air show. They were to dispatch a Land Rover, with driver and passenger on board, from the rear of an RAF transport aircraft. It would float gently down on four parachutes, land on the airfield and drive off to the applause of the crowd. In charge of the operation was 2nd Lieutenant 'Rupert Newboy'. At the last minute it was decided that the vehicle would be manned by dummies, a good decision.

Approaching the airfield the pilot gave 'the green light', and the Land Rover slid out into space and dropped; parachutes deployed. "How is it, Hockenhull?"

"Sir, I think we've missed the airfield. Two 'chutes' are OK, that's all…And there's a great cloud of dust."

"Good God! I'll be court-martialled."

The nineteen-year-old had only just been commissioned. Rupert was not disciplined. The squad crossed the Channel to take up their duties with the Army of the Rhine.

Driver Hockenhull adopted a casual attitude to his role as a Cold War warrior and left the worrying to politicians and readers of the *Daily Mail*. To show his platoon what it was all about Lieutenant Newboy organised a trip to the 'front line' in Berlin. They arrived by train and transferred to the S-Bahn, the rapid-transit system that circled the city. There were stops in every sector. Map in hand the young officer ushered his men into a carriage. "This is the Interzonenzug," he announced confidently. "Templehof, American Sector."

"Where are we now, sir, there's lakes and woods?"

"Treptower Park, nearly there, be ready to disembark." With all the authority of a school prefect Rupert called out, "This is it, our stop."

They lined up outside the surprisingly large station and marched off boldly along Friedrich Strasse. They were outshone by a squad stamping along in the opposite direction.

"Sir, they've got stars on their caps. What regiment would that be?"

"Have they really? About turn!"

How they managed to avoid the border guards and march out into the Russian sector was a mystery. The purpose of the visit was to observe the procedures at the various checkpoints around the city. The Lieutenant would make his report, omitting to mention that he had examined the border from both sides.

Even the Royal Army Service Corps could not avoid schemes and manoeuvres although they didn't have to charge around like Hussars. They just had to play hide and seek and not draw attention to themselves, something they believed they were good at.

The 'Sudwerker' was a massive truck. White balls at the end of steel rods mounted to left and right in front of the bonnet were supposed to help the driver avoid running into things. The squaddie in the passenger seat could help by standing up to get a better view through a circular hatch in the roof of the cab. The platoon sergeant found the perfect spot to hide, in a shallow ravine surrounded by woodland. Mick drew up behind with the Bedford ration truck. They left nothing to chance; camouflage netting was draped over both vehicles, leafy branches piled on top and wheel tracks, made on the soft ground, carefully disguised. Well satisfied with their work the platoon retired to the cab of the Sudwerker to celebrate with fags all round. Trucks and armoured cars scurried along the road and a helicopter circled overhead. They held their breath, drew on their fags and puffed away. "He's getting close, why doesn't he buzz off?"

There was thump on the top of the cab. A lump of black rubber, the shape of a small rugby ball, bounced down into the woodland clearing. "We've been spotted, but how?"

The Gazelle had been given a smoke signal from half a dozen 'Craven A'. The nicotine addicts had produced a column of smoke that was funnelled up through the hatch in the top of the cab and out above the woodland canopy into the clear blue sky. Bombed from above, they were out of the game. It was only a game.

The best of times were when Mick was driving alone. Later, when he examined the map of Europe, he was surprised to see how much ground he had covered in eighteen months. One cool morning Driver Hockenhull was rattling along a perfectly straight road taking in the view over the perfectly flat Dutch countryside. A heavy mist covered the ground; grazing cows had disappeared. It was unworldly. Trees

325

stood out on shortened trunks, and houses had no doors. High up in his cab Mick was above it all and glided on mentally counting 'days to do' before he returned to Civvy Street. The surrounding mist reminded him of something his instructor had said at the end of the driving course. There was a question and answer session that no one took very seriously. "Hockenhull, you are driving in fog. How can you tell if you are driving too fast?"

"You run into something, Corporal."

"Correct! If you hit a big grey elephant and its backside ends up on your bonnet you are going too fast."

It all came flooding back when Mick saw the elephant wandering about in the mist and looking anxiously around the eerie landscape. He slowed down, drove cautiously past, and watched in the mirror. Flapping ears and waving trunk faded away. He must have been seeing things. Up ahead, above the mist, there were tent tops and flags and banners. Mick bounced off the road and into the field. Strange people speaking a strange language surrounded him. An army truck with a soldier in it, had they done something wrong? He tried to explain, raised his hands behind his ears and waved. *"Elefant, verstehen Sie?"*

They didn't understand a word of German. Mick waved his arm in front of his nose and 'the penny dropped'. The ringmaster, the trapeze artist, lion tamer and dwarfs scampered out onto the road and disappeared into the morning mist. Mick backed onto the road and went on his way. Driver Hockenhull carried on driving when he came home from Germany. He didn't dismember any more dead sheep or see any more stray elephants.

Chapter 29

Sunshine Island

E.O.K.A

The situation on the sunshine island of Cyprus, in the 1950s, was complicated. Greeks and Turks had been at each other's throats for centuries. In 1925 the island became a British Crown Colony and the administrators managed to get Greek and Turk to rub along together for a while. In the post-war period, Britain was in the process of granting independence to several of her colonies. Cyprus was considered strategically important and worth hanging on to. The Greek community started to talk about *Enosis*, union with Greece. It was easy to see that this was something that the Turks would never agree to.

In the conflict that erupted Brits and Turks were allied against the Greeks. Reporting the troubles in the daily papers was simple because there were two easily recognisable 'pantomime villains' for the British public to jeer at. There was the Archbishop, dressed all in black with a grisly beard and a funny hat, and there was the wild-eyed old Colonel with a ridiculous moustache. What they got up to was no joke.

Colonel Georgios Grivas retired from the Greek Army and slipped secretly back to the island of his birth in 1954, and set up the National Organisation of Cypriot Fighters (EOKA). He inspired them to commit acts of terrorism. Archbishop Makarios was more politician than priest and gave vocal support to Grivas and his campaign. The British couldn't shut him up so they deported him to the Seychelles. After a year he was allowed to move to Athens. 'Black Mak' did not return to Cyprus until 'the troubles' were over. Grivas evaded capture a number of times and after nearly five years 'Uncle George' walked out of hiding. There were no winners, the island was eventually partitioned and Greeks and Turks carried on squabbling for the next fifty years.

At the height of the EOKA campaign there were in excess of thirty thousand British troops stationed on the island. Apley sent a small contingent of airmen: AC Snow, a one time evacuee; SAC Jones, from Windmill Lane and Corporal Eddie Cook, an estate carpenter. Their presence on the island had little impact on the outcome of the campaign.

SMART LAD

The woodland held no secrets for Ted Cook; generations of the family had worked at Apley. As gamekeeper he knew every tree on his beat and the ways of every creature, pheasant and partridge, fox and stoat, rabbit and grass snake. For satisfaction in life he saw no reason to look beyond the boundaries of the estate. As a soldier in the Great War he had served in the dangerous tribal areas of British India on the border with Afghanistan. He had seen enough of 'foreign parts'. Sergeant Ted Cook had little to say about his time in uniform.

When his son, Eddie, left school, Ted found him a job as a forester. It was not to his liking. The agent was sympathetic and moved him to the Estate yard where he began his apprenticeship as a carpenter. Repairs to farms and cottages took him to every corner of the Estate and in touch with scores of people. This he enjoyed, Eddie was a sociable lad. When work was done Eddie got back on his bike and went off for more socialising. He took to the dance floor at every opportunity and was never short of a partner. He could make the clumsiest girl appear elegant. Not every carpenter was comfortable in an evening suit and a black tie; perhaps he was not suited to the trade.

In the summer of '56 he was out of his apprenticeship and into Air Force blue. He signed on, for better pay and choice of trade. RAF Spitalgate was home to an officer cadet training unit in the 1950s and here the staff handed on all the skills needed for Eddie to be an officers' mess steward. No sooner was Eddie Cook's training complete than he was sent on embarkation leave, dispatched to Southampton, boarded a Cunard liner and sailed to Cyprus. Most of the lads who sailed with him spent their tour of duty sharing a dusty tent, not Eddie. At Episkopi on the south coast of the island he had a room to himself in the sergeant's mess, sheer luxury.

The security situation did not improve. 'Uncle George' Grivas directed his band of terrorists from a series of hideouts and evaded capture. Makarios, the 'troublesome priest' had been deported. He was not the only 'man of God' to give their blessing to bombers and snipers. When there was clear evidence they too were arrested. Taking the opportunity to see something of the island Corporal Cook volunteered to escort one of them to Nicosia. It was just as well to know how to react if anything unexpected cropped up. All servicemen on the island were issued with a 'little red book' with advice on when to open fire and what to aim at. The biggest target, the middle of the body was recommended. This was the 'licence to kill' and everyone was assured that if they truly believed they were doing the right thing the military authorities would back them up. Eddie checked the regulations just to be on the safe side. The journey to Nicosia was uneventful. Eddie and the driver chatted; the priest maintained a stony silence.

Alarming articles appeared regularly in the papers reporting bombings, ambushes and murders. Folks at home might have been anxious but, for the most part, servicemen on the island accepted the situation and made the best of their time in the sun. Staff at Episkopi had a fine beach to lounge about on. Most days Eddie was off duty at midday and could saunter down the cliff path and bathe in the Mediterranean. He was lying in his bunk one evening listening to *Two-way Family Favourites* when he heard his name mentioned. "We have a request for a piece of music for Corporal Eddie Cook from a girl back home." By the time he had recovered from the shock the music faded away and the announcer was nattering on about another couple.

The only dangerous incident he could recall during eighteen months of 'active service' was on the camp outside the Astra cinema. A queue of young airmen was waiting for the doors to open and admit them to the world of Hollywood. Someone casually kicked an empty beer can across the road; it bounced against the side of an upturned cardboard box. The box flipped over and a parcel of explosives was revealed. The queue scattered in all directions. Nothing happened, there was no explosion. The RAF police arrived from the guardroom. There was no need for 'the Snowdrops' to worry about crowd control; no one was going near the dangerous-looking package. Lads from the station armoury arrived and made it safe.

It was all the luck of the draw; airmen could be posted anywhere in the world. Eddie could have gone to Kinloss with the murky Moray Firth to the north and the Cairngorm Mountains behind him. Now if he wanted snow he could go to the Troodos Mountains for a day or two and return to the beach to warm himself up.

Sailing home again with Cunard, Eddie had time to consider his next move. He had the training and experience to make him the ideal candidate to be a Cunard steward. Back home he applied and was accepted. There was a snag. The ship he should have joined was weeks away from port and Eddie was strapped for cash. He had to find something more immediate. Much to his father's dismay, Eddie made a decision. He was not going to take up his carpenter's tools again and return to the Estate.

Eddie was a 'people person' and spent his working life solving problems for social services. For this work and his voluntary work as welfare officer for the local RAF Association, he was awarded the Imperial Service Medal to pin up alongside the campaign medal awarded to all who had served in the EOKA campaign.

Tony's Tour

Eddie Cook's cockney cousin, Tony Snow, did not complete his engineering apprenticeship. When his call-up papers came he did not hesitate, he wanted to get it over with. Most lads from around the Elephant and Castle had never heard of RAF Bridgnorth, but Tony certainly had. Evacuated as a toddler to the safe haven of Apley, he knew the fields and lanes that surrounded the recruit training camp very well. Off duty at weekends he could walk away and visit aunts and uncles, enjoy home cooking and meet up with old school friends.

These were anxious times for the nation in the build-up to the Suez invasion. After brief training at RAF Odiham in Hampshire, Tony was put on standby for Suez. Orders were changed and he found himself in the belly of a Beverly bound for Cyprus. It was a stop-start flight. Taking off from Abingdon they spent half an hour in the air over the home counties before returning to base with 'a touch of engine trouble'. They returned to the skies and made it as far as Italy. From there it should have been a short hop to Cyprus. The pilot, worried by the same 'dodgy' engine, decided to put down again at Idris in Libya. Eventually they arrived at Nicosia.

Within the perimeter of the airfield there were scores of tents. Tony spent six months in one close to the RAF Police post. Aircraftsman

Snow's duties were simple: he 'rode shotgun' on vehicles provided for officers being ferried around the island. As escort he sat with a Sten gun across his knees, admired the scenery and kept an eye out for any suspicious-looking characters. Not everyone was comfortable handling a loaded gun. Off duty Tony made up his meagre pay by standing in on guard duty for anyone who didn't like the idea of being a target.

In this tense atmosphere some of the security forces 'overstepped the mark'. Tony recalled one unpleasant incident involving a member of the RAF Regiment. An unfortunate Greek youth was discovered in a boiler house on the camp. He shouldn't have been there. When Tony came on the scene he was being given a beating by the gunner. Tony intervened. "Lay off 'im, he's had enough." It has to be acknowledged that there was brutality on all sides.

Tony tried skiing in the Troodos Mountains. After forty-eight hours practise he gave up rather than risk a broken leg. He was much more at home in the camp pool. Few lads were competent swimmers but Tony's boyhood training in the Worfe Brook and the River Severn paid off. The RAF had given Tony an action holiday in the sun. The weather after Christmas was rather dull.

Tony boarded another Beverly; this one was more reliable and he made it back to England without incident. Appropriately, Aircraftsman Snow arrived at RAF Lyneham in the snow. After leave he reported to RAF Old Catton, near Norwich. He was to receive his discharge papers and then return to the sensible world of the engineering workshop.

By chance one day on London Bridge Station, Tony met the man he had tussled with in the boiler room at Nicosia. Tony tackled him again over the incident. The 'Rock Ape' (member of the RAF Regiment) was unrepentant. He still believed that any Greek youth, terrorist or not, deserved a good hiding. No amount of reasoning was going to change his view.

As I Recall

Senior Aircraftsman Jones didn't keep a diary and so his recollection of events was not always accurate. That was his excuse for making slight exaggerations and adopting stories he had heard and making them his own.

His earliest memories were of wartime. There was nothing remarkable about that because he couldn't remember a time when there wasn't a war. Men in uniform, bombers in the air, convoys on the main

331

road, Land Girls in the fields and evacuees in the village school, this was normal. Without any warning the evacuees all went home. If there was a farewell party he missed it.

When he graduated from the village school a whole new world of knowledge was revealed at Bridgnorth Grammar School. There were really important sounding subjects like Physics and Chemistry, even Scripture was interesting. Mr Pearson had actually been to Palestine with the army and hardly ever mentioned Jesus.

Schooldays came to an end and the world of work had to be faced. Father and brother worked on the land, so did most of his uncles. It was hard work and he didn't like the feel of it. Harold Evans, the blacksmith, came to the rescue. "I'll get you a job at the Friar's, in the warm."

'Young Jonah' completed his education in the riverside factory of the Carpet Manufacturing Company. The men of the maintenance department and their apprentices were a protected species. They worked inside a wire cage. Teenage boys were outnumbered twenty to one by cheeky girls and wanton married women capable of doing shameful things to innocent lads. For their own protection they took refuge in the safe haven of the machine shop. For the apprentices carpet production was not important. Things worth considering were sport, the hidden charms of some of the comely young weavers and the call-up. There were two ways to approach this: wait for the letter or volunteer.

He jumped the gun. One Saturday afternoon he took the bus to Wolverhampton walked into the RAF recruiting office and signed on. At every stage in his training he earned a 'satisfactory' grade. His would not be a glittering military career. The aim was to serve overseas, anywhere, but because he had jumped the gun he was too young to be sent abroad, and was posted to RAF Colerne instead. He had hardly settled in when there was an alarming incident.

Stretched out on their 'pits' after lunch, ground crew mechanics were only half listening to 'Digger' Bryden as he described some of the more unusual treats offered by Chinese maidens in the brothels of Singapore. An engine fitter at the end of the billet jumped up. "I don't like the sound of that. She's lost an engine." He strode out of the billet, no one moved, he was back almost immediately. "She's crashed!"

Pete Horden was one of the first on the scene. Riding his motorbike across the airfield he had also spotted the problem. Hastings TG 615 was attempting to land with one engine 'feathered', and he knew she wasn't going to make it. Well short of the runway she bounced on one wheel and careered across a couple of fields and came to rest on the edge of a patch of woodland. Horden alerted the fire crew and made for the crash site. The clanging of the fire bell brought airmen out of their billets and scampering across the airfield. In minutes the aircraft was in flames and the crew in danger. With great presence of mind Horden snatched up an axe and attempted to smash through a Perspex panel in the nose, he could see one of the crew trapped inside. His battledress began to burn. The fire crew hauled him away and sprayed him with foam.

Taffy Jennick, wearing protective clothing, managed to drag Flight Sergeant George Lee clear just before one of the fuel tanks exploded. The rest of the crew were badly shaken but managed to make their escape unaided.

The last resting place of Hastings TG 615 on Bannerdown Hill.

"Is there anything worth saving?"

When 'Digger' and 'Jonah' arrived on the scene the crew were picking their way across a field of turnips. They glanced back and appeared to be chatting casually as if they had just executed the perfect landing. It was a memorable scene; brilliant balls of fire erupted from the undercarriage when the magnesium alloy castings began to melt.

Pete Horden's heroism was not rewarded, hair was singed and tunic ruined. He was interviewed by his squadron leader. Instead of a pat on the back for a brave effort he got a 'bollocking' for damaging his precious RAF uniform. LAC 'Taffy' Jennick got his name in the paper the next day.

A choice of overseas postings was offered to volunteers. There was Korea and Malaya. Senior Aircraftsman Jones didn't like the sound of either. He chose Ceylon, safe and exotic. He was posted to Cyprus.

Kitting out for overseas service was organised at RAF Cardington, famous for its enormous airship hangars that dominated the Bedfordshire landscape. The organisation was impressive; kit issued and 'jabs' given all on the same day. There was no time for volunteers to have second thoughts. Weighed down by the extra kit, batches of young airmen were assembled in the railway sidings. Jonah had seen old newsreels of prisoners of war (usually Italians) being herded around and had often wondered why one or two didn't just slide off into the nearest patch of woodland. He went along with the crowd and boarded the train for Liverpool. Brummies on board were excited by the prospect of getting one last glimpse of their beautiful city. They were disappointed. No one was quite sure where they were at any stage of the journey. On some stretches of the track there was grass growing between the sleepers. At Liverpool the train puffed straight onto the quayside. He could not be sure but Jones 238 thought the train actually went down Lime Street, making a screeching noise on the little-used rails. They arrived at the dock.

Her Majesty's Troopship, *Oxfordshire*, was big and it was full of 'Pongos'. Boys in blue were heavily outnumbered by lads in khaki. Communications on the troop deck were difficult. 'Jocks' of the Black Watch were hard to understand and Green Howards, from just south of the border, were impossible. The passage across the Bay of Biscay was rough. In the bunk next to Jonah was a hairy Scotsman. They were thrown together and tossed about for twenty minutes. Neither of them enjoyed the experience.

The seas were calm when the *Oxfordshire* passed through the Straits of Gibraltar. The young airman recalled images of the Rock he had seen in his stamp collection. Now he was getting somewhere. Was that a dhow near the coast of Morocco or flying fish south of Malta? When he came to tell of his adventures he couldn't be sure. Distinguishing fact from fiction, and fantasy with reality he always found difficult.

The troopship dropped anchor in Larnaca Bay. Troops were ferried ashore in the lifeboats and they stepped off onto a wooden landing stage and down onto the beach. This was great, just like D-Day without the danger. Trucks were backed up on the edge of the sand and once they were full shot off inland in convoy. There wasn't much to see out of the back; orange groves and old blokes with big moustaches and baggy black trousers.

The transit camp at Nicosia was dire. The only good thing about it was that it was a transit camp and no one expected to be there very long. The 'bell tents' were ancient. The site, in a dusty hollow, looked as if it had been overrun by a tribe of Zulus. Draining away from behind the catering tent was a sluggish stream of grey oily liquid with an uncountable number of flies sipping at the edge. The cooks must have done something terribly wrong to have been condemned to serve there.

Luckily, within a week, 238 Jones and 239 Massey appeared on a list and were sent off to meet Flight Lieutenant Lampton, CO of the Levant Communications Flight. This was a very happy little unit tucked away in the corner of the airfield. The Pembroke ferried the Governor General and other VIPs around, and 'Lambkin' kept up his flying hours in the night fighter version of the Meteor.

Rather than confront the EOKA threat head-on, Levant Communications Flight personnel sometimes flew around dropping leaflets to explain to the terrorists that what they were doing was pointless, and that what Colonel Grivas had to offer at the EOKA Restaurant was not very appetising.

335

This had no effect and Greek hooligans carried on murdering Turks and taking pot shots at British troops.

The billet, a stone-built barn, was cool and airy. This was first-class accommodation compared with the tents that sprang up from time to time to be filled with disgruntled infantrymen. Catering was still an issue. The best fed on the island were undoubtedly the flies. The only time they moved away from the cookhouse was when they followed the cart used to empty the latrines. They soon returned and dabbled their dirty little feet on everyone's plate. There was one condition the medical officers never had to prescribe for and that was constipation.

A night out in Nicosia was not the same as a night out in Bridgnorth. Flight mechanics were not front line troops but they still had to carry a weapon to visit the bars on Ledra Street. They were issued with Lee-Enfield rifles that could have been used by their fathers in the Great War. The press referred to Ledra Street as 'murder mile' because squaddies had been shot from the window of a newspaper office. The culprit was eventually caught.

Entertainment was limited. There were one or two enterprising young women available and some not so young. Even casual romance could be dangerous. A lad could lose his innocence, his wallet or his life. One local beauty invited an RAF Sergeant to her flat. When he stepped in EOKA gunmen killed him. It was best to stick to Keo, the local beer. It produced a shocking headache but nothing worse.

A lot of lads relied on the local taxi drivers to get them safely back to base before midnight. You had to admire the Greeks heroism. They were inviting into their taxis half a dozen drunks armed with a variety of weapons. Most of the bearers were incapable of handling these weapons safely even when they were sober. And at the end of the journey there was no guarantee that the fare would be paid.

Over the years Cyprus became the ideal holiday location; not too far from home, perfect climate, history, varied culture, good food, wine and sandy beaches. The northern port of Kyrenia was particularly attractive with its harbour and ancient castle. Richard the Lionheart captured it on his way to the third crusade, and it was subjected to numerous attacks throughout the centuries that followed. When Flight Lieutenant Lampton's lads went down to the harbour to help him with his dinghy it would have been nice to have a look inside the castle, but that was not allowed. On the top of the battlements were coils of barbed wire, not to stop intruders getting in but EOKA prisoners getting out. Kyrenia Castle was the police training school and prison.

On the Kyrenia Pass, between the port and Nicosia, the RAF career of 238 Jones took a tumble. You couldn't call it an action or even an incident. It was just a 'brush' with a carload of Cypriot youths. The following day Jonah was not himself. He was an early riser, once awake he was out of bed. On this miserable morning he couldn't move. He was whisked away to the British Military Hospital. An army medical officer assessed his condition and recommended 'bed rest'. The nice comfy bed prepared for him was a thick sheet of plywood with a thin sheet of cotton on top. Resting on this would have been difficult had it not been for the wonder drug morphine.

He wished he could have taken in the atmosphere of the ward more clearly. The ward sister was a vision of loveliness, moving gracefully round the ward in her pure white uniform, filling young lads' heads with impure thoughts. 'Jonah' was unmoved; he could hear the card players behind him talking about dangerous incidents and near misses. He couldn't join in and neither could 'Scouse' or 'Pop'.

They said Popadopoulos was in the British military hospital to be treated for a wound and an anxiety disorder. Someone had shot him; he didn't say who or why. Maybe he had been a bit too pally with the British. 'Pop' went around the ward with a worried look on his face. Outside the security of the hospital compound there was the real possibility that someone would shoot him again. For the good of his health his best bet was to fly to London and get a job as a waiter in a backstreet café in Fulham.

It was hard to say whether the Scouse squaddie was unlucky or just plain stupid. The decision of the court martial was that he should be detained in Wayne's Keep, another ancient monument that had been converted into a military prison. He didn't really want to go because it was rumoured that forms of torture were still practised there. Bumping along the road in the Military Police jeep he snatched a Sten gun from the escort and shot himself in the thigh hoping for a flesh wound. He was very unlucky the round shattered his femur and because his leg was bent the round flew on and passed through his shin. This self-inflicted wound would be added to the charge sheet at his next court martial. He had few friends but he did have his uses. As he hopped about the ward he kept Jonah informed of events as he lay about waiting for a miracle cure. The Scouse gave him a first-hand account of a particularly tragic incident. "Shot in the back on foot patrol, they reckon. No use, can't do anything for 'em. They're laying 'em out now."

Jonah was unmoved. He was still stuck on his sheet of plywood, and still enjoying his morphine. It was a very seductive and comforting drug. From what he could remember he pieced together a story he would repeat many times.

Telling the Tale

The QA Nursing Sister glided round the ward with a clipboard and a charming smile. "You are 238 Jones, RAF, I believe? Have to say goodbye to you. 'Casevac' in the morning."

As he was being manhandled into the Hastings Jonah glanced up at the squadron markings, 511, his old squadron from RAF Colerne. That was disturbing. He had made modifications to the control system of one of these aircraft and it might have been this very one!

Safely back in England, Senior Aircraftsman Jones spent a few weeks in the RAF Hospitals at Wroughton and Cosford. He had returned from active service as a casualty which sounded quite heroic so he was given a compassionate posting to RAF Shawbury. He was on permanent 'light duties', which meant he did very little. He came home most weekends and set himself the mission of having a drink in every pub in Bridgnorth, although not all on the same night.

The pubs were full of 'boys in blue'. The last of the National Servicemen were square bashing on the camp at Stanmore. SAC Jones stood out from the crowd in his slightly worn battledress. As the evening wore on and the pints of beer pushed him into a world of fantasy he was ready to tell the story once again. Noticing the ribbon of the General Service Medal over the breast pocket an unsuspecting 'erk' might say, "Were you in Malaya?"

"No, Cyprus."

He leaned back clutching his elbows so that the badges of rank of a Senior Aircraftsman and his marksman's badge could be admired by the young recruits. He was now ready to tell the tale with one or two extra touches. He began. "They were Red Caps but they weren't in uniform,

338

just strolling about in Famagusta. I was in the BMH at Nicosia, nothing serious. Medics shot out and piled the pair of them onto stretchers and dragged them out of the back of the garry, that's a jeep. One of them QA sisters all starchy and efficient appeared, and they were whisked off into one of the huts. It was blazing hot outside; must have been good to get into the shade. Word went round, they'd been shot, poor bastards, seriously. It was serious, they were both dead…It was quite wild out there."

His delivery was not always totally convincing.

After eighteen months of light duties Jonah was detached to paradise, RAF Chessington. Excellent food, light exercise routines under the supervision of a beautifully proportioned WAAF Sergeant – "Nothing wrong with her body." There was occupational therapy in the afternoons. Lovely girls with cultured southern accents helped out with watercolours, basket weaving and other hands-on activities. There were trips out to the zoo next door. On one occasion, 'the walking wounded' were whisked off to the centre court at Wimbledon to be applauded by the crowd. TV personalities put on entertainments and signed autographs. At the weekends there were free tickets to West End shows paid for by Lord Nuffield. This could not last. Senior Aircraftsman Jones was sent back to Cosford, fitted with a lovely new corset, then back to Shawbury to hand in everything except his tropical kit and his cap badge. He was discharged 'unfit for service'. His glorious military career was at an end.

THE TRUTH AT LAST

A grateful nation gave him a demob suit and sent him off for training behind the Hoover factory on the Great West Road. He was going to be converted from airframe mechanic to instrument maker. All the trainees in Mr Cobley's workshop were 'unfit for service'.

"What brings you here?" Unusually for him, Jonah didn't have much to say. He only made vague references to the British Military Hospital in Nicosia.

Phil had a short leg crushed by a tank in Germany, an accident. Ron was paralysed from the waist down, a casualty of friendly fire in the billet. Ted only had one foot; he left the other one behind in Cyprus. The bomb incident that caused this was reported in national newspapers so everyone knew the story. Jonah had a corset with steel bands in it, so he kept quiet. A bad back was hardly a war wound.

Years and years and years went by; marriage, children, work, travel, a whole new series of stories were put into the memory bank. 'The Murder of the Red Caps' was only revisited when Mr Jones was on a morphine trip which wasn't very often. Then he stopped telling the story altogether because he began to doubt the truth of it. "Did I make it up? Was I there at the time?" This went through his mind as he stared at the ceiling of the orthopaedic ward in Christchurch Hospital. He was listening to an old New Zealander telling about his conversion to Christianity.

"The shell must have got stuck. There was this almighty bang. When I turned back I could see the barrel, solid steel, opening up like a tulip. I walked back, all the gunners were dead. Their officer, only a boy; his cap was blowing about in the dust. I thought someone up there must be looking out for me."

Graham Jones was discharged from hospital and spent six months watching TV, shuffling about on a Zimmer frame and playing on the computer. This uncomfortable period of convalescence wasn't a complete waste of time because, through the magic of the internet, SAC Jones discovered the truth about Lance Corporals Cameron and Turvey. All was revealed at Woodside in Telford by John Paskin. "We were born on the same day, me and Brian. We could have been twins."

John Paskin and Brian Turvey arrived at the Royal Artillery Depot at Oswestry on the same day and travelled together to Inkerman Barracks to join 582 Squad and begin their training as military policemen. They sailed together on the *Empire Orwell* to disembark at Limassol, crossed the island to Famagusta and began their tour of duty with HQ 227 Provost Company. These two young Lance Corporals were in each other's company daily. They shared meals, drinks, jokes, days on the beach and the dangers of patrolling Varosha, the Greek district of Famagusta.

Brian Turvey was going home. He had taken his last 'snaps' of the town and expected the prints to be ready for collection at the chemists. "John, let me do your shift today. I want to pick up those pictures."

John Paskin stayed in Warburg House, Brian Turvey and Bill Cameron went out on 'Q' Patrol. They were in plain clothes. This was no disguise. They were familiar figures known to the local children, the shopkeepers and the local EOKA commander and his men. The gunmen made no mistake. They were shot in the back at close range, and died there on the street on a sunny Sunday afternoon in May. Comrades in uniform were on the scene in minutes and they were carried away with all speed to BMH Nicosia and laid in the mortuary. As he quietly left the room one of the escorts recalled hearing the steady tick of a wristwatch; 'life goes on'. No family members were present when they were buried, side by side, a few days later at Wayne's Keep.

At Kyrenia in 2009, fifty years after the end of the conflict, a memorial was unveiled to commemorate the three hundred and seventy-one who died during the campaign. The names of Lance Corporal Turvey and Lance Corporal Cameron also appear again on a panel at the National Memorial Arboretum. They are carved at waist height and can easily be touched if anyone wanted to confirm that they were real people. 238 SAC Jones is satisfied that this is one story he did get right.

Chapter 30

Part-timers and Professionals

The Terriers

Anyone joining the Territorial Army in the 1930s must have known that sooner or later they would be asked to do something more serious than playing soldiers. The call to arms soon came and they performed well.

Play was resumed in the 1950s. The Cold War didn't put off half a dozen village lads who turned up for parade once a week at the Drill Hall in Bridgnorth. An annual camp was arranged to test their ability to survive in the open air after a heavy night's drinking. Similar skills were tested at the annual dinner.

The Falcon had seen better days. Wines, spirits and ale had been served there for over four centuries. The trade had its ups and downs. When Cromwell's Puritan Parliament ran the country trade was down. It perked up when the monarchy was restored, and up again as trade on the river increased. To the dismay of churchmen and sober citizens, an alarming number of pubs sprang up in the town. In the dismal days that followed the Great War the publicans suffered like everyone else. Then came the RAF to set up a camp nearby and train recruits, and the landlords rejoiced.

Members of the 4th Battalion King's Shropshire Light Infantry (TA) arrived in twos and threes. The Falcon sign was taken from the coat of arms of the Whitmores of Apley and swung on-high from an ornate wrought iron bracket, all very suitable for men of quality. To enter the Falcon in its heyday customers had to be appropriately dressed; no open-necked shirts. At the time this was not a suitable place for men who worked in the weaving sheds of the carpet factory on the opposite bank of the river. The management provided a discreet little room for officers of the Royal Air Force with a bar at one end, an upright piano at the other and a dance floor for smooching around with girls of good character. Crib, darts, dominoes and factory girls were on offer elsewhere, at any one of the sixty-odd pubs in the town. When the camp closed the Falcon had to open its doors to all sorts.

The 'Recce Patrol' arrived. "What do you lot think you lot are doin' in here?"

"Terriers' Dinner, don't be rude. Camp's closed, you ought to be grateful."

The barman was subjected to more abuse until Captain Peter Shaw arrived, greeted his men cheerily and ordered drinks. They settled down and began to chatter again. They patted the bread rolls that had been carefully set out with the cutlery four hours earlier and were drying out nicely. There were paper serviettes in wine glasses and half a dozen drooping flowers in a lager glass. The Falcon had definitely seen better days. Someone who could bring cheer to any gathering was 'Merve' Roberts.

Ever Ready

Private Mervin Roberts joined the ranks of the 4th Battalion of the King's Shropshire Light Infantry (TA) in September 1961. He went on to serve for over thirty years. In all that time he missed only one summer camp.

Merve Roberts on a TA exercise doing what he did best, keeping up morale.

Permission given by Val Roberts

"Did I say something funny?"

When compulsory National Service came to an end in 1962, the government offered TA soldiers a bounty of £150 if they would agree to serve anywhere in the world at short notice.

There had been troubles in many of Britain's old colonies as they demanded independence. The anti-colonial movement in South Arabia focused on the port of Aden. This was not a simple affair. Egypt gave support to the National Liberation Front (NLF). Other rival groups attacked both the NLF and British servicemen and their families. The first serious incident was a bomb attack targeting the British High Commissioner in 1963. For the next three years, until the last of the British forces withdrew, Aden was a very unpleasant place to be.

Merve and half a dozen 'Ever Readies' flew out in 1965 to serve alongside regulars of the Royal Anglian Regiment. Their trip was well publicised in the local press. They drew their tropical kit and were photographed. They posed for the camera on the railway platform at Shrewsbury, and as they boarded an RAF Britannia at Lyneham they were photographed again.

When the aircraft doors were opened at RAF Khormaksar, Merve's reaction was the same as many who had gone before. "Like stepping into a bloody oven, it was."

It wasn't exactly a war but it wasn't very pleasant walking the dusty streets, and driving along barren tracks not knowing who was friend and who was foe. Merve made the best of it like he always did, out on patrol, manning a checkpoint, and keeping up everyone's spirits. By now four of Bill Roberts's sons were in uniform. Tommy and Michael were regulars; Mervin and John were with the TA. Their paths crossed a number of times. Michael, a REME fitter, put Merve's truck on the road in Germany. On peacekeeping duties in Cyprus Tommy met up with his part-time brothers. Taken together, the military service of father and sons must have amounted to at least seventy-five years. Few families could make this claim.

FOLLOWING IN FATHER'S FOOTSTEPS

The Honourable James Hamilton had a year out after Eton to do some travelling. With the money he made as a truck driver at a uranium mine in Canada he bought a motorbike and drove around the States. Scruffy and bearded he returned to the family home in Surrey. "A spell with the Coldstreams, that'll smarten him up."

344

No other regiment could be considered, family tradition would be maintained. His father, the 3rd Baron Hamilton of Dalzell, had distinguished himself in the Second World War. He had been wounded and decorated with the Military Cross. Even with that sort of background receiving a commission was not a forgone conclusion. One Old Etonian, Tam Dalyell, expected to be commissioned into the Royal Scots Grey; one of his ancestors raised the regiment in 1678. Tam managed to 'lose an armoured car' on a training exercise and completed his National Service as a trooper.

The staff of Eaton Hall were satisfied with James Hamilton's performance and he was commissioned. Next there was the question of a posting. This was a worry for Lady Hamilton. She knew what young officers in barracks in London got up to in their spare time. "I'm going to speak to George."

The 3rd Battalion Coldstream Guards was in Germany and the Guards Brigade was commanded by George Burns, best man at Lord and Lady Hamilton's wedding. Strings were pulled and James was plucked away before any real damage could be done to his reputation. He was given a job as liaison officer at the Guards' Headquarters with the British Army of the Rhine where the long-suffering Brigadier Burns could keep an eye on him. This came as a relief to Lady Hamilton.

It was becoming obvious that he was not going to be a conventional officer. He was most comfortable wearing his father's old forage cap and wellington boots. Well over six feet tall, he was not the sort of man who couldn't be overlooked. Supervising his platoon one day as they enjoyed a spot of target practise, James was approached by the range commander. The Major was short in stature and short-tempered. "Don't you salute Majors in your regiment?"

With a casual hand James gently brushed the side of his father's cap and replied, "Most certainly, I will salute anyone if it gives them pleasure." No reply.

The British Army of the Rhine spent a lot of time 'on exercise'. This meant manoeuvring around the German countryside in all weathers. Headquarters was made mobile, clerks packed up their typewriters, cooks packed up their stew pots and senior officers packed anything that would make their spell 'in the field' more comfortable. In a score of trucks they moved from one location to another at the whim of staff officers.

Ensign Hamilton was given a map reference which he managed to misread. Guardsmen piled out of the trucks and started to pitch tents over rows of sugar beet. "Sir, this can't be right!"

It seemed alright to James dressed as a gamekeeper and wearing his favourite black gumboots. In the evening Brigadier Burns opened his ration pack, took off his boots and tried to get some rest on his camp bed. James had made other arrangements. He made contact with local gentry who could offer better accommodation, a hot meal, fine wine and very comfortable sleeping arrangements. Despite his 'odd' behaviour James Hamilton proved to be an efficient young officer, but he was clearly not cut out for a career in the army.

A FINE PAIR

Old soldiers sometimes think back and ask themselves, "Whatever happened to 'Chalky' White? We were big mates. We lost touch years ago." James Hamilton and Jimmy Ferard never lost touch. They met in Germany and struck up a friendship that lasted a lifetime.

The life of a National Service officer could be a miserable one. How could they, in less than two years, earn the respect of their men and complete a military career to compare with their father's? Jimmy's dad had been a Lieutenant Colonel and Lord John Hamilton had won the Military Cross.

The menu in the officers' mess was better and the battledress of the subaltern was better tailored than that of the squaddie. That said, for eighteen months the most junior officers could expect to be looked down upon by regular officers, and treated with contempt by most senior NCOs. If the platoon sergeant took a liking to them all would be well, and they would be able to cope with the indifference and lack of enthusiasm of the troops counting the days to demob. To survive they need a sense of humour and plenty of outside interests.

Together Jimmy Ferard and James Hamiliton made the most of what the jazz clubs or the opera house in Dusseldorf had to offer. Always on a tight budget James still managed visits to Vienna and the ski slopes of Switzerland. Away from mud and map-reading organised by the army, there were ducks to be shot on the Rhine and geese in Yugoslavia. Jimmy and James shared soldiering and sporting experiences and their friendship grew. They both had a love of nature, and the traditional way of life of the English countryside.

In retirement Jimmy Ferard moved into the Manor House at Ewdness and over the years created a living memorial. In the orchard he cultivated a collection of fruit trees, pruning and grafting rare varieties of apple and plum. The orchard is neglected now but some of the stock he so carefully tended may find another place to flourish when the restoration of the Apley walled garden is complete.

James Hamiliton was a generous man remembered in many ways. He supported numerous charities. He wasn't 'a soft touch', but he was always open to suggestions. Plans were made to build a replica of the Globe Theatre on the banks of the Thames. Traditional materials would be used, blacksmith-made nails, lime plaster, thatch and a vast amount of English oak. An appeal was launched and James responded. Somewhere in the timbers of the theatre are beams and planks of Apley oak; the bench seats for the audience are durable and very hard.

A Colourful Career

In 1963 Mick Roberts cleaned the mud off his farm boots and hung them up. The army gave him some new ones to keep brightly polished for the next twenty years. He became a heavy plant specialist with the Royal Electrical and Mechanical Engineers. Tanks, trucks, even trains, Mick could handle them all.

His first taste of travel was to Germany where, even after twenty years, there were still reminders of war. Nuns ran a mental hospital in a castle at Liebenau. Hitler ordered the patients to be exterminated. Some of the rooms had not been redecorated since the Nazis left. There were ornate pillars, intricate plasterwork and swastikas painted on the ceiling. "This was one of Hitler's love camps," Mick was told.

Here strapping young storm-troopers were encouraged to breed with blue-eyed blonde beauties. It was hard to believe that swastikas on the ceiling would make the lovemaking more passionate. Hitler had some funny ideas.

For two years REME fitters kept the 'Stollies' of the Scots Guards rolling along. The Alvis 'Stalwart', a six-wheeled amphibious truck, was a complicated machine, far too complex for mere guardsmen to understand.

After specialist training on earthmoving equipment, Mick was off to Singapore to celebrate his twenty-first birthday with his brother, Tommy, who was serving there with the KSLI. He quickly recovered from the binge at a Changi bar. Soon he was on his way, north into Thailand and east up to the Cambodian border.

Royal Engineers and REME technicians toiled to build roads through tropical forest, and bridges over tributaries of the Mekong River. To help with this difficult work they brought in local labour and their 'pets'. The elephants knew what they were about; they had been handling logs for centuries. As these placid animals cleared roads and built pontoon bridges, American jets screamed overhead flying east to Vietnam on bombing raids. Fighters from the airbase at Ubon engaged in dog-fights with communists over what was supposed to be neutral territory. This was close enough to the unwinnable Vietnam War.

Michael rose steadily through the ranks. Mary Ann spotted Sergeant Roberts when he arrived at Manobier in south Wales. She must have thought he had potential because she agreed to marry him. After eighteen months in the classroom Michael was qualified for the top job and Artificer Sergeant Major Roberts T. Eng. became a law unto himself.

The British Army sent the newly-weds on safari to Kenya – not for a fortnight like most tourists – for three years. They were given splendid accommodation, a lavish bungalow, freshly painted, no swastikas on the ceiling required.

Sergeant Major Roberts supervised training for the Kenyan Army and gave support to British troops sent out for a taste of the tropics.

A constant problem was pilfering, not just small things like khaki shorts and spanners from the workshops, but even sand-coloured Land Rovers sometimes disappeared in a cloud of dust. "I'll see to it they don't take mine."

Michael ordered pots of non-regulation pink paint. No one was going to steal his famous pink Land Rover even if he left the keys in it.

Britain granted Cyprus independence in 1960. Greeks and Turks continued to squabble. Generals in Athens still wanted the island to be part of Greece. They arranged a military coup that changed the government in Cyprus to one that shared their aims. Within a week Turkey responded by landing an invasion force on the north coast of the island. The invasion ended in partition along the UN-monitored Green Line which still divides the island.

When British troops took up peacekeeping duties they wore the blue beret of the United Nations. There were few incidents. Servicemen and their families could relax and enjoy the sunshine, and Ann and Michael Roberts certainly did. Their last tour together was not so agreeable. In Northern Ireland it was not so easy to keep 'the men of violence' apart.

Sergeant Major Mick Roberts helping a Kenyan soldier with at tricky technical problem.

Permission given by Michael Roberts

"If you find any money in there it's mine."

Mick Roberts returned to civilian life after more than twenty years with the British Army. A brief history of the military service of Artificer Sergeant Major Michael Roberts was set out in his red pay book. He had worn jungle green in the Far East and khaki in Europe, patrolled the Green Line in Cyprus wearing the blue beret of the United Nations and painted his Land Rover pink in Kenya. His had been a colourful career. In Northern Ireland he crushed a yellow Mini. How did that happen?

Chapter 31

The Troubles

OPENING UP OLD WOUNDS

The Troubles in Ireland stretched back over centuries. Old wounds were regularly opened up and used to provoke more violence. At the end of the seventeenth century the catholic king, James II, and protestant, William of Orange, squabbled over who should rule England, Scotland and Ireland. The scene was set for three hundred years of intolerance.

The rural poor of Ireland, predominantly catholic, remained poor largely due to exploitation by protestant landowners. Many of these were absentee landlords living in England. They left the dirty business of collecting rents to their agents in Ireland. Most of the grain produced was for export. The staple diet of the poor was potatoes and when crops failed they starved. The famine of 1845 was a defining event in the history of Anglo-Irish relations.

The British Prime Minister denied state aid to starving Irish citizens. The man responsible for overseeing a policy that discriminated against the catholic poor was Charles Trevelyan. When the famine was over a million were dead, masses fled the country in search of kinder lands and hundreds of 'troublemakers' deported. Trevelyan's wickedness was recalled in a popular song, 'The Fields of Athenry'.

Political pressure for an independent Ireland grew. After decades of agitation Home Rule for Ireland was agreed in 1914, but suspended at the outbreak of the Great War. One of the founding political parties, Sinn Fein, could not wait any longer, and in 1916 public buildings in Dublin were occupied. The Easter Rising was brutally suppressed by British forces. The IRA (Irish Republican Army) was formed following this incident. Negotiations took place after the Great War and in 1922

350

the Irish Free State was established, but the six predominately protestant counties in the north were excluded.

Apley farmhand, Frank Jasper, had served in the trenches of Flanders with the county regiment. He was wounded, and then 'to cap it all' he spent the last months of their military service in Ireland. The 2nd Battalion KSLI was the last British Regiment to leave Dublin Castle, and hand it over to the newly created Irish Free State.

Following the Second World War Ireland left the Commonwealth but still enjoyed open access to mainland Britain. The dominant political force in Northern Ireland was the Unionist party. A system that discriminated against the catholic minority was created. Throughout the 1950s there was an undercurrent of discontent and isolated terrorist incidents.

Within a year of leaving school, Hugh Dyas arrived in the province as a newly commissioned Lieutenant in the Royal Artillery. Little did he, or anyone, imagine at the time how ugly the conflict would become and how long it would last.

AN OFFICER OF THE BRITISH EMPIRE

When the time came to respond to the call-up, some lads were at a loss. They didn't know what they wanted to do; not Hugh Dyas. His Uncle Jim had flown Meteors for the RAF and one of his brothers flew Vampires. Another brother flew an Auster with the Royal Artillery and Hugh wanted some of the same.

In a dusty billet in Walsall in the company of Black Country labourers, a metal-basher and few farmhands, he filled in forms and was interviewed by a barking Sergeant. "Flying with the gunners, and the best of luck, lad!"

He packed him off to the depot at Oswestry and almost immediately there was disappointment. The Royal Artillery was not training National Servicemen as pilots anymore so that meant no flying for Hugh, his boyhood dream gone.

Hugh had been a keen member of the Cadet Force at Bradfield School; even Field Marshall Montgomery had been impressed when he came to inspect the detachment. With his School Certificate the young recruit had the qualifications to apply for a commission. After basic training at Park Hall, Oswestry, he was dispatched to Durham in the depths of winter.

Way back in history Barnard Castle must have had stout walls and a blazing fire in the hall. The young gunners were housed in a hut with an asbestos roof and a coke stove to crouch over. This was a precious source of heat. It was a temperamental device that needed constant attention.

The boys went out on Saturday night and left the only teetotaller in the billet in charge of the stove. Pleased with his efforts as a stoker he greeted his mates when they swayed in under the influence just before midnight. "Look at that, feel the heat. I kept it in, didn't I?"

The billet was dimly lit with half a dozen naked light bulbs and illuminated by the glow of the white-hot stove. There was a chorus of, "Jesus Christ Almighty, what are we going to do with that?" Before a decision could be made the stove fell apart and a lava-stream of coke poured out of the gaping cracks and onto the billet floor. By now everyone was stone-cold sober. The fire was quenched, the coke cleared away and the fractured stove examined. Everyone was of the same opinion. "We are in the shit!"

"We can't leave it like that, it's got to be hidden somewhere."

One perceptive lad said, "They'll notice it's gone."

There was no immediate answer to that. Another brighter lad said, "I know where there's a new one, in that billet behind the cookhouse."

"Yes, but it's locked up."

In any group of men there are those with special talents: leaders and loafers, singers and sinners, hard men, craftsmen, conmen, thieves. They all have a part to play. The Black Country was famous for its locksmiths and safe makers. The team swung into action, the lock clicked open, and the stoves were exchanged, the new one given its first coat of polish. The fractured stove was put together and patched up with cardboard. They admired their handiwork and went to bed. Above the coarse grey blankets their smooth baby faces glowed with innocence.

A few days later Hugh left their company and went before the War Office Selection Board not for a reprimand but to apply for a commission. He was young. Many of his competitors had been deferred, training for the professions, fresh out of university, Oxford and Cambridge graduates.

After days of frustration and anxiety the selection process was over and the Colonel called the hopefuls in, one by one. "Ah, Dyas, at ease.

Have to tell you, sorry, failed the Board."

"Sir."

"Not to worry, lot of clever chaps about. Apply again, you'll know what to expect the next time."

"Thank you, sir."

Six weeks later Hugh was back again, and this time he was successful and sent on his way to Mons OCTU at Aldershot. Officer cadets were browbeaten by some of the most unforgiving Company Sergeant Majors in the British Army. Not everyone was 'up to the mark', so they were RTU'd, (Returned to Unit). Cadet Dyas was fine on the parade ground but he had a problem in the classroom.

When an officer in the Royal Artillery shouts 'Fire' he is expected to have some idea where the shell will land. The calculations involved to dispatch the shell from the artillery piece are not absolutely straightforward. Hugh must have been dreaming when the mathematics master at Bradfield was explaining the intricacies of trigonometry. Help was close at hand, in the next bed in fact. His neighbour, Cadet Tim Whiteway, was a trained accountant. Figures were his speciality. His weakness was 'bullshit', keeping his buttons bright, his tunic pressed and his boots polished was beyond him. They came to an arrangement. He taught Hugh trigonometry and in return his kit was cleaned and maintained in perfect order. Both men amazed their instructors. "My, my, you gentlemen have certainly bucked your ideas up." They passed out into the wider world.

A TASTE OF THINGS TO COME

No sooner had the cadet tabs been taken from his collar, and the 'pips' of a 2nd Lieutenant stitched on his epaulets, than Hugh Dyas was sent off to get a taste of 'The Troubles' that were brewing in Northern Ireland. Troop Sergeant Cox, recently returned from the Korean War, was there to give guidance.

The Gunners worked side by side with the Royal Ulster Constabulary, setting up roadblocks and patrolling the narrow lanes around Clogher near the border with the South. Most of the incidents were more entertaining than dangerous. Any stand-up comedian can get a laugh if he puts 'Irishman' and 'drink' together in a joke.

Returning home in the dead of night after a boozy day at the market, with no light and more stout in his belly than fuel in the petrol tank, a merry hill farmer ran into one of the patrols. "Got ya! What have you got to hide, I wonder?"

"Nuthin."

"You've no lights."

"I'm not needin' lights, I knows the road."

The gunners searched and it was soon clear that this man had nothing to hide. For his own safety and that of other road users the smallholder was escorted home. The house and the adjacent cowshed were almost identical with stone walls, ill-fitting doors and litter on the floor. A glance around the living room confirmed that, with plates and a frying pan in the sink, this was the home of a bachelor. The place was comfortable enough for the cat on the open hearth in front of a dead fire, and the dog in a sagging armchair. The hound slid out from under his master's rear end as he lurched backwards down into the chair.

One of the gunners came in. "Sir, the cattle are playing up."

Lieutenant Dyas stepped out into the yard. Hugh knew why the cows were complaining and he knew the very man to put it right. "They want milking. That's a job for you, Davies. You haven't forgotten how to milk have you?"

"No, Sir."

"Then I leave it to you; fresh milk in the cocoa tonight."

At least one Irish countryman was persuaded that the presence of British troops was not all bad. In the towns there was tension in the streets; there was nothing to distinguish friend from foe. The security services knew the tactics of the IRA, and often knew who they were. The ones most easily identified were the braggarts and bullies who specialised in extortion and intimidation. Behind these were the planners and fundraisers who in the years to come would travel to America to meet wealthy sympathisers. Others travelled to Libya and persuaded Colonel Gaddafi to supply arms and explosives to create havoc in the Province. To finance their activities at home the terrorists threatened shopkeepers and lifted their takings from the till, and there was always good old fashioned 'smash and grab'.

Everyone looked forward to payday, the day when the company safe was opened and accounts clerks lifted out trays filled with precious pay packets and carried them off to 'the workers', their reward for a week's hard work. The men in black balaclavas were always on the lookout for ready cash. If they could open the company safe on the day before payday it was there for the taking.

Sitting in the District Inspector's office one evening, Lieutenant Dyas was manning the two-way radio to keep in touch with his men out on patrol in the narrow lanes near Strabane. He was rudely interrupted by the loud, black Bakelite phone shaking on the Inspector's desktop. The 1950s ringtone was not a charming little jingle, it was an alarm call which demanded, 'Get up now, and answer me!' The Inspector snatched it up. "Jeasus! They've blown up the bloody gasworks!"

Constables and Gunners raced nose to tail in their Land Rovers. They expected to see flames forty feet high issuing from the huge gas tanks. Nothing, the tanks were dark silhouettes against the night sky. Cautiously they made for the manager's office overlooking the yard. Hugh led his men into the office block. All were armed, the lads clutched their Lee-Enfields, their commander drew his service revolver; the lanyard bounced against his side as he charged up the stairs. Since the weapon had been issued to him Hugh had fired only about a dozen rounds from it at a target, never in anger.

The scene might have been staged in Hollywood for a low-budget gangster film. MANAGER had been painted boldly on the frosted glass of the office door, behind it lurked a shadowy figure. The young Lieutenant paused. Safety catch off, he barged in. A hulk of man, brandishing a shotgun, stood before him. "Put that bloody thing away, son. They tried to blow up the safe, they've gone, and they got nothing." The manager summed up the situation in a few words. This little drama was over. There was more to follow that same night.

The IRA had packed a lorry wheel with explosives and rolled it against the wall of the Customs house in Strabane. There was a mighty bang. Hugh Dyas and his men rushed to the scene. The building had been shaken and there were a few cracks but little real damage. The terrorists had fled but the troops still trod carefully. Before the IRA got their hands on SEMTEX they used nitro-glycerine if they wanted to cause a big bang. This was tricky stuff to handle, the slightest knock set it off and then the bomber himself became the victim. Sergeant Cox warned his men. "Don't start stamping about in those hobnailed boots."

The Royal Artillery knew all about setting off explosives but making them safe was someone else's job. "I'll call in the Sappers, sir.

"Excellent idea, Sergeant."

Lieutenant Dyas ended his military service with a bang, scores of bangs; he lost count. During a six-week NATO exercise at Stonebridge Ranges, his battery fired more twenty-five pound shells than the battery fired throughout the Korean War! The experience of National Service was never going to be life-changing for Hughie Dyas. He returned to the farm to work alongside his father and old codgers, veterans of past campaigns. Now he had a few tales of his own to tell.

Farming was in the blood. Curious to know how the crops on neighbouring farms were progressing Hugh might have leaned over the fence. Instead he flew over it. He learned to fly, it was in the blood. He built an airstrip at the Leavenhalls and took off in his light aircraft. Soaring above Apley lands with white clouds above, the greens and browns of fields and woodland, and the silver of the Severn below, this put the whole world in perspective.

Hugh involved himself in sugar beet research which meant travelling all over England and into Europe. One day on Wolverhampton Railway Station he was shaken by a rude voice from the past. "Hughie! Remember me?"

"Brummy Harris, Barnard Castle."

"Yo' did right leavin' when yo' did. We wus all in the shit."

The cardboard coke stove they had so carefully constructed in the next billet did not last long when the first fire was lit. There was an investigation; the culprits could not be identified so the heavy hand of the Royal Military Police delivered a blanket punishment. Hughie and Gunner Harris boarded the London train. Brummy got off at Brum and was never seen again.

A campaign medal for service in Northern Ireland was first issued in 1969. Lieutenant Dyas missed out, but it didn't matter. He got his reward in 1998 when, for long service to agricultural education and research throughout Europe, he was awarded the OBE. He was an Officer of the Order of the British Empire.

THE OPENING SHOTS OF THE CAMPAIGN

In 1963, Viscount Brookeborough, the Prime Minister of Northern Ireland, stepped down after twenty years in office. He had much to answer for. Terence O'Neill took over and tried to bring Protestants and Catholics together. His efforts were openly attacked by the Reverend Ian Paisley, another man with a lot to answer for.

Clashes between the communities often flared up during the 'marching season' when the protestant Orange Order paraded through the streets. In August 1969 they organised the annual Apprentice Boys March, commemorating the successful defence of Derry from attack by the catholic King James II.

On this occasion a street battle broke out between catholic and protestant youths on the streets of Londonderry. Police were stoned and petrol bombed when they attempted to separate the factions. They moved in with armoured vehicles and water cannon. The 'Battle of the Bogside' lasted two days, violence also erupted in Belfast. The Royal Ulster Constabulary could not control the riots, and a small contingent of British troops was sent in. They were welcomed by the catholic community. The honeymoon period was brief.

To outsiders the conflict was inexplicable. Men who declared themselves Christians and prayed to the same God were still prepared to commit evil acts against each other. 'Sectarian violence' was a phrase that would appear regularly in the press for the next thirty years. Of all the campaigns involving British troops this must have been one of the most difficult. There was no clear battlefront; there was no way of distinguishing friend from foe. Frequently lads sent to keep the troublesome factions apart were caught in the crossfire. This was nothing new to troops of the Light Infantry.

The County Regiment

Colonel William Whitmore of Apley Hall raised a Regiment of Foot in 1755, and in 1881 this regiment joined with the 85th King's Light Infantry to form the King's Shropshire Light Infantry. Local lads served with the county regiment throughout its history and were there at the end. In July 1968, on parade under a bright sky over the Indian Ocean, Corporal Brian Jones witnessed the final hour of the county regiment when the 1st Battalion KSLI became the 3rd Battalion of the Light Infantry. He flew from Mauritius back to Malaysia, the battalion came home. The colours of the King's Shropshire Light Infantry were laid up in Saint Leonard's Church in Bridgnorth in April 1970.

The Light Infantry, largely made up of boys from Durham and Yorkshire, Somerset and Shropshire, were constantly on the move; Canada and the Caribbean, Germany, the Mediterranean, Africa and the Far East. In March 1971 they were patrolling the streets of West Belfast and they would return to the troubled province many times. For over thirty years hardly a month went by without an 'incident'. There were casualties on all sides. The IRA lost men and so did their Protestant opponents of the Ulster Volunteer Force; impartial soldiers and innocent civilians died.

This senseless conflict was felt by families throughout Britain, in housing estates in Belfast, on crofts in the Scottish Highlands, by cockney mothers in the East End and the Queen in Buckingham Palace. The Queen's cousin Lord Louis Mountbatten had survived the Second World War only to be killed by the IRA whilst on holiday in the west of Ireland. Airey Neave, one of the few to escape from Colditz Castle, was killed by a car bomb at the Houses of Parliament. In May 1973, another booby trap bomb killed John Gaskell on the Donegal Road in Belfast. More young soldiers of the Light Infantry would die in the years that followed.

To Ulster Time and Again

There were none of the comforts of home for the foot soldiers who patrolled the streets. Fort George in Londonderry, with a dismal view across the River Foyle, was no place to spend Christmas. The prospect was no better for the officers billeted on board HMS *Rame Head*, tied up nearby. This tour for 3LI was mercifully short. When they returned to the streets of Belfast accommodation for the members of the 'close observation patrol' was even more basic. They lived in derelict houses off the Falls Road. This was a very unhealthy place to be. Two days after they arrived in the province Michael Harrison and Richard Turnbull were ambushed by the IRA and killed in North Howard Street. This was in the year of the Queen's Silver Jubilee.

The Jubilee was celebrated with street parties and pageants. Cheering crowds and waving flags greeted the Queen as she travelled the country. She knew there would be huge risks involved when the visit to Belfast was planned, but knew there were thousands of loyal subjects in the city ready to welcome her. The Falls Road and the Shankill Road were often in the news, scenes of riots and atrocities; above them was the Divis Tower with two thousand residents, some of them IRA sympathisers. The top two floors were occupied by the British Army; they were 'behind enemy lines'. They made no secret of it. An observation post was set up on the roof. Sinn Fein called it a 'spy post', and they were right.

David Thomas and his platoon had a fine view as the Royal Yacht sailed in to Belfast Lough and put down her anchor. On the street twenty floors below, a known gunman was spotted. "Shall I shoot him, sir?"

"No, you might miss. We'll deal with him later."

The Queen was about to have a new experience. She flew into Belfast from the deck of the Royal Yacht by helicopter. Security was precarious; the people she came in contact with were all carefully vetted. She called on the people to 'live and work together in friendship and forgiveness'. Her wish was not immediately fulfilled. Loyalists in the province celebrated. Lads of the Light Infantry came down off the tower for what David Thomas described as 'a punch-up' with the Republicans.

The 3rd Battalion became part of the UK Mobile Force based at Tidworth; they deployed to South Fermanagh in 1982 for yet another tour of duty. Three years later they became the resident battalion in barracks at Omagh. They were experienced men able to deal with most situations, routine patrols, stop and search operations, surveillance and support for Special Forces, and keeping an eye out for anyone who might harm the 'Clones Cyclone'. Barry McGuigan, world featherweight boxing champion, was born in Clones, just over the border from County Fermanagh. He represented Northern Ireland in the Commonwealth Games and Ireland at the Moscow Olympics. A Catholic married to a Protestant, he refused to choose sides in The Troubles. For this reason alone he was threatened by the IRA. The threat had to be taken seriously; a company of the 3rd Battalion were assigned to give protection, and they did.

Fortunately there were times when IRA operations failed because their troops were ill-disciplined or simply inept, like the lad who used an alarm clock to detonate the bomb, set the time but failed to wind up the clock.

An ambitious plan hatched by three clowns was a spectacular failure. They stole a Transit van and packed it with explosives, drove it to a border post and parked close by. Two crept from the cab and stole away leaving the demolition specialist in the back to set the timing mechanism. All was going according to plan until the bomber discovered that the back door was locked. He hammered on the side of the van to alert the RUC to let him out, then fell into their open arms.

It has to be admitted that there were times when the security forces made mistakes.

A Case of Mistaken Identity

Apley lad, Tommy Roberts, of the 3rd Battalion Light Infantry, completed a number of tours, more than most, in Northern Ireland. His brother, Michael, completed just one, with the REME.

During his six-month tour of duty, Artificer Sergeant Major Roberts and his team were given a number of tasks; to support search and rescue operations on Lough Neagh and to clear the streets of Belfast of suspicious vehicles. These might be booby trapped, or be used to build a barricade.

If a bomb was suspected, bomb disposal experts were called in. When the all-clear was given, the REME moved in. There was nothing subtle about the way they handled suspect vehicles. They picked up the whole car, dumped it in an armoured trailer, drove to a quarry, crushed it or blew it up. The Allis Chalmers grab-truck was a formidable machine capable of picking up a double-decker bus.

One evening, ASM Roberts was being guided down the Falls Road by Intelligence Corps lads on foot patrol. "Suspicious vehicle, Yellow Mini, can't miss it." The Allis Chalmers got stuck in, the windscreen and side window were shattered and the roof crushed by steel claws as the canary-coloured car was swung over the trailer and dumped. Minutes later the Intelligence Corps sent another message. "Sorry about that, wrong Mini, another yellow one further on." This was not the way to win the hearts and minds of the owners of yellow Minis.

Terrorism on the Mainland

Troubles in Northern Ireland spread to mainland Britain. The Provisional IRA targeted pubs in Guildford and Birmingham, popular with off-duty servicemen. In total twenty-six people were killed by the bombs. In Brighton five more were killed when the IRA attempted to assassinate the Prime Minister, Margaret Thatcher. Two small boys were killed in Warrington. Evil acts were committed all over England.

Shrewbury Castle was fire-bombed in 1992. The museum held the records of the King's Shropshire Light Infantry and precious mementos of the county regiment's history. This was a soft target. Regular battalions of the Light Infantry had disrupted many IRA plots over three decades. Bombing the Regimental Museum may have been a childish attempt by the terrorists to get their own back. The Territorial Battalion (5LI) were much involved in the investigation that followed the Shrewsbury bombing.

Members of Scotland Yard anti-terrorist squad were called in. Suspicion fell on Harper Adams College. Students sympathetic to the IRA cause may have formed a 'cell' behind the stately home façade of the college. Whether this was true or not, the barman, posing as an MI5 agent, convinced three students that there were terrorists in the college and that they were all in danger. He took them to a series of squalid 'safe houses'. The wealthy families of the gullible students financed the playboy lifestyle of the conman, Robert Hendy-Freegard. He was eventually convicted for a string of similar offences in 2005. This was a remarkable tale. The true identity of the Shropshire bombers may never be known.

THE HONOURABLE MAJOR

The State Opening of Parliament is quite an event, and the Queen is probably glad it doesn't happen very often. She has to read a speech she did not write, parts of which she may not agree with. Members of the House of Lords and the House of Commons sit together in rather cramped conditions. The Queen and the Duke of Edinburgh look down on them, as you would expect, from the top of a wide flight of steps. Before the Queen arrives the cellars of the Houses of Parliament are searched to make sure there is no repeat of the Gunpowder Plot.

Preparations for the ceremony are elaborate. The Queen is dressed for the occasion. She wears the Imperial State Crown, which cannot be comfortable, and the bejewelled Robe of State with its long unwieldy train. The Queen needs help with all this. Lords and Ladies in Waiting are very willing but too tall. The Queen is quite petite. Step forward the Pages of Honour, lads like Harry Legge-Bourke, Malcolm Mclean, Piers Blewitt and The Honourable Benjamin Hamilton.

To stay composed in front of a vast audience requires special qualities; pop stars and politicians might need a shot of whisky from a hip flask. The pages were given a little bottle of smelling salts just in case they felt faint. Ben Hamilton was eleven when he took up his duties. He was in attendance at Garter Ceremonies and the State Openings of Parliament, and put on a solo act – behind the Queen of course – in Saint Paul's Cathedral. He was taller than the Queen, so after two years he had to give way to someone shorter.

A well trodden career path used to be Eton, Sandhurst and the Guards. Benjamin Hamilton wisely had a gap year in Africa after Eton, and then three years at Newcastle University. The Officer Training Corp threw the best parties and had the cheapest bar in the university. This was excellent preparation for service in the army. Ben joined the OTC and spent weekends charging about Northumbria in old Land Rovers, sleeping rough in barns and woods, and forging life-long friendships. He arrived at Sandhurst with twelve others from the Newcastle OTC to begin the commissioning course in September 1997.

When he entered Sandhurst Cadet Hamilton carried with him a most important piece of kit, his own personal ironing board. Ironing was an essential part of the process of producing an 'all-rounder'; calm under fire, confident, decisive and capable of producing a sharp crease down the leg of a pair of trousers. Careful grooming by Captains Graham and Gerrard-Wright and loud barking by Colour Sergeants Christie and McCabe transformed the raw recruits. The day came for fond parents to turn up for the passing-out parade to see what the staff of the Royal Military Academy had done to their offspring. It was an emotional occasion, but excessive hugging and 'air kissing' were frowned upon. Nevertheless, there was real pride in a job well done. The parade ground, the pillared entrance to the Old College and the surrounding lawns provided the perfect backdrop for commemorative photographs. Giggling girls in garden party hats queued up to pose beside smirking cadets, splendid in dark tunics with red sashes and gleaming brass buttons. The drill sergeants had paid particular attention to the Sovereign's Platoon which had the honour of carrying the Sovereign's banner on parade. Cadet Hamilton was one of the escorts.

The ball in the evening was the time for letting hair down and another opportunity to pose for less formal pictures. BH was a very lucky man; he waltzed and jigged around all evening with his wife-to-be,

Miss Charlotte Purchas. Less fortunate cadets had to make do with a sister, the sister of a friend or the latest 'flame' that would fizzle out after the event.

Lieutenant Hamilton was commissioned and joined the Coldstream Guards. There really was no alternative; father, grandfather and uncles had all served in the same regiment. The staff at Sandhurst had done all they could, now it was up to Sergeant Dart to make sure Lieutenant Hamilton carried out his ceremonial duties at Windsor without making too many obvious blunders. This has been the task of senior non-commissioned officers for centuries. 'Getting to know the men' was one of the most important parts of the young officer's duties. This meant acting as a social worker, sorting out problems, behavioural, financial and, the trickiest of all, matrimonial.

It was during six weeks of jungle training in Belize that he really got to know the lads under his command. From the School of Jungle Warfare on Mountain Pine Ridge, they were sent out to crawl about in leech-infested streams, hack through thorny scrub in combat gear and return in the evening to brush the scorpions out of their tents before they lost consciousness. This was called team-building. Everyone was warned that the slightest scratch in the tropics could become infected and fester. A very dangerous place was Raul's Rose Garden where local beauties lay in wait. Guardsmen were advised to protect themselves with a rubber sheath if they planned to brush against the prickly little blossoms in the Garden.

A FINE VIEW OVER THE BORDER

Back home in Victoria Barracks, the Coldstream Guards prepared for deployment to Northern Ireland. Romeo 21 was not as romantic as it sounds. It comprised three watchtowers overlooking the 'Bandit Country' of South Armagh. From the lookout tower at Fork Hill there were fine views to the Slieve Gullion Mountain in the north, and Black Mountain across the border. The Coldstreams were not there to admire the view. With the latest surveillance equipment they scanned the neighbourhood day and night. Military Intelligence provided them with a file of characters, 'IRA sympathisers, known to the security services'. Their movements were monitored and any ugly customers were stopped at roadblocks or by foot patrol.

To continue their operations the IRA were always looking for ways to raise funds. They dabbled in drugs, property deals and any scam that would pay; one such scheme was smuggling fuel. This may have been one of their least harmful activities but, nevertheless, it had to be stopped. The RUC and BH and his guardsmen made life difficult for these wicked men. Everyone was wary but there were no serious incidents during the six-month tour.

First tour of duty over it was back to Victoria Barracks and another severe test of discipline for the guardsmen. They had to remain steady and show no emotion in the face of cameras and mobile phones thrust at them by clamouring tourists. There were rehearsals for the Queen's Birthday Parades, and a celebration for the three hundred and fiftieth anniversary of the founding of the regiment and, in between, long stints of public duties. It almost came as a relief when the battalion were sent back to Londonderry for a second tour.

The Coldstreams took over from the Royal Anglian Regiment at Eglington Barracks on the banks of the River Foyle. It was disturbing to find that repairs to the officers' mess had not been completed. The IRA had lobbed in a mortar bomb a few weeks earlier, but they seemed to have lost their touch because it failed to explode. The Guards were expected to patrol the street round the clock but this proved to be unsustainable. Captain Hamilton devised a more workable routine, and at the same time organised a wedding at long distance. He thought that once the date was set all he had to do was turn up on the day. Fine details were discussed late at night over the telephone. Ben adopted an 'agree-to-everything' policy and this seemed to work.

Captain Hamilton turned up with two days to spare. Fellow officers who might have formed a guard of honour were still on duty in Northern Ireland. It turned out to be a rather unmilitary affair. Two fine young Coldstream musicians made the day by playing the regimental slow march to greet the bride as she entered the church, and excerpts from Handel's Water Music as the newly-weds went arm in arm back down the aisle. Their feet hardly touched the ground, at least until they reached Reunion in the Indian Ocean for a ten-day honeymoon. Then it was back to reality and back to Londonderry for the Captain, leaving his bride behind in the New Forest.

They were soon together again and enjoying a bit of slalom at Val d'Isere. Ben was captain of the battalion ski team. Accommodation was arranged for the competitors and 'camp followers'. This was Charlotte's first experience of married quarters. She shared a small flat with her husband, another officer, a lance corporal and two guardsmen. Being married to the regiment had not been mentioned at the wedding ceremony.

Ben returned briefly to Londonderry to hand over his command and then it was back to Chelsea Barracks, and a return to ceremonial duties. 'Charlie' was happy. She settled into a family flat instead of making a home in a concrete tower block belonging to the Ministry of Defence.

JUST THE MAN FOR THE JOB

The Queen Mother died and the Coldstream Guards were very much involved in the arrangements for her funeral. During the lying-in-state in Westminister Hall, thousands of mourners passed by the coffin throughout the day. At night Captain Ben Hamilton's men mounted the guard. All were moved by this experience in the silent hours of the early morning.

Number 7 Company had a break from ceremonial duties when the firemen threatened to go on strike. They were packed off to Faslane for three weeks to be taught fire-fighting skills by the Royal Navy. Fortunately the newly acquired skills were never put to the test.

Not one for getting stuck in a rut, BH heard of a vacancy at the Palace and thought it was 'worth a shot'. He let it be known that he was interested in the position of Equerry to the Queen. Months went by, and then one day he was told to report to the CO. "Morning, Hamilton, do sit down. Equerry to the Queen, only temporary."

"Sir?"

"Previous experience?"

"I was a Page of Honour, sir."

"Well, that settles it then. You've got the job."

The initial audience with the Queen was arranged for the 14th of November 2002. This was a bit awkward because that was the day when Alexandra, Ben and 'Charlie's' daughter, was due to arrive. Conveniently for all concerned Alexandra arrived in the early hours. Father had no sleep, he 'freshened up' and changed into his morning coat, made sure mother and baby were tucked up in bed and made off to Buckingham Palace for his eleven o'clock appointment with Her Majesty.

The year 2003 was a very interesting year for BH; there was a lot of meeting and greeting. "President Putin and Mrs Putin, ma'am." The State Visit by the Russian leader passed off without a hitch.

The Queen's ambassadors leaving to take up posts abroad all had an audience at the Palace, and foreign ambassadors arriving in the country presented their credentials. Captain Hamilton briefed them on how to behave when they were greeted by the Queen. There were garden parties and investitures to attend, and very little spare time for the equerry. At Windsor, BH had a private lunch with the Queen and the Duke of Edinburgh. Affairs of state and diplomacy were not on the menu. Farming, the trials of running a country estate, such as Apley, and the conservation of plants and gardens were topics that everyone had an interest in. Lunch over; Captain Hamilton ushered in Hamid Karzai, President of Afghanistan, who didn't have much interest in plants, except growing poppies.

When BH returned to the battalion he was promoted to Major and became the CO's right-hand man. Preparations were made for deployment to Iraq. The battalion were dispatched to Iraq and there was no place in the command structure for an Acting Major. BH stayed in London, no doubt to the great relief of his wife.

By the Centre Quick March

Perhaps it was time to consider a change of career. For those who have enjoyed life in the services coming out of uniform is a sad moment. When it happens it is best to march off the parade ground with head up, chest out, arms swinging and the band playing. The last hurrah for Major Hamilton was as a 'tour manager' in the USA.

The Regimental Band of the Coldstream Guards and the pipes and drums of the Royal Scots Dragoon Guards went everywhere from Niagara Falls on the Canadian border to the Deep South, visiting twenty-eight different states. They gave seventy-eight concerts including one in front of an audience of geriatrics in Palm Springs, and another near an 'aircraft graveyard' at Tucson, both equally lively. There were visits to the island prison of Alcatraz and the gambling dens of Las Vegas.

There were logistical problems but happily few disciplinary problems. A faultless performance is only made possible by hours of practise. To be a military bandsman requires extra discipline and BH was grateful. He knew that had he taken eighty 'ordinary' guardsmen on tour it would not have been without incident. Booze, brawling and 'broads' would all have featured on the American tour.

There was one notable breakdown in discipline in San Francisco when Bill Calderhead hired a 'muscle car'. He wished it could have been a 1968 Ford Mustang GT like the one Steve McQueen drove in *Bullitt*. Captain Calderhead and Major Hamilton did their very best to recreate the car-chase scenes from the film on the switch-back streets of San Francisco. No disciplinary action was taken against the senior officer or his second in command.

Ben was reunited with his family in San Antonio. They were given front row seats at two concerts and a rodeo. The most memorable concert must have been the one played in the Metropolitan Museum of Art in New York. The backdrop was the Temple of Dendur built in Egypt, and relocated to the United States when the Aswan Dam was built. The Coldstreams and the Scots Dragoons knew how to put on a display. Ceremonial duties in London and at Windsor ensured that they did not disappoint the crowds in America. Major Hamilton left the army on a high note.

Every year the British Army shrinks; outposts are abandoned. The skills of jungle warfare are no longer practised in Belize. Armadillos and jaguars roam the jungle trails undisturbed by blundering squaddies. The watchtowers in South Armagh have been taken down, the army base at Fork Hill is now a children's playground. Service in Northern Ireland had a lasting effect on some soldiers. They suffered flashbacks. Reflecting on his ten years service with the Coldstream Guards, Ben Hamilton's flashbacks were truly memorable. There were few dark places to revisit. "I wouldn't have missed it for the world."

Chapter 32

In their Element

THE WANDERING ALBATROSS

The masters at the Grammar School were not very inspiring. It wasn't easy to make Latin and Scripture interesting to teenage boys. 'Sticky' Pearson did try; at least he had been to Palestine and knew the 'little town of Bethlehem'. He had actually stood there on the streets, in khaki shorts with an army revolver on his hip.

Mr Wells stood, wooden pointer in hand, in front of the world map to remind his dozing pupils where Crete lay in relation to Alexandria. Everyone suspected that he did this to remind himself of his Navy days. As an aside he would say, "There is much to be said for seeing the world at government expense." Ken Morris woke up and took note.

In September 1955, at the Royal Naval barracks at Lee-on-Solent, Ken signed on. Then he turned his back on the sea and went inland to a Naval Air Station that pretended to be a ship by calling itself HMS Gamecock. The Royal Navy was totally different from the other services. They all marched about and polished things, but no soldier or airman would ever salute a white line in the road and call it the quarterdeck, at least not when they were sober. From Gamecock he went to Bulwark for 'sea training', in a dry dock.

To begin his training as a photographer he arrived at Royal Naval Air Station Ford just in time to see an aircraft fly into the Captain's greenhouse, killing the pilot. At last, after thirty-eight weeks learning the art and science of photography, Ken put to sea aboard HMS *Dalrymple* to examine the seabed around the British Isles. Scientists took soundings as they sloshed about, and Leading Airman Morris captured the routine tasks of life on board ship in black and white. This was not the romantic see-the-world adventure Ken had dreamed of.

When *Dalrymple* sailed back for a refit, Ken hopped off. The Admiralty had something mysterious in mind for this young sailor. He was called to the capital. HMS *President* was a 'virtual ship', the crew didn't even look like sailors; they were dressed as civilians and lived in 'digs'. There was no quarterdeck to salute, not even a white line.

The signals section was a lively place, in contact round the clock with ships and outposts of the Royal Navy worldwide. Photographic negatives arrived in envelopes marked 'secret'. Ken developed them, printed them and slid them into envelopes stamped 'top secret'. There were aerial photographs, shaky 'snaps' of bits of military equipment and long-lens shots of shady characters. There didn't seem to be much to get excited about. No one questioned what they were doing. All these files and folders had to be stored somewhere. From time to time Ken strolled round the corner to 26 Whitehall, showed his get-you-into-anywhere pass at the door and left behind another package. The Admiralty Building was huge with endless corridors and dusty offices with plenty of space to store brown envelopes. Working for Naval Intelligence could be dangerous. The 'spooks' spent long hours in an atmosphere of fag smoke; there was the ever present threat of lung damage.

Luckily, for the good of his health, after a year in London Ken was whisked off to Lossiemouth to join a Squadron of Scimitars, and then put to sea on board HMS *Ark Royal*. They cruised around the Mediterranean and then crossed the Atlantic to 'show the flag' in New York. Ken took in the sights and plenty of pictures. The view from the top of the Empire State Building was spectacular. Walking down 5th Avenue he recalled the words of his old geography teacher. Ken said to himself, "Now it is happening, I am travelling the world at government expense."

Back in Portsmouth there was a period of monotony to be endured before the next adventure. The photographic unit was housed in one of the forts built as a defence against a possible invasion by Napoleon. The forts were substantial buildings but not very comfortable. The ratings slept in the moat. The moat had been drained and billets erected. Processing and printing fifty thousand identity card photographs – twice – was repetitive but it didn't last long, and Ken was off to Cape Wrath where the Royal Navy and the RAF were pounding the coast with live shells. He was there to record the damage if they managed to hit the target.

Back in London in the offices of the *Daily Mirror,* press photographers, wearing raincoats and trilby hats, taught Ken how to take pictures of celebrities, in other words how to be one of the *paparazzi.* Then he was given a most exclusive badge, the Royal Yacht shoulder flash. The royal family were privileged to have Ken Morris on board when they sailed to Cowes to show off their yacht, and then went off to Scotland for their summer holidays. Ken left them to it and flew off to the Caribbean to meet SNOWI.

Senior Naval Officer West Indies was on a tour of inspection and he liked to be photographed to prove that they had done the job. They visited a lot of islands but not Cuba. This would have upset the Americans who viewed their new communist neighbour with suspicion. Fidel Castro had taken over in Cuba. His regime was certainly an improvement on the previous one, but his politics didn't suit everyone. Some disgruntled Cubans sought refuge in Florida.

The American Government used the CIA to organise a return trip for these refugees. The invasion of the Bay of Pigs was a tragedy; at least two thousand lost their lives. The planning was farcical. When the CIA selected the 'troops' from exiles living in Florida some of Castro's men volunteered. They helped in the planning and were able to provide all the information necessary to ensure that the operation would be a complete disaster. Ken, the Commodore and his team spent some time fishing invaders out of the water and ferrying them back to Miami.

In the Bahamas Ken was on hand when Harold McMillan, the Prime Minister, and John Kennedy, the American President, met to discuss the Cold War and the Cuban question. After rubbing shoulders with the 'top brass', Ken jetted home on a Boeing 707. Leading Airman Morris had now been in uniform for nearly seven years. He had seen a lot. There was more to come.

Back at Portland he was attached to a unit which did 'working up'. To make a ship fit for service there were sea trials after which everything was supposed to work efficiently and the crew knew what they were doing. Gunnery practise involved shooting at a canvas target towed by a tug. The photographic section took pictures of the damage, if any. Once or twice the gun crew mistook the tug for the target. Perhaps this was done on purpose so that the crew knew what it was like to be under fire. Ken came away unscathed and was then drafted to RNAS

Brawdy, a place of little importance in his naval career but life-changing nevertheless. Here he met his wife-to-be.

The wedding of a close friend always gives single girls ideas. Joan was overwhelmed by the gaiety and romance of the occasion, the convivial uniformed company and the bubbling champagne, and there was Ken. "Then followed a most interesting experience."

No great romantic, Ken was talking about HMS *Protector*, a survey ship. Aboard *Protector*, he sailed to the Great Southern Ocean which encircles Antarctica. The strongest most persistent winds on Earth propel cyclonic storms over the mountainous seas. It freezes in winter and yet there is abundant life. Tiny life forms, plankton and krill, sustain multitudes of fish which in turn provide a living for birds and seals.

In the South Atlantic Ken Morris captured a lot of wildlife on film. There was no shortage of birds, penguins and gulls and the giant albatross. Sometimes he used a long lens and sometimes he moved in close. On the beaches were seals and it was easy to see why this one was called an elephant seal.

Photograph by Ken Morris

"Oh my! You are a big boy."

Vast colonies of penguins compete with seals for space on the shores of rocky outcrops. Above on the cliffs are the nesting sites of gulls, cormorants, giant petrels and a bird with a wingspan wider than

371

any other. The wandering albatross is no ordinary bird; it is the bird of legend. The tale is told, in Coleridge's 'The Rhyme of The Ancient Mariner', of a sailor who killed an albatross and brought a curse on his ship. Ken took aim with his camera and pressed the button.

Protector was on hand when Francis Chichester rounded Cape Horn sailing *Gypsy Moth*. Ken had taken many photographs from the air and he was preparing to capture this moment in history. The forces of nature were against him, the strength of the wind was such that the helicopters could not take-off and he failed to get his 'world exclusive'. The yachtsman got his reward. When Francis Chichester, the first man to sail around the world single-handed, arrived in England, he was greeted on the quayside by the Queen. She gave him a knighthood there and then.

Protector ploughed on around the South Atlantic for a while and put into Port Stanley, in the Falklands, for Christmas. They put on paper hats and sat down to turkey and all the trimmings. "Tastes a bit oily. It's not penguin is it?"

Back in Portsmouth Ken was given a choice, under or over. Leading Airman Morris refused the offer of a spell under the waves in a nuclear submarine. Sitting in the open door of helicopters had been an exhilarating experience. The drafting officer made him an offer "Morris, search and rescue, aircrew. Interested?"

It was a dream come true. The aircraft carrier HMS *Eagle* was once featured in the *Eagle*, a popular comic. Schoolboys pored over the cut-away drawing and memorised some of the details, such as the two-acre deck, and accommodation for a hundred aircraft or two hundred and sixty-three double-decker buses. Did a fourteen-year-old schoolboy ever imagine that one day he would be flying off the two-acre deck and sailing round the warm waters of the Indian Ocean and the Persian Gulf?

Never a dull moment, Buccaneers, Sea Vixens and Gannets shot off the deck almost daily and the helicopter crews ferried personnel and supplies to the carriers escort vessels and most importantly the daily bread baked on board *Eagle*. She toured the Far East so that the crew could add to their collection of postcards at Cape Town, Singapore and Hong Kong, and at the same time keeping an eye on Russian 'trawlers'.

They knew there wasn't much room to store fish on these vessels because all available space was crammed with electronic equipment. As the British Empire shrank the Russians expected their empire to expand. In November 1967, *Eagle* and her escorts covered the withdrawal of British troops from the port of Aden. When British forces withdrew the Soviets jumped in and took over the airfield within weeks.

HMS Eagle, *45,000 tons and pride of the Royal Navy.*

"Full steam ahead!"

Ken decided to sign on but there was no more cruising in tropical seas. Life was tough as a member of the Commando Squadron. Sleeping on Dartmoor in the snows of winter must have been unpleasant. If it could be arranged, helicopter crews flew back to a cosy bed at Brawdy. For twelve months he was involved in real flying, air sea rescue working in co-operation with the other emergency services, lifeboat service, air ambulance and police.

Then a real shock. Joan agreed to marry him. Nest-building is never easy for newly-weds especially when it is the Admiralty that decides where the nest is to be built. They were settled at Culdrose, and with a sensible shift pattern enjoyed a sensible sleep pattern in a nice warm bed. "Pity the poor Marines at the School of Arctic Warfare."

He spoke too soon. HMS *Hermes* was converted to fill a commando assault role, all part of Cold War strategy. Where better to practise than in the North Atlantic, and who more acclimatised to Arctic conditions than Petty Officer Morris? With Ken on board, *Hermes* toured Norway, Iceland, Greenland and the Canadian coast.

Meanwhile, back in Redruth Hospital, Joan was awaiting a new arrival. In the maternity ward party balloons, left over from Christmas, were taken down. Joan had deflated and was left with just a few wrinkles and a fine new baby. *Hermes* put in to New York for some sightseeing. Ken picked up a few souvenirs. He pictured the happy smiles when they were unwrapped in the family home. Heading back he expected to catch a glimpse of familiar landmarks as they made their way to port.

To airlift civilians to safety Royal Navy helicopter crews had to negotiate with the Turkish invaders. Petty Officer Morris remains calm.

© Daily Mail

"Yes, your papers do seem to be in order."

"New orders, we're off to the Med, spot of bother." The Greeks and Turks were at each other's throats again. Twenty years earlier the

374

Greek Cypriots had wanted union with Greece. Britain wanted none of it and neither did the Turkish Cypriots. After four years of terrorism there was a sort of agreement. At least the British were no longer involved. Tensions remained, the Greeks were 'pushy' and they pushed the Turks in the north a bit too far. They asked for help from the Turkish mainland. The response was a full-scale invasion.

Caught up in this minor war were British residents and tourists. *Hermes* and her crew were trained for just this sort of rescue operation. Marine Commandos were landed in the midst of it flown in on the Wessex Mk5 helicopters. That calmed the situation immediately, gunship diplomacy from the air. The helicopter squadron now got to work ferrying distraught civilians of all ages and nationalities to places of safety.

It was the job of PO Morris and other crewmen to negotiate with Turkish soldiers. A few days earlier Greek Cypriots had been up to their old tricks taking pot shots at anything British. Fortunately, no one had been 'winged'. The United Nations intervened and *Hermes* sailed home. Christmas presents, bought on Fifth Avenue, were finally unwrapped.

Time to settle down. Ken was drafted to the Aircrewmans' School at Culdrose as an instructor, and there he stayed until the end of his service in 1977.

In flight the albatross is superb. Above the Great Southern Ocean it glides effortlessly for miles. It spends so little time on land that when it does touch down it often stumbles, crumpling uncomfortably to the ground. Petty Officer Ken Morris was out of uniform and grounded. He glided in through the gates of the Central Ordinance Depot at Donnington and stumbled against a desk. He sat there rather uncomfortably for twenty years. Now and then a stiff breeze from the Welsh Mountains sent clouds scudding across the sky. He watched them through the office window. He was off again, soaring and swooping, over the pack ice pushing its way north from Antarctica.

SITTING UNDER THE ICE

Ports and dockyards are fascinating places. Everything is on a large scale; massive cranes, powerful tugs capable of turning round an oil tanker, ropes and chains far too heavy for a man to lift. There are great warehouses to store everything a ship might need to sail around the world. At the harbour entrance there may be the remains of ancient forts and defences against all-comers, Phillip of Spain, Napoleon or Adolf Hitler. For peaceful purposes there may be a towering lighthouse with a lamp that can be seen twenty miles away.

Catstree Farm was far from the sea. At the time of ploughing, when the weather was bad on the Welsh coast, gulls appeared and followed the plough back and forth across the fields that Mapps had tilled for generations. Wheeling above the ploughman and squabbling in the furrow behind him the gulls made strange angry cries. This was not the place for them and soon they were off over the Shropshire Hills and the Black Mountains near Brecon, to Swansea and out into the great Atlantic Ocean. The ploughman was content to remain. Most lads born into farming families were never tempted by 'the call of the sea'.

Adrian Connolly and Gary Drew were mates at school and army cadets together. At sixteen Gary became a boy seaman and Adrian became a cowman. One day they met in Bridgnorth High Street. "You want to join up, do something different, and see the world."

"I might, the army maybe."

Adrian changed his mind. In November 1984 he signed on for twenty-two years in the Royal Navy, and off he went to HMS *Raleigh* at Torpoint across the Tamar from Devonport and Plymouth. These were historic waters.

Polishing boots, laying out kit very neatly, marching up and down and handling a rifle, Adrian had been through all that with the army cadets. He sailed through basic training without distinguishing himself or drawing attention to himself, the aim of every sensible recruit. He chose to join the catering branch. At Aldershot he learned that hot food was good for morale. He also learned about inter-service rivalry. Paratroopers and Royal Marines were attending the same course and when they weren't preparing batter to make 'toad in the hole' they were battering each other. Adrian kept his head down while 'booties' and 'paras' practised what they did best – aggression.

Ordinary Cook Connolly's first taste of life on the ocean wave was on board *Hecate*. Over a hundred crew and half a dozen scientists had to be catered for. HMS *Hecate* was a deep-ocean survey vessel. Scientists on board were there to map the ocean bed to provide vital information for the submarine service, and useful information for geologists looking for oil.

Captain Edwards set course for Iceland. For more than twenty years the coastal waters of Iceland had been a 'war zone'. *Hecate* had to proceed with caution. The waters around Iceland were teeming with cod. Trawlers of many nations came to gather the harvest. This was a million pound industry and essential to the Icelandic economy. The opening exchange in the Cod War followed the decision of the Icelanders, in 1958, to extend the fishing limit around their shores from four miles to twelve. There was relative 'peace' for over ten years, then the limit was extended to fifty miles and a war of words followed. Britain had to accept the new limit and restrictions on the size of the catch for her fishing fleet. The new agreement lasted for only two years before Iceland extended her fishing limits to two hundred miles.

Britain's response was to send frigates, tugs and support vessels to protect her fishing fleet. The bows of the frigates were reinforced with stout timbers to protect them when they rammed the coastguard vessels of the Icelanders. The opposing forces were supposed to be NATO allies and a solution had to be found. Diplomatic pressure from NATO members, the US and the Nordic Council forced Britain to back down. The end result was unemployment for fifteen hundred fishermen and the loss of seven thousand jobs on shore. Iceland's action was not easily forgotten.

HMS *Hecate* arrived off the coast of the old enemy. She was the first Royal Navy vessel allowed into Icelandic waters after the Cod War. The work she was about to carry out benefitted both nations and, needless to say, she was unarmed and unharmed. They set about their task ploughing through seas that were often very rough, scanning the seabed with their instruments and building up a picture of the ocean floor. In 1980, *Hecate* played a part in locating the wreck of the *Titanic*.

In rough seas the full English breakfast is something that does not go down well on a delicate stomach. Adrian was a lucky man; seasickness was one thing that never bothered him. He could serve up a nice piece of fatty bacon with a runny egg no matter how high the waves.

Hecate put in to Reykjavik to give the lads a 'run ashore'. Beer was not on tap everywhere, but there was no shortage of spirits – at a price. Adrian ordered a round, "Three Bacardi and Coke and one gin and tonic, please."

"That will be twenty pounds, please."

They sipped the drinks very slowly and crept back to *Hecate*, topped up on British beer and returned to town in search of nightlife. In the bars there were fine young women, blonde, blue-eyed, full-bodied. The blokes were built like bulldozers, the sort of men who competed in the 'Strongest Man in the World' competition. They could hold a blacksmith's anvil above their head with one hand. This was what stood between the crew of *Hecate* and a good night out in Reykjavik. They sailed away.

Eyjafjordur, an inlet on the north coast of Iceland, was wide enough to allow free passage in and out of the port of Akureyri . There must have been some tension on the bridge as HMS *Hecate* sailed the fifty miles from the open sea and manoeuvred towards her berth. A collision with a trawler would have been a diplomatic disaster. Adrian and his shipmates had another opportunity to take in the sights. Snow-capped mountains, volcanoes in the distance and pools of boiling mud, unforgettable sights. These were all to be added to Adrian's list of 'things I saw when I was in the Navy'.

It was time to have a taste of the tropics. Next stop, Freetown, Sierra Leone. From the sea the coast of West Africa appeared lush and inviting but in the mangrove swamps at the water's edge there was an enemy that threatened all who ventured ashore. The colonisers, the British, French, German, Spanish and Portuguese, all came and claimed lands along the coast. Hundreds died, killed off by the mosquito. The Europeans were drawn to this unhealthy coast by the riches that were there for the taking – gold from the Gold Coast, ivory from the Ivory Coast, mahogany from the forests and men, women and children from wherever they could snatch them.

The Royal Navy were no strangers to the folk of Freetown. They had been sailing into the great natural harbour for two centuries and were very welcome. In 1792, Lieutenant John Clarkson arrived off the coast of Sierra Leone with fifteen ships packed with immigrants to establish a new colony. They had crossed the Atlantic with over a thousand freed slaves and landed them on the shore. The first task was to clear the bush for the new settlement. They stopped when they reached a large cotton tree and prayed, thanking God and the Royal Navy for arranging their freedom. One of the things the Royal Navy could be rightly proud of was the determination shown in stamping out the slave trade. The cotton tree still stands in the middle of Freetown.

Hecate sailed on, west past the coast of Liberia and then called in to the port of Abijan. It seemed rather odd to hear 'the locals' speaking French. Cote d'Ivoire had been an independent state for twenty years but still had strong ties to France, the old colonial power. No one could be sure if they got value for money when they changed the pound sterling for the Ivory Coast franc, but they certainly got plenty of them. Adrian and his mates set off, clutching bundles of grubby notes, in search of 'a bit of local colour'. In the shanty town dark-skinned barmaids relieved them of their wads of notes, and everyone was happy.

Sailing due south *Hecate* made for Ascension Island and St Helena. Adrian was crossing the equator for the first time and had it not been for the tropical climate he might have thought he was back in Iceland when he arrived at Ascension Island. It was a wasteland of lava flows and cinder cones. The runway of Wideawake Airfield had been widened and extended by the Americans to be used as an emergency landing strip for the space shuttle. The RAF was very grateful. Ascension Island was a vital staging post during the Falklands War. It was the base from which Vulcan bombers launched their attacks on the runway at Port Stanley to show the 'Argies' they meant business.

Heading south again, *Hecate* arrived off the coast of St Helena. For those who were interested it was time for another history lesson. The Battle of Waterloo was the end of Napoleon's military career and just to make sure he didn't cause any more trouble he was exiled to St Helena. He moaned about his accommodation. Longwood House was damp and dilapidated that was true, but he did have considerable freedom to wander about the island. He carried on complaining, for five years, to readers of *The Times* until he died. He wanted to be buried in Paris on the banks of the Seine, instead the British Governor laid on a modest funeral in the Valley of Willows. Adrian went ashore as a tourist. He visited Longwood House where Napoleon spent his dying days, and his burial site.

The highlight or the high spot of the tour was undoubtedly High Knoll Fort, not a place for anyone with a fear of heights. This was built as a retreat into which the defenders of the island could withdraw if they were unable to hold off invaders. It had a moat and a drawbridge just like castles of old. It had been rebuilt in Victorian times so it wasn't really that old, certainly not as old as Jonathan.

No one knew exactly how old Jonathan was. Jonathan arrived with three other giant tortoises from the Seychelles in 1882. They took up residency on the lawn of Plantation House and started to munch away at the Governor's grass. Governors came and went, Jonathan's companions faded away, he just kept on munching. He lost count of the number of times he had been photographed with visitors. He remembered the first time; it was with South African prisoners of war, brought to the island during the Boer War. When Adrian met him he was probably the oldest living animal on Earth.

Sailing on again, south west, across the Tropic of Capricorn, *Hecate* steamed into the mouth of the Rio de la Plata to sample the hospitality on offer in the bars of Montevideo. They were once again made very welcome; sailors of all nations had been entertained and given refreshment in this busy port for centuries. To give young naval officers something to be proud of they may well have been lectured on the Battle of the River Plate. The Royal Naval action here ended with the sinking of the *Graf Spee* on the 17th of December, 1939. "So this is where it all happened."

The survey work continued. From time to time the crew were given glimpses of the long, long coast of Brazil. They sailed past Rio de Janeiro and Copacabana Beach, famous for tiny bikinis and large bosoms, and on to Salvador. With a High Town and a Low Town, there was some resemblance between Salvador and Bridgnorth except 'Low Town' had a golden beach and golden-brown girls on it.

Hecate crossed the equator again and the Tropic of Cancer, and then made a brief stop in the Azores before heading home to Plymouth. Cook Connolly had completed his second 'trip of a lifetime'. He had cruised the Atlantic and been to places that could be visited only by the most adventurous tourists.

For some unaccountable reason Adrian decided to take a different view of the world. Some curious sailors want to know what life it is like below the waves so they volunteer for the submarine service. The first thing the Royal Navy teaches them is how to get out. On the waterfront at Gosport Naval Dockyard there is a tower like no other, more than a hundred feet high with long narrow windows from top to bottom. Visitors on a harbour tour might enquire, "What's that over there?"

"Ah, that's full of water. Matelots swim about in it." This is the SETF (submarine escape training facility) at HMS Dolphin.

The diving instructor gave Adrian some advice. "Take a deep breath, then let it out gently as if you were blowing through a straw. If you don't do that your lungs will explode and I will thump you! Off you go."

Watching other trainees from the top of the tank it did look possible. Concentrating on the steady stream of bubbles coming from between his lips, like a silent whistle, Adrian began his ascent up through eighteen feet of lukewarm water. He bobbed up on the surface and filled up his lungs again, pleased with his performance.

"That's fine, now let's have go at thirty-two feet."

Adrian took a deep breath. He thought, *It must be possible or we wouldn't be here.*

He was 'out of puff' before he had reached the halfway mark, but just as his instructor had said he seemed to get a second wind. The depth markers slipped by; fifteen, ten, five and out on top for a welcome gulp of air. Escape from a depth of one hundred feet was only possible with a pressurised suit.

The experience was exhilarating. In a rubberised suit with mask and goggles, Adrian could breathe normally in the chamber at the bottom of the tank. He turned the valve and allowed the chamber to fill with water. Divers above opened the hatch and he floated up like a Michelin man. The ascent began slowly, as the air in the suit expanded the rate of ascent increased until the 'red balloon' shot right out of the water and plopped helplessly back onto the surface. Everyone hoped that they would never have to repeat this exercise for real.

At Faslane, Adrian joined the crew of 'The Conk', HMS *Conqueror*. Within three days she had sailed down Loch Gare and dived down into the Firth of Clyde. Adrian was going under for the first time; it was too late now to have a change of heart.

Where they went nobody knows; they were not called the 'silent service' for nothing. The Cold War was coming to an end but Russian submarines were still nosing around the British Isles and had to be warned off. Adrian's contribution to all this was to keep up morale by preparing four meals a day for one hundred and twenty men. *Conqueror* and other submarines of the hunter-killer class were capable of staying submerged for three months at a time. It was a miracle that the catering staff could find space for all the provisions, but they did. Salads and fresh fruit lasted for about a fortnight. The shift system, or 'watches', meant that it was easy to lose track of time. The menu helped; it was fish on Friday, roast on Sunday.

HMS Conqueror in home waters at Faslane.

"Getting a breath of fresh air."

Tracking the Russians, chasing them across the North Sea and under the Arctic ice, was not for the faint-hearted. In the galley they knew when they were getting close to a Soviet sub because they were not allowed to operate 'Peter the Eater'. He was vicious, he could rip the skins off a sackful of potatoes in minutes, and he made a dreadful noise when he went into action. The vibrations from the potato peeler would have been picked up by the Russians, so the chefs always had to ask permission to use Peter the Eater.

To qualify as a submariner every member of the crew had to complete the Task Book. They had to know the details of every department and the duties of 'stokers', 'writers' or even 'tactical systems operators'. In his off-duty hours Adrian toured *Conqueror* and familiarised himself with the positions of valves and switches that he might be called upon to operate in an emergency. He knew he was never going to fully understand the workings of a nuclear power plant so before he visited the control room he prepared a tasty little snack for the Petty Officer who was going to sign his Task Book. The bacon butty went down very well and the Petty Officer Stoker was happy to sign the book and declare that Cook Connolly understood the propulsion system very well. After six months the Task Book was complete. A simple ceremony was arranged in the officers' quarters. Adrian smartened himself up for the occasion. The Captain presented him with 'The Dolphin Badge'. He was now a submariner.

The Dolphin Badge worn by those who travel in an underwater world.

"Even dolphins have to come up for air."

When Adrian came home after his first tour of the seabed he was greeted by his mother with, "Where have you been, a prison camp?"

He was unnaturally pale, he had lost a stone and his hair was on his shoulders. Adrian explained he could not have his hair cut on the sub because loose clippings would get into the air conditioning system and cause problems. Of course he was pale. He hadn't seen the sun for months. He couldn't explain the weight loss; he was a chef and should have been plump and jolly like most TV chefs. On the next tour everything was fine.

Conqueror went under the ice again. They knew they were there because it was cold. They knew they were in warmer waters when the spuds started to sprout, so it was no surprise when they surfaced and there was the Rock of Gibraltar. The crew could now go on a 'jolly'. The Royal Navy was generous; bed and breakfast in a good hotel was arranged. The bed was much appreciated; it was bliss. This was the reward for months of 'hot bunking', sharing the same bunk and mattress with another submariner working a different shift. The sleeping bag was personal and slipped under the mattress 'in the morning'. Off the coast of Morocco they submerged and headed south, far south to the Falkland Islands.

Five years earlier, in 1982, the *Conqueror* had sailed with the British task force to reclaim the Falkland Islands. She was there to patrol a two hundred mile total exclusion zone around the islands. It was soon realised that this was too small and through diplomatic channels it was made clear to the Argentine Government that any vessel anywhere in the area would be considered 'fair game'.

The task force was threatened by carrier-borne aircraft and destroyers with Exocet missiles. Also in the area was the *Belgrano* with over a thousand troops on board, and protected by Sea Cat missiles. This was a highly dangerous situation. Admiral Woodward was concerned that his fleet would be caught in a pincer movement. Submarines tracking the aircraft carrier had lost contact, but in the meantime *Conqueror* had the *Belgrano* in her sights. The order to engage the enemy was authorised by the War Cabinet in London and a signal sent direct to Commander Wreford-Brown. He ordered torpedoes to be launched; it took less than a minute for the first torpedo to travel the three quarters of a mile separating the two vessels. A second torpedo followed almost immediately. This caused catastrophic damage and accounted for most of the casualties. Nearly eight hundred took to the lifeboats and were saved; over two hundred lost their lives. At the time the sinking of the *Belgrano* created a political storm, now it is accepted, even by the Argentine Navy, that it was a legitimate act of war.

The next visit to the Falklands had to be discreet. To avoid detection by submarines of the Argentine Navy, the *Conqueror* settled gently on the seabed next to a wreck. When it was all clear she slipped into one of the many coves on the ragged coast of the Falklands. The crew were bussed across the island to see the sights of Port Stanley and enjoy the hospitality of the RAF. The submariners picked up parcels and letters from home which was rather strange because no one was supposed to know they were there.

From the Falklands they headed north under warmer waters. Still submerged *Conqueror* passed along the coast of Brazil. 'Billy' Connolly reminisced about his earlier tour on board *Hecate* and described the delights on offer on the beaches and in the bars of Salvador, Recife and Forteleza. "Don't go on about it, Billy. We'll get some of that in the Caribbean."

They did get a glimpse of it as they cruised on by the tourist resorts. No one went ashore. The sea was an unnatural blue, the beaches bright gold, the sunshades rainbow striped, the loungers covered with female forms glistening with suntan oil. Binoculars were passed around. "Come on, let's have a look."

"No, don't torment yourself."

The chefs did their best to cheer everyone up. They arranged a barbeque on the deck. As the beefburgers and sausages sizzled so did some of the crew. After months in the depths of the South Atlantic they crept out of the sub, looking as if they had crawled out from under a stone. In less than half an hour they were blistered red meat. "You won't get any sympathy, that's a self-inflicted wound."

Florida was different. Comfy beds, sights to see and visitors. Among the nearest and dearest flown in by the Ministry of Defence was Kim, the girl of Cook Connolly's dreams. During the refit Adrian did have some duties but there was still time to visit the tourist spots, Disneyland, Sea World (as if he hadn't seen enough of it) and Cape Canaveral. The roads for miles around were blocked with traffic. Car radios gave a commentary so the visitors were well prepared. "Three, two, one, lift off!" What a sight it was, the launch of the Space Shuttle.

Holiday over, loved ones parted and *Conqueror* made for home. It was decision time for Adrian. Did he really want to spend three months every year chasing Russians under the ice? The 'game of chicken' was not without risks. When rival captains confronted each other someone had to back down. The winner of the game was the man who held his nerve. If neither captain turned away at the last minute then inevitably there was a collision. On one occasion the 'Conk' had to make a swift return to Faslane to have damage to her conning tower repaired. Then there was 'friendly fire' to contend with. As part of a seek and destroy exercise, the *Conqueror* was the target to test a new missile system. It didn't take long for the helicopter pilot to spot *Conqueror* and once the weapons system had locked on to her he couldn't miss. The only thing missing was the explosive warhead. Even so the casing of the missile hit the sub with a considerable clatter and it was back to base again to be patched up.

Then there was something mysterious that 'went bump in the night'. It turned out to be more embarrassing than sinister. Cruising along gently one dark night, at periscope depth, *Conqueror* ran into something. No one panicked, the officer of the watch gave directions and a well-rehearsed routine was put into operation. When they surfaced the situation became clear. They had cut a yacht in half! A rescue boat was launched and the four passengers were brought on board. They were dried out and warmed. The Captain apologised. "Sorry about all this. I'm told you were not displaying navigation lights, or any lights come to that. These two young ladies, your daughters, nieces, perhaps?"

The Captain was a 'man of the world'. The skipper of the yacht was himself a retired officer and his male companion was a clergyman. Their relationship to the ladies was not entirely clear. The Captain did not enquire further. He had heard many tales that ended with, 'And the actress said to the bishop'. The incident was not made public.

Once or twice 'odd bods' appeared who were not members of the crew. They settled into spare bunks in the weapons bay, turned up for meals regularly, kept themselves to themselves and then disappeared. Were they part of what the military call 'covert operations'? Nobody knew.

Cook Connolly's service with the Royal Navy had been a 'Boys' Own Adventure', but the tug of war between the Royal Navy and the loyal Kim was over. Adrian divorced the Navy, married Kim and came back to Catstree Farm.

Adrian does sometimes have flashbacks when he looks out over the green fields and wooded valleys of his boyhood and watches the gulls making for the river and down to the sea. In the kitchen, helping to prepare a meal on a Friday, he leans over the freezer and takes out a few fillets of cod from the very bottom.

Toddlers are strange little creatures, very unstable, liable to fall over without warning. They often lurch about hands high above their heads hoping to attract attention. Alwyn's mum skipped after him as he tottered towards the river. He spun round on the bank and his sturdy little arms shot straight up, fingers spread, pointing to the sky. "Mum, where are they all going?"

"They're going home to America."

The sky was full of bombers, in loose formation, droning west like a flock of migrating geese. There was peace in Europe at last and all efforts to end the war were now turned to the Pacific and the war with Japan. In later life, when asked about his earliest memories, this was the scene Alwyn described. Clearly it made a lasting impression on Air Commodore Barnett.

George and Hilda Barnett were keen cyclists. At weekends they checked the brakes and oiled the chain of their tandem and swept out of the streets of the Black Country and into the country lanes of Shropshire. These were happy days before the outbreak of war. When bombs began to rain down on Birmingham they looked for a place of safety for baby George. The family lodged first in the Station Master's house at Linley, and then moved on to Winscote Hills.

The hollow in the woodland was a suntrap in summer. In this 'chocolate box' setting Joe Williamson's bees hummed around the flower beds and foraging hens clucked with satisfaction when they discovered something tasty on the side of the sandy lane. From the cottage chimneys thin columns of smoke drifted up into the clear blue sky and faded into the treetops. A Victorian artist might have captured this on canvas and made twenty-first century townsfolk envious.

In reality the conditions were primitive. The summer suntrap was a frosty hollow in winter. All year round the range, for heating and cooking, was lit and fuelled with fallen branches from the surrounding woodland. There was no electricity. Water was carried from a standpipe thirty yards from the house. The dwelling was built over the mouth of a cave that made up part of the living quarters. There was nothing romantic about this way of life.

Huge snowdrifts filled the lane that led to the main road during the memorable winter of 1947. Britain was icebound for months but

Sid Foxall still managed to negotiate Newton Bank in his Bedford bus, and carry children down the lanes to Worfield School. The Barnett boys, farm boys and the children of airmen from Stanmore Camp responded well to the teaching by young men recently returned from the war, even the aptly named Frank Bangham. He was not just a man who commanded respect. He was the owner of a Riley sports saloon that small boys could admire in the corner of the schoolyard, and dream of driving.

Waiting for the school bus there was an almost daily reminder of wartime. First a Spitfire and then a Mosquito flew over. Their mission was to check weather conditions on their flight path between Woodvale and Pershore. At the sound of the Merlin engines, Alwyn looked up and studied their progress across the sky. So began a life-long fascination with air traffic.

A cheeky, cheery lad, he was always ready for an adventure. The river, a hundred yards from the garden gate, was the obvious place to start. Under the sandstone cliff the water raced through the channel cut in the riverbed to allow the passage of Severn Trows a century earlier. Downstream the river widened and slowed. Alwyn and his mate Mick spent days making the old bathtub seaworthy, surrounding it with planks and oil drums. They fashioned a wooden bung to replace the bath plug and hammered it home before the launch. The primitive technology Alwyn and Mick used to construct their craft meant that this was not going to be a long voyage. With paddle and pole they pushed from the bank. Sabrina, goddess of the Severn, took the controls and carried them downstream. They ducked under the overhanging willows and swept past bemused cattle standing knee deep in the shallows. The boy sailors knew the river and the tricky currents that lay ahead under High Rock. Wisely they headed for the bank and beached the rudderless craft in the nick of time. Plodding back, a mile through the meadows, the lads discussed the problem of sailing against the current. This had not been part of the original plan.

Few schoolboys have a clear life plan but parents know that a sound education is the first step on the ladder to success. George and Alwyn progressed from the village school to Bridgnorth Grammar School. Sacrifices had to be made to allow the boys to stay on, even to the age of sixteen. It was not easy for Hilda Barnett who was now a lone parent.

At sixteen Alwyn 'got on his bike' and rode to Jackfield to work alongside the press shop supervisor at Maws, the famous tilemakers. He was a management trainee and this was excellent grounding for a leader of men. The workforce was overwhelmingly female. He learned a lot about ceramics and the techniques of tilemaking, and a new vocabulary from the ladies who had specialist knowledge of courtship and baby-making, and were willing to educate any young lad. The company could not survive in the modern world. Just before the factory closed, Alwyn left and set off into the wider world.

NEW VENTURE

He arrived at the RAF station at South Cerney in July 1962 to begin his training as a pilot. Horatio Nelson was a great admiral but he wasn't a great sailor. In a letter written to Lord Camden he admits, *I am ill every time it blows hard and nothing but my enthusiastic love for the profession keeps me one hour at sea.*

With Officer Cadet Barnett the problem was airsickness, particularly when carrying out aerobatics. He persevered and had the unforgettable experience of flying solo. Unfortunately, the condition did not improve and it was decided that he would be 'grounded'. This was deeply disappointing.

While the authorities were considering a new direction for Alwyn's RAF career, he discovered an unexpected talent in the control tower at Middleton St George. This was the home of the Lightning, the RAF's fastest fighter. To handle air traffic that flew at well over a thousand miles an hour required lightning reactions. Controllers had to be capable of handling any emergency, and at the same time stay calm, speak clearly and confidently. He loved the atmosphere in the control tower and was delighted when he was offered the chance to train as a controller.

At the Central Air Traffic Control School at RAF Shawbury, Alwyn threw himself into the course with enthusiasm. The failure rate was high. There were casualties; the fearful who could not handle the responsibility, the indecisive, the ditherers and mumblers were all weeded out. Pilot Officer Barnett excelled and was posted to RAF Honington in Suffolk. This was the base for a squadron of Handley Page Victors that carried Britain's nuclear deterrent. With bombs on board they stood ready at all times to counter any threat from the other side of the Iron Curtain. Aircrew, ground crew and air traffic controllers were on duty around the clock.

No sooner was the Emergency in Malaya over and the new nation state of Malaysia created than there was trouble on the island of Borneo. British North Borneo, the protectorates of Sabah and Sarawak, became East Malaysia. To the south was Indonesia and it was along this border that most of the action took place between 1963 and 1966. Alwyn was posted to the island base of Labuan just off the East Malaysia coast.

Flying Officer Barnett talking them down in Borneo.

Permission given by Alwyn Barnett.

"Look at that, my knees are so brown."

Here the busy airfield provided support for the ground operations against the Indonesian forces that crossed the border to harass the villagers and ambush Malaysian and British troops. Most actions were small scale but frequently deadly, and coffins were a regular cargo item on the flights to the British forces HQ eight hundred miles away in Singapore.

Guard duty at Labuan was something no one looked forward to. Cooks, clerks, mechanics and airmen of every trade were required to act as infantrymen, and junior officers were expected to supervise. Sleeping on duty was a serious offence, even more serious when 'on active service'. The young airman looked so peaceful propped against the wall with just a hint of a dreamy smile. His loaded rifle had slipped from his fingers and lay just out of reach. Flying Officer Barnett kicked the sole of his boot. "Wake up, will you! If this was the Zulu War you'd be court-martialled and probably shot!"

"Sir, won't happen again, sir."

Since the surrounding jungle contained all sorts of nasties, recreation was restricted to water sports and fishing. Alwyn compared the temperature of the clear tropical waters with the murky Severn at Winscote where he first practised with rod and line. At least there he wasn't troubled by sea snakes or the evil stonefish that lurked on the bottom with deadly spines along its back. These could be avoided by moving into the nearest bar and resting bare feet on the rungs of a tall stool, which may airmen did.

When the Malaysian armed forces took over border security and the RAF presence reduced, Alwyn was posted to the Seletar air base in Singapore. There was so much here to enjoy in the newly-independent city state; wonderful food, plenty of sport and a vibrant nightlife. Two years flashed by.

BACK TO BASE

After three years in the Far East, Flying Officer Barnett returned to the UK for up-to-date radar training and put this into practise on airfields in East Anglia. Then he returned to Shawbury, not as a student this time but as an instructor and then as an examiner. From the Central Navigation and Control School, Flight Lieutenant Barnett visited all RAF flying units to check on their safety and efficiency. These units were spread over much of Europe and the Middle East. One particular inspection in Oman was interrupted by incoming rocket fire launched by angry tribesmen. It was decided to withdraw and continue discussions in a slit trench rather than the easily targeted red and white painted control tower.

Ten years later, and promoted to Wing Commander, Alwyn returned to Shropshire once again to take over responsibility for the training of all air traffic controllers. Very few of the trainees were familiar with the geography of south Shropshire. Explaining some of the exercises the CO might point out on the map the course of the Severn from Shrewsbury to Bewdley. What the young airmen could not see was the slide show that flickered through the mind of Wing Commander Barnett as he ran the pointer over the chart: the playing fields of Bridgnorth Grammar School, the woody hollow at Winscote, the country lanes where he first ventured out behind the wheel of his 1932 Morris Minor on his way to the Maws factory at Jackfield. "And there you have it. Clear to everyone?"

Alwyn's career had never taken a backward step, but now he was tempted to glance back to where it all began.

Memory Lane

Alwyn got in touch with the Apley Estate Office to arrange a visit. The Land Agent said, "The General won't mind, I'm sure." Alwyn and Fiona wandered around taking it all in. The sandstone caves at the riverside, the buttercup meadows, the sandy lane, the peaceful shade of the woodland; little seemed to have changed. There were new tenants in the cottage at the bottom of the lane. Luigi, the fiery ex-POW, his wife and his dark-haired, dark-eyed, adored-from-a-distance daughter, Rosanna, had all moved away, back to Italy perhaps.

Old Joe Williamson had kept his garden in perfect order. Fruit trees and flowers beds, bean rows and beehives, and the weed free vegetable plot were all gone, and Joe was gone as well. He 'came to grief' when an MG sports car knocked him off his bike one dark night on the way home from the pub. An artist with the scythe, if only he could have been there with Al and Fiona as they worked their way through the undergrowth until, at last, they found the remains of the family home.

When returning to scenes of childhood, schools, churches, cottages often seem smaller. Number three Winscote had always been cramped. Standing in the crumbling remains of the living room it was hard to believe how the family could have been so comfortable there. Al recalled the scene: his mother preparing dinner on the primitive cast iron range, her boys reading and completing their homework by the light of an oil lamp.

Alwyn and Fiona drove away in their VW convertible (he had an enduring passion for open-topped cars) through the lanes to Worfield.

They drove slowly past The Dog and the village shop, turned in front of Saint Peter's Church and drew up in front of the school. "That was where Mr Bangham parked his Riley. Shop and post office still the same."

The same red post box, embossed with GR, and set in the wall by the shop window, was a reminder of the day when a ten-year-old schoolboy went in to buy sweets in February 1953. The postmistress said, "Will you take this letter up to the Smiths on your way home? Thank you, Alwyn." He turned the brown envelope over a few times as he walked towards their cottage. It didn't have a proper stamp but a crown in a black circle, and On His Majesty's Service printed across the top. It wasn't exactly good news but it was better news. The War Office was able to tell the family that their son, Alec, serving with the Durham Light Infantry in Korea, was safe. Wounded on the front line he had been flown to a military hospital in Japan and was 'out of danger'.

A remarkable chain of events had taken a boy from a secluded hollow on the banks of the Severn to command hundreds of airmen. There must have been a turning point that led to this. Wing Commander Barnett looked into the Shawbury archives and read his own original training reports. His old instructor, a veteran fighter pilot, had made an unusual comment on Alwyn's performance. "This boy is a revelation."

How right he was. There was still more promotion, to Group Captain and finally to Air Commodore. With gold on the peak of his cap, and one broad ring on his sleeve, Alwyn became the head of air traffic control for the Royal Air Force with responsibility for over two thousand personnel, two large Control Centres and forty-four airfields. He served thirty-three years in the Royal Air Force, was introduced to several members of the Royal Family and dined with Princess Anne – twice. He met many politicians; the most frightening was Gwynneth Dunwoody. Al had to face her across the table in the House of Commons when she was chair of the transport committee.

He was a grounded pilot and not given to flights of fantasy. "I never forgot those happy formative years at Apley, and I think that helped me to retain a sense of perspective in later life."

Retired from the RAF in 1995, Al and Fiona moved to Luxembourg where he became head of training for the European Organisation for Safety of Air Navigation. Now settled in Surrey he returns regularly to Shropshire, to the haunts of his youth and to have his sports car serviced.

Chapter 33

Back to Basra

KNOW HOW TO HANDLE A GUN

Botley, Ewins and Draper sound like a firm of solicitors, but they were not. They did all have something in common. They were soldiers and they all passed through the port of Basra to do battle between the Tigris and Euphrates. These two mighty rivers that flow into the Persian Gulf were well known to pupils at the Grammar School in Bridgnorth. They were taught that in the fertile lands between the rivers was Mesopotamia, the Cradle of Civilisation.

Tom Botley learned just enough at Worfield School to get by in the world. He was not a stay-at-home boy. In the reign of Edward VII he learned to handle a gun. From his keeper's hut in woodland near Newbridge-on-Wye, he went about his duties. He was a true countryman. In his lifetime he came to know the ways of all things in the natural world. On daily patrol of his 'beat', with a shotgun over his arm, he might look across the River Wye and observe sand martins and kingfishers as they skimmed back and forth in search of fish and flies.

At the outbreak of the Great War, from this place of peace and harmony, Tom came back to Hartlebury. Reports of casualties in the great battles on the Somme and the Marne were enough to convince anyone that the young men of Europe were engaged in a dangerous game. Like it or not Tom was called up and reported to barracks at Gosport in May 1916. He signed the form of engagement and gave his trade as rabbit catcher and farm labourer. In a matter of weeks he had a new trade, gunner in the Royal Garrison Artillery.

The troopship with Tom and his battery on board sailed from Devonport. Troops had been sailing away from the port on every tide for the past two years. There were no cheering crowds, perhaps just a casual wave from an old sailor, on the quayside, as he let slip the hawser, the last link with the homeland.

German U-boats had been a menace from the start of the war. In the first ten weeks five British cruisers had been lost to them. In the spring of 1915 two battleships were sunk in the Eastern Mediterranean during the Gallipoli campaign. This was no secret; the painful details of all the ships lost to the U-boats were reported in the daily papers. It was a great relief to all on board when they entered the Suez Canal. The Canal was surely one of the Wonders of the Modern World. Sailing through a sandy desert; it didn't seem possible. Troops were everywhere, at times close enough to the ship to exchange greetings "…and the best of luck in Mesop."

BETTER THAN BOOK LEARNING

With friendly faces all around, the threat of U-boats left behind in the Med and more than enough sunshine, the troops relaxed and took in the scenery, sand and palm trees, and the hills above Ismailia on the Crocodile Lake. They sailed on south with desert to east and west.

"Somewhere out there they say there's a holy city with some sort of monument, a tomb. The Gipos and the like stop what they're doin', twice a day, and get down on their knees, praying and chantin' facing in that direction. What do you make o' that, Tom?" The customs, the landscape of the orient, palms and palaces, scenes of daily life with camels, men in flowing robes, women heavily veiled with only a narrow view of the world; this was all new to farm boys and lads from grimy towns in England. Even their young officers, with the benefit of some classical education, had learned little from the dusty books in the school library. Now they were all experiencing it at first hand. "Makes y'u think, don't it, Tom?" Once they entered the Red Sea they were given only the occasional glimpse of land. Seabirds following in the wake of the ship, pods of dolphins and flying fish were commonplace. The sailors tried to explain that below the surface of the sea there was another world. "Coloured fish, not just silver. Blues and yellows, some even black, allsorts. There's coral, hard as rock, with patterns like lace. You see bits of that washed up on the shore." It was impossible to describe the wonders of the coral reefs fringing the Red Sea, or the startling colours of the angelfish darting in every direction.

The sun set early, the lads drifted about on deck enjoying the cool of the evening and wishing that the last meal of the day had been a bit more substantial. They lit up a last 'fag' before turning in for the night. Along the rail the tips of their cigarettes glowed like fireflies. Lights from the portholes below lit up the waves spreading out from the prow of the ship as it churned on its way.

"The sea's all aglow, Tom, how's that? There must be something spilling out from the ship. P'rhaps we're leaking oil." An uncountable number of tiny organisms, each one capable of producing a speck of light, gave the sea surface a ghostly glow when conditions were right. Bioluminescence was something that didn't happen in Worfe Brook or the River Severn. At certain times of the year sea sawdust, bacteria very useful to the coral below, produced 'red tides' in the Red Sea.

Once they emerged from the Red Sea the captain changed course, sailing to the east past the port of Aden then north across the Arabian Sea towards the Strait of Hormuz. More palms and grand palaces came into view, and by contrast the simple earth-coloured dwellings of ordinary people. Even at a distance the gulf between rich and poor was clearly wider here than at home in England. At last they entered the Shatt al-Arab and tied up at the port of Basra, in Mesopotamia.

Basra 1917. Turkish prisoners passing along the bank of Ashar Creek, near Whiteley's Bridge.

"They don't look a bad lot."

Gunner Botley's world had been between the River Worfe and the Severn, not the Tigris and Euphrates. This voyage had been an education for Tom. He had learned more in a month at sea than he had in six years at Worfield School.

Striking Back

Things were going badly for the British. The Turks had thrown in their lot with the Germans, and although their empire was in decline it still extended from Istanbul to the Persian Gulf. The flow of oil from the region had to be protected, so at the outbreak of war a force was dispatched from India to take the town of Basra and secure the oil refinery nearby at Abadan.

In the opening months of the war forces under the command of General John Nixon sailed into Basra and set up a garrison in the town and built defences around it. The Mesopotamian Expeditionary Force was made up largely of troops of the Indian Army. The Turks mounted a series of attacks hoping to retake Basra and drive the invaders into the sea. All attempts failed.

Nixon went on the offensive, at least he sent General George Townsend off to do the job for him. With an armoured column, supported by gunboats and supply vessels, Townsend moved inland along the valley of the Tigris. He captured the town of Kut, about a hundred and eighty miles inland from the port, and pressed on towards Baghdad. Townsend and his Indian troops became the victims of their own success. With supply lines extended they could not maintain the momentum. In November 1915 they were defeated at the Battle of Ctesiphon and fell back to Kut. The Turks laid siege to the town. George Townsend was confident he could hold out until a relief column arrived. Two attempts were made to raise the siege, both failed. At Kut the beleaguered troops faced starvation. The number of sick and wounded rose until Townsend had no alternative but to surrender, unconditionally, in April 1916.

Gunner Botley to the Rescue

British and Indians troops licked their wounds, and by December 1916 they were ready to go on the offensive and push the Turks back along the Tigris.

Artillery pieces of the Royal Field Artillery were assembled to support the infantry. Heavy guns of the Royal Garrison Artillery were brought out. Tom Botley patted the barrel of the eight inch howitzers. It was capable of firing a shell seven miles. This was a very comfortable distance away from the enemy. A few flimsy aircraft of the Royal Flying Corps buzzed overhead and reported any damage inflicted on the enemy. Kut was recaptured in February 1917. General Maude made a triumphant entry into the town. Gunner Botley retired to Basra and allowed General Maude to carry on up the Tigris.

In less than a month General Maude had taken Baghdad. To make the British position more secure expeditions were sent up the Tigris to Samarrah, famous for its golden mosque, and up the Euphrates to Ramadi. Then the General himself became a casualty. He died of cholera, a disease which claimed the lives of many. In all there were over forty thousand casualties in Mesopotamia, victims of a variety of diseases that thrived where there was overcrowding, poor diet, poor sanitation and heat.

How Tom passed the time over the next twelve months we will never know. Basra was a busy place. Vessels of every shape and size were tying up and casting off daily. Fresh troops arrived to replace the sick and wounded. Tons of bully beef and biscuits were offloaded on the quayside to sustain the garrison.

By the spring of 1918 it was clear that Germany was losing the war. Their Turkish allies were all but defeated and Britain and France had a new ally, America. Gunner Botley was granted a month's leave. In April 1918, Tom sailed to India on the *MT Aronda* and back to Basra on the *Sicilia*, both ships provided by the Italians, our allies in the Great War. He made what tourists today call 'the trip of a lifetime'.

The freighters, gunboats and troop carriers tied up at Basra were grimy, cheerless vessels often needing oily tugboats to tow them away from the quay. Bobbing about alongside them were the floating market traders offering snacks and souvenirs. More stately and serious were the 'dhows' with triangular white sails, the style and shape unchanged for centuries. For as long as anyone could remember they had been trading across the Arabian Sea and along the coast of Africa carrying any cargo that would turn a profit, and that included human cargo.

The dhows leaving Basra alongside the *Aronda* added colour to the scene with garlands on the prow and decorations in the rigging, offerings to the gods for a safe passage. The captains, serious men in white robes, did not respond to the cheers or insults thrown at them by the cheerful 'Tommies'.

Everyone was used to the heat of the Gulf but the sea breeze created by the movement of the ship as it got underway had a very pleasant cooling effect. The atmosphere on board was relaxed. "What do you reckon to the tea, Tom?"

"Well, there's plenty of sugar in it, but it could do with a drop o' milk, and why 'ave they've put it in these piddlin' little glasses?"

"Perhaps we shall get a nice bit of fish shortly."

There was no shortage of fish in the Persian Gulf. They came to feed on the waste from the ports, and in turn sharks fed on them. Lads like Tom who had never seen the sea until they were called to serve their country lost count of the number of sharks they had seen slicing through the waters alongside the ship.

Refreshed after a month's leave Tom sailed back to Basra. The Turks melted away and peace was declared in Europe. Guns fell silent and slowly troops began to return home. The Indians sailed back across the Arabian Sea, the heroic Anzacs made their way to Australia and New Zealand and, in March 1919, Tom Botley and others of the Mesopotamian Expeditionary Force took ship to Dover.

He was still in Dover three months later, languishing in the military hospital. General Maude and hundreds of his men had died of cholera and Tom Botley must have been suffering from something similar. It was six months before he was fully fit. His brother Harold was mystified "Can't make out what's up with our Tom. There's not a mark on 'im."

Harold Botley had a nasty scar; a German infantryman had dug his bayonet deep into his side. Many had received similar wounds, few had survived. "Basra must be an unhealthy place."

Two decades later Gunner Ern Ewins was preparing for a trip to the Gulf.

ALL ABOUT OIL

Ern Ewins couldn't help it. Even when he was being serious he still looked cheeky. He was full of energy and there was no better place for him to work it off that on the cricket field. Batsmen defending their wicket steeled themselves when Ern came storming towards them to deliver hard leather at high speed. He was a truly fast bowler. At work he had to steady up. Painting was a job that couldn't be rushed.

Young tradesmen, painters, plumbers, carpenters and bricklayers, all prepared to follow the example of their fathers and take up arms again as the Second World War approached. Billy Ewins, Ern's father, and others like him who had survived the Great War, muttered words of caution. "It won't be no picnic, my lad." One by one they left the estate and went by sea and air to distant battlefields.

Following the collapse of the Ottoman Empire the victorious allies carved up the region. Britain had a mandate to govern both Palestine and Iraq; the French had control of Syria and the Lebanon. The British mandate for Iraq ended in 1932. Military bases were still maintained not to protect the fruit and vegetables growing in the fertile fields on the banks of the Tigris, but for the oil underground. The Iraqis did not have full independence. The movement of troops and the flow of oil were dictated by Britain, and this rankled.

With France defeated and Britain tied up in North Africa, Rashid Ali, the Iraqi Prime Minister, took the opportunity to stage a coup in 1941 deposing King Faisal. He refused to allow British forces to enter Iraq believing that if it came to armed conflict the Germans would intervene on his side. There was some diplomatic wrangling but it was clear that he could not be allowed to get away with this. Oil supplies had to be protected and maintained.

The British presence in Iraq consisted of two air bases, RAF Shaibah, near Basra and the other at Habbaniya . Gunner Ewins and his company arrived and set up their battery at Shaibah. Twenty years earlier this had been the site of a battle with the Turks when Tom Botley was a young gunner.

About a thousand troops were based at RAF Habbaniya about fifty miles from Baghdad. The RAF flew Gloster Gladiators from the airfield. Of the eighty aircraft less than half were capable of engaging in serious warfare. The Iraqi Air Force that had been trained by the RAF and were no better equipped. They also flew the Gloster Gladiator, the same biplane fighter that stood on the tarmac at Habbaniya, with the RAF roundel painted on the side. Ern Ewins wore something similar on his shoulder, a roundel with an arrow pointing upwards. The Royal Artillery was there to protect the airfields.

Rashid Ali ordered his forces to attack British bases within Iraq and to oppose any attempts to land troops at the port of Basra. The Royal Navy was called in and Indian troops landed unopposed. Royal Artillery Field Regiments were attached to the 10th Indian Infantry Battalion. Lancashire lads of the 'King's Own' flew in to RAF airfields, more aircraft arrived. The Anglo-Iraq war began officially on the 2nd of May 1941.

The RAF airfield at Habbaniya was surrounded by Iraqi forces. A pre-emptive air strike was launched against them. A number of Iraqi planes were destroyed on the ground. With no effective air cover the besieging forces began to withdraw to Fallujah. Attacked by about forty aircraft the Iraqis suffered further casualties. The Luftwaffe sent a small force to Mosul but it was too little too late. British troops from Habbaniya pursued the Iraqis, and after five days fighting pushed them out of Fallujah.

The war was barely three weeks old and already British forces had the upper hand. A dozen Italian aircraft arrived but had little impact on the conflict. British forces began to advance on Baghdad on the 27th of May. Rashid Ali fled the country. The Mayor of Baghdad surrendered to British forces and the brief Anglo-Iraqi War came to an end. Basra, Baghdad, Fallujah, Mosul were place names that would be heard of again in far more serious conflicts.

Gunner Ewins moved on to North Africa. His ant-aircraft battery dug in on dusty airstrips to fend off enemy aircraft. The battlefront swung back and forth but in the end the Desert Army and the Desert Air Force pushed Rommel and his Afrika Korps out of Africa.

At home on the Estate Ern Ewins took up his old trade and the sport he loved. Apley's 'demon bowler' terrorised nervous batsmen for another decade. He set up home in the heart of the village with his young wife and they lived happily together for the rest of their days.

A Soldier's Life for Me

Russian, American and British diplomats were agreed Saddam Hussein had gone too far. He had occupied some of the oil-rich land of his tiny neighbour Kuwait, and in August 1990 his tanks rolled into Kuwait City itself. The United Nations declared that Saddam must withdraw. An international force assembled in Saudi Arabia and prepared for battle.

At Soltan, north of Hanover, the 7th Armoured Brigade was given its marching orders. Six thousand troops were issued with desert camouflage kit complete with 'Desert Rat' shoulder patch, and one hundred and fourteen battle tanks were given a respray. On arrival in Saudi Arabia they began serious training. Small boys all over Britain watched reports on TV with keen interest. One lad, seven-year-old Steven Draper, decided there and then, "I'm going to join the army."

Desert Rats swept into Kuwait and delivered a left hook manoeuvre to Saddam's Republican Guard. Operation Desert Storm lasted forty-two days. The problem didn't go away.

Steven Draper moved on from Ringmere Primary School in Sussex to Bridgnorth Endowed School and made preparations for his military career. At school Steven was bright enough to pass the necessary examinations to enter the Army Foundation College at Harrogate. He passed out in August 2002 and went on to Catterick to complete infantry training before he began serious soldiering with the 2nd Battalion, the Royal Regiment of Fusiliers.

When Fusilier Draper arrived in Belfast, infantrymen of the British Army had been patrolling the streets for over thirty years. The modern conflict in Northern Ireland began in 1969 before most of the fusiliers of C Company were born. Protestants of the Orange Order put on regular parades and IRA sympathisers always reacted in the same way. Public order operations were the responsibility of C Company which meant keeping a lid on the riots.

For years newspaper articles had been written trying to explain 'religious extremism' and 'sectarian violence'. Outside observers found it difficult to understand. In other parts of the world even more violent forms of religious extremism disrupted the lives of peace-loving folk. Sunni and Shi'a Muslims had been at odds with each other for centuries. A cycle of atrocities between the rival communities flared up in Iraq in the aftermath of the Second Gulf War.

Saddam Hussein was still in power in 2003. The Americans believed that he had failed to destroy his WMDs (Weapons of Mass Destruction). He expelled teams of weapons inspectors. In March 2003, American and British forces aided by Australian and Polish troops invaded Iraq for the second time. Within a month Baghdad had fallen and so had the statue of Saddam Hussein in the centre of the city.

It was months before the man himself was captured.

Attempts were made to set up a democratic government. Agreement between the various parties proved to be impossible. The Coalition Forces were attacked by Saddam loyalists inspired by Osama bin Laden. Both Sunni and Shi'a Muslim extremists attacked soldiers and civilians who cooperated with them. The situation escalated; a virtual civil war developed when the religious factions fought amongst themselves.

Fusiliers Steven Draper and Donal Meade had been serving together at Palace Barracks in County Down for two years. Northern Ireland was still an explosive place. Donal Meade's early memories were of a very big bang. The Soufriere Hills volcano on the island of Montserrat in the Caribbean had been dormant for five hundred years. It began to stir in 1995. Eruptions became more violent until it 'blew its top' and covered more than half the island in ash. The capital, Plymouth, became a ghost town; thousands lost their homes. Families dispersed to neighbouring islands, the USA and Britain. The Meades made the best of it and settled in south London.

Donal Meade and Steven Draper were big mates on duty. On leave they enjoyed family hospitality in Plumstead or on Windmill Lane. It was time for a change of scenery.

The Royal Regiment of Fusiliers was on the move. They packed their kit and flew out to Jordan to prepare for deployment to Iraq. At Shaibah, near Basra, they began their tour of duty serving alongside the Coldstream Guards. To police the surrounding area patrols were sent out. Usually they returned without incident. As the end of the tour approached everyone was looking forward to moving with the battalion to Cyprus.

Members of C Company set out on a two vehicle patrol from Shaibah on the road to Az Zubayr. Donal Meade and Richard Manning were acting as 'top cover' sentries. It was routine, there was nothing around to cause alarm.

The shockwave from the IED shook the vehicle; it stopped in its tracks. Meade and Manning died together on the 5th of September 2005. It was little consolation to the families that the incident was reported by the BBC. It only served to confirm that the lives of two bright young men had been snuffed out. At battalion headquarters in Belfast their commanding officer paid tribute to both of them. Saddened by the loss of this good friend Steven Draper came home. The battalion enjoyed their tour of duty in Cyprus. It was something Donal Meade had been looking forward to.

The Iraqis were left to their own devices. The conflict in Afghanistan dominated the news. It was often depressing; good men died. The latest high-tech equipment could not save them because someone had to go out on foot patrol. As in all wars this was the job of 'the poor bloody infantry'.

Many of the fusiliers deployed to Afghanistan in 2007 already had battlefield experience; they were well prepared when they were sent in to Sangin. The town had long been under Taliban control. Opium poppies grew well in the in the surrounding 'green zone'. Farmers, local tribesmen, drug traffickers and the Taliban all profited from the drug trade, and were fearful that ISAF (International Security Assistance Force) troops might destroy the crops.

A cornfield in Helmand Province.

National Archives, Open Government Licence

"There's no poppies in here, Sarg."

Movement along any of the roads out of Sangin was dangerous. Supply convoys and patrols were ambushed and roadside bombs were common place. Local Afghans were targeted by the Taliban who assassinated many who worked for the Central Government. Relatives who came to collect their bodies also risked being killed.

Troops were sent in to enforce the authority of the Afghan Government that set up offices in a dusty compound half a mile from the town centre. This became the base for a hundred and twenty troops. Royal Engineers, working under enemy fire, surrounded the compound with 'Hesco' barriers and cleared a helicopter landing pad. This was essential when all roads into the town were under Taliban control. Foot soldiers dug in and fortified their positions with sandbags. The DC (District Centre) came under attack almost daily from small-arms fire and rocket attack. Despite repeated efforts by coalition forces Sangin remained under Taliban control for months.

British units manning the district centre rotated – Parachute Regiment, the Royal Marines, and the Light Infantry. It was the turn of Steven Drapers 'mob', the 2nd Battalion, Royal Regiment of Fusiliers. In their first twenty days in Sangin, the fusiliers were attacked at least sixty times. Steven came away unharmed.

Back on home soil Steven was promoted, retrained and 'rebadged'. Sergeant Draper of the Royal Electrical and Mechanical Engineers returned to Afghanistan in 2012 and came home safely the following year.

Chapter 34

Learning from History

A COSTLY GAME

All the strife and conflict in Afghanistan began as a game between Britain and Russia, both countries seeking to expand their empires. In 1842 the first Anglo-Afghan War ended in defeat for British forces, massacred by tribesmen, when they retreated back into India. A second invasion secured a treaty with the Afghans and Britain was given control of foreign affairs. A dividing line between Afghanistan and British India split the Pashtun ethnic group, and laid the foundations for cross-border conflict in the future.

There was constant diplomatic and military manoeuvring by the French, the British and Russians, and the Great Game of espionage began. Rudyard Kipling's novel, *Kim,* tells the tale of the game played by all sides in attempts to control Afghanistan. Kipling knew the border area well and gathered material for his book when he worked as a young journalist in Lahore in the 1880s.

In 1918, at the end of the Great War, the Afghan Army attacked British troops in the 'tribal regions' of India. Tired of war, Britain gave the Afghans full independence. Afghanistan slowly began to modernise. At the end of the Second World War the government asked for help in the process. The Americans refused; the Afghans turned to the Russians who gave them economic and military aid. This proved to be an uneasy relationship that exploded into guerrilla warfare in 1979. For ten years Russian conscripts fought a no-holds-barred campaign against the Mujahideen. Several nations including America and Pakistan supplied these Islamic extremists with arms and financial support.

The last Soviet troops left Afghanistan in1989. Within five years the country was under the control of the insurgents, and the name Osama bin Laden became infamous. His training camps, for Taliban fighters, became the target for missile attacks by the Americans. Bombing raids intensified three weeks after the 11th of September attack on New York in 2001. British troops were soon engaged in a campaign that lasted more than ten years. Trooper Jamie Chater was just one more local lad to serve in this part of the world. He never had a chance to compare notes with Tom Welsby or Ted Cook, they were long gone.

Sergeant Cook plodded up the Khyber Pass from Peshawar towards the Afghan border in 1917. His company came to within a hundred miles of Kabul and he could have told Jamie that soldiering in this part of the world was a miserable business. He might have told him of an incident similar to many that would be repeated decades later.

In May 1919, a band of Afghans crossed the border and occupied a number of strategically important villages with reliable water supplies. They were warned to withdraw. The Dragoon Guards were mobilised. Local police and Army Intelligence advised them that the postmaster in Peshawar was organising an uprising to coincide with the invasion. The Dragoons dealt with this terrorist threat and secured the town in a matter of hours. They moved on into hostile enemy territory, their final objective was the village of Dakka. An air strike by the RAF was very effective. The Afghan rebels abandoned their positions leaving behind only a handful of troublesome snipers. 'B' Squadron, under Captain Cooper, was sent out to deal with them. Lieutenant Card was slightly wounded. The Royal Artillery gave the insurgents a pounding and this particular skirmish was all over in a fortnight.

Corporal Tom Welsby had a similar experience during the Second World War. He was stationed twenty miles from the Afghan border in the 'tribal territories'. Here the main pastime of the Masuds and Pathans was killing each other, or anyone else that got in the way. To keep an eye on the warring tribesmen troops of the Indian Army manned a string of primitive forts and outposts. They were supplied from the army base at Razmak. Six thousand feet above sea level the weather varied between scorching hot and bitterly cold. Tom Welsby and his platoon escorted columns of trucks or mules along the dangerous road to Bannu.

Corporal Welsby bringing in supplies.

"Where's the green pasture I was promised?"

After a stint on the North-West Frontier, Tom was off to somewhere really unpleasant – Burma.

Corporal Tom Welsby and Sergeant Ted Cook put up with dust, freezing temperatures, sweltering heat, monsoons, encounters with insects, reptiles and dangerous men. They put it all behind them and returned to the peaceful fields and woods of Apley. Next it was the turn of Trooper Jamie Chater.

THE WELSH CAVALRY

In 2011, the Dragoon Guards were preparing for another tour of duty in Afghanistan. The importance of the border area between Afghanistan and Pakistan was explained to junior officers. When the time came to put the lads in their own troop in the picture they didn't go into details. "Our job is to protect the Afghan people from the insurgents, simple as that." It wasn't that simple but it wasn't easy to explain why there had been so much trouble in the region for more than a hundred years.

Year thirteen is decision time for teenagers preparing to leave school. Within a fortnight of leaving Bridgnorth Endowed School, Jamie Chater had found a job with Len Foxall who sold all things electrical in the High Street. It was a good start but not his chosen career. "I always wanted to join the army."

In January 2008, Jamie made his way to Bassingbourn where the army guaranteed that after fourteen weeks training the recruits would be 'fit, motivated and capable of carrying out local protection tasks in an operational environment'. A military career always comes with a health warning. Anyone joining had to be prepared to serve in a place where acts of terrorism by the Taliban were reported at least once a month. Afghanistan was always in the news. Jamie went to Germany.

The Prussian Army established a training camp for cavalry at Sennelager in 1851, and there has been a military presence there ever since. A few British fishermen arrived at the beginning of the Great War captured by the German Navy and made prisoners of war, the first of many. Hitler's famous Tiger tanks practised manoeuvres on the heathland nearby. When they were defeated in 1945 the British took over the barracks. It was not the most romantic place for Jamie to bring his young bride, Adele. This was her first experience of life abroad with the British Army. She was welcomed by other soldiers' wives and quickly settled in. The 'regimental family' were always there to give support, particularly when the men were away.

A TRIP TO THE THEATRE

The Queen's Dragoon Guards began preparations for deployment to a war zone. Trooper Chater was packed off to Canada. He was learning all the time and so was Lieutenant Boyce. The training staff at the Royal Military Academy had been impressed by this young officer; he had done well at Sandhurst. He now faced a more critical and demanding team, the senior NCOs and veterans of earlier campaigns. Men like 'Shag' Scanlon who had already served in Bosnia and Iraq. They asked the question, "Was Mr Boyce up to the job?" Tall, athletic and decisive, he quickly earned the respect of all.

Final preparations for deployment to Afghanistan were made in Pembrokeshire, on the ranges at Castlemartin. The main armament of the Scimitars was a thirty millimetre cannon capable of spraying a target at the rate of seventy rounds a minute. It was exhilarating stuff. All concerned were now keen to put training into practise. Arrangements were made to fly out from Brize Norton.

Everyone knew about Brize Norton and Compton Bassett. TV cameras were there regularly to relay tragic scenes from the airfield. In living rooms all over Britain the blurred image of an RAF Hercules, banking on final approach to the runway, would appear. Minutes later the next shot would show the ramp of the loading bay lowered and a medalled warrant officer giving instructions to a party of guardsmen, riflemen, troopers or airmen. The coffin appeared carried with such tender care down the ramp and onto home soil. The union flag ruffled by an English breeze. It always happened to some other formation. "Not to worry, we'll all be fine."

Loading troops and equipment onto the C-17 was a well-practised routine at Brize. Ground crew of 99 Squadron had lost count of the number of troops they had packed off. The flight path to Camp Bastion was well travelled. The take-off over the Oxfordshire countryside was as smooth as silk and in no time at all the Globemaster was making a leisurely descent over the Mediterranean, and trundling along the runway at Akrotiri towards the startling white passenger terminal. So far the journey compared well with a package holiday flight. The inflight entertainment wasn't very good, just childish banter and dark army humour, but there was plenty of legroom and no obese tourists hogging the armrests.

Anxiety began to build up on the next leg of the journey from 'Aki' to 'Afgha'; no one let it show as the mighty aircraft ploughed on over Iraq and Iran. "We're getting there. Be over Helmand soon."

A long slow predictable flight path made any aircraft vulnerable to attack from hostile forces on the ground. Landing at Camp Bastion the pilot faced the same problem that had troubled US Marines besieged at Khe Sanh during the Vietnam War. Planes carrying fresh troops and supplies dived from altitude to avoid anti-aircraft fire, and on take-off the pilot pulled back hard on 'the stick' as soon as the wheels left the ground. The young troopers were warned that the pilot would use the Khe Sanh approach; this would be different from an EasyJet landing. Even so it came as a shock when the Globemaster put her nose down and dived steeply leaving stomachs in the rear compartment. The ground shot up at the last minute and the aircraft levelled out. They had arrived.

The Welsh Cavalry moved in to 'MOB Price' just outside the Green Zone. This Mobile Operating Base was small compared with the sprawling Camp Bastion. Danish troops had built a log cabin in the centre of the base with an outdoor seating area where anyone could enjoy coffee or a 'slushy' in the sun. There was little time for this sort of luxury. The Dragoons were busy, keeping supply routes open, flushing out the Taliban, supporting and training the Afghan National Army and trying to win over the local population.

RUNNING INTO TROUBLE

The war against the Taliban was a serious business and no less dangerous to front line troops than any of the campaigns that local lads had served in before. The Dragoons quickly settled in and set about their task. After days out on patrol, living on ration packs and sleeping on hard ground, they were ready for a 'slushy'. Families at home watched the news on TV every night. Images from the battlefront were of dusty roads, scrubland, dry muddy walls and irrigation ditches, and then there was the Green Zone. This was not the place to be.

The Green Zone was home to the Taliban. The Afghans here were either active supporters or under threat. It was referred to as a 'kinetic area' which meant that patrols could expect trouble every time they ventured in. "We were always getting into scraps there," Jamie said.

They were doing a good job even if this meant no sleep for forty-eight hours at a stretch. With every week that passed confidence grew. Patrols became routine.

War artist, Dan Peterson was embedded with the Queen's Dragoon Guards during their tour of duty in Afghanistan, 2011.

© Dan Peterson

"There's nothing to worry about, lad."

411

Official War Artist, Dan Peterson, accompanied the Dragoons. His lightning sketches captured 'the moment' as no camera can. He shared the dangers and won the confidence of all. Officers and men were only too pleased to pose for him. Over fifty of them can be shuffled together. To honour the men he served with, Dan has created a pack of playing cards. The cheeky faces of Welch Cavalry might be a distraction for those who take gambling seriously.

On the 17th of November 2011, 'B' Squadron were motoring steadily along an old MSR (Main Supply Route) in the direction of Khani Khua. Dust billowing up from the tracks of the leading Scimitar blew back over Lieutenant David Boyce and Lance Corporal 'Shag' Scanlon standing side by side in the turret. They scanned the surrounding countryside on the lookout for anything that might spell danger. There was nothing out of the ordinary, nothing to worry about.

The explosion lifted the Scimitar clean off the ground and flipped it over. The reaction of the driver to the rear was instantaneous. He veered off the road as dust and debris settled. The lead vehicle tore away then slewed around to face the tragic scene. The troop sergeant took command. Distress calls went out and in came the 'Pedros' in their Pave Hawk helicopter. These American paramedics wear a shoulder patch with the cartoon figure of a Mexican in a straw hat, but there was nothing silly about them. They were the best. Despite their efforts David Boyce and Richard Scanlon died at the scene. Their driver, Corporal Donaldson, a TA soldier, nearly drowned in diesel from the ruptured fuel tank but escaped with a few bruises.

Jamie Chater's troop had just completed twenty days on patrol. They were called out immediately to form a cordon around the area. Bomb disposal specialists arrived and found three more devices. No one could be sure what had caused the explosion. It may even have been an old Soviet mine, a legacy of the nine fruitless years the Russians had spent fighting against the same enemy.

"Bad news travels fast," the BBC presenter read from the autocue. "The Ministry of Defence...regrets...both of the Queen's Dragoon Guards...The next of kin have been informed." It was days before Adele was able to speak to Jamie and be assured that he was safe and well.

At Camp Bastion, Lieutenant Colonel De Quincy Adams spoke of the heroism and commitment of Lieutenant Boyce and Lance Corporal Scanlon. They flew home together back to Brize Norton. Their comrades returned to duty.

Within a month the Colonel had the satisfaction of planning a raid on a bomb-making factory. The Brigade Reconnaissance Force made up of his Dragoons, infantrymen from other regiments and supported by helicopter crews and Afghan commandos mounted a dawn raid on a Taliban stronghold. Heroin, a large amount of cash and ex-Russian small arms were discovered but, more importantly, the chemicals and materials used to produce IEDs. Before the Dragoons tour of duty came to an end patrols set off three more Improvised Explosive Devices and were involved in several 'exchanges' with the Taliban, but mercifully suffered no more casualties.

Enjoying the Freedom

The freedom of the city had already been granted to the Queen's Dragoon Guards and so, on the 30th of May 2012, the regiment exercised the right to march through the streets of Swansea. The Mayor and the Lord Lieutenant addressed the parade at the Guildhall before they set off through the city. The band of the Prince of Wales' Division struck up with the Radetzky March and they swung through the streets accompanied by waves of applause from the crowds lining the route. It was a memorable day for lads who had spent seven months in a dusty and dangerous place.

Later that week a memorial service was held at Llandaff Cathedral for comrades lost in Helmand Province. To celebrate the Queen's Diamond Jubilee the regiment were on parade again in Cardiff's Millennium Stadium. The crowd gave them a standing ovation. It seemed unthinkable that the government should consider disbanding this regiment with a history stretching back to the Battle of Waterloo. The sacrifice of David Boyce and Richard Scanlon may have saved The Welsh Cavalry from extinction.

Queen's Dragoon Guards had played their part in Operation Herrick 15. Jamie came home to be reunited with Adele and pampered by his mum before he went back to Germany and the serious business of soldiering. His experiences had not put him off army life.

It was easy enough to pick out the serious competitors preparing for the Bridgnorth Walk. They were the ones with chunky trainers on the end of sinewy legs and serious expressions on their faces. They looked disapprovingly at giggly schoolgirls wearing tight tee shirts and fancy dress wigs. Nonetheless, they all had a common purpose: to raise money for charity. If anyone was interested it was printed on the front of the girls' tee shirts, and a lot of people did show an interest. Lightly clad, carrying no more than a bottle of water, the walkers set off on the Mayor's command. He was swept aside as they surged down the High Street.

A few silly boys had hired costumes for the day. There were gorillas and pirates, Batman and Robin put in appearance. Jamie Chater was outstanding. Tall, athletic, every inch a soldier in battledress, and carrying a full pack. He didn't get this outfit from a party shop; this was the real thing, the same kit he wore during his tour of duty in Afghanistan.

Twenty-two miles later the race leaders came strutting confidently back along the High Street to enjoy the applause and, with hands on hips, explained why they were not in the first three. Less athletic bunches of grinning fundraisers panted up to the finishing line. Youngsters in the crowd scurried about with disposable cameras taking blurred snaps of confused dogs, dragged along to greet their owners. Teenagers with mobile phones flashed images around the world of friends sticking their tongues out. The staff photographer from the Shropshire Star dashed about looking for something out of the ordinary.

Jim Hall-Gough joined the walk two hundred yards before the end. On gleaming black shoes he covered the final stretch with confident strides. He was in full regalia, blazer and beret, badges and medals, carrying the blue and gold standard of the Royal British Legion. Jim fell in alongside Trooper Jamie Chater, who appeared as fresh as when he set off. He was back in the High Street. In the crowd there were old school friends who had never left the town, and in Len Foxall's shop they were still selling kettles and fridges. Jamie had been to a war zone and returned unscathed but determined that those less fortunate should not be forgotten. The funds he raised from the walk he donated to the Legion.

Jamie Chater had witnessed disturbing scenes and yet appeared to accept the danger and the loss of comrades as a part of being a soldier.

414

Not everyone can do this. Some are plagued by flashbacks; they dwell on past events and cannot 'move on' with their lives. They can be helped. 'Fishing for Heroes' is an unusual charity set up to help men 'burned out' by service in a war zone. They find some peace, sharing a few thoughts in tranquil surrounding with someone who understands. Jamie knew he could help.

Jim Hall-Gough and Trooper Jamie Chater arriving in the High Street at the end of the Bridgnorth Walk.

© The Shropshire Star

"Try to keep up, Jim!"

Home on leave he made for the river to brush up his angling skills and perhaps have some time to reflect on the memorable events of the recent past. With rod in hand he walked down Cheswardine Lane and found the perfect place near the suspension bridge. On the way down to the river he passed the doors of old soldiers who over the years had similar experiences to his own.

Close by, veteran of the Great War, George Sargent, lived with his son, Norman, and his wife, Doris. Norman always limped. Some said he 'put it on', but there was no doubting that he has been shot in the leg on the way to Berlin. Further down the lane in a thatched cottage, long demolished, Jack Leith found peace and put his years as a POW behind him. In every dwelling, farmhouse and the Hall, there had once been men in uniform, and Jamie could see as he approached the river where they had been active. The Home Guard dug trenches in woodland near the pill box that guarded the bridge. The barbed wire had gone from the roadside but there may still have been fragments of sacking from the sandbags lying under the carpet of leaves. If only the woods and cottage walls could talk.

A kingfisher flew by and found a perch in one of the willows. He turned his head on one side, scanned the river and flew on. Jamie didn't catch anything either. He strolled back and sat down in the kitchen. His mum made him a cup of tea. Sam Coles had spent his whole life in this same house except for the six years he spent with the Royal Engineers, making bombs safe.

AND FINALLY

An orderly withdrawal is planned for British forces serving in Afghanistan.

The retreat at the end of the first Afghan War was a disaster. The garrison at Kabul was surrounded by hostile tribesmen. General William Elphinstone, the commanding officer, ordered the withdrawal in 1842. British and Indian troops, their wives, children and camp followers began the long trek through the Khyber Pass to Jalalabad. There were sixteen thousand in all. When Surgeon-Major William Brydon arrived he had a sorry tale to tell. A handful of Indian soldiers had survived, and he was the only European.

Sergeant Ted Cook came away 'none the worse for it' in 1919, and Corporal Tom Welsby's trip through the Khyber Pass was uneventful.

Steven Draper and Jamie Chater may have the distinction of being the last Apley men to fight in Afghanistan. Returning from this dangerous place, they must have had mixed emotions: anxiety, elation and grief, but also warmth, comradeship and good humour. It is always best to look on the bright side when telling tales of men in uniform.

Notes and Acknowledgements

THE COVER STORY

The nature of Apley has changed but it is still possible to feel the presence of generations past. The varied scenes and seasonal changes have been captured by Vicki Norman. The cover illustrations are adapted from two of her paintings. Echoes Hill is viewed from the front drive of the farmhouse at the Leavenhalls. The farmer, Hugh Dyas, served in the Royal Artillery. An officer's greatcoat it is draped over a fence of steel mesh once used as matting on a wartime grass runway. Above the hill a Lancaster bomber is towing a Horsa assault glider towards the airfield at RAF Cosford.

In tropical lands the works of man are soon hidden if the rapid growth of plants and creepers is not kept in check. Seedlings take root in the stonework of temples, the masonry crumbles and any evidence of the ancient civilization may lie hidden for centuries. In a cabinet in the corner of the Northgate Museum, in Bridgnorth, local historians have arranged a small collection of items to remind visitors of the Civil War. There is a dagger together with cannon balls, musket balls and the metal moulds the soldiers used to form them. Among these relics of war, but much more difficult to date, is a flint arrowhead made by a Stone Age hunter. It is perfectly formed, as sharp as the day it was made in a settlement near Astley Abbotts. This quiet corner of England enjoyed well over two hundred years of peace after the Roundheads and Cavaliers had settled their differences. A closer look at the landscape reveals evidence of more recent conflict.

Nature tries to hide the pill-box guarding Linley Bridge but once in a while woodland seedlings and brambles are cut back and the brickwork and the concrete roof are revealed. No shots were ever fired in anger from this sturdy structure. In the darkest days of the Second World War uniformed bands of labourers appeared in the fields, German and Italian prisoners, Land Girls in corduroy breeches working alongside veterans of the Great War. In the evening the Apley company of 'Dad's Army revived old skills. When peace came village boys took over the duties of the Home Guard and slaughtered an imaginary enemy attempting to cross the river. Returning from foreign fields to take up there old trade again the farmhands sometimes looked like a gang of mercenaries dressed in 'army surplus'. The fabric grew threadbare until only the heavy greatcoat remained, used to keep the frosts of winter out of the car radiator. Ships, tanks and aircraft were all surplus to requirements, scrapped or sold off.

Rupert Hockenhull could never resist a bargain and when the gliders, assembled at Cosford, were being disposed of he went back and forth with tractor and trailer and passed on body sections to friends around The Estate. The Agent, 'Paddy' Roney-Dougal, declared, "We can't have this, they look like gypsy caravans."

Hidden away, several survived as hen-houses and tool sheds; those with cockpits attached made little boys' war games feel like the real thing. One old Horsa, hidden in the rhododendrons at Winscote survived for years. The skin of the grounded war-bird withered and cracked and in time fell away from the hooped skeleton of the body until that also collapsed and was lost in leaf mould.

In the days before traffic noise drowned out country sounds, the ploughman singing to his horse, the skylark overhead and the laughter of children at play could be heard for miles. When lessons were over and they spilled out of the school door the whole village knew about it. They scampered off in all directions in gangs of three or four. A handful, still squealing and giggling, turned off the road and down the track to Echoes Hill.

It's hardly a hill at all just a bump in the fields of the Levenhalls Farm, just as well for Squadron Leader Jim Cooksey when he performed his tree-top aerobatics. He had commanded a squadron of Meteors, the RAF's first jet fighter and on his retirement, after a distinguished war-time career, became one of the Gloster Aircraft Company's test pilots. This was a serious business but Jim still managed to perform juvenile antics in the air. Taking off from Moreton Valence Jim would buzz over his neighbour's rooftops, do some 'wing-wagging' to his wife and head north up the Severn Valley. It wasn't that far from Gloucester to Apley as the crow flies. As the Meteor flies it probably took no more than a quarter of an hour. There was time enough to try out a few stunts at the Leavenhalls, over his sister's home, in preparation for the Farnborough Air Shows. These displays over Echoes Hill were very popular with lads labouring in the fields. Jim was less popular with nervous housewives and the normally placid cows. The Gloster Aircraft Company was ahead of the game; the Meteor set a world record time for a 1000km closed circuit. The man responsible was Jim Cooksey. The flight path from Moreton Valance to the Firth of Forth and back took him directly over the Wrekin and Echoes Hill.

War-time relics remained in every corner of the Estate for years. Eventually the barrel sized concrete cylinders that lay at the roadside disappeared. They were never rolled out; the Tiger tanks never came to disturb the peace of the country lanes. The largest and most durable relic was buried deep and ran the whole length of The Estate, its presence marked by concrete pillars in the hedgerows. Petroleum vital to the war effort was transported by every means possible to storage depots nationwide; by road, rail, river and canal. Safer and more efficient were the underground pipelines. An important branch was laid under Apley fields. Fuel discharged from oil tankers on the Mersey flowed south below meadows and cornfields down the Severn valley to Avonmouth. Some must have been pumped on to the Isle of Wight and under the Channel to the French coast to supply the advancing armies after D-Day. PLUTO, the Pipeline under the Ocean, had a short life but the system that fed it lived on and was extended during the period of the Cold War. It is still in use today.

THE ARTISTS

Vicki Norman, one time artist in residence on Apley Estate, has produced a whole gallery of paintings capturing the changing moods of nature. The view of Echoes Hill on the front cover and the Queen's View on the back are hers.

Christine Bradshaw, another local artist, accepted the challenge of illustrating the map of Apley to give the reader a sense of the location of the Estate in the Shropshire landscape. To capture history it is possible to pick almost any point on a map of England, draw a five-mile circle around it and examine the lives of the people who lived within. On a red sandstone outcrop on Apley Terrace William Whitmore's men cut a socket to hold a stout pole and flew a flag to show their loyalty to King Charles. About half of Apley lands can be viewed from this lookout; north to the Severn Gorge, west across the river, south to the market town of Bridgnorth.

War artist Dan Peterson has given permission to reproduce 'Drop Off' in the final chapter. This is one of the sketches he made in Helmand Province. He accompanied the 1st Queen's Dragoon Guards on their tour of Afghanistan in 2011.

THE AUTHOR

Graham Jones spent his childhood and youth on Apley Estate. He attended the village school, shared a classroom with evacuees from Liverpool and watched convoys of American troops pass by to help liberate Europe. He travelled the world but was always drawn back to the fields of his boyhood. A member of the Apley Park Branch of the Royal British Legion for more than fifty years he knew personally many of the characters in this book. He says:

"I cannot believe now the freedom we were allowed then. We were free to roam the woods and explore every track and watery hollow, build dens and sail rafts on the Severn. We committed acts of vandalism, lit fires, stole garden produce, poached rabbits in the hedgerows and fish from the river. With knives, catapults and airguns we killed wildlife and practised tribal warfare. Now we would be rewarded with an anti-social behaviour order but then we were kept in order by the village bobby, and had respect for old soldiers of the Great War and our heroes who had returned from far-flung battlefields in 1945. This book is dedicated to their memory and to the generations that followed, the lads who served in Malaya, Korea, Northern Ireland, the Gulf and Afghanistan."

MANY THANKS

Special thanks go to my wife, Pat, who does not share my enthusiasm for all things military. Nevertheless she has been most supportive and listened patiently as I retold many of the stories.

In compiling this history I made many mistakes. There were errors of fact, grammar and punctuation. A dear old school friend, Ruth Darby, did her very best to make corrections. I am responsible for any that remain. She died shortly before her task was complete. I will be forever in her debt.

Thanks to all those who have been so generous, allowing me access to precious family photographs and documents. I have tried to be truthful and accurate but I know there are defects. Remarks made by some of the characters are mine not theirs but I honestly believe they would have used similar words. I have listened to many stories and retold incidents that I suspect have been 'added to' over the years. I have thought it best not to enquire too deeply but to accept 'this is how I remember it' or 'so I was told' as the truth.

My aim was not simply to catalogue the military records of men associated with a country estate. It is about comradeship and continuity. Apley men travelled far and witnessed great events. On their return they said little. In quiet moments; resting on a spade in the garden or listening to birdsong in the woods something would remind them of the campaigns of their youth.

Apley was a place where old-fashioned values were maintained and that might have meant a place where snobbery and class distinction were preserved. In Victorian times the generosity of the Fosters improved the lot of the community. This spirit has been handed down to the present day. I am most grateful to Lord Gavin Hamilton and his family for the help and encouragement given to me.

PLATES AND PUBLISHING

Many of the photographs have been loaned by the families of the servicemen and I am most grateful for this. The staff of a number of museums and libraries have also been most helpful and I must mention in particular:
Sally Richards, the Imperial War Museum
Kate Swan, the National Army Museum
Dawn Watkins and Clare Carr, the RAF Museum
Peter Duckers and John Taylor, the Castle Museum in Shrewsbury
Ms E M Bregazzi and Mr N Parks, Durham County Records Office
Anne Buchanan and Dan Brown of the Bath Library Service

I have found this enterprise a great challenge but with help and encouragement on all sides the task is now complete. The final process of publishing was made possible by Helen Hart and her team at SilverWood Books. Working with Sarah Newman has been a particular pleasure, thank you for all your help and guidance.

Graham Jones
January 2014